Lester Ward

and the Welfare State

THE AMERICAN HERITAGE SERIES

THE

American Heritage

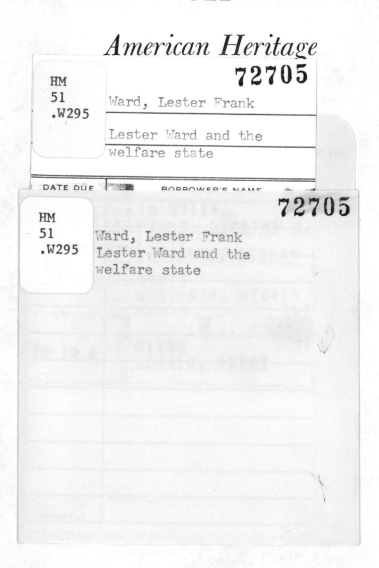

Lester Ward
and the Welfare State

EDITED BY

HENRY STEELE COMMAGER
Amherst College

THE BOBBS-MERRILL COMPANY, INC.

INDIANAPOLIS AND NEW YORK

FOREWORD

A half century ago, scholars described Lester Ward as an intellectual Gulliver among the Lilliputians, even as an American Aristotle. Bridging more than the "two cultures," he mastered the natural sciences, the social sciences, and languages. An educator, he was also a geologist, a botanist, and a paleontologist; a social statistician, he was a systematic philosopher too; a linguistics expert who could read Sanscrit, Hebrew, and Latin, as well as modern European languages, he was a founder of the discipline of sociology. He called one of his courses at Brown University "A Survey of All Knowledge," and he entitled the six-volume encyclopedic collection of his minor papers *Glimpses of the Cosmos!* Ward published many books and some six hundred papers, yet his works are largely unread today and not one of his books is now in print.

Ward may not be honored in his country, but he was a prophet nonetheless. He predicted and championed the coming of the welfare state, which he called a "sociocracy," the rule of society by society and for society. If the details of his vision have not proved exact, and if his forecast has not yet materialized in fullness, time may yet validate him. The direction of the nation is clear enough: the New Deal, Fair Deal, and New Frontier have now brought us to the edge of the Great Society that Ward would have found kin to his sociocracy. He was a militant liberal, a self-confessed "apostle of human progress" who believed in the efficacy of "scientific" planning by a democratic government advised by experts on the legislative needs of society. "There is no need of having any slums," wrote Ward, nor disease, ignorance, or poverty either. If he did not invent the welfare state, he was, in the opinion of Henry Steele Commager, its foremost philosopher, protagonist, and architect. "His formulation of its philosophy," remarks Professor Commager, "is what has proved to be the most lasting and significant of his many contributions." This selection of Ward's writings demonstrates what is usable in Ward and relevant for the future, as well as for our own time. From the standpoint of scholarship, this selection of Ward's writings makes conveniently available the evidence that may be used to place him in our history as one of the giants in social thought.

This book is one of a series created to provide the essential primary sources of the American experience, especially of American thought. The series, when completed, will constitute a documentary of American history, filling a need long felt among scholars, students, libraries, and general readers for authoritative collections of original materials. Some volumes will illuminate the thought of significant indivduals, such as James Madison or Louis D. Brandeis; some will deal with movements, such as the Antifederalists or the Populists; others will be organized around special themes, such as Puritan political thought, or American Catholic thought on social questions.

Many volumes will take up the large number of subjects traditionally studied in American history for which, surprisingly, there are no documentary anthologies; others will pioneer in introducing new subjects of increasing importance to scholars as to the contemporary world.

The series aspires to maintain the high standards demanded of contemporary editing, providing authentic texts, intelligently and unobtrusively edited. It will also have the distinction of presenting pieces of substantial length that give the full character and flavor of the original. The series will be the most comprehensive and authoritative of its kind.

Leonard W. Levy
Alfred Young

CONTENTS

INTRODUCTION

The student of the American Constitutional system is confronted, at the very outset, by a paradox. The term "general welfare" is written twice into the Constitution: once in the Preamble, as part of the broad statement of the purpose of the Constitution itself; once, in what may (or may not) be a more restricted sense, in that Section Eight which confers power on the Congress. For that matter, the injunction on government to serve the general welfare was not new; the phrase appears twice in the Articles of Confederation as well.

Yet notwithstanding the broad statement of purpose and the more specific grant of power to raise money "to provide for the common defense and general welfare," Congress allowed the authority—if it was indeed an authority—to "provide for the general welfare" to go by default, while courts and commentators alike disputed the meaning of the phrase. When, from time to time, Congress did find it desirable to expand its legislative powers, it did so under either the commerce clause or the war power—authorities whose effectiveness varied (as the Passenger, the Prize, and the Legal Tender cases revealed) with the character of courts and judges.

And here is a further paradox: Not until the eighteen-eighties did Congress begin in any serious fashion to explore those grants of power specified in the Constitution. There had been tariffs, and internal improvements, and railroad legislation, and an occasional assertion of power in the territories; but though these exercises of power inspired acute constitutional controversies, they were far from exhausting constitutional potentialities. Not until a century after the original constitutional grant did Congress exercise its power over immigration, or enact a general commerce law, or make even tentative gestures toward the regulation of business and industry. In the meantime, the Supreme Court had formulated the principle of affectation with a public interest, but when states attempted to test, somewhat gingerly, the contours and the limits of this principle, courts hastened to discourage them, while the principle itself was held not to apply to Congressional authority.

By this time a constitutional and political crisis was upon the country, a crisis that was to test whether government in America had the power to do those things that governments elsewhere took for granted, and whether such powers as government did have were national or local.

Three interrelated aspects of the crisis enlist our attention: the economic, the political, and the philosophical.

The economic crisis was brought on by the speedy and unregulated growth of industry, transportation, and capital; by the chaotic upsurge of cities; by mass immigration (over five million in the eighties); and by concentration in industry, transportation, and capital without a comparable concentration among farmers or workers—or consumers.

The political crisis resulted from the failure, or the incompetence, of government to deal with the economic crisis. The explanation of that failure is complex. It was in part the tradition of dual federalism, and the emergence of a twilight zone in which neither state nor Federal government operated. It was in part that those who controlled national politics were not interested in effective regulation of the industrial order. It was in part that the courts seemed to be engaged in a kind of conspiracy to paralyze governmental power, denying states the authority to regulate corporate business by a broad construction of the "due process" clause of the Fourteenth Amendment, and denying the national government authority by a narrow construction of the commerce and the tax clauses.

By what theory did the courts declare so many labor and

welfare laws unconstitutional? It is forbidden in most state constitutions and in the Fourteenth Amendment to the Federal Constitution to deprive persons of liberty or property without due process of law. As no reform can be effected without depriving someone of something that he may deem to be a liberty or a property right, the courts early elaborated the doctrine of a superior "police power"—the reserved right of the state to protect the people's health, safety, morals, and welfare. The police power was held to justify even confiscatory legislation, such as the prohibition of lotteries or of the sale of alcoholic liquors. But when, in the seventies and eighties, labor and factory laws began to appear on the statute books, judges discovered second thoughts about the scope of this power. Corporations found it easy to convince courts that such laws were not a proper exercise of the police power, but rather a violation of the "due process" clause of the Fourteenth Amendment. Thus, half a century after Reconstruction, such judges as Field, Brewer, Peckham, and Sutherland, and their disciples in the state courts turned the judicial bench into a dike, against which the surging tides of welfare legislation beat in vain. They interpreted the Constitution as a prohibition rather than an instrument, and read into it limitations on the scope of governmental authority that were in fact merely the conclusions of natural-law syllogisms. Insisting that they were without discretion, and that their functions were purely mechanical, they struck down hundreds of state police laws which appeared to limit freedom of contract without the due process of law. Thus, for example, a Pennsylvania act forbidding payment of workers by orders on company stores was voided as an "infringement on natural inherent rights and an insulting attempt to put the laborer under a legislative tutelage," and a West Virginia court, confronted by a similar act, held that "the evil was in the hands of the employee, since he is not compelled to buy from the employer"—this in the face of the fact that the company owned the town, the houses, and the stores. A New York act fixing the hours of labor for municipal contracts was nullified because it "created a class of statutory laborers," and a Colorado act regulating hours in the smelting industry was voided as an interference with liberty of contract. The New York Court of Appeals prohibited a workmen's compensation law because "it did nothing to conserve the health, safety or morals of employees," and a constitutional amendment was required to enable the legislature to deal with this problem. An Illinois court declared unconstitutional a statute limiting the hours of labor for women in sweatshops, on the ground that women had the same liberty of contract as men.[1] And a few years later, the New York Court of Appeals declared void a law prohibiting night work for women. "When it is sought," said Judge Gray on behalf of the court, "under the guise of a labor law, arbitrarily, as here, to prevent an adult female citizen from working any time of day that suits her, I think it is time to call a halt." In 1905 the Supreme Court of the United States, in the case of *Lochner* v. *New York*, took a similar view of a New York statute prescribing the hours of labor in bakeries. If, said the Court in effect, bakers' long hours could be shown to affect the quality of bread, something might be said for the regulation under the police power; but bakers were sufficiently intelligent to make their own labor contracts in their own interest, and "we think the limit of the police power has been reached and passed in this case."

---

[1] The decision inspired the Chicago *Evening Post* to protest that "when Dora Windeguth, her employer at her elbow, says that she cannot earn enough in ten hours to live, our whole chivalry rises to her defense; let her work twelve hours then. We have always contended that nobody need starve in America! It is interesting to reflect that while Dora's feudal forebears fought for the right to work, it has been left for Dora's generation to fight for the right to work overtime. But there is still a chance—if we stick together—to save this state from the fate of Massachusetts . . . and other commonwealths, which, given the choice between healthy womanhood and cheap paper boxes, are now going without paper boxes."

The philosophical crisis was fundamental. The roots of laissez faire went down deep into American history and experience. To the generation that won independence from the Old World, nothing was more dramatic or more edifying than the contrast between the roles of government in the Old World and in the New. In the Old World, government maintained standing armies and indulged in incessant wars; supported an established church and rigorously enforced religious conformity; levied crushing burdens on the poor for the benefit of the rich; administered one standard of justice for the powerful and the privileged, and another for the weak and the underprivileged. There, government was indeed the enemy to liberty, to toleration, to equality. But in the New World, government was, in very fact, almost nonexistent for fortunate America: no king, no court, no aristocracy, no armies, no church, no inquisition, no levies on the poor or crushing taxes. The lesson was plain for all to see: that that government is best which governs least; that government, like dress, is the badge of lost innocence.

Besides, Americans were able to fend for themselves without government, or so it seemed. Men could take care of themselves and did, through voluntary associations. Thus they provided for their own religious needs by building churches and supporting them; they provided for their educational needs by setting up schools and academies and colleges; they provided for defense through the militia, or—along perilous frontiers— by organizing their own military companies; they organized companies to build roads and bridges and canals. "Wherever," as Tocqueville later observed, "at the head of some new undertaking, you see the government in France, or a man of rank in England, in the United States you will be sure to find an association."

Federalism, too, or what came to be called dual federalism, contributed to and facilitated the habits of laissez faire. For federalism distributed powers among governments, and inevitably this distribution precipitated controversies that delayed or discouraged the application of power and created a twilight zone in which no government appeared to have power. Whether this was logically necessary is a matter of dispute, but none can deny that institutions like slavery, or corporations that desired to avoid any regulation, did take refuge in the interstices of the federal system.

Another ingredient in the development of laissez faire in America was the special position and power of the business community. For a variety of reasons, business had, almost from the beginning, greater prestige and power in America than in the Old World. In Old World countries—Britain or France, for example—business was a newcomer and had to adjust itself to a political and social world already dominated by the crown, the church, the aristocracy, the army, the guilds, and other ancient institutions. It accepted such terms as these were prepared to grant and accommodated itself to ancient laws and practices. Not until the nineteenth century did it command social prestige; in France, for example, the aristocracy was not permitted by law to engage in business; in England, successful merchants hastened to provide themselves with landed estates and to marry into the landed gentry. But in the New World, commerce, trade, and business had few competitors for power or prestige. There was no court, no aristocracy, no church, no army or navy, no guild system. There were few barriers, legal or otherwise, to the indulgence of private enterprise, and many incentives. In America the merchant, the entrepreneur, the banker did not so much fit into the rules as make the rules. They did not have to adapt their activities to some traditional doctrines of public interest; what they did was clearly in the public interest. A later generation was to look back on the railroad builders, the captains of industry, the titans of finance as "robber barons," but most of their contemporaries regarded them as public benefactors.

By the eighteen-seventies and eighties business had developed its own philosophy, one which levied arrogantly on economics, law, biology, and even religion to justify the special privileges that it enjoyed. We have come to call this philosophical potpourri Social Darwinism. It was made up of five not wholly harmonious ingredients. First was the principle drawn from Jeffersonian agrarianism and Manchester liberalism: that that government was best which governed least, and that government should keep its hands off business. "All experience," wrote the most vigorous of the Social Darwinists, Professor William Graham Sumner of Yale University, "is against state regulation and in favor of liberty. The freer the civil institutions are, the more weak and mischievous state regulation is." Second was the principle of the peculiar sanctity of property—including, of course, corporate charters and franchises—in our constitutional and economic system. Third was the quasireligious principle that the acquisition of wealth was a mark of divine favor, and that the rich therefore had a moral responsibility both to get richer and to direct the affairs of society. Judge Elbert Gary, who had refused to talk to representatives of steel workers who worked twelve hours a day, seven days a week, in his mills, put it simply: "Moral principles," he said, "are the base of all business success."

Fourth was the principle of white—and Nordic—supremacy, which seemed to justify the exploitation of the Negro by Southern whites and of newly arrived immigrants from Italy, Poland, Rumania, and other non-Nordic countries by industry, and which, on a larger scale, was invoked to throw a halo around imperialism and the White Man's Burden. The findings of social workers and the teaching of sociologists commonly supported this principle of Nordic supremacy, for somehow their findings showed that "new" immigrants and Negroes contributed far more than their proportionate share to crime, vice, and disease.

Fifth was the principle of the survival of the fittest, derived from Darwinian biology and applied to the affairs of human society by Herbert Spencer and his many American disciples, notably John Fiske and Edward L. Youmans, who presided over the *Popular Science Monthly* and the immensely influential International Scientific Series. Spencer's basic principle was that society is an organism, like all other organisms, and subject to the same evolutionary laws as all others. Any attempt, therefore, to remove human society from the laws that operate uniformly and implacably upon nature is foredoomed. Makers—political schemers, he called them—who look on society as a "manufacture" rather than a natural growth, and who attempt to "supercede the great laws of existence," may do incalculable harm.

Indeed, where government was concerned, Spencer was not merely a Manchester Liberal; he was almost an anarchist. He believed that because government is based on the necessity of dealing with evil in man, it is itself a reflection of that evil; if men could but learn to cooperate with nature, they would not need government at all. Like the Marxists, he looked forward with confidence to the eventual withering away of government. Meantime there were a few—a very few—things that government might rightly do: defend the nation, keep the peace, enforce justice. But that about exhausted the legitimate arena of governmental activities; all others—even the postal service, public health, education—were misguided. They were misguided on natural grounds, for they encouraged the survival of the unfit, while nature preferred, and progress required, the survival of the fit.

It requires an effort of the imagination, now, to appreciate the dominion that Spencer exercised over American thought in the quarter century or so after the Civil War and, in some quarters, down to the eve of the First World War. Henry Holt testified that "no other philosopher ever had such a vogue as Herbert Spencer"—he was speaking of his own country, to be sure—and John Fiske asserted that Spencer's genius surpassed that of Aristotle as the telegraph surpassed the carrier pigeon. Andrew Carnegie considered Spencer more important than Charles Darwin, and Frederick Barnard was prepared to insist that his was "the most powerful intellect of all time." As late as 1916, Truxton Beale brought out a new edition of *The Man Versus the State,* and great national figures like William Howard Taft, Henry Cabot Lodge, Elihu Root, and Nicholas Murray Butler were honored to contribute introductions to single chapters.

Even more impressive—and certainly more revealing—were the tributes that came from the business community and its spokesmen, like William Graham Sumner of Yale University, and Edward Youmans, editor of the widely read *Popular Science Monthly.* When in 1881 Henry Demarest Lloyd launched his first attack on the Standard Oil Company, one great industrialist indignantly wrote that "the donkeys who can't see the operation of natural laws in fixing the rates of transportation now, rely mainly on the Standard Oil Company as an example. [But] the Standard Oil Company is simply a product of natural laws which it is not safe to touch." Clearly John D. Rockefeller agreed with this interpretation. "The American beauty rose," he said, "can be produced in the splendor and fragrance which bring cheer to its beholder only by sacrificing the early buds which grow up about it. This is not an evil tendency in business. It is merely the working out of a law of nature and of God."

It is interesting to reflect that Spencer enjoyed no comparable vogue in Britain or on the European continent. The explanation is simple enough. First, European economic and social thought was more mature and sophisticated than American, with traditions that traced back to Johann Wolff and Vico and Montesquieu. Second, Europeans had long been habituated to assuming that they had the authority and the responsibility to hold a just balance between conflicting interests and orders and to carry through whatever reforms were called for. Third, Social Darwinism made little sense in the highly urbanized and industrialized Britain of Gladstone or the Germany of Bismarck; where it did seem to make sense, and where it flourished, was in the colonial empires of these two powers. But the American tradition was one not of strong but of weak governments, not of governments that held or imposed a balance of power in society, but of multitudinous interests, groups, factions, which themselves balanced out. And in America, which was still wide open and still in the making and which still offered immense scope to individual initiative, much of what Spencer and his disciples had to say seemed but a reformulation of familiar experience.

Yet every year America was getting more and more like Europe, economically, socially, even intellectually. America, too, was becoming urbanized and industrialized and was facing problems very much like those that Western Europe faced. It was almost inevitable that sooner or later, Americans would find the simple solutions of Spencer irrelevant to the realities of life.

Though Americans borrowed Social Darwinism from abroad, where it was not popular, they did not look abroad for the counterphilosophy, which was popular. To an astonishing extent, America's counterphilosophy was indigenous. Though Europe first created the welfare state—Germany and Scandinavia and Britain—it is no exaggeration to say that Americans were the first to develop the philosophy of the welfare state. This was something of a reversal of customary roles, but a reversal natural enough in the light of the needs and circumstances of the two Atlantic societies.

For at no time did the Spencerians have things their own way in America. So overarching is the fame of Spencer that we tend to underestimate, or to forget, the strength and pervasiveness of the revolt against his teachings and those of Manchester. From the mid-seventies on, protest welled up from every part of the nation and in many voices, which in the end found their own harmony. Most eloquent perhaps, was the social-gospel group, the clergymen and their allies outside the church—men like Washington Gladden of Columbus, Ohio; Lyman Abbott of New York; Octavius Brooks Frothingham, who was a proper godson to Theodore Parker and who developed a religion of humanity; and Walter Rauschenbusch, whose *Christianity and the Social Crisis* was one of the vital documents of the Progressive movement. Equally important were the economists, pioneers like Henry George, whose *Progress and Poverty* touched a responsive chord in a dozen countries, and the pioneering Richard Ely of Wisconsin, and his colleague John R. Commons, and the hard-bitten Thorstein Veblen, and the philosophical Simon Patten down in Philadelphia, and E. Benjamin Andrews and Edward Bemis, who were forced out of their academic posts because of their radicalism. The jurisprudents were fewer, but even more distinguished: young Louis Brandeis, who was already becoming the people's counsel, and the German born Ernst Freund, and Judge Walter Clark in North Carolina, and at Harvard two erudite deans, James B. Thayer and Roscoe Pound. They had this in common, these men of the law: They distrusted the theories and fictions of natural law and the pretensions of judges, and thought that law, like other institutions, should be required to serve the needs of society. There were the social workers, the wonderful Jane Addams at their head, and her associates at Hull House, Florence Kelley, Dr. Alice Hamilton, Julia Lathrop, and Sophia Breckenridge, and settlement-house workers throughout the country; their influence was nation-wide. There were reformers such as Jacob Riis of *How the Other Half Lives* fame, and the sociologist E. A. Ross at Wisconsin, and the defrocked Congregationalist minister, George Herron. There were the politicians, most of them more at home in the Populist or the Socialist than in the "major" parties, which were engaged in a kind of conspiracy of silence: men like Governors Altgeld of Illinois and Pingree of Michigan and the incomparable La Follette of Wisconsin; and in Ohio,

"Golden Rule" Jones of Toledo and Tom Johnson of Cleveland; and scores of others who refused to accept the dominance of the great corporations as somehow ordained by nature and by God, and who tried to rally farmers and workingmen and intellectuals to a common cause. For the intellectuals were involved too: philosophers William James and young John Dewey; the Georgia-born poet Sidney Lanier, whose "Symphony" was one of the earliest assaults on the sins of industrialism; the transcendental New Englander William Vaughn Moody, whose "Gloucester Moors" raised fundamental questions about the social order; and most of the leading novelists —Mark Twain and William Dean Howells and Frank Norris and Stephen Crane and Hamlin Garland among them.

Of them all—the economists and the jurists and the political reformers, the Christian socialists and the philosophers and the men of letters—none contributed more to undermining Social Darwinism and to laying the foundation for the welfare state than the government clerk whose business was with immigration statistics, with the census, with the flora and fauna of the West, with fossils—Lester Ward.

Lester Ward has some claim to being regarded as the philosopher, the protagonist, even the architect, of the modern welfare state. Neglected in his own day (though never quite as neglected as he liked to suppose) and almost forgotten since, he was, like so many of the leaders of the intellectual revolution at the turn of the century—Thorstein Veblen, for example, or Charles Beard, or Frederick Jackson Turner, or Louis Brandeis, or Roscoe Pound, or Frank Lloyd Wright—a product of the Middle Border. His father was an engineer of sorts, untrained, like Ward himself, a mechanic who specialized in building locks and dams. He had fought in the War of 1812— how quickly we get back to the generation of the founding fathers—and many years later he was able to collect a quarter section of land out in Iowa for his military services. Born in

1842, young Lester Ward grew up in what was still frontier country, along the banks of the Desplaines and the Rock and the Fox rivers in Illinois and Wisconsin, getting what schooling he could, which was not much, and learning from nature what he could, which was a great deal. In the mid-fifties the family moved to that quarter section in Iowa, but Ward was not attracted to farming, and after his father's death he and his brother Cyrenus, another unsung genius, went east to Pennsylvania to work in a wheel-hub shop. It was a thankless job, but somehow Ward managed to pick up a bit of Latin and Greek and French, and mathematics as well, and when the wheel-hub venture failed, he took to schoolteaching; he began and closed his career that way. He was very conscious of the ragged and desultory character of his education:

Perhaps the most vivid impression that my early experience left on my mind was that of the difference between the educated and the uneducated person. I had had much to do with the uneducated, and I could not believe that the chasm between these and the educated people was due to any great extent to their inherent nature. . . . The influence of education and environmental conditions, took an ever stronger hold on me.[1]

He took a few courses at the Susquehanna Collegiate Institute; he continued his own studies of Greek and Latin and added German; he kept a diary in French, partly for practice, partly for privacy, for he was indulging in a romantic and passionate love affair, and the diary told all. When the Civil War came he enlisted in the Pennsylvania Volunteeers and marched off to Virginia, where he managed to get himself wounded three times; if he did not read quite as much into that experience as did Justice Holmes, for whom it was central, he did, like Holmes, draw from it a sense of the national power.

Out of the Army, Ward found himself a job with the Bureau

---

[1] *Glimpses of the Cosmos* (New York: G. P. Putnam's Sons, 1913–1918), III, 147.

of Statistics, and after that with other government departments—the Bureau of Standards, the Census Bureau, the Bureau of Immigration. Meantime he was busy educating himself,
faithfully attending night classes at the Columbian University,
now the George Washington University, and somehow managing to pick up degrees in both medicine and law. The degrees
were not much, but he was able to win admission to practice
before the bar of the Supreme Court—quite an accomplishment for a self-educated young man from the Illinois frontier.

Somehow, too, he found time to launch a jejune little magazine, named, prophetically enough, the *Iconoclast,* and dedicated to embalming the ideas of Tom Paine and echoing those
of Bob Ingersoll. He edited it and wrote most of it, but soon
he tired of it and turned to more serious interests. For by now
Ward was settling down. He had earned his degrees and he
had married (alas, he lost this wife, whom he loved, and his
next marriage was not very successful). His interests were
turning increasingly to science, especially to geology and
paleontology and paleobotany, and he found himself a job in
the United States Geological Survey under the dynamic and
inspiring John Wesley Powell, to whom he was to dedicate his
first book. But more and more—all very unusual, this—he
found himself distracted from science to larger social problems. He was a child of Darwin, to be sure, a committed evolutionist, a scientist who worked by preference in the field, off
on one expedition after another, jogging along dirt roads in
Alabama, or exploring the Bad Lands of the Dakotas just at
the time Theodore Roosevelt was discovering them, or floating
down the Missouri River in a flatboat. Clearly he was a product of the age of science and of evolution; but he was a
product, too, of the new spirit of unrest and revolt against
Victorian complacency and the triumph of the new plutocracy,
a product of the age that produced the Greenbackers and the
Grangers, the Populists and the Socialists, and it was with
these that he could cast his lot. He lived in Washington, where

he could watch politics at first hand, but Washington meant to him not politics but government, not spoils but power, and if he took little interest in the politics of the Gilded Age, he learned well the lessons of power. But mostly Washington provided Ward with a great company of scientists. No university of that time could boast a scientific faculty the equal of that which worked in the Smithsonian and in the various departments of the government; here was surely the best scientific laboratory to be found in the nation. As early as the seventies, when Ward himself was barely in his thirties, he began to make those contributions to science and to social science that were destined to mark him, eventually, as one of his generation's leading explorers in both realms.

Nothing is more astonishing than how early Ward found what were to be his lifelong interests, unless it is the assiduousness with which he cultivated them. As early as 1869, he had drawn up an elaborate prospectus of the book that was to appear, fourteen years later, as *Dynamic Sociology*, and this while he was still working for those degrees. He gives us a chapter by chapter account of the composition of that book in one of the autobiographical notes in *Glimpses of the Cosmos*, and gives us, too, without the slightest embarrassment, the three reviews that he himself wrote of his book in various journals. If we take 1869 as the starting point of Ward's inquiries into science and sociology, we can say that the scholarly monument that he built engaged his undivided attention for forty-five years.

There was, indeed, a formidable intensity about the young man, and the old man, too, and with it a hard, almost an implacable quality; there were few grace notes in Ward, few concessions to style, and for all his concern with the psyche, little interest in the life of the imagination. We see this in the boy who took up the study of Greek and Latin, French and German, and mastered them; we see it in the relentless pursuit of academic degrees; we see it in the unswerving commitment to the one great principle of sociology that he formulated early in his studies and upon which he played variations for the rest of his life—the principle of the psychic control of evolution.

Ward never really outgrew his early suspicion of the respectable elements of society; indeed, that suspicion grew deeper with the passing years. He was, almost by instinct, a dissenter and a come-outer, even something of a dreamer. It is hard to see a dreamer in that hard-bitten, humorless, prematurely old government clerk, busy with his immigration statistics and his fossils. Yet there was romance there, and excitement. He knew America intimately, knew her as did only a handful of his contemporaries—explorers and scientists, men like Major Powell, Clarence King, Ferdinand Hayden, and Raphael Pumpelly, all, at one time or another, connected with the Geological Survey. As a boy he had grown up on the frontier of the Middle Border, and later he was to crisscross the plains and the mountains of the Far West, the Yellowstone, Colorado, Utah, and Arizona, sleeping out under the stars and writing his books by the flickering light of log fires, studying the flora and fauna of the west, building up fossil collections for the Geological Survey. He knew the plain people, too, those who rode coaches instead of Pullman Palace cars, or who rode no cars at all, farmers and cattlemen, workingmen, privates in the Army, the humble civil servants of Washington, the immigrants, the poor, the denizens of the slums, whom he thought potentially the equals of the rich and the privileged.

Somehow, in the midst of all his professional activities, he mastered a dozen fields of knowledge, until he became, in the end, perhaps the most variously learned man in the country. And except in a few areas, that learning was not superficial but professional. What he knew, he knew thoroughly; what he did, he did not only well but expertly. A master of half a dozen fields of science, he was a master, too, of social science—in a sense he may be said to have created it. When, at the end of his life, he attached himself to Brown University, he gave a course which he called—perhaps it was his one gesture of humor—"An Outline of All Knowledge."

The protest movement was, to be sure, well under way when Ward enlisted in it, but it was disparate and amorphous and even fortuitous in the sense that it took its tone from the evils which it attacked rather than from the virtues which it extolled. That is one reason why, compared with the great sweeping reform movement of the pre-Civil War years, this one appears so miscellaneous. It was—the historical name is right here—an era of social protest rather than an era of social achievement, and a disproportionate amount of its energy was devoted to criticism. What it lacked was a philosophy that would bind together its disparate activities and enthusiasms.

It was this which Ward undertook to provide, a philosophy that could be relevant, comprehensive, fundamental, and positive. First came the book which, he hoped, would sum up the problem, and settle it too: *Dynamic Sociology*. "All things considered," wrote the Chicago sociologist Albion Small years later, "I would rather have written *Dynamic Sociology* than any other book ever published in America." A decade later, in 1893, came *Psychic Factors of Civilization,* in some ways Ward's most important book, succinct, original, and persuasive. This little masterpiece was followed, in turn, by *Outlines of Sociology* (1898), *Pure Sociology* (1903), and *Applied Sociology* (1906). There was, in addition, that curious hodgepodge which Ward, with unconscious vanity, called *Glimpses of the Cosmos*. Originally designed to fill twelve stout volumes but restricted, in the end, to six, it was a collection of almost everything of a fragmentary character, scientific, sociological, or merely occasional that Ward had written.

Few men of his day ranged so widely or saw so deeply as Lester Ward. In the realm of social economy he anticipated Thorstein Veblen, who owed much to him. In the realm of education he anticipated John Dewey and supplied him with a scientific basis for much of his educational philosophy. In the realm of politics he provided the intellectual foundations on which such men as La Follette and Wilson and Franklin Roosevelt were later to build.

It is Ward's political thought that particularly concerns us, for this collection does not attempt to represent the whole range of his intellectual or professional interests, nor the whole of his philosophy. It is confined to the presentation of what was, in retrospect, the central thrust of his social thought, and what has proved to be, in our current situation, the most lasting and most significant of his contributions: his formulation of the philosophy of the welfare state.

Ward's sociology was all of a piece. Like so many great social thinkers, Comte for example, and Herbert Spencer, and perhaps even Veblen, he was a man of one great idea, he was consumed by this idea, he devoted much of his life to advancing it—that part left over, in any event, from the demands of his professional work. And what was that one great idea? It was this: That man is not the subject but the master of nature, and that all progress is achieved by the conscious exercise of that mastery over the impersonal and chaotic forces of nature. This mastery over nature distinguishes man from all creatures here below. All of nature and all forms of life are subject to the iron laws of evolution, but man and man alone, through the psychic forces of mind and spirit, can control and direct those laws.

Almost all of Ward's voluminous writings in the sociological arena were variations on this theme. Certainly this was true of his first book, *Dynamic Sociology,* a book that he had hoped would sum up the whole of his message. That hope proved mistaken; Ward found that he had to restate his case, over and over, in different ways. And that is what much of his later work was: the penetrating *Psychic Factors of Civil-*

ization, the abstruse *Pure Sociology,* the intensely practical *Applied Sociology.* Like so many great philosophers and social thinkers, Ward had a habit of cannibalizing himself: he nourished himself on his own ideas, digested them well, and brought them out again in new forms and patterns. But along with the exposition of his own philosophy went another task, time-consuming but unavoidable. That was to clear away the debris which, he thought, littered the sociological landscape.

"A growing sense of the essential sterility of all that has thus far been done in the domain of social science," he wrote, in the preface to *Dynamic Sociology,* "has furnished the chief incentive to the preparation of this work. Just as Comte could complain that the philosophy of Hobbes, Locke and Voltaire was negative, so it may now be maintained that the school of Mill, Spencer, and Fiske is almost negative. . . . The latter has only advanced to the passively dynamic stage which recognizes only the changes wrought by nature, unaided by art; but before the science of society can be truly founded, another advance must be made, and the actively dynamic stage reached in which social phenomena shall be contemplated as capable of intelligent control by society itself in its own interest." Ward had no doubt, from the beginning, that he had made that advance, and in the notice that he himself wrote of *Dynamic Sociology* he staked out his claim:

Seizing upon the new conception of universal development or evolution [he wrote], Mr. Ward fits everything into its appropriate niche in his progressive scheme of having man in his highest social stage at its head in showing how this system of things has been evolved, the higher from the lower forms, our author is in entire harmony with most of the modern philosophers who set out with the facts of the known universe as the basis of their ideas, but at this point he finds himself compelled to diverge from the main path of the most advanced modern thought, and to introduce new elements which he regards as being of paramount importance. Without ascribing to man any divine attributes not originally attained through spontaneous evolution like all the rest, he does maintain that the development of the psychic faculty, and especially the appearance of the rational intellect of man, introduced a set of factors into the general problem of evolution. . . .[2]

"Is it true," Ward asked, "that man shall ultimately obtain dominion of the whole world except himself?" Those who subscribe to the doctrine of *Social Statics* as formulated by Spencer were forced to confess that it was. But sociology, Ward insisted, was a positive and dynamic science, and, properly applied, it would enable man to control the evolutionary process. The psychic factors, he maintained, count more than the natural, for they condition and control the natural. "The advent with man of the thinking, knowing, foreseeing, calculating, designing, inventing and constructing faculty, which is wanting in lower creatures, repealed . . . the law of nature, and enacted in its stead the psychologic law, or law of mind," he wrote. The capital error of the Spencerian system was its failure to appreciate the role of mind in creative evolution, and this error Ward set about to repair. "Thus far," he wrote, "social progress has in a certain awkward manner taken care of itself, but in the near future it will have to be cared for. To do this, and maintain the dynamic condition against all the hostile forces which thicken with every new advance, is the real problem of sociology considered as an applied science."

More clearly than any of his contemporaries, Ward saw that though environment transforms animals, man transforms environment, and he insisted that the transformation be not haphazard but planned—and so planned as to produce not only material abundance but intellectual and spiritual well-being. He set himself, therefore, to rescue evolution from the creeping paralysis with which Spencer had infected it, to

---

[2] *Glimpses of the Cosmos,* III, 232–233.

release its energies for the use of society and make it the servant rather than the master of man. Throughout all Ward's writings there runs, his fellow sociologist Frank Giddings wrote, one dominating and organizing thought: "Human society as we who live now know it, is not the passive product of unconscious forces. It lies within the domain of cosmic law, but so does the mind of man; and this mind of man has knowingly, artfully, adapted and readapted its social environment, and with reflective intelligence has begun to shape it into an instrument wherewith to fulfill man's will."

If the mind of man was to function in this benign fashion, it was necessary to rid it of those superstitions that still held domain. Of these, laissez faire was the most stupefying, and it was on the doctrine of laissez faire that Ward trained his heaviest guns. Laissez faire, Ward argued, was incoherent, fragmentary, and futile, scarcely consistent with the law of nature and wholly inconsistent with the law of man. It repudiated the past and condemned the future, denied scope to the creative faculty of man and barred the road to progress. For civilization, as we know it, is the triumph of man over the blind forces of nature and the deliberate application of human genius to the task of emancipating man from the tyranny of those forces. "We are told," Ward wrote, "to let things alone, and allow nature to take its course. But has intelligent man ever done this? Is not civilization, with all it has accomplished, the result of man's not letting things alone, and of his not letting nature take its course?" Nature is prodigal and ruthless, indifferent to man's fate and to time; it is only when man breaks in upon nature's course that he can free himself from the fate to which all other forms of life are condemned:

This iron law of nature, as it may appropriately be called, was everywhere found to lie athwart the path of human progress, and the whole upward struggle of rational man . . . has been with this tyrant of nature—the law of competition. And in so far as he has progressed at all beyond the purely animal stage he has done so through triumphing little by little over this law and gaining somewhat the mastery of the struggle. In the physical world he has accomplished this through invention, from which have resulted the arts and material civilization. Every implement or utensil, every mechanical device . . . is a triumph of mind over the physical forces of nature in ceaseless and aimless competition. All human institutions—religion, government, law, marriage, custom—together with innumerable other modes of regulating social, industrial and commercial life are, broadly viewed, only so many ways of meeting and checkmating the principle of competition as it manifests itself in society.[3]

The notion of the "survival of the fittest" Ward repudiated as either meaningless or pernicious. Assuredly, said Ward, mere fitness to survive is no criterion that civilization can accept, and here he echoed Huxley's statement that "social progress means a checking of the cosmic process at every step. The more advanced a society becomes the more it eliminates the struggle for existence." It was only when man intervened that nature's products became fit for man, and it is only when society or government intervenes, Ward asserted, that man's products become fit for society. Competition is, in fact, not the law of life, as so many of Ward's contemporaries believed, but the law of death: the whole of medicine and surgery is a violent interference with biological competition. Man, thanks to the possession of mind, repudiates nature and applies art—or that which is *art*ificial. "The constant tendency," Ward pointed out,

is to render everything more artificial, which means more and more perfect. Human institutions are not exempt from this all-pervading spirit of improvement. They, too, are artificial, conceived in the ingenious brain and wrought with mental skill born of inventive

---

[3] *Psychic Factors of Civilization* (Boston: Ginn and Co., 1893), pp. 261–262.

genius. The passion for their improvement is of a piece with the impulse to improve the plow or the steam engine. Government is one of these artificial products of man's devising, and his right to change it is the same as his right to create it.[4]

Ward protested equally the inconsistency and the insincerity of the doctrine of laissez faire as applied in America. It was applied to public associations but not to private, and Ward had been too long a civil servant to accept the curious theory that a peculiar iniquity attached to governmental activities from which the comparable activities of corporations were miraculously free. He knew that laissez faire was a rationalization rather than a first principle: business did not embrace competition in response to philosophical precepts; those precepts, rather, flowed from the felt needs of business. Laissez faire was rather the validation than the inspiration of the economic conduct of the age of corporate business. And Ward saw, too, what even William Graham Sumner, for all his hostility to the protective tariff, had failed to see: that business had already made a travesty of the doctrine of laissez faire, invoking it only to prevent regulation that might interfere with profits, but rejecting it out of hand whenever questions of tariffs, patents, copyrights, or corporate charters were at stake.

All this meant, inevitably, an enlargement of the role of government. Unlike most of his contemporaries, unlike many of our own contemporaries, Ward did not fear this but looked upon it with approbation.

Government was, as Ward saw, the most fundamental and the greatest of man's inventions, the one without which all the others were doomed to futility. Man and the state were not incongruous, as Spencer had insisted, but interdependent. Imagine man without the state! Ward, to be sure, did not think of "man," but of "mankind"; a collective title for his

---

[4] *Psychic Factors*, pp. 287–288.

books might have been "Society and the State." His political philosophy—we can use the term for Ward as for Montesquieu or Rousseau or John Stuart Mill—can be stated succinctly, though he himself argued it elaborately and pervasively. First, all invention is an intervention in nature, and all invention is social. Second, government is the greatest of all inventions for intervening in and controlling nature. Third, almost everything government undertakes—in a democracy, in any event—it does better than private enterprise can possibly do. Fourth, the major factor of government, so far, has been caution and ineffectiveness, and as long as government is controlled by private and selfish interests it will continue to be cautious and ineffectual. And, finally, the function of government is not negative but positive, not merely the prevention of crime or subversion or conquest but the organization of the energies of society for beneficent purposes. Government must, of course, guard against crime and injustice and chaos; these duties are elementary. But the larger end of government is the manufacture of intelligence and of happiness, and the advancement of the general welfare.

"Modern society," wrote Ward, "is suffering from the very opposite of paternalism—from under-government. . . . The true function of government is not to fetter, but to liberate the forces of society, not to diminish but to increase their effectiveness." It was a bold thing for a scholar to announce in the eighteen-nineties, when even the Interstate Commerce Act seemed vaguely socialistic, and when Henry Wood, whose *Political Economy of Natural Law* purveyed Spencer in capsule form, was insisting that "Freedom of the individual contract is the chief cornerstone in the structure of any system of liberal government. . . . Any legislation or even prevailing custom, which tends to its impairment, is tyrannous."

William Graham Sumner had said the same thing. "All experience is against state regulation," he asserted roundly. But Ward was not inclined to apologize for the state. Government had already extended its jurisdiction over broad areas of life—justice, national defense, agriculture and the public domain, science and education—and no one could say that it had done badly. "In all those affairs which the state can manage more advantageously than the individual," he concluded, "it has in fact managed well, and such as have passed from private to public control are better administered by the state than they were by the individual."

The question of government intervention, as Ward saw, was one not of theory but of fact, and the wisdom of particular legislation was to be determined by experience rather than by a priori reasoning. The realization of this made him impatient with discussions of abstractions like centralization, paternalism, bureaucracy, socialism, and similar terms that lost all their meaning when they were treated as absolutes rather than as techniques. Ward had the same test for legislation that James had for truth: Good legislation was what worked. Nor was his political pragmatism less idealistic than James's philosophical. What worked was what contributed most, in the long run, to the spiritual and the intellectual as well as to the material welfare of mankind.

The trouble with legislation, as Ward saw it during the last quarter of the nineteenth century, was threefold: it was limited in scope and in imagination; it reflected the will of special pressure groups rather than the needs of society as a whole; it was haphazard and unscientific. What was needed, therefore, was a positive program, one not hamstrung by those predatory interests that were so ready to use government for their own advantage and so reluctant to permit society to use it for social advantage. Ward himself was not tempted to shift from his study to the political hustings. He was more concerned for the establishment of right principles than for the agitation of current issues. "It is not indifference, now, that resigns me to events," he wrote, "but a sense of the infinitesmal effect of anything I could do, especially of the utter powerlessness of the hortatory method." For he had no faith in mere tinkering with the political or the economic machinery of society. What was needed was new machinery altogether, machinery to "manufacture intelligence" and to apply it scientifically to the needs of society.

One way to begin was to formulate a science of politics and to provide scientific training for legislators and social scientists.

Before science taught man the nature of physical laws, all attempts at invention except of the simplest kind, were just such wretched miscarriages as attempts at progressive legislation are today, and for the same reason, viz., that the inventors possessed no science of the field of natural forces over which they sought to exert an influence. Before progressive legislation can become a success, every legislature must become, as it were, a polytechnic school, a laboratory of philosophical research, into the laws of society and of human nature. No legislator is qualified to vote on or propose measures designed to affect the destinies of millions of social units until he masters all that is known of the science of society. Every true legislator must be a sociologist.

The legislation of the future, Ward wrote elsewhere, "will consist of a series of exhaustive experiments on the part of true scientific sociologists, and sociological inventors, working on the problems of social physics from the practical point of view." As a contribution to this end, Ward proposed the establishment of a national academy of the social sciences, to train public administrators and study the great social problems of the age.

For intelligence, too, was a manufacture. "The origination and distribution of knowledge can no longer be left to chance and to nature. They are to be systematized and erected into true arts." This, as Ward saw it, was the major task of society: to provide education for all, to discover talent and develop it and enlist it in the attack on social problems. Faith in education was nothing new in America, but no earlier American educator—neither Jefferson nor Horace Mann nor Henry Barnard—had based his education program so firmly on scientific foundations or had faced so clearly its logical implications and consequences. He believed both in the potential equality of intelligence and in the manufacture of knowledge. There is, he asserted, no aristocracy of talent; intellectual ability is the product of opportunity and privilege, not of native capacity. "The denizens of the slums," he asserted, "are not inferior in talent to the graduates of Harvard College," and criminals are "the geniuses of the slums. Society has forced them into this field, and they are making the best use they can of their native abilities." Nowhere is Ward's quarrel with Spencer sharper than here. "It is a frequent delusion," Spencer had said in reply to an inquiry about the future of America, "that education is a universal remedy for political evils." But for Ward education was "the great panacea." And it was, like civilization itself, a violent and calculated interference with nature. It was, of all the activities of civilized man, the most thoroughgoing departure from laissez faire.

Ward's significance as prophet has been overshadowed by his role as critic. The first sociologist to challenge the doctrine of laissez faire on scientific grounds and to articulate social to natural evolution, he was the first, too, to embrace the full implications of pragmatism and to give sociology a scientific foundation. From the beginning he ranged himself on the side of the plain people, fighting their battles with weapons more formidable by far than those that Sumner and his followers could muster. He inspired a generation of scholars and social workers to believe that it was possible to rebuild society on sounder foundations, with more honest materials, and on a more symmetrical plan; and new generations that did not know him fought with his weapons and built with his tools.

He lived long enough to hear Woodrow Wilson inaugurate the New Freedom in words that might have been taken directly from his own writings:

There can be no equality of opportunity if men and women and children be not shielded in their lives, their very vitality, from the consequences of great industrial and social processes which they can not alter, control, or singly cope with. . . . Society must see to it that it does not crush or weaken or damage its own constituent parts. The first duty of law is to keep sound the society it serves.

If this was not the end of laissez faire, it was the beginning of the end; if it was not the triumph of the welfare state, it was the mere beginning of that process. For the New Freedom was to be succeeded by the bolder and more far-reaching New Deal, and that by the New Frontier, and that in turn by the Great Society—a term and a concept first formulated by Ward's fellow worker, Graham Wallas, back in 1914. It is no hyperbole to call Ward the prophet and the protagonist of all those movements that looked to the reconstruction of the American economy and society through governmental inter-vention—the most striking development of American politics in the past half-century—or to name him the philosophical architect of the welfare state.

H. S. C.

Amherst, Massachusetts
August 1966

BIBLIOGRAPHY

Arnold, Thurman. *The Folklore of Capitalism.* New Haven: Yale University Press, 1937.

Beard, Charles A. *Public Policy and the General Welfare.* New York: Farrar and Rinehart, Inc., 1941.

Childs, Marquis. *Sweden, the Middle Way.* New Haven: Yale University Press, 1936.

Chugerman, Samuel. *Lester F. Ward, The American Aristotle: A Summary and Interpretation of His Sociology.* Durham: Duke University Press, 1939.

Commager, Henry S. *The American Mind.* New Haven: Yale University Press, 1950.

Davie, Maurice R. *William Graham Sumner.* New York: Thomas Y. Crowell Co., 1963.

Dealey, James Q., *et al.* "Lester Frank Ward," *American Journal of Sociology,* XIX (July 1913), 60–78.

Fine, Sidney. *Laissez Faire and the General Welfare State.* Ann Arbor: University of Michigan Press, 1956.

Faulkner, Harold Underwood. *The Decline of Laissez Faire, 1897–1917.* (*The Economic History of the United States,* Vol. VII.) New York: Rinehart, 1951.

Gerver, Israel. *Lester Frank Ward.* New York: Thomas Y. Crowell Co., 1963.

Glueck, Sheldon, ed. *The Welfare State and the National Welfare: A Symposium on Some of the Threatening Tendencies of our Times.* Cambridge: Addison-Wesley Press, 1952.

Hawkins, Richmond Laurin. *Auguste Comte and the United States, 1816–1853.* Cambridge: Harvard University Press, 1936.

Hofstadter, Richard. *Social Darwinism in American Thought (Revised).* Boston: Beacon Press, 1955.

Keezer, Dexter, and Stacy May. *Public Control of Business.* New York: Harper and Brothers, 1930.

Kirkland, Edward C. *Business in the Gilded Age: The Conservative's Balance Sheet.* Madison: University of Wisconsin Press, 1952.

Lippmann, Walter. *An Inquiry into the Principles of the Good Society.* Boston: Little, Brown and Co., 1937.

Loewenberg, Bert J. "Darwinism Comes to America, 1865–1900," *Mississippi Valley Historical Review,* XXVIII (December 1941), 339–368.

Lutz, Karl. "The General Welfare Clause," *Journal of the American Bar Association,* XXXVI (1950).

McCloskey, Robert Green. *American Conservatism in the Age of Enterprise: A Study of William Graham Sumner, Stephen J. Field, and Andrew Carnegie.* Cambridge: Harvard University Press, 1951.

Odum, Howard W., ed. *American Masters of Social Science: An Approach to the Study of the Social Sciences Through a Neglected Field of Biography.* New York: Kenaikat Press, Inc., 1951.

Parrington, Vernon Louis. *The Beginnings of Critical Realism in America. (Main Currents in American Thought,* Vol. III.) New York: Harcourt, Brace and Co., 1930.

Schlesinger, Arthur M., Jr. *The Vital Center.* Boston: Houghton, Mifflin Co., 1949.

Shannon, David A. *The Great Depression.* Englewood Cliffs, N. J.: Prentice-Hall, 1960.

Small, Albion W. "Fifty Years of Sociology in the United States, 1865–1915," *American Journal of Sociology,* XXI (May 1916), 721–864.

Swados, Harvey. *Years of Conscience.* Cleveland and New York: World Publishing Co., 1962.

Ward, Barbara. *Freedom Under Planning.* Chapel Hill: University of North Carolina Press, 1945.

Ward, Lester F. *Applied Sociology.* Boston: Ginn and Co., 1906.

————. *Dynamic Sociology.* 2 vols. New York: D. Appleton and Co., 1883, 1897.

————. *Glimpses of the Cosmos.* 6 vols. New York: G. P. Putnam's Sons, 1913–1918.

————. *Outlines of Sociology.* New York: The Macmillan Co., 1898.

————. *The Psychic Factors of Civilization.* Boston: Ginn and Co., 1893.

White, Morton G. *Social Thought in America: The Revolt Against Formalism.* New York: Viking Press, 1949.

EDITOR'S NOTE

This selection from the writings of Lester Ward does not purport to be representative. Ward published altogether six stout volumes of sociology and another six volumes of miscellaneous writings, plus scores of substantial articles in journals, learned and otherwise. These reflected a great variety of subjects, and it would not be difficult to cull from Ward's voluminous writings substantial books on sociological theory, the history of sociology, gynecocracy or the superiority of the female, the nature and geography of genius, and education, as well as on botany, geology, and paleontology. This collection is confined to a single subject—one that Ward himself thought pervasive, imperative, and significant—the welfare state, a term that he himself, curiously enough, did not use. To be sure, I have not imposed a rigorous consistency on myself in this matter but have included some autobiographical pieces and some educational. Though I have consulted the Ward papers at the Brown University library, I have not found it feasible to levy upon them: Ward's correspondence is interesting but discursive and miscellaneous, and it throws relatively little light on the subject of this collection. Had his voluminous diary survived, it would have illuminated not only Ward's intellectual history but the intellectual history of his generation. But alas, only one volume did survive, and that carried the story only to the threshold of his professional career, 1869. Because this collection addresses itself to a single coherent subject, I have adopted a chronological rather than a topical arrangement, one that permits us to follow the development of Ward's thinking on this problem so central to his own philosophy, and to ours as well.

Lester Ward
and the Welfare State

1

AUTOBIOGRAPHICAL

SKETCH

1913

Ward wrote this sketch of his life sometime in 1912 or 1913, as part of the preface to what was designed to be a complete collection of his miscellaneous writings, somewhat grandiloquently titled GLIMPSES OF THE COSMOS. *This collection, which originally was to have run to a dozen or fifteen volumes, was eventually limited to six. Fortunately, most of Ward's nonscientific essays are included in these volumes, and it is from this rich storehouse that we have drawn most of our material.*

. . . My father was a mechanic, especially a millwright and wheelwright, but generally inventive, and a "jack-at-all-trades." He was also musical and played the fife. He was fife-major in the army during the War of 1812, and served in the battle of Buffalo, for which service, before the homestead days, he obtained a land warrant for 160 acres of land in Iowa. The whole Ward family early settled in Western New York, and there is a nest of Wards there still. But my father moved to

Glimpses of the Cosmos (New York: G. P. Putnam's Sons, 1913–1918), I, lxviii–lxxviii.

3

Illinois after the birth of most of the children. My next older
brother Erastus, and I, the tenth and last, were the only ones
born in that State. My father sought a mill-site in Northeastern
Illinois, first on the Dupage River, and later on the Des Plaines
River. The Illinois and Michigan Canal, now the great Drainage Canal, was being cut through to connect Lake Michigan
with the Mississippi, and he secured the contract to build many
of the locks. He settled in Joliet, where there were fine beds
of freestone, bought a quarry, and built the locks. My next
oldest brother, Loomis, assisted him in this work. It was there
that I was born. On Aug. 31, 1893, I visited Joliet in company
with my brother Loomis, and he showed me the house in which
I was born, and also the locks that they built. He pointed out
the spot where the stone was quarried, but the State Peniten-
tiary now stands over my father's quarry! For all the time that
I lived in Illinois the State Prison was at Alton. But it has now
been so long in Joliet that people sometimes smile when I tell
them I was born there. As the family moved away from Joliet
one year after I was born, I tell them that I *escaped* at an
early age.

The Des Plaines (or Aux Plaines, as it was locally called)
flowed over a long swamp or low, wet region of country, called
the "Sag," for many miles in its course. This occurred mostly
in what is now called Downer's Grove, then known as Cass.
It lies some distance above Lockport and Lamont, and extended to within fifteen miles of Chicago. It was impossible to
build a towpath along this region, and my father and older
brothers obtained the contract to build a long towpath-bridge,
called the "Sag Bridge," raised on timbers above the swamp.
It had to be ten miles long. To do this work it was necessary
to erect a sawmill near the spot. A brisk-flowing stream came
into the river from the north with sufficient fall to make an
overshot wheel possible, which will drive a saw with the minimum of water. The site was located, the mill built, and the
work begun. We moved to a place on this stream a mile above

the mill, and my father bought a farm there and built a house. The stream had never been named, and it was thenceforth known as Ward's Creek. It was at this place, in this new-built house, on this stream and farm, that I first came to consciousness, and here are stamped on my memory all the scenes of my earliest boyhood. Here we lived till I was nine years old, here I first went to school in the schoolhouse a mile north of the Cass farm. My recollection of every detail, and of the precise topography of the whole region over which I so freely roamed, is exceedingly vivid. From the date of our next removal, viz., in 1852, this time to St. Charles on the Fox River in Kane County, to the day above mentioned, Aug. 31, 1893, I had never returned to that spot, and I was anxious to do so. Before we went to Joliet, my brother Loomis and I, on that day revisited the whole region. Getting out of a way train at the station nearest the mouth of Ward's Creek, we followed it up to the mill-site, of which only the faintest traces remained, and on up to the farm and the house. But all was changed. The brook was dry and the whole region was transformed. Forty years had made their ravages, and nothing was left but the house and the ground around it. I will not dwell on such a theme, but I was glad to have once more seen even the spot, if not the scenes, of my childhood.

St. Charles was only headquarters in the next act of the drama, a place for my brother, Erastus, and me to go to school, a place to live in the winter, and for my parents to have social and religious society. The objective point was another mill-stream two miles north of the village, in fact, a mill already built, Norton's Mill on Norton's Creek, which my father had purchased along with a large tract of land, and where for three years more I was destined to struggle with nature. I had to work, both in the village and at the mill, but I had much leisure time for play and for roving where I pleased. Here, on the pretty Fox River, I learned to skate, and in its clear waters in summer, to swim. Here my brother Erastus and I abandoned our bows and arrows, our cross-guns, and our bow-guns, and bought with nuts we gathered, a shotgun, which we owned in common, and "took turns" in shooting! Our interest was transferred from insects to birds and mammals. Finally we got each of us a gun, and how we did pursue the small game of the place! For there was no large game there then. We did also much fishing. It was there that occurred the event recorded in *Pure Sociology* on page 182. I enlarge upon it in the sketch of that work, in dealing with the burlesque article in the New York *Sun,* where it is characterized as a "fish-story." In all this I always had the companionship of my next older brother, Erastus, who, though three and a half years older than I, seemed the same age. I was already larger than he, and I well remember when I first threw him in a wrestle, and ever after that I could easily "handle" him. But we were exceedingly congenial, and very fond of each other—a true Damon and Phintias[1]. Our minds were also about equivalent, though very unlike, he running to mathematics, and I to languages, but we were both fond of nature, and spent most of our time in the woods and fields. We attended school in St. Charles in winter, and got the elements of an education.

This lasted about three years, when in 1855 my father sold the Norton's Mill property, and we moved to Iowa. We traveled there in a small covered wagon, not a large "prairie schooner." My father and mother slept in the wagon and my brother and I on the ground. We thus traveled through the State of Illinois to Galena, crossed the Mississippi to Dubuque, took a northwest course to the Maquoketa Creek, through Dubuque and Delaware Counties, and settled in the northeast corner of Buchanan County, where my father preëmpted a quarter-section of land, which was subsequently deeded to him on his land warrant for service in the War of 1812. The journey was made in May and June, 1855, and was one of the most memorable, as well as most enjoyable events

---

[1] Pythias.

of my early life. My brother and I had our guns; there were many water-fowls and other birds, some rabbits and squirrels, and we occasionally got a duck. We lived on our game all the way. My mother prepared it and we fairly feasted. It was the greatest opportunity I had ever had to see the world, and no passion was stronger in my nature than that of adventure. I never have been entirely free from that passion.

Two summers and two winters were spent in the new home. They were years of work, of course, but, as I look back upon them, it seems as though most of my time was spent in roaming over those boundless prairies, always with a gun, killing the game both for sport and for the table, and admiring nature. I believe I was born a naturalist, but the opportunity to be scientific was meager—no teacher, no books.

In January, 1857, my father died. My mother did not wish to live longer in Iowa, and my oldest brother, Lorenzo, who lived near us, was made administrator of the estate, and took charge of it. My mother, my brother Erastus, and I returned to Illinois. There was then a railroad most of the way, and we went by rail. The little homestead in St. Charles still remained in my mother's name, but she preferred to live with her only daughter in Geneva, two miles below on the Fox. We arrived in the spring of 1857, and my brother and I found work to do, but could not be together. He worked in a machine shop, and I on the farm of a man named Rufus Smith near Lodi, ten miles west of St. Charles. In the fall we resolved to go to school in St. Charles, a sort of grammar school having recently been introduced, in which we could study algebra, geometry, grammar, and some other branches that we had not been able to pursue before for want of a teacher. I also studied French. My employer, Rufus Smith, had lived in Canada and spoke Canadian French. I found a little book and studied it evenings on the farm, and he offered to teach me the pronunciation, but I found I had it all to unlearn later.

My brother and I "kept bachelor's hall" all that winter in the little house in St. Charles, and we studied hard, for we were both ambitious to "get an education." But we found time to read stories, and became intensely interested particularly in the story of Mrs. E. D. E. N. Southworth, entitled: "The Hidden Hand," which ran through the New York *Ledger* that winter. We also read a good deal of the "yellow covered" literature, including some blood-curdling tales of crime and murder. One of them, I remember, was entitled: "The Banditti of the Prairies." We had nothing else to read, and we did not know any better than to read such things. After reading them, for me to sit down and write a story was scarcely more than reflex action. I do not think Erastus wrote any, but I wrote several, I do not know how many. I have in an envelope labeled "Stories," filed with my "unpublished manuscripts," five of these, all apparently complete, but not one of them bears a title! I never have read them since, and probably never shall. This is exclusive of "The Spaniard's Revenge," which chanced to get printed. . . .

In the spring of 1858, my brother Cyrenus Osborn, nine years my senior, having set up a wagon-hub factory at Myersburg near Wysox, five miles from Towanda, Bradford County, Pennsylvania, and needing help to conduct it, Erastus and I, at his urgent request, and with "great expectations" as to pecuniary results, left our native State once more, and went to join our fortunes with his. I was engineer, but did every other kind of work. I had *Ollendorff's Greek Grammar,* and went through it while about my work. I could then conjugate all the irregular Greek verbs! It was then, too, over the arch, that I studied Loomis's *Physiology* and several other textbooks. I was also all this time studying French, German, and Latin.

But the business proved a failure. We had to take our pay in wagon-hubs which we could not sell, and in the winter of 1860–61 I left my brother and taught a school. In the spring of 1861 I entered the Susquehanna Collegiate Institute at Towanda. There I had my first surprise, for, autodidact as I was, I did not suppose that the knowledge I had picked up in that way would count for anything in an institution of learning. But I found that in Greek and Latin, at least, I had distanced the foremost scholars in the school, and had to be advanced over class after class, to Livy and Herodotus. My *Anabasis* and *Æneid* I took home and read them for the history and the poetry. I could not say as much for mathematics, for mine is not a mathematical mind.

I worked on a farm during the summer of 1861, took the fall term at the Institute, and taught school the winter of 1861–62. I took the spring term of 1862 at the Institute, and was preparing to go to Lafayette College, when a great change came over all my plans. The war had broken out and raged all the spring. I had hoped it might end, but when the President called for "three hundred thousand more," I could resist no longer. I enlisted as a private soldier, and the next twenty-seven months I was in the service of my country. . . .

After the war I entered the civil service of the Government, where I remained for over forty years; but I filled many posts, and the last twenty-four years were devoted to scientific research. I first intended my clerical service for the Government to be merely a stepping-stone to the completion of my academic studies, and I expected still to go to college as soon as I could gain the wherewithal. But with a wife and child to support, this was a slow process. The difficulty was overcome when, in the spring of 1867, I persuaded Columbian (now George Washington) University, which had long had evening classes in law and medicine in order to accommodate the Government employees, to establish an academic school of the same kind. I entered it from the beginning in March, 1867, with thirty others. I was examined and classed as a sophomore, and the year 1867–68 was my junior year. I pushed through and graduated in 1869. The next two years I took the law course, graduating from that in 1871. After that I studied two more years in a prescribed course for the degree of Master of

Arts, which I took in 1872. It included qualitative chemistry (laboratory work) and practical anatomy (dissection).

I was then determined to go into science, and I immediately commenced the study of botany. I also took lessons in taxidermy and learned to make skins. In three years' time I had a respectable herbarium and a collection of some hundred bird skins. My scientific career had begun, and after my Utah campaign of 1875, I commenced contributing to the scientific journals. But all this time, from June 18, 1869, I had also been writing the book which was to be called *Dynamic Sociology,* a full history of which is given in its place. My botanical work is described in the history of my *Guide to the Flora of Washington and Vicinity,* and my geological and paleobotanical labors are set forth in the sketches of he large illustrated memoirs published by the U. S. Geological Survey. The histories of my sociological books following the *Dynamic Sociology* are also complete, and sufficiently biographical for all purposes.

I will therefore close this biographical sketch here, believing that the reader who is curious to know the details of my life will be fairly well satisfied with what I have here furnished. It is plain and unvarnished and contains nothing of any very remarkable interest. Details and anecdotes that I could have introduced would have been much more pithy and spicy than the mere historical facts, but this is clearly not the place for such things. I will end this part, as I began it, by repeating that, but for a certain estimate that any reader may make to himself of my contributions to human thought, the life history of the author would be practically jejune. . . .

2

THE NATURE OF

DYNAMIC SOCIOLOGY

1883

These remarks, preface to DYNAMIC SOCIOLOGY, *set forth succinctly what Ward thought were his important contributions to the analysis of social theory and practice. They are placed here out of their chronological order because of their general character.*

A growing sense of the essential sterility of all that has thus far been done in the domain of social science has furnished the chief incentive to the preparation of this work.

While this sterility is certainly very manifest in the superficial and unorganized labors of those who especially claim that field as their own, still it is not wholly or chiefly such that are open to this impeachment, but also and equally the quite opposite class, who indeed employ scientific methods in obtaining the true data of social science, but who not only fail to apply the data when obtained, but persist in teaching that no application of them can be made. Not that the results

---

Dynamic Sociology (New York: D. Appleton and Co., 1883), I, Preface.

attained by either of these classes are without value; they have a great and permanent value, but it is thus far potential only, and can not be converted into actual value until truer views shall prevail respecting the nature of social phenomena and social forces.

Just as Comte could complain that the philosophy of Hobbes, Locke, and Voltaire was negative, so it may now be maintained that the school of Mill, Spencer, and Fiske is also negative. From the purely statical stage of the former the latter has only advanced to the passively dynamic stage, which recognizes only the changes wrought by Nature, unaided by Art; but, before the science of society can be truly founded, another advance must be made, and the actively dynamic stage reached, in which social phenomena shall be contemplated as capable of intelligent control by society itself in its own interest.

The indictment of sterility has lain against all the great systems of thought. Theo-teleology is sterile, because, however viewed, it paralyzes effort; metaphysical-ontology is sterile because it ignores the mediation of material things and builds on pure ideas; and now even the philosophy of evolution thus far proves sterile also, because, while justly claiming a social science, it falls short of admitting its complete homology with other sciences, and, while demonstrating the uniformity of social as of physical phenomena, it denies to the former that susceptibility to artificial modification which, applied to the latter, constitutes the only practical value that science has for man.

Perhaps it is more correct to say that the new school fail to comprehend the true nature of *art* as applicable to all departments of science. Perceiving that natural processes are genetic, they erroneously conclude that Nature's ways should be man's ways. They thus confound the essential idea of fine art with that of useful art, the imitation of Nature with the control of Nature. They teach the natural as the proper human method, whereas the latter is necessarily an artificial method.

Sociology is reproached, even by those who admit its legitimacy, with being impracticable and fruitless. The prevailing methods of treating it, including those employed by its highest living advocates, to a great extent justify this charge. There are dead sciences as well as dead languages. The real object of science is to benefit man. A science which fails to do this, however agreeable its study, is lifeless. Sociology, which of all sciences should benefit man most, is in danger of falling into the class of polite amusements, or dead sciences. It is the object of this work to point out a method by which the breath of life may be breathed into its nostrils.

It has been found sufficiently difficult in any age to contribute any thing new to the thought of the world. In the present age, with its accumulations of learning and its intense intellectual activity, such an attempt would, indeed, be presumptuous. Henceforth it can be only in the direction of improved methods, and new forms of presenting old truths, that novelty and successful innovation, in any but the domain of original scientific research, are to be expected. The only positive claim here made is of this nature—that while the world's present stock of known truth, the generous tribute of many great minds, has been freely but appreciatively employed, it has been woven into a unique fabric, and one by which, to continue the figure, society may be completely rehabilitated.

If, in the detailed unfolding of this system, any comprehensive principles have been announced, to which attention has not heretofore been specially directed, the chief of these will, perhaps, be recognized in—

1. The law of Aggregation, as distinguished from that of Evolution proper.

2. The theory of the Social Forces, and the fundamental antithesis which they imply between Feeling and Function.

3. The contrast between these true Social Forces and the guiding influence of the Intellect, embodying the application

of the Indirect Method of Conation and the essential nature of Invention, of Art, and of Dynamic Action.

4. The superiority of Artificial, or Teleological, Processes over Natural, or Genetic, Processes; and, finally—

5. The recognition and demonstration of the paramount necessity for the equal and universal Distribution of the extant Knowledge of the world, which last is the crown of the system itself.

While there certainly have been adumbrations of many of these truths, it is believed that thus far no one of them has been systematically formulated or distinctly recognized. . . .

THE RISING SCHOOL

OF PHILOSOPHY

1870

Written when he was just twenty-nine, this is the first "formal" statement of the social and philosophical position toward which Ward was already gravitating. "I was steeped in the old philosophy," he later wrote, "but I was wholly unsatisfied with it, and fairly panting for a fresh breath of science."

The age of speculation has gone by. The age of investigation has begun. The philosophies of the past have at last culminated in a system which, while it still retains the name philosophy, is in truth, science. The Ionian and the Eleatic schools of philosophy, the great Platonic and Peripatetic schemes, the religio-philosophical scholasticism of the Middle Ages, and the grand metaphysical systems of modern Europe, have all passed away, and the myriad volumes of their profound elaboration lie moulding upon the shelves of our libraries. Thales and Pythagoras, Plato and Aristotle, Aquinas and Descartes, have all in turn shed their lustre upon the world, and left it to

---

The Iconoclast (Washington, D.C.), Vol. I, No. 10 (December 1870), in *Glimpses of the Cosmos*, I, 110–112.

monuments which stand as true representatives of the condition of the human mind at the respective epochs in which they figured. But they are monuments only. They are no longer fingerposts. They are no longer authority. All these schools of philosophers are extinct. There is none to revive them—none to mourn their loss. The profound disquisitions of Sir William Hamilton must be regarded as their last triumph for all time; while the vigorous but unsuccessful effort of Cousin to extract from their vast accumulations an eclecticism adequate to the demands of the Nineteenth Century affords ample proof that the world has outstripped them in its march and left them behind it to take their places among the relics of antiquity.

The rising school of philosophy, as distinguished from practical scientific labor, and the one which may be said to have already succeeded the French, German, and Scottish schools of metaphysics, is that which for want of a better name is styled the Positive. Deriving its principles from the teachings of Bacon, Galileo, Newton, Franklin, and Humboldt, it had an illustrious founder in Auguste Comte, and is to-day illuminated and adorned by the intellects of John Stuart Mill and Herbert Spencer. Darwin, Buckle, and Lyell labored in its ranks, as do now Huxley, Tyndall, and a great number of other distinguished scientists and thinkers in Europe and America. We have already laid before our readers the fundamental principles of this new school of philosophy, as laid down by its founder, and its chief exponents. It remains to add, that besides being scientific in its methods and rational in its doctrines, it is eminently practical in its objects and its results.

Its aims are all utilitarian, and its principles humanitarian. It is neither dogmatic nor visionary, but liberal and exact. Taking nature as its only source of information, and the phenomena of the universe as the material for its deductions, it seeks in the observation of their uniformities in the present, to trace all things back to their true origin in the past, and calculate their true destiny in the future.

In this two-fold view it passes in review all the systems and institutions of man upon the earth, follows them back to their natural source in his remote history, and predicts with all necessary certainty their ultimate collapse or triumph. Premising a reign of law as absolute and certain over the affairs of men and nations as over the movements of the celestial spheres, the new philosophy grapples as successfully with the questions of human society, law, government, morals, and religion as with those of astronomy, chemistry, or physics. To reform humanity is the grand object of this system. Its expounders realize their power, by this method, of accomplishing this object; and if his followers do not all avow it as openly and as repeatedly as Comte did, they certainly practice it since his death with equal sincerity and far greater results. They have caught the true inspiration, as their exact inquiries have revealed to them the great and hitherto hidden secret of human progress in the transcendent majesty of knowledge over all other sources for securing this end; and from each and all of the recognized lights of the Positive Philosophy the cry has gone up for more knowledge, better knowledge! Education, and of the true sort, is what they demand, and that for all mankind.

Education is the key-note of the sociological system of this school of philosophers, and they intend to ring the changes upon it till all the world shall be awakened to its incalculable importance.

Such is a brief review of the history, nature, and aim of what we denominate the rising school; and we confess we cannot, as Liberals, ignore the existence or achievements of this noble movement. Its laborers are Liberals in the widest sense who, in the very act of building a grand structure with knowledge for its corner-stone, are removing in the most effectual manner the rotten timbers of theological error and popular superstition.

4

SCIENTIFIC LAWMAKING

1877

This brief piece was originally part of an article on the Bureau of Statistics, where Ward had worked for some ten years. The first two paragraphs, he tells us, were the contribution of his fellow employee, Edward Peters.

In a recent article on the province of statistics we showed that to social science statistical facts have the same relation which the observations of investigators bear to physics, and we pointed out the necessity of increased attention to such facts and increased effort in their collection and classification as a means of securing for sociology some share in that splendid progress by which the physical sciences have been distinguished since the Baconian method of investigation and study began to be applied to them.

The science which deals with humanity, and a proper understanding of which would lead to a vast amelioration in the condition of the human race, is surely as worthy of public encouragement as any of those which deal with the laws that govern inert matter; and there are special reasons why more

---

National Union (November 3, 1877), in *Glimpses of the Cosmos*, II, 169–171.

than any of the less complicated sciences it is in need of active public assistance. Such assistance can only be adequately rendered through the direct agency of government, since it must consist mainly in the collection of statistics, which can only be obtained in obedience to governmental authority. Something is already done in this direction by our own Government and by a number of the States, but nothing in comparison with what the importance of the subject would warrant. No appropriations made by Congress have been made more grudgingly than those for the National Bureau of Statistics, and yet none of them are applied to work in the results of which that body is so directly interested.

The primary object of statistics should be to influence and direct legislation. The facts of statistics point out the laws of trade and of all other movements in society. The true function of legislation is to remove all obstructions from these social movements and to cause their free operation to effect the least possible injury to public and private interests. In order to legislate to this end these natural laws must be understood. They can only be understood by the study of the facts which they present, i. e., of statistics. Every movement of whatever nature going on in the country should be regularly reported to a central office, and all such facts should be there systematically elaborated and published in tables, charts, diagrams, &c., and regularly laid before Congress for its use in framing laws for the benefit of the general public.

The director of this central office or bureau should have charge of all branches of statistics. He could thus directly compare the operations of different movements and coordinate all the facts found to possess a common bond. The phenomena relating to different kinds of production should be frequently placed in juxtaposition with a view to showing which branches should be stimulated and which checked. For while agricultural production cannot, perhaps, ever be too great, manufactures frequently far exceed the needs of the country before the fact is made known by the operation of natural laws.

Again the phenomena of production should be constantly compared with those of transportation and exchange, and statistics of all these branches of industry would suffice to indicate what legislation is necessary to harmonize the workings of them all.

In like manner financial statistics would show the condition of capital in the country and suggest the requisite legislation to bring it into its proper relations with labor. Vital and sanitary statistics of immigration and emigration as well as of internal migration so far as obtainable should be given a prominent place. Indeed, the taking of the census, which is preëminently a statistical work, should be placed under the Bureau of Statistics, where uniformity and method could be made to replace our past irregular and chaotic mode of taking the census. The Bureau of Statistics could thus become, as it should be, a large and influential bureau. It should take a high rank among the bureaus of the Government and the highest talent should be secured not only to direct it but also to fill the subordinate positions in it. Finally, a liberal policy should be pursued towards the Bureau of Statistics, and especially should it be exempted from those sudden changes which sometimes affect certain branches of the Government, caused by great and abrupt reductions in the force and change of *personnel*. Such cataclysms would here more than anywhere else tend to destroy the accumulated labor and thought of years, and to overthrow useful systems of valuable records, whose chief value consists in the length of time they have been recorded. We are informed that a Bureau of Statistics was created in 1845, and that for several years important statistical reports were made and published, embracing mining statistics, bank statistics, &c. But this bureau soon fell a prey to mistaken "retrenchment," or to some other of the unfortunate vicissitudes to which representative governments are unhappily subject, and the memory of it had well nigh been blotted out.

But suppose this bureau had been permitted to stand and to grow with the natural growth of the nation under a liberal patronage of Congress and the management of competent officers, who can estimate the value of such a bureau to-day and that of the uninterrupted series of recorded facts of vital national import that would have accumulated?

5

"THEORY AND PRACTICE

ARE AT WAR"

1881

This essay, which Ward called "Political-Social Functions,"
was first read to the Anthropological Society of Washington, in
March 1881. It is an early analysis of the double standard of
public and private philosophy and morality to which Ward
returned again and again, and which his nephew, E. A. Ross,
was later to explore in SIN AND SOCIETY.

It is a sign of approaching crisis in social opinion, when prevailing theories become widely at variance with prevailing
practices. While a certain amount of general depravity may
be conceded, even to a progressive and apparently prosperous
people, it is quite too much to insist that, because they are
almost universally running counter to the received philosophy,
they must necessarily be pursuing a downward course. They
may simply be following social instincts; and when social instincts are found to be powerfully opposed to social tenets, it

---

The Penn Monthly, XII (May 1881), 321–336, in *Glimpses of the Cos-*
mos, II, 335–353.

is time, while deploring the former, to pause, also, and examine the latter.

In one view, all truth is relative. Doctrines that were true for one age cease to be true for a later one; principles which really worked the salvation of the last century cannot be utilized in the present one. The conservative tendencies of society, which perpetuate customs and ceremonies after their usefulness has ceased, preserve also the great social theories by which past ages have been redeemed, and they hand them down to later times, with which they no longer stand in legitimate relationship. Feeling is more powerful than intellect. Society is always moved by the great tide of sentiment long before the voice of reason declares the nature of this motive power. When the tide once fairly sets in in one direction, the philosopher knows that there must be a force behind it; but ere he can investigate that force by the slow and cautious methods of science, and announce its true character, long steps will have been taken in the direction of the inevitable. This is a critical period. The interval between action and reason,— between new practice and new theory—is one full of dangers to society. For all the forms of feeling, as well as the particular form called love, are equally blind; and blind sentiment sweeping through new tracks, and encountering old theories and old practices, must inevitably produce innumerable conflicts and perpetually jeopardize the great interests which are at stake.

The second half of the nineteenth century is precisely such a period as that described. Theory and practice are at war. The only social philosophy that exists is one that condemns the bulk of the social action taken. The libraries of the world are filled with arguments against the very course which events are blindly taking. The whole weight of the greatest social writers of the past is massed against the social movement of the age. The works of Adam Smith and Ricardo, of Pitt, Cobden and the two Mills, of Jean Baptiste Say and Michel

Chevalier, and of the train of political economists who have followed these leaders, while they abound in discords and contain many conflicting views, are, in the main, hostile to all those schemes of regulation which characterize the action of modern States. The political science of these masters is all there is to be taught in the colleges and universities, and it continues to be so taught. The representatives of science have joined their forces with the ones already named, and, with the added power which science has justly come to wield, stand boldly in the track of current events. There is also an able corps of living writers who are earnestly protesting against the tendencies of the times. The commercial and financial journals are filled with hostile flings at "Government meddling," and "bureaucracy"; the organs of transportation, telegraph, and insurance companies are daily holding up the dangers of "State regulation." The Cobden Club and other "Free Trade" societies are scattering tracts with a liberal hand, in the hope of stemming the tide. Victor Boehmert warns, Augustus Mongredien shouts, and Herbert Spencer thunders. What is the result? Germany answers by purchasing private railroads and enacting a high protective tariff. France answers by decreeing the construction of eleven thousand miles of Government railroad, and offering a bounty to French ship-owners. England answers by a compulsory education act, by Government purchase of the telegraph, and by a judicial decision laying claim to the telephone. America answers by an inter-State railroad bill, a national education bill, and a sweeping *plebiscite* in favor of protection to home manufactures. The whole world has caught the contagion, and all nations are adopting measures of positive legislation. A large amount of crude lawmaking is being dictated by this blind impulse. Vast internal improvements are undertaken by Government, and millions are appropriated for commercial and industrial schemes. The wildest financial measures are seriously advocated, and both at home and abroad the public credit of the world was at one time seriously imperilled by Socialistic theories of national financiering. Cernuschi said "Nomisma"; and a large but irresponsible party sprang up in every civilized country and demanded that the State should create and distribute an abundance of the circulating medium!

What conclusion is the thoughtful student of social events to deduce from all this? The prevailing school of political economists think the world is temporarily mad, but hope that it will soon return to itself. They declare the entire movement baseless, and believe that all efforts should be directed towards diffusing and reinforcing existing theories, and they insist that there are no grounds on which the events described can be logically defended. In this they are undoubtedly sincere. Reform with them means simply a halt and reversal of prevailing tendencies.

But there is another possible policy, practicable also for those who really desire reform. It is an adage that reforms never go backward. It is always well to inquire whether, underlying a great movement, however perverse it may appear, there may not be a basis of truth concealed by the errors that lie on the surface. In such cases true reform may not consist in open opposition. This may often be fruitful of harm, and usually is fruitless of good.

In the present state of society, the movement above sketched is irresistible. This is sufficiently proved by the powerlessness of the influences allied against it to check it. It behooves all true reformers, therefore, to cease factious opposition, and settle down to the soberer task of studying the causes of the phenomena observed. Society needs less to be told that it is doing wrong than to be shown what it is really doing. If there must be a movement in a given direction, let its true nature be made known. The jars and evils are due, not to the advance itself, but to the clashing of interests which ignorance of their existence and of the whole field swept over renders inevitable. The true need is for enlightenment respecting the causes and consequences of action, by the aid of which alone these conflicts can be avoided and the movement intelligently guided.

In what consists this schism between theory and practice? It is after all a schism between two theories; for all action is based on theory, if it is nothing more than a blind intuition of selfish and momentary benefit. In the present case it is much more. Fundamentally formulated, it is the theory of natural, against that of artificial regulation. The belief in some form of regulation is one deeply implanted in the human mind. A supposed divine regulation of human affairs was the first form in which this belief manifested itself. Then, when government was exercised chiefly by one man or a few men, the belief in the power of these rulers to regulate society was long supreme. It is only since the civilizing agencies of printing and of science have been at work, that this illusion has been dispelled. But in its place the only alternative clearly perceived has been accepted, viz., the idea that nature and the laws of nature are alone competent to regulate the affairs of men. This theory was plausible. It was supported by the spontaneous growth of numerous great industries; it was strengthened by the failures of human regulation in the past, and by the continuance of such failures in the present. It was thought to be in full accord with all the teachings of science which had so greatly contributed to relieve the world of the yoke of despotic regulation. Science taught the uniformity of all of nature's processes. It taught that the universe was controlled by fixed and unchangeable laws which could not be violated with impunity. Progress in nature was due to the secular operation of these laws, which could neither be slackened nor accelerated. Political science followed strictly in the path of physical science. It declared that commerce and industry were controlled by uniform laws of nature which man must interfere with at his peril. The laws of trade must be allowed to take their course. The improvements necessary to further civilization, to be real or substantial, must be spontaneous. Great systems of commercial intercourse, of productive industry, of transportation, intercommunication, finance, and education, would naturally work themselves out, provided the potential qualities necessary for them existed in society. Every attempt on the part of Government to interfere with these great processes of nature only recoiled upon the agent and imperilled the safety of the State. Government must protect—it must not control; it may forbid—it may not command.

Such was the theory which very naturally grew up at a time when it was greatly needed, and emancipated society to such an extent from monarchical and oligarchical rule, that nearly every one of the pretended monarchies of Europe is to-day a virtual democracy. And this is none other than the present prevailing theory of political economists; the one which is embodied in our masterpieces of literature and philosophy, is taught in our colleges, preached in our pulpits, echoed from our rostrums, served up daily by the press, and advocated by many of the most learned men of the time. And now, in these later days of republican institutions, which, as already remarked, it has done much to secure, it finds itself again confronted by an enemy which it cannot distinguish from the old one that it formerly encountered and drove back.

Just here is the great mistake. In so far as artificial regulation in itself is concerned, the modern theory is indeed indentical with the original one; but here the parallelism ceases. Government under a real autocrat is the interference by one man with the affairs of millions. Government by popularly chosen representatives is the management by society of its own affairs. This may be true only in theory, but it approaches realization in proportion as representative government approaches perfection.

Now, precisely the conception which vaguely, but not the less obstinately, inspires all the apparently rash tendencies of our times, is that society ought to take its affairs into its own hands, check the abuses of unrestrained competition and combination, and consciously work out certain of the problems of civilization. Against the negative theory that nature must be left to bring about social progress in its own time and way, it holds that nature may be assisted by organized social action, very much as the *vis medicatrix naturæ* may be assisted by intelligently directed applications of the healing art. . . . There is no fixed set of doctrines laid down to govern this movement. Acts advancing it are not defended by argument. It is an impulse without a philosophy; an instinct rather than conviction. Yet it is deep-seated and ineradicable, and its smouldering fires often burst into view in the form of prejudices and passions. There is a sentiment that something is wrong, and a feeling that something should be done. The opposition school does not share these feelings. It condemns every attempt to *do* anything. *"Laissez faire, laissez passer,"* said De Gournay; and with these words was christened the *laissez faire* school of political economists. These writers deride the mistakes of Governments in the past in trying to perform positive functions, and show that such attempts have usually resulted in failures, and often in mischief. All their utterances and teachings imply that it is folly to undertake the control of social events, and wisdom to leave them wholly to the untrammelled influence of what they call natural laws. As above remarked, almost everybody, if separately questioned, would admit this position, so completely has it become part of the education and thought of the present age; and yet, often without perceiving the inconsistency, many entertain a vague but powerful sentiment in favor of mending existing evils, of regulating social events, and of doing something very decisive in many ways.

It is this insidious manner in which these two incompatible theories coexist, often in the same individual, and permeate society, that complicates the problem and creates the urgent need of a clear presentation of their respective claims and a thorough acquaintance with their nature and aims. If man was really, as is often claimed, a rational being, in the sense of always acting upon reasoned-out conclusions, there would be no difficulty. It would then resolve itself into a simple trial of strength between two well defined parties. But as it is, every house is, as it were, divided against itself. . . .

Science and natural law to the contrary notwithstanding, it remains, and always has remained, a patent fact, that social events, left to themselves, are always attended with glaring evils. There is no necessary harmony between natural law and human advantage. The laws of trade inevitably result in enormous inequalities in the distribution of wealth. It may, with much truth, be argued that considerable inequality is the better social condition; but the degree and kind of inequality which is actually reached cannot be defended on this ground. The fact is too apparent that all this inequality is not due to the superior intelligence or industry of those who possess most, which, thus limited, many might be disposed to declare just. It is obvious that mere accident of birth or position is sufficient to account for the great bulk of this inequality; that real intelligence, beyond the coarse cunning inspired by avarice, has little or nothing to do with it; that the primary producers—that is, the discoverers and inventors of the laws and appliances by which the production of wealth is accelerated—have generally enjoyed few or none of the advantages of their intellectual efforts, but that these are reaped by men of very moderate abilities beyond a certain business shrewdness and tact; that the immediate creators of wealth—the bone and sinew of labor—are, in nearly all cases, poor, while princely fortunes fall, for the most part, to the class who, far removed from all the objects of production or exchange, busy themselves solely with the medium of exchange or with mere transfers of entries representing the value of commodities produced and exchanged. . . .

It is not true that all attempts at Government regulation and State management have failed or wrought only mischief.

State postal management is admitted by nearly everybody to have proved a success. City corporations now universally undertake the work of extinguishing fires, as being too closely connected with the interests of all to be entrusted to private enterprise. There are still a few who condemn the public school system, such as it exists under State and municipal regulation, but it is generally conceded that the people are considerably better educated than they would have been had education been left entirely to private efforts. These exceptions, if such they may be called, together with some others, apply to the United States with a very weak Government, which is jealously watched by a suspicious democracy, ready to hurl its *personnel* from power for the slightest departure from their prescribed duties. But when we look to the Old World, we see that these so-called encroachments upon individual rights have progressed much further.

Our mother-country—Great Britain—is most like us in this respect, but it has carried the work of regulation and State management so far as to embrace the telegraph system, along with the post-office; and recent reports show that, for the eleven years during which this has been the case, the results have been in the highest degree satisfactory. In this brief period the telegraph-system and operations of the United Kingdom have about quadrupled in all directions; the lines have been self-sustaining, and uniform rates, much lower than the former ones, adapted, like those of the post-office, to the common people, have been established.

Great Britain has not purchased any railroads, although it has long held this sword of Damocles over them in the form of a Parliamentary enactment reserving the right to do so. It has, however, enacted an entire code of regulative railway laws, and for the past eight years there has existed a special judicial commission or railway court, which is an integral part of the Government. By these means rates are established and innumerable details are arranged by the State to insure just dealings between the railway companies and the public.

These are fixed measures which the British public could not be induced to rescind, and which may therefore be regarded as successful.

If we go to the Continent, we find a still greater advance in this direction. The greater part of the railroads of Germany and Belgium are owned and worked by the State; in the former case mostly by the separate States of the Empire. In France, while the most of them are still nominally in the hands of private companies, such is the degree of national supervision that all rates and even time-tables are fixed by the Government, and no new private lines are allowed to be constructed. Moreover, the charters of many of these lines are soon to expire, and by the terms of the concessions the State has the right of purchase. This it has announced its intention to do, so that before many years the entire network will be in the hands of the Government. Add to this that France has already planned and commenced the construction of 17,700 kilometres of new Government railroad, and has also purchased several of the former lines which it is itself successfully managing.

Prussian statistics show that freight is carried on an average fifteen per cent. cheaper on State than on private lines, and that passengers are carried ten per cent. cheaper, while no road is run at a loss and all are a source of revenue to the State. Italy, in the matter of railroads, is following the example of France in almost every particular, and other countries are moving in the same direction.

As regards the telegraph, many Continental countries have handed it over wholly or in part to the control of Government, and the tendency is steadily in this direction and nowhere in the opposite one.

Government savings-banks, in which the poor mechanic's earnings are rendered perfectly secure, are now almost universal in Europe, and these, as might be easily foreseen, have proved a complete success.

Everybody knows something of the system of public instruction in Germany. Nothing could induce the Fatherland to surrender it. Something closely approaching it exists in Austria and Hungary, as well as throughout Scandinavia, while France, Italy, and Belgium are rapidly extending their educational systems. Even England has taken a long step in this direction, in which it persists, against the attacks of many eminent writers. In 1870 it created School Boards, which it empowered to require parents to send their children to school; and, in 1876, it made it obligatory on all parents to provide elementary education for their children. The result has been that in that time the number of schools, of pupils, and of teachers, has increased over 100 per cent. . . .

But we may go much farther. Of what does government consist? It consists, when rightly understood, simply of a collection of just such cases in which matters of general public interest have been taken out of the hands of individuals and assumed by the central authority. As soon as one such industry becomes permanently established as a proper object of national administration, it drops out of the list of those which it is deemed necessary to defend against Government encroachment. Each one of the body of regulative agencies which constitute the present accepted sphere of normal government functions has passed through this stage before settling down into its present place. We see this clearly in the history of finance and the bitter opposition to national banking. We may see it still more plainly where no one ever thinks of looking—in the progress of jurisprudence. It is, comparatively speaking, only recently that in Europe people were obliged to administer their own justice, both civil and criminal; and this is still the prevailing custom among many barbaric peoples and savage tribes.

Government has ever been constantly encroaching upon these supposed private rights, in the interest of the public good; and, though always opposed, it has always been slowly gaining ground. And, whether we like it or not, this process is destined to continue until, one after another, all the important public operations of society shall come more or less directly under the power of State regulation. Contrary to the general belief, this result is not often reached before the time is ripe for it. Such is the aversion to innovation, that the evils of private management usually become well-nigh intolerable before the State is able or willing to step in and relieve them. While, therefore, progress in the direction of enlarging the sphere of Government operation should be very slow and cautious, such is the constitution of society and of the human mind, that there is less danger than is generally supposed that this will take place too rapidly.

The objectionableness of this movement is in great part attributable to the necessity of applying to it terms which, during the transition period above described, have come to receive a certain stigma or reproach. The administration of justice is now regarded as a highly proper function of Government, one which society is in duty bound to perform. The carrying of the mails has already become a recognized Government duty. Only those who desire to profit by issuing private bank notes now wish to return to that system of banking. The State management of railroads in Belgium has proved so satisfactory to the public that petitions are pouring in praying the Government to expropriate the remaining private lines, and there, at least, this, too, will probably soon pass to the side of legitimate national operations. As much may be said, in a large portion of Europe, of Government telegraphing, of national savings-banks, and of public education; and the world will probably wonder in the future that a patient public should so long have permitted the avarice of individuals, under the legitimate operation of natural laws, to play havoc with the public health in the adulteration of food, medicines, and dyes, etc., and in the improper constructions of private and public buildings. The maxim, *caveat emptor,* of the common law, is simply a premium on dishonesty, and a proper understanding of its workings must reverse it and substitute *caveat vendor,* who is supposed to know the quality of his wares and deserves their confiscation for the offence of misrepresenting it.

The stigma which now attaches to the term "Government regulation," is, therefore, simply that which individuals, seeking to profit by the absence of it, have ingeniously fastened upon it. It applies only so long as there is hope of defeating State interference in the excesses of private competition and combination. As soon as this hope is definitely surrendered these operations become legitimate Government functions, and Government is then abused, if at all, only for not performing them in a wholly infallible manner.

What term, then, shall be employed to express this conception free from reproach and with sufficient latitude to embrace both classes of cases, viz., those which are now recognized Government functions and those which are still disputed and characterized as Government encroachments upon the domain of private enterprise? It is clear that there is no such term now in common use. The conception, though a simple one, requires not only a circumlocution, but an elaborate explanation, to make it intelligible to the popular mind. For the popular idea of Government is extremely crude. It is looked upon objectively—as an outside power—hostile rather than friendly to the interests of society; and it must be confessed that this manner of looking at Government goes far towards making it what men are willing to regard it, and towards giving to the holders of political power the impression that they are above, and independent of, society. But every theory of Government must regard it simply as the agency by which society transacts those affairs which are recognized to be of a public character. All the difficulties of which we have spoken, therefore, have arisen from the effort to determine the boundary line between affairs of an essentially public and those of a private nature.

Regarded as the agency of society, it is clear that the acts of Government, theoretically at least, are simply the acts of society through its chosen agents; and Mr. Herbert Spencer has ably shown that even the most despotic forms of Government really reflect the average will and character of the units composing such societies. Opposition to Government regulation is, therefore, in the nature of an attempt to frustrate the will of society as it is constituted to express it; but so long as such opposition is successful, this is itself the proof that the acts opposed do not properly represent the social will as thus constituted, since the only test of this will is the power to enforce it, no matter what the form of Government.

Thus viewed, the entire movement of which we have spoken becomes a social movement, and the conflict must be between individuals and society at large. The question in each case is, then, shall individuals continue to control this industry, or shall society henceforth control it? We have seen that the sphere of social control has been gradually expanding throughout the periods of civilization, sometimes, perhaps, too rapidly, but usually too slowly; and now we find that for more than a century the English school of negative economists has devoted itself to the task of checking this advance. This *laissez faire* school has entrenched itself behind the fortifications of science, and while declaring with truth that social phenomena are, like physical phenomena, uniform and governed by laws, they have accompanied this by the false declaration and *non sequitur* that neither physical nor social phenomena are capable of human control; the fact being that all the practical benefits of science are the result of man's control of natural forces and phenomena which would otherwise have run to waste or operated as enemies to human progress. The opposing positive school of economics simply demands an opportunity to utilize the social forces for human advantage in precisely the same manner as the physical forces have been utilized. It is only through the artificial control of natural phenomena that science is made to minister to human needs; and if social laws are really analogous to physical laws, there is no reason why social science may not receive practical applications such as have been given to physical science.

To distinguish this general movement in the direction of regulating social phenomena from all other facts in human history, and at the same time to avoid all objectionable terms and express the conception in its widest sense, it may be appropriately denominated *Sociocracy*. It is too late now to object to this new term on the ground of its hybrid Greco-Latin etymology, since the Greek language is known to be deficient in a proper root for its first component, and several kindred terms are already in common use by the best authorities. It means something quite distinct from Democracy, which points, as this term does not, decisively towards a definite form of organization. The term Socialism, too, which might seem akin to it, aside from its unpopularity, has by far too great definiteness, and looks too much to fundamental change in the existing status of political institutions. All of these forms of social organization stand opposed to other existing forms, while Sociocracy stands opposed only to the absence of a regulative system, and is the symbol of positive social action as against the negativism of the dominant *laissez faire* school of politico-economic *doctrinaires*. It recognizes all forms of government as legitimate, and, ignoring form, goes to the substance, and denotes that, in whatever manner organized, it is the duty of society to act consciously and intelligently, as becomes an enlightened age, in the direction of guarding its own interests and working out its own destiny.

6

THE WASTEFULNESS

OF NATURE

1882

These pages are an excerpt from an essay on "The Scientific Basis of Positive Political Economy," later incorporated into Dynamic Sociology. *The excerpt is presented here as one of the earliest statements of the idea of a biological basis for a positive sociology that Ward was later to develop so elaborately.*

. . . The negative school of political economists insist upon nothing so strongly as that the natural processes of society be left undisturbed. All attempts to influence the operation of these laws of nature, which they so greatly admire, are depreciated with a warmth which might make one doubt the sincerity of their avowed faith in their immutability. But these natural processes are neither more nor less than the form which genetic phenomena assume when seen in the superorganic world.

The International Review, XII (April 1882), in *Glimpses of the Cosmos*, III, 32–35.

It was once supposed that nature's methods were the most economical ones conceivable, and constituted perfect patterns for men to copy from. It was while this view prevailed in all departments of science that political economy had its origin as such. Since then biologists have abundantly demonstrated the error of this belief, and had sociology been thoroughly grounded in biology, as Comte so justly insisted that it should be, it would have kept pace with the other sciences in rejecting this fundamental error. But this has not been the case, and we find social science writers still lauding the stern economy of nature's laws. That economy, however, consists only in this, that while no measure is adopted which does not at the time produce some result, however slight, the amount of energy expended in producing such result is wholly disregarded, and bears no proportion to the value of the result. Nature acts on the assumption that her resources are inexhaustible, and no amount of expenditure is too great to be made provided any good, however small, be thereby accomplished.

No system is maintained at greater expense than the reproductive; yet consider nature's prodigality in this. The octopus, in order to hold its own, must lay 50,000 eggs; a single sturgeon emitted 921,600 ova at one spawning, as counted by Dr. Buckland; the codfish hatches 1,000,000 young fish each year, that two may survive and the species not become extinct; the oyster spawns 2,000,000 embryos in a season, if all of which could reach maturity two or three individuals might supply the markets of the world. Professor Baird has estimated that an eel may contain at one time 9,000,000 eggs; a nematode was found to hold 60,000,000, and a tape-worm more than 1,000,000,000 ova. Similar facts confront us in the vegetable kingdom, but we need only mention that a single plant of the common mold, *Penicillium crustaceum,* was found to possess 3,200,000,000 spores.

The apparent peace which is supposed to reign in organic

nature is highly illusory. Even the vegetation is at war, and the result of that strife is immensely to lower the possible standard of every living species of plant. In the animal kingdom the struggle is desperate and unceasing, and the result is not different from that in the vegetable. Not only is the waste of reproductive power enormous in proportion to the amount of life brought forth, but of the latter by far the greater part meets with premature destruction. Animals, as all know, prey upon each other, producing universal and indescribable suffering, and placing every living thing in a state of chronic terror in the midst of its countless enemies. But even this tells less heavily upon the vital energies than does the silent conflict which results from the competition for the means of subsistence. It is here that occurs the greatest waste, if the cost of producing and developing an organism is counted at anything.

That the same laws have operated in the superorganic as in the organic world is too clear for contradiction. Not only the progress out of barbarism into civilization, but the march of civilization itself, has been attended with the same incidents that characterize the development of a species or of an individual. The archaeologist digs the remains of extinct civilizations out of the earth in much the same manner as the paleontologist does those of extinct animals and plants. Besides his wars with the elements and with wild beasts, man has been perpetually afflicted by wars with his own kind. *Homo homini lupus.* And yet these wars of men with their surroundings, with wild beasts, and with one another, are the strict analogues of those of the lower forms of organized existence. Even the silent battle for subsistence has its counterpart in the competitive struggles of industry. The same wasteful methods prevail in society as in the animal and vegetable kingdoms. The natural resources of the earth are squandered with a wanton disregard of the future. The forests are cut down to supply temporary wants, consumed by escaping camp fires, or purposely cleared for tillage, until the habitable portions of the earth are successively transformed into lifeless deserts. The soil is rapidly exhausted by the first occupants, who consider and know only the immediate present. *Après nous le déluge.* The wild animals useful to man are soon extinguished by the heartless destruction of the fertile females and helpless young. Population distributes itself to great disadvantage. Cities grow up with narrow, crooked streets, which must from time to time be widened and straightened at large absolute cost. Filth and disease-germs, due to dense, unregulated population, bring pestilence and sweep away at rhythmic intervals the excess. Famines come to scale down the ranks of such as have forced their way in during years of plenty. Bitter partisanship everywhere prevails throughout society, the nearly successful effort of each party being to undo what the other has done. Labor and capital, whose dependence upon each other is absolute, are constantly found in open hostility, which greatly reduces the productiveness of both. Exchange of products is largely carried on by redundant third parties, who, through no fault of their own, are allowed to absorb the largest share of the wealth produced. Trade consists to a great extent in unnecessary and duplicated transportation. Wealth is not only distributed unequally, but inequitably. In short, all the functions of society are performed in a sort of random, chance manner, which is precisely the reverse of economical, but wholly analogous to the natural processes of the lower organic world. Great results, it is true, are accomplished, even in society, by these unregulated natural forces. But are they the best possible? The optimistic view leads to stagnation by discouraging effort, while all true progress springs from that restless skepticism which dares even to question the methods of nature.

7

DYNAMIC SOCIOLOGY

1883

This was the great work that Ward began in 1869 and brought to fruition some thirteen years later. He himself tells us:

In all my early life I was always thinking on the deeper problems of nature and of man, and in various debating clubs I often ventilated my views. It always seemed to me that the last word had not been said on many of the most vital of these, and I instinctively inclined to express my own thoughts. I also wrote a good many academic papers in which I did express some of them. But I had the feeling, common to many young men, that what was called an 'education' was a condition precedent to any serious effort. I do not know when I became fully resolved to begin some systematic work as soon as I should receive my first degree, but I know that I long carried that resolution with me. When at last that consummation was approaching in the last semester of my collegiate course, this sentiment took a firm hold of me and found expression not only in my diary, but also in some pencilings which are happily preserved.[1]

With some justice, Ward regarded this book as the most important of his works, the one which most fully presented his thinking about social science, and he devotes no less than eighty-five pages in GLIMPSES OF THE COSMOS to tell the story of its composition and publication. The book was dedicated to Ward's chief in the U.S. Geological Survey, Major John

---

[1] *Glimpses of the Cosmos*, III, 147.

W. Powell. DYNAMIC SOCIOLOGY *was, with the possible exception of Lewis Morgan's* ANCIENT SOCIETY, *the first major sociological work of American scholarship; it was, too, the first major attack on the high priest of sociology, Herbert Spencer, whose first book in turn had been called* SOCIAL STATICS. *Hopefully Ward sent a copy of his book to Spencer, but he had to content himself with a brush-off:*

38 QUEENS GARDENS, BAYSWATER

LONDON, JULY 2/83.

My Dear Sir:

I have to acknowledge with thanks the copy of your two volumes on Dynamic Sociology *which recently reached me.*

I am at present so much out of health that I neither can do any writing nor any reading; and I fear it may be long before I shall be able to give any such attention to your work as it well deserves. From such few glances at the heads of chapters and their contents as I have allowed myself, I infer that you have a good deal more faith in the effects of right theory upon social practice than I have. The time may come when scientific conclusions will sway men's social conduct in a considerable degree. But as you are probably aware, and as, in fact, I said very emphatically when in America, I regard social progress as mainly a question of character, and not of knowledge or enlightenment. The inherited and organized natures of individuals, only little modifiable in the life of a generation, essentially determine for the time-being the type of social organization, spite of any teaching, spite even of bitter experience.

In respect of this belief I gather that you are at issue with me, and hence hope much more from a constructive social philosophy than I do. Nevertheless, I regard all works which draw public attention to sociology, scientifically considered, as calculated to raise useful discussion, and I hope your work will be widely read.

I am truly yours,

Herbert Spencer

Glimpses of the Cosmos, III, 214.

DYNAMIC SOCIOLOGY *appeared originally in two stout volumes of seven hundred pages each. Limitations of space force us to be content with some of the arguments from Volume II that bear more directly on what is to us the central issue: the role of government in social evolution.*

A. SOCIAL PROGRESS

There has been progress in civilization just as there has been progress in organic life, because the highest and best has been selected and preserved, and the lowest and poorest has perished. It is simply that man, as a progressive animal before the human period, and before the historic period, did not cease to be a progressive animal after reaching these periods. His progress has been the progress of nature, a secular and cosmical movement, not the progress of art, the result of foresight and intelligent direction. In short, man has not yet ceased to be an animal, and is still under the control of external nature and not under the control of his own mind. It is natural selection that has created intellect; it is natural selection that has developed it to its present condition, and it is intellect as a product of natural selection that has guided man up to his present position. The principle of artificial selection which he has been taught by nature, and has applied to other creatures, more as an art than as a science, to his immense advantage, he has not yet thought of applying to himself. Not until he does this can he claim any true distinction from the other animals.

Notwithstanding the failure of all systematic attempts thus far made to secure artificially the improvement of society, still, cheerless as the prospect may seem, the only hope of

Dynamic Sociology (New York: D. Appleton and Co., 1883), I, 15–16, 20–22.

success in this direction is in other systematic attempts made
in the same manner, and according to the same methods as
those by which these have been established and carried on;
that is, placed in the power of the feelings which alone are
capable of propelling any social operations. If this is hopeless,
then must the race be left to drift on under purely natural
influences, and reach any stage to which the conditions found
on the planet may be capable of carrying it. Let no one, however, be deluded by the thought that this cosmical progress,
even in its own slow way, can continue for ever. It will here-
after be shown that this swarming planet will soon see the
conditions of human advancement exhausted, and the night
of reaction and degeneracy ushered in, never to be again
succeeded by the daylight of progress, unless something
swifter and more certain than natural selection can be brought
to bear upon the development of the psychic faculty, by
which alone man is distinguished from the rest of the fauna
of the earth and enabled to people all parts of its surface.
The resources of the globe are not inexhaustible unless zeal-
ously husbanded by the deliberate foresight of enlightened
intellect. . . .

The fundamental law of human nature, and therefore of
political economy, is that all men will, under all circumstances,
seek their greatest gain. All the alleged exceptions to this
rule are apparent only, and experience has a thousand times
over established their entire unreliability as grounds of public
policy. But, where the intellectual and the moral forces of a
great social movement are separated, the temptations to self-
aggrandizement on the part of those wielding the former are
wholly irresistible. They never have been resisted, and it
would be folly to expect that they ever would be. In such a
movement, therefore, every individual must be both a force
and a rein for himself. But it must be apparent to all that
intellectual activity, coupled with enthusiasm, could never
alone accomplish the great object of utilizing the materials

and the forces of nature. Of course, originally, this is all that could have initiated this movement. But every one can not originate such work for himself. The originators must always remain a mere handful as compared with those who follow and elaborate. Whatever has been thus far done in this direction has been the work of nature. Necessity has led man to adopt a thousand ingenious means of supplying his needs. The inventions and discoveries that have thus far been made are, in one sense, the products of natural selection as much as are the improved nests of certain birds, or the dams of beavers. True, they have all been due to the guiding force of the intellect applied in aid of the propelling forces of hunger and want. And if the world is left wholly to nature, these agencies will continue for a great while to produce progress. The case is comparable to that which exists in plants and animals. Many of them are still in a progressive state. As the vegetable kingdom has for millions of years been slowly rising from seaweed to moss, from moss to fern, from fern to cycad, from that to pine, and so on to the oak and the apple, and as the animal kingdom has, in like manner, continued to exhibit forms of a higher and higher organization from the monad to the man, so it may be expected that both these kingdoms will, for perhaps an indefinite period of time, continue this progressive differentiation. Yet how long, under nature alone, would it require to develop the wheat, the maize, and the apple, that human agency has brought forth? how long to produce the Ayreshire, the Devon, the Cheviot breeds of animals? And while the cases are not strictly parallel, since nature would never select just the qualities that man selects, still it gives us a faint idea of the enormous acceleration which we may imagine human progress to acquire if it could be made the subject of artificial instead of natural selection. I do not speak here either of generative selection, as it is practiced on animals and plants, with a view to improve the physical quality of humanity, although I recognize this as one of the great considerations that can not much longer escape the serious attention of those who lead the thought of the world. I desire to confine the comparison now wholly to society as an organism. The problem is to apply the vast emotional forces which are ever striving to improve society, but failing for want of the proper intellectual guidance, to some truly progressive system of machinery that shall succeed in accomplishing the desired end. As above remarked, the intellect alone can not do this. It must be joined to facts. In short, what is really required is *knowledge*. Knowledge is simply truth apprehended by the intellect. Intelligent mind, fortified with knowledge, is the only reliable form of the directive force. The only proper knowledge for this purpose is that which can be acquired of the materials and the forces of nature. As it is the utilizing of these which alone can secure the end sought, so the knowledge of these is the prime necessity in the exercise of a directive control over human zeal for the improvement of mankind. Hence the diffusion of this kind of knowledge among the masses of mankind is the only hope we have of securing any greater social progress than that which nature itself vouchsafes through its own process of selection. But the knowledge referred to is just that which is embraced in the word *science*, and the diffusion of it is the process which goes by the name of education. Therefore, the first element of a truly progressive system is *popular scientific education.*

It is thus clear how wholly different must be both the nature and the plan of operation of a truly progressive system from those of any of the non-progressive systems which have divided up the energies of the world in the past.

B. ERRONEOUS IDEAS RESPECTING LIBERTY

. . . There is very little perceptible amelioration of the condition of society at large. The world does, indeed, enjoy thousands of material blessings which this unorganized progress has scattered over it; but when we consider the proletariat, when we look into great cities or out on large plantations, or visit those immense centers of production, the factories, we realize that, while the intellectual and material condition of society has reached almost giddy heights, the moral or emotional condition of man has scarcely advanced at all. There still remain the overworked millions on the one hand, and the unemployed millions on the other. There are still all the depths of ignorance, poverty, drudgery, and nameless misery that have ever been the baneful concomitants of human civilization. I am aware that it will be said that all this is a necessary evil, that it arises out of the inherent depravity, the idleness, or the perversity of human nature in some of its phases, and that it is incurable. This, however, is precisely the issue. There are some who think it quite unnecessary and the result of the wholly unorganized state of society itself—that these wretched ones are simply the unfortunates who, in the great soulless struggle for existence and scramble for gain, are crowded to the wall. There are those who believe that the organization of society on such a basis as shall put these evils in the way of immediate mitigation and ultimate removal is not a chimera. In fact, almost every one, without admitting it, entertains notions more or less definite of this kind. Such conceptions were far more prevalent in past ages than they are in our own. The failure of all the attempts in this direction has led to much skepticism in these later times. All the moral and religious systems of which mention has been made have been nothing more or less than so many attempts to realize a teleological progress. Even if the hope of securing any improvement in this world were renounced, and all efforts concentrated on obtaining the same results in a future life, the labors of missionaries and propagandists would still be simply teleological attempts to secure artificially this great good for man.

But not moral and religious systems alone belong to this class; government, too, with all its usurpations and oppressions, has always avowed, and still avows, as one of its primary functions, the temporal advancement of citizens and subjects. It has thus expressly declared for the feasibility of this teleological improvement. That it has almost without exception failed to realize the results claimed has not prevented nearly all mankind, not in the past only but in the present, from giving in their adhesion to this doctrine, so that even those who repudiate it in the case of religious institutions generally accept it in the case of political ones. . . .

Let us content ourselves here with the most general survey of the doctrine which has in modern times been indicated by the term *laissez faire*. Indeed, let us expand this notion beyond the limits usually assigned to it, and embrace not only the question whether human government can rightfully or successfully undertake to initiate and conduct reformatory and progressive measures, but with this the wider one, whether society, no matter by what means, whether through political, moral, religious, or any other system of institutions, regulations, or measures, can, either rightfully or successfully, prosecute any plans having the improvement of its own condition for their object. The question of right can be disposed of with a word. We do not care to discuss the question as to whether society or any other organism has a right to manage itself. Throughout nature the rights of individuals to carry out their desires are limited only by their power to do so. Man only *pretends* to do differently. A bird's-eye view of human history shows him to have acted on the same principle as the rest of nature, the principle that "might *makes* right."

Not until we have succeeded in banishing the metaphysical conception of abstract right, and taken down the unrealizable standards of an imaginary disinterestedness in action, shall we be prepared to discuss intelligently the conditions of man's progress conceived as capable of accomplishment by his own efforts. The first step in this movement is the recognition of the primary law that in the last analysis all results are accomplished by force. Although this proposition may shock the minds of many when brought forward as a law of society, it is really no more than saying in other words that all effects are produced by causes, which is a truism. But its effect as a law of sociology is to establish the necessity for a paramount source of power in human society.

It is here that the new science is destined to be strongly antagonized by the growth of erroneous ideas respecting liberty. The so-called "abstract rights" of mankind must be denied if society is ever to become the arbiter of its own destiny—in theory, that is, for it is impossible that the real enjoyment of liberty should be thereby in the least diminished, while the sum of human happiness must be greatly increased, and this is the only conceivable object of any right. All the prevailing theories of human rights are but ideal conceptions which not only have never yet been realized, but in the nature of things never can be. In point of fact, all things are now and always have been governed by force, and all the attempts to disguise it under the color of abstract right have only served to make it easier for the unscrupulous to accomplish their personal aggrandizement. Government has always wielded an iron scepter, which the forms of law have only rendered the more inexorable. The most complete recognition of the right of force in human society—the only rule known to the rest of the sentient world, and the only one ever acted upon by mankind—could by no possibility render matters worse than they are. But this recognition would put it in the power of the controlling authorities in society to introduce progressive elements into government, and make the coercion which is now so fruitless a positive and increasing future benefit. Under the negative system of government which has prevailed thus far, the world naturally looks round and asks what return it has received in exchange for all this sacrifice, and it is no wonder that many insist that the account is against government, and would gladly dissolve the partnership and annul the "social compact." . . .

But our problem was, whether it is possible for society to improve itself. Society is simply a compound organism whose acts exhibit the resultant of all the individual forces which its members exert. These acts, whether individual or collective, obey the fixed laws. Objectively viewed, society is a natural object, presenting a variety of complicated movements produced by a particular class of natural forces. The question, therefore, simply is, Can man ever control these forces to his advantage as he controls other, and some very complicated, natural forces? Is it true that man shall ultimately obtain the dominion of the whole world except himself? I regard society and the social forces as constituting just as much a legitimate field for the exercise of human ingenuity as do the various material substances and physical forces. The latter have been investigated and subjugated. The former are still pursuing their wild, unbridled course. The latter still exist, still exhibit their indestructible dynamic tendencies, still obey the Newtonian laws of motion, still operate along lines of least resistance. But man, by teleological foresight, has succeeded in *harmonizing these lines of least resistance with those of greatest advantage to himself.* He has made the winds, the waters, fire, steam, and electricity, do his bidding. All nature, both animate and inanimate, has been reduced to his service. One field alone remains unsubdued. One class of natural forces still remains the play of chance and from it, instead of aid, he is constantly receiving the most serious checks. This field is that of society itself, these unreclaimed forces are the social forces, of whose nature man seems to possess no knowledge, whose very existence he persistently ignores, and which he consequently is powerless to control.

C. IDEAL GOVERNMENT

Let us now see if we can find a *rationale* for all these paradoxes. When we have admitted the necessity of government, we have, of course, established its utility. The evils which it engenders are all extraneous, they do not belong to government proper; yet, as they are wholly due to it, they are styled the evils of government, and properly. But, were government restricted to its legitimate sphere, no evils would arise. Hence, what we call the evils of government are, after all, only the evils of false government, or misgovernment. They are the blemishes of the system, the evils of governments as they are and have been, not of government as it should be. We must conclude, therefore, that existing governments are defective, and, if so, we should inquire what would be a perfect government. The answer has already been hinted at.

A true government should be in most respects the precise opposite of existing ones. In the first place, it should originate in a manner directly the reverse of that in which all have originated. All governments thus far have been devised, and established by, and in the interest of, those desiring to govern. A true government would be demanded, created, and put in force by, and for the benefit of, those desiring to be governed. In the second place, as regards the light in which the governing class and the class governed regard government, the present state of things should be exactly reversed. Whereas, now, the people look up to the government as a master, and beg of it to vouchsafe them liberty and rights as a matter of favor, and the government looks down upon the people as its "subjects," and denies their petitions, or, granting them reluctantly, lays them thereby under a perpetual debt of gratitude; in a true government the people would regard the officers of government as their remunerated public servants, and require of them that they faithfully perform the service for which they were employed and in the manner in which they were directed; and they in turn would not fail to comply, on pain of removal. Again, the strange and incomprehensible distance which now separates the government from the people would be entirely removed by a true system of government. As governments are now constituted, there is no other relation recognized than that of authority on the one hand and subjection on the other. The people, at least the great majority of them, submit to the burdens of service and taxation which government imposes, not as a duty, not as a *quid pro quo*, but simply as a necessity. They are not considered, not even requested—they are simply coerced. They comply, without the least idea of ever receiving a return. They consider it in precisely the same light as if required by force to give of their substance and earnings to a stranger who possessed the power to exact it. And government encourages this sentiment, and treats them in all respects as though this were the only relation subsisting between them. In a true system of government all this would be reversed. The people, having created their government for their own convenience, would understand what was the real relation in which they stood to it, and the government would understand this relation also. It would be an intimate relation of immediate interest, not that of a foreign power. Society would be the source of authority, and the government its agent; but this relation, being a true one, could never be attended with those interminable quarrels for the mastery which now characterize the opposite and false relation. If the people paid money, it would be into their own treasury, kept by their own chosen agents, who would not dare or desire to appropriate it otherwise than as instructed. If a war must be waged (and under such a government this would be a very rare event), it would be the people's own war, and not the war of ambitious rulers; and it would be cheerfully fought. And thus it would be throughout, the present system being supplanted by one entirely different, and in most respects the very antithesis of it, founded on the principle that the people desire to be governed, which is diametrically opposed to that upon which all existing governments are based, viz., the fact that certain persons desire to govern.

The theory of government is very simple. Where many

individuals are situated in narrow, local compass, those acts which tend to satisfy the desires of one must in many cases produce pain to others. The individual thus injured resents the injury, and conflict is the result. Where each individual acts in his own case, it reduces itself to a question of mere force, and this is an effectual bar to the existence of society. But man reasons, and perceives that justice is not always with the strong. Hence there arises a demand for a tribunal for the decision of cases according to reason. Every demand brings after it a supply. In this case the supply came too soon, and from the wrong quarter. If ambition could have been kept down, society would, perhaps, have ultimately erected a government, and the government which society established would have been the true theoretical one described above.

But this is the primary quality of government which is necessary for the existence of society, viz., protection. If this were no longer required, if mankind were grown so wise as to be able to live in peace *in* society, as was once possible *without* society, still there would be need, not of government, but of *organization*. Society would need agents to transact its common business, and this is what I have called the secondary function of government, or accommodation. This, too, is all that will one day be left of government. It is toward this that all nations have been steadily drifting. The other feature of government must necessarily be odious, however indispensable, and the sense of this odiousness, aggravated by the perpetual usurpations of the ruling class, is what accounts for the incessant warfare which society has always been waging against government.

But, whatever be the objects of government, it is clear that it can have no other just origin than the *will* (not the "consent," which is merely negative and permissive, but the positive, declared will) of society. A class of individuals possessing wealth, intelligence, or lineage, can not be called society. It is not even an aristocracy, it is an oligarchy. It only increases the number of rulers, and thereby increases the burdens of the people. Neither can it be called society when, where distinct races occupy the same territory, one race excludes all others, or when any race or class is excluded. It is not the will of *society* which governs when the individuals of one sex are prevented from the expression of their will. This is only a rule of sex, and, although logically the most radical defect, this *andrarchy* is the form of government which the world has always had to endure, even in those nations which have called themselves democracies, where not only one half of society is excluded, but an entire class with all its peculiarities. It would be far better were every second individual excluded without regard to sex, since then there would be equilibrium. . . .

D. THE SUPERIORITY OF GOVERNMENT OVER PRIVATE ADMINISTRATION OF PUBLIC CONCERNS

. . . The question whether any enterprise should be undertaken by the state or left to individuals is one which must be determined on the intrinsic merits of each individual case. The transfer of functions from the latter to the former simply marks the expansion of the jurisdiction of the state, a process which, when correctly viewed, has been going on steadily from the earliest ages of political history. Nearly every present acknowledged function of government has once been intrusted to private enterprise. It simply shows that, little by little, society has risen to the consciousness of its needs, and has, one by one, assumed control of the more important public interests. Whether it be its finances, its criminal jurisprudence, its customs regulation, its postal affairs, its telegraphs, or its railroads, whatever it fairly perceives to need state administration, it proceeds to assume and add to the functions of the government.

Dynamic Sociology, II, 578–580, 582–585, 590–591.

Now, of all the enterprises which the state has thus appropriated to itself, there is not one which it has not managed
better and more wisely than it had been managed before by
private parties. Most of them are such that the world has
entirely forgotten that they were ever private enterprises.
Others have become cherished public institutions which no
future revolutions can again remand to private direction. And
there are others which are still debating-ground or on trial
in some states. The transportation question is one of these
latter. Telegraphic communication is another. Education is a
third. Other social operations still, not now looked upon except
by a few as belonging to this class, are destined to pass through
the stages of agitation and governmental assumption. These
facts should not, however, lead to the conclusion that government should immediately assume charge of all private enterprises which concern the general public. There must be a
gradual maturing of the conditions, both on the side of the
state and of the individual, before this can successfully be done.
The question in each case must always be, Is the age ripe for
this change? As society is constituted, however, premature
action of this nature can scarcely occur. So strong is the force
of established custom, that it much more frequently happens
that the event is too long postponed, and the state does not
step in until the crying evils of private mismanagement and
individual incompetency have thoroughly aroused it to the
necessity.

The superiority of governmental administration over private
management, in large enterprises of a general public character,
has been clearly seen and frequently pointed out, but the
progress of popular opinion on such questions has been powerfully counteracted by the special nature of the case. Private
enterprise is ever jealous of governmental encroachment upon
its domain, and the more lucrative the enterprise is—that is,
the greater the need that it be conducted by society in the
interest of its members—the stronger will be the influence

brought to bear against such a result. This influence is exerted by the creation of a public sentiment against state interference. In this, private enterprise always has matters almost entirely its own way. The state has little interest in the subject. The people at large rarely attribute their burdens to the proper source. Things must reach the point of unendurableness before the public will appeal to the state for assistance. Meanwhile a constant stream of opposition to all forms of state interference, more or less ingeniously supported by plausible argument, is being poured out by interested parties. The result is, according to the principle already laid down, that current views which are unopposed will be generally accepted, that the state must overcome an immense mass of prejudice before it can act in any case. . . .

It might similarly be shown that all the functions of government are usually performed with far greater thoroughness and fidelity than similar functions intrusted to private individuals. If any one will take the trouble to examine the various reports published by the several executive departments of any government, and to compare them with efforts of a like general nature made by individuals, he will doubtless be willing to confess that the latter fall below the former in many important respects. The peculiar weight which every body attaches to the word "official" has something more to sustain it than that mere blind worship of great names. It is instinctively felt that, whether absolutely reliable or not, an official statement is the very most reliable to be attained; and between two statements, one official and the other unofficial, the strongest opponent of governmental encroachment on private territory would not hesitate to prefer the former. It is fashionable to declaim against the so-called "bureaucracy" of modern times, but this is only a part of the attempt of sagacious capitalists to manufacture public sentiment to counteract the steady current of rational conviction toward the conclusion that society must arouse to its own interests, and take the welfare of its members more directly into its own hands.

There is one class of work extensively performed by the state which has proved its adaptability to this method more completely perhaps than almost any other. This is work of a scientific character. Whatever scientific undertakings have been intrusted to the government have almost invariably been ably and thoroughly prosecuted. This is abundantly illustrated by the exceptional efficiency of our Coast Survey and Light-House Service, by the labors of the Naval Observatory, of the Signal Service, of the Patent-Office, of the Geological Surveys, and of every other bureau to which work of this class has been intrusted. The same is true of all other countries. The scientific mind appears to be peculiarly adapted to faithful service in situations where great practical interests are involved. Scientific men are, from their very education, earnest men, and fully aroused to the importance of putting their knowledge to the best practical use. Though making no professions of philanthropic principles, they really have the welfare of society more at heart than many who talk loudly of social reform. They only ask an opportunity to apply scientific principles to great things, and when this is offered they, as a rule, devote themselves completely and unreservedly to their work.

Then, again, science is ill-adapted to the competitive and feverish methods and sentiments that obtain in nearly all departments of private life. Success in science depends on the ability to await results. Science can not be hurried. Forced to make haste, it is in danger of degenerating into charlatanism. It must also be independent. No one can influence it or warp its conclusions. There is no substitute for exact truth. For all these special characteristics of all scientific work, the service of the state is admirably adapted.

All that has been said of scientific work and much more will apply to educational work. Education is essentially a scientific labor, and this in the highest sense. It is not only the science of sciences, but the art of arts.

Without repeating the considerations set forth in the preceding paragraphs, we may proceed to enumerate a few of the special reasons why all educational work should be intrusted to the state.

Education can not be successfully conducted on the competitive system. It is an enterprise so wholly dissimilar from those of ordinary business life that an entirely different set of principles must be applied to it throughout. In the first place, it is not prosecuted in order to supply any of the demands of the physical being. No true social force can be named as its original motive. It is from first to last the result of cold calculation based on observation and experience. There exists no natural desire for education. Even admitting the natural craving of the youthful mind for knowledge, this would never be sought in any of the ways in which education requires it to be conferred.

Again, the recipients of education are not the same individuals as those who really desire that education be given. Where this desire is more specialized than in society itself, it inheres in parents or guardians, viz., the desire that their children or wards receive it. This is obviously a wholly anomalous form of enterprise, and finds no analogue within the whole domain of social undertakings. This radical difference of nature, therefore, clearly requires a radically different form of treatment, and the principles and formulas that apply to other enterprises are wholly inapplicable to this one. Adam Smith excepted education from the law of supply and demand, and similarly it must be excepted from every other established law of politico-economics. . . .

. . . State education is far better for the pupil. It is distinguished fundamentally from private education in dealing with all in a strictly impartial manner. The lowest *gamin* of the streets here meets the most pampered son of opulence on a footing of strict equality. Nothing counts but merit itself. Pupils take their places according to what they are, not what they are called. Public education operates as a gauge of the capacities of the mind. Each mind is, as it were, measured and its capacity recorded. A thorough trial of it would doubtless be of the highest value, merely as a means of eradicating popular errors respecting the fancied superiority of birth, rank, and station. But this is not its aim. Its aim is to diffuse intelligence. The fact that, under its undiscriminating rule, each mind must find its natural level, wholly regardless of conventional circumstances, is simply an incident to its operation. The child comes to look upon it as he looks upon other processes of nature, as something over which he has no control. He feels that in coping with it, as in coping with other natural forces, his success will be determined by his power. It is not something which can be accommodated to his whims. His tasks can not be shirked, or imposed upon other more willing ones. Violations of its requirements, like violations of the laws of health, bring their own certain penalties, and he learns to regard it, as he regards the other natural forces to which his life is subject, as both inexorable and irresponsible. This kind of discipline is the most valuable that could be administered, and does more to square up the character than any amount of moral teaching.

Lastly, public education is immeasurably better for society. It is so because it really accomplishes the object of education, which private education does not. What society most needs is the distribution of the knowledge in its possession. This is a work which can not be trusted to individuals. It can neither be left to the discretion of children, of parents, nor of teachers. It is not for any of these to say what knowledge is most useful to society. No tribunal short of that which society in its own sovereign capacity shall appoint is competent to decide this question. To the teacher duly trained for his work may be left certain questions of method, especially of detail; but even the method must be in its main features unified with a view to the greatest economy in its application. This must necessarily also be the duty of the supreme authority.

If society ever collectively realizes what the ultimate end of its being is, and comprehends the true relations of the hierarchy of means to that end, it will necessarily regard the distribution of knowledge as the one great function, outside of its regulative functions, which it is specially constituted to perform. It will concentrate its entire dynamic energy upon it, to the neglect of all those ends which, as we have seen, must follow from this one initial motive power. . . .

E. EDUCATION AND SOCIAL REFORM

. . . The distribution of knowledge underlies all social reform. So long as capital and labor are the respective symbols of intelligence and ignorance, the present inequity in the distribution of wealth must continue. It may be urged that, since there exists so great inequality in the natural capacity of the human mind, there must still ever exist, even after knowledge shall have been equally distributed, a corresponding inequality of intelligence, and that therefore the proposed change will only substitute one species of inequality for another. The answer is twofold:

First, the differences in native capacity, though admittedly great, are small compared to the differences of information. The supposed intellectual inequality is greatly exaggerated. The large fund of good sense which is always found among the lower, uneducated classes is an obtrusive fact to every observing mind. The ability with which ignorant people employ their small fund of knowledge has surprised many learned men. While there may doubtless be found all grades of intellect, from the highest philosophic to the lowest idiotic, the number who fall below a certain average standard is insignificant, and so, too, is the number who rise above it. The great bulk of humanity are fully witted, and amply capable of taking care of themselves if afforded an opportunity. In fact, it is out of this class that the majority of the great names of history have been taken. It is a mistake to suppose that the sole element of excellence is superior intellectual power. It is usually an average intellect joined to an indomitable will, a tenacious perseverance, or an unquenchable ambition. It is *emotional* force, not intellectual, that brings out exceptional results. This is unfortunately often too apparent in the labors of so-called "self-made men," whose real intellectual mediocrity, though overlooked when accompanied with so great energy, renders the results achieved comparatively worthless and shortlived. On the contrary, the really best minds are not the ones that accomplish most. They usually lack inspiration, they are too critical, too sensitive to the least defect. Great causal penetration and all-sidedness are antagonistic to energetic, independent effort under difficulties. Contrary to the common belief, the most permanently useful and solid work that has ever been done has come from such minds when so circumstanced as to find themselves in the very current of their labors. Had they not been so placed, they would probably never have made the effort necessary to place themselves there. The best minds require to have opportunity brought to them. Those who seek opportunities and create circumstances do so by virtue of emotional forces which usually accompany only average talents.

It is a prevalent belief that so-called self-made men attain their distinction in consequence of the adverse circumstances against which they are compelled to contend. The phenomenon so frequent in modern times of men working up from obscurity to eminence is supposed to support this view. Looked at more closely, however, this argument is found to involve a fatal fallacy. It must first of all be remembered that "obscurity" embraces all but a minute fraction of the human race. The proportion to their class of those who thus rise out of it is next to infinitesimal. On the other hand, the class having means and leisure is numerically very small. One case of distinction from this class would be relatively equal to all that can be named from the other. Yet no one can deny that there are many great names belonging exclusively to the latter class. It is sufficient to mention Lord Bacon, Sir Isaac Newton, Alexander von Humboldt, Sir Charles Lyell, or Charles Darwin, in order to show that leisure is not, as is claimed, a detriment to aspiration. It shows, on the contrary, that the want of it is the great barrier to intellectual excellence; that poverty and monotonous toil crush out millions of potential luminaries in society. Yet the phenomenon of self-made men is not without its lessons. It teaches the average native capacity of all men, without regard to rank or circumstances, a truth which is also generally ignored or denied, and whose denial is often made an argument against universal education, as is the fallacy just pointed out. The other fact of the relatively frequent rise of men of leisure to eminence, and the great achievements of such men, also teaches a useful truth, viz., that if the true merits of mankind are to be all brought out, it must be done by equalizing the opportunities of all. And it should be remembered that, while the work of the so-called self-made men has generally possessed only a temporary and fleeting value, that of men of leisure has usually possessed a permanent and lasting value. This is partly because all truly useful work requires *preparation*, and this the mushroom growth of the self-made man can not provide.

Thus some of the most specious arguments against education in general, and universal education in particular, are seen to rest upon facts which, rightly interpreted, really argue powerfully in their favor. . . .

8

"THE

LAISSEZ FAIRE DOCTRINE

IS SUICIDAL"

1884

By the 1880's Professor William Graham Sumner of Yale University had emerged as the most vigorous and influential of Herbert Spencer's American disciples. This review of Sumner's WHAT SOCIAL CLASSES OWE TO EACH OTHER *opens the great debate between these two antagonists over the role of government in society and economy, a debate in which Ward increasingly took and held the offensive. Note, in passing, that Ward wrote this essay at a moment when he had been converted to simplified spelling. He later abandoned this reform but chose to retain the simplified spelling in his reprint of the review.*

This little book, from its very smallness, wil probably be widely read. It may do good or it may do harm. We think it

Man, Vol. IV, No. 9 (March 1, 1884), in *Glimpses of the Cosmos,* III, 301–305.

wil do good. We say this, however, not because we agree with its general tone. On the contrary, we regard it as founded on radically false assumptions, but they ar assumptions which ar popular and ar supported by current theories. There is nothing new in the *matter* of the book. Every statement it contains has been made a thousand times, and nearly every illustration used is already threadbare in the same service. It is the *manner* alone that can hope to attract attention, and this, we must confess, is at least original.

The book is a sort of final wail against the modern practices of states and peoples which run counter to these current theories. The argument is simply the old cry: *"Laissez faire, laissez passer!"* It is the renewed appeal to State and other social agencies to cease their interference with the natural laws of society as expressed in unrestricted private enterprise and freedom of trade. Notwithstanding the powerful array of alleged scientific theory by which this argument is supported, and the great and confessedly useful influence it formerly exerted, its rallying cries hav for many years lost much of their effectiveness, and, without any very large body of doctrin to act from, states and nations, driven to it by popular demands, hav largely adopted the policy of restriction, regulation, and supervision. The countries of Continental Europe, less influenced by theoretical economists, led the way by many decades, and to-day most of the important public agencies, telegraphs, railroads, etc., ar under state control. In England the Liberal party resisted until it came into power, but was then compelled to yield to popular demands for interference. We now see there, in the land of Adam Smith, regulation of railroads, state education, postal telegraphy, the parcels post-law, temperance laws, landlord and tenant laws, an Irish land act, and a great body of legislation arising in large part from what is popularly called the "national conscience." In general, foreign commerce is there left free, as is obviously the true policy for an almost exclusively commercial nation; but when it is wished to discourage the importation of luxuries or injurious commodities, such as distilled liquors, the duties ar unsparingly laid on, often amounting to prohibition.

In America, to secure national self-dependence, develop mineral and other resources, encourage inventiv talent and home manufactures, diversify population, and avoid redundant transportation, duties hav from the first been levied on certain commodities and ar still so levied. We hav had a national postoffice, which Prof. Sumner probably admits to be a success; and we hav state, if not national, education. Other forms of state action ar demanded, among which ar those against certain monopolies, particularly those of transportation.

The various enterprises named, and many others which different states hav assumed, have not been the wretched failures which the theorists describe, but successes of the most important kind, and it is experience and facts that continue to embolden men to demand additional ones. It is beginning to be recognized by many people that not only ar individuals often incompetent to manage those operations which specially affect the general public, but that the state *is* competent to manage them. This is strikingly shown in numerous instances; hence a form of mild but rather business-like popular clamor to be relieved of certain serious evils arising from the greed and incompetency of private individuals and corporations.

The practice is to listen to this form of appeal and cautiously but securely to adopt regulativ measures. So far has this tendency gone that the doctrinarians hav taken the alarm. They feel that practice is running counter to theory. *Laissez faire* has with them become a creed, and they feel as do religious devotees when they see their faith breaking down and their creed superseded by a more liberal and progessiv one. They hav already long ago said all there was to say. They can now only protest, threaten, and vituperate. All effect must henceforth come, if at all, from new forms of warfare, and this book aims to secure it in this way. Its method is thoroly *ex parte* and aggressiv. There is no attempt to conciliate, no hint at concession. The style is pungent and incisiv. All attempts at social reform ar unsparingly condemned, and reformers of every kind ar lashed and goaded in a merciless manner. The reader feels that the schoolmaster is indeed abroad, and so pointed and almost personal ar the author's assaults that there is scarcely any one who can fail to perceive that he is himself the unhappy victim. The laboring class and "the poor" in general ar handled with especial severity. These ar given no quarter, and one is inclined to believe that they ar regarded as sheer intruders and cumberers of the earth.

The whole book is based on the fundamental error that the favors of this world ar distributed entirely according to merit. Poverty is only a proof of indolence and vice. Wealth simply shows the industry and virtue of the possessors! The very most is made of Malthusianism, and human activities ar degraded to a complete level with those of animals. Those who hav survived simply prove their fitness to survive; and the fact which all biologists perfectly understand, viz.; that fitness to survive is something wholly distinct from real superiority, is, of course ignored by the author because he is not a biologist, as all sociologists should be.

Laissez faire is "translated" into "blunt English" as meaning "mind your own business," and this injunction he drives home to almost every one who has ever done anything except to write about "what social classes owe to each other"; the salutary reservation of Sir Joseph Porter, "except me," seeming to be constantly kept in mind.

It would be wholly profitless to attempt to meet such an argument. Nearly every proposition in the book involves a fallacy, and one that has been repeatedly, as it is easily, pointed out. The author inveighs, as is the fashion, against meddling with natural laws, and interfering with the natural flow of events. He seems never to hav reflected that practical art as the product of applied science, and which alone constitutes man a civilized being, is the exclusiv effect of his meddling and interfering with the natural course of physical phenomena. The inventor is just the "meddler" he is belaboring. Or else he thinks that social phenomena form a complete exception, and ar not a domain of practical science such as can be put to any use. If so pray, why waste time in cultivating such a pseudo-science?

But his inconsistency is not confined to questions so profound. His own idea of true functions of government must condemn that institution even in its ideal form as an interference with the natural course of things. It should, he says, secure to all equal chances to pursue happiness. But would not nature secure this without such institutional interference? Clearly, consistency must condemn all government, and proclaim anarchy pure and simple.

Again in his severe condemnation of the "friends of humanity," as he sneeringly calls all who believe in the attainment through human effort of a higher social state, he seems to forget that these very troublesome persons ar merely products of society and *natural*. To hear him, remembering his premises, one would suppose that these men either had invaded the world from some outer planet or had artificially created themselves. But they belong to society as much as the hated paupers and worthless invalids whom he would turn over to nature. Why then not let them alone? Why meddle with the natural course of things? In fact what is the *raison d'être* of this earnest book that wants to hav so much done? On his own theory, the author should let his deluded victims alone, should *laisser faire*—we omit the "translation."

We said we believed the book would do good. It wil show, as nothing else has done, that the *laissez faire* doctrin, if it could be carried to a logical conclusion, would be nihilistic and suicidal. This work goes to the utmost possible extreme short of complete consistency, and the network of absurdities in which this attempt has involved the author must serve to condemn the whole doctrin in the eyes of all readers whose opinions ar not already irrevocably fixed, *i. e.*, all whom it aims to convince.

This result wil be especially salutary at the present time, since it is only quite recently that the modern current of public policy has ever received anything like a theoretical analysis from a strictly philosophical standpoint, such for example as that which Mr. Lester F. Ward has given to it in his "Dynamic Sociology." For when thus fundamentally analyzed it appears that, after all, this is the really scientific side of the question, and is sustained by an impregnable bulwark of truly cosmical principles.

9

"ART IS

THE ANTITHESIS

OF NATURE"

1884

This essay, which Ward himself called "Mind as a Social Factor," was first read to the Anthropological Society of Washington, and later that same year to the Metaphysical Club of the Johns Hopkins.

After many centuries of exclusive study of the soul the thinkers of the world turned their attention for some centuries more to the study of the intellect. During all this time, the true influence of mind as a social factor was left quite out of view. At last there rose up the scientific philosophy which essayed to explain the nature of mind. Its dependence upon organisation in general and upon brain in particular was proved by scientific experimentation, and the domain of metaphysics became that of psychology. Mind was shown to be a function of body

Mind, IX (October 1884), in *Glimpses of the Cosmos,* III, 563–573.

and psychology became a department of biology. Man has now taken his true position in the animal world as a product of development. Brain, which alone raises him above other animals, has been developed in the same manner as the other anatomical characters. The brain is the organ of the mind, its physical seat and cause. Mind is therefore a natural product of evolution, and its achievements are to be classed and studied along with all other natural phenomena. Such is the scientific conception of mind.

The modern scientist places all objects in the midst of an infinite series of antecedents and consequents. Organic forms as well as inorganic must take their places in this series—the animal no less than the plant, the man no less than the beast. Mind itself is a link of this endless chain. Its activities consist in the transmission of the properties of its antecedents to its consequents. The quantity of force in the universe is constant. No power can increase or diminish it. All attempts on the part of the creatures of this constant and unchangeable force to modify its normal effects are not less vain because such creatures happen to have acquired the faculty of observing the changes going on in nature.

The protracted study of nature's processes leads to admiration of them, and the belief has become prevalent that they are not only unalterable but also in some way necessarily beneficent. Nature has made great progress in developing organised beings and is assumed to be still working in this direction. The natural method is always the true method, and to find it out is the aim of all scientific investigation. Out of this earnest and laudable strife to discover the true method of nature has grown, logically enough, the assumption that when found it must be something of great worth. It is commonly supposed that the highest wisdom of man is to learn and then to follow the ways of nature. Those dissatisfied people who would improve upon the natural course of events are rebuked as meddlers with the unalterable. Their systems are declared utopian, their laws *bruta fulmina*. All efforts in this direction are held to be trifling and are stigmatised as so many ignorant attempts to nullify the immutable laws of nature.

This general mode of reasoning is carried into all departments of human life.

In government every attempt to improve the condition of the state is condemned and denounced. Curiously enough, here the claim is illogically made that such measures are harmful. In fact, unfortunately for the whole theory, they have often been proved to be so. But this, of course, proves their efficacy. This glaring inconsistency is, however, overlooked, and government is implored, not to adopt wise and successful measures, but to refrain from adopting any, to let society alone, and thus allow the laws of nature to work out their beneficent results.

In commerce and trade absolute freedom is insisted upon. Free trade is the watchword of this entire school. The laws of trade, they maintain, are natural laws. As such they must be better than any human rules. And here again we find them insisting that regulation is injurious to trade, although it is at the same time declared to be nugatory.

In social affairs these doctrines are carried to their extreme logical outcome. The laws of nature as they manifest themselves in society must be left wholly untouched. The passions of men will neutralise and regulate themselves. Competition can be depended upon to correct abuses. The seller must be allowed to exaggerate and misstate the nature of his wares. This has the effect to sharpen the wits of the buyer, and this develops the brain. To dilute, adulterate, or even poison food and medicine for personal gain is not objectionable, since the destruction thereby of a few unwary consumers only proves their unfitness to survive in society. As in general commerce, so in private business, competition must be free. If a dealer, by selling at a loss, can hold out until all his competitors have been driven from the field, in order then to recover more than his losses by the monopoly he will enjoy, his right to do this must not be questioned. It is under such conditions and by the aid of such discipline that man and society have developed.

Education must be that of experience. Knowledge must be gained by efforts to avoid the consequences of ignorance already felt. The intellectual development of the child must be an epitome of that of the race. It is thus only that nature operates, and surely nature is greater and wiser than man.

All schemes of social reform are unscientific. Public charities tend to bolster up unworthy elements in society that nature has declared unfit to survive. Temperance reforms tend only to abridge individual liberty—for even the liberty to destroy one's self should be respected. Philanthropy is zeal without knowledge, while humanitarianism is fanaticism.

This general class of views antedated by many years the publication by Spencer and Darwin of their formulated doctrines of the "survival of the fittest" and "natural selection." But it cannot be denied that these doctrines, supported as they were by facts fresh from nature, have greatly strengthened this habit of thought. Nature's method is now much better known than formerly, and it is now well understood that an utterly soulless competition constitutes its fundamental characteristic. Surely man cannot go astray in following in the footsteps of nature. Let him learn from the animal world. He has descended from some of the humble stocks which he is now studying. Nature's plan has raised him from the condition of a beast to that of a rational being. It has created and developed society and civilisation. Unless tampered with by "reformers" all the operations of society would be competitive. Competition is the law of nature out of which progress results. Sociology, as its founder insisted, must be based on biology, and the true sociologist must understand this biologic law. Those who propose to apply methods to society which are opposed to the methods of nature are supposed to be ignorant of these fundamental truths and are called empiricists, "meddlers," and "tinkers."

Such, I say, is the tenor and tendency of modern scientific thought. I do not say that all scientific men hold these views. I merely maintain that leading ones have formulated and inculcated them as natural deductions from the established facts of science, and that the public mind is rapidly assimilating them, while scarcely any attempts are being made to check their advance.[1]

Is there any way of answering these arguments? Can the *laissez faire* doctrine be successfully met? That all attempts to do this have been timidly made cannot be denied. That these have been few and feeble is equally certain. While there has existed in the minds of many rational persons a vague sense of some hidden fallacy in all this reasoning, none have felt competent to formulate their objections with sufficient clearness and force to warrant pitting them against the resistless stream of concurrent science and philosophy of the nineteenth century. There has, however, been developing of late a more or less marked apprehension with regard to the possible consequences of this mode of thought. The feeling is distinct in the best minds, and to a large extent in the public mind, that the tendency of modern ideas is nihilistic. It is clear that if they become universally accepted they must work stagnation in society. The *laissez faire* doctrine is a gospel of inaction, the scientific creed is struck with sterility, the policy of resigning all into the hands of Nature is a surrender.

But this recognition is by no means proof that the prevalent opinions are false. At best it can only suggest this on the ground that true doctrines should be progressive. But this would be a *petitio principii*. Nature is not optimistic, still less anthropocentric. For aught we know, the laws of nature are such as make a recognition of strict scientific truth a positive

---

[1] The social philosophy of Mr. Herbert Spencer possesses this tone throughout, and his disciples, particularly in America, delight in going even farther than their master. The most extreme statement of the *laissez faire* doctrine known to me is that of Prof. W. G. Sumner, in his recent work *Social Classes*.

barrier to social advancement. The argument we have been considering must be refuted, if at all, by legitimate counter-argument.

The present attempt to meet some parts of this argument is made in full consciousness of its strength as a factor in modern thought and with due deference to the great names that stand committed to it. The scientific facts which its defenders have brought to its support are, in the main, incontestable. To answer by denying these would be to abjure science and deserve contempt. The method of nature has been correctly interpreted. The doctrines of the survival of the fittest and natural selection are perfectly true doctrines. The law of competition is the fundamental law. It is unquestionably true that progress, not only in primary organic development, but also in society, has resulted from the action of this law.

After conceding all this, the attempt, notwithstanding, to stem the tide of modern scientific thought must, indeed, seem a hopeless one. At the outset it must be frankly acknowledged that if the current views are unsound the fault is not chargeable to science. If there is any defect it must lie in the inferences drawn from the facts and not in the facts themselves. To what extent, then, is the *laissez faire* doctrine, as defined and popularly accepted, an inference? If the method of nature is correctly formulated by that doctrine, wherein lies the fallacy when it is applied to man and to society?

In order to grapple at once with the whole problem let me answer these questions by the open charge that the modern scientific philosophers fail to recognise the true value of the *psychic factor*. Just as the metaphysicians lost their bearings by an empty worship of mind and made philosophy a plaything, so the modern evolutionists have missed their mark by degrading mind to a level with mechanical force. They seem thus about to fling away the grand results that the doctrine of evolution cannot otherwise fail to achieve. Far be it from me to appeal to the prejudices of the enemies of science by casting opprobrium upon scientific deductions, but when I consider the tendencies which are now so unmistakable, and which are so certainly the consequence of the protracted study, on the part of leading scientists, of the unquestionable methods of nature, I think I can, though holding precisely opposite opinions, fully sympathise with Carlyle in characterising the philosophy of evolution as a "gospel of dirt."

But I need not longer dwell upon the blighting influence of this construction of the known laws of nature. Let us approach the kernel of the problem.

The *laissez faire* doctrine fails to recognise that, in the development of mind, a virtually *new power* was introduced into the world. To say that this has been done is no startling announcement. It is no more than has taken place many times in the course of the evolution of living and feeling beings out of the tenuous nebulae of space. For, while it is true that nature makes no leaps, while, so long as we consider their beginning, all the great steps in evolution are due to minute increments repeated through vast periods, still, when we survey the whole field, as we must do to comprehend the scheme, and contrast the extremes, we find that nature has been making a series of enormous strides, and reaching from one plane of development to another. It is these independent achievements of evolution that the true philosopher must study.

Not to mention the great steps in the cosmical history of the solar system and of the earth, we must regard the evolution of protoplasm, the "physical basis of life," as one of those gigantic strides which thenceforth completely revolutionised the surface of our planet. The development of the cell as the unit of organisation was another such stride. The origin of vertebrate life introduced a new element, and the birth of man wrought still another transformation. These are only a few of nature's revolutions. Many more will suggest themselves. And although, in no single one of these cases can it be said at what exact point the new essence commenced to exist, although the development of all these several expressions of Nature's method of concentrating her hitherto diffused forces was accomplished through an unbroken series of minute transitional increments continued through eons of time, still, it is not a whit less true that each of these grand products of evolution, when at length fully formed, constituted a new cosmic energy, and proceeded to stamp all future products and processes with a character hitherto wholly unknown upon the globe.

It is in this sense, and in this only, that I claim development of mind—of the thinking, reasoning, inventing faculty of the human brain—as another, and one of the best marked, of the great cosmic strides that have characterised the course of evolution and belong to the legitimate methods of nature.

It is, for example, only to a limited extent and in the most general way that we can apply the same canons to the organic as to the inorganic world. It is usually, but falsely, supposed that the student of biology need know nothing of physics, the assumption being that they have nothing in common. While this error is fatal to all fundamental acquaintance with the laws of life, it well illustrates the immensity of the advance from one realm to the other. The same could be said, in varying degrees of obviousness, of every one of the ascending steps to which reference has been made. I freely admit that the theologians and metaphysicians commit the most fatal error in treating the soul, or mind, as independent of the body, but this enormous fallacy is scarcely greater than that of the modern evolutionist, who, finding out their dependence, ignores the *magnitude* of the step by which mind was made a property of body, and proceeds as though no new factor had entered into the world.

But all this may be regarded as mere generality. Let us come to something more specific.

It has always been a marvel to my comprehension that wise men and philosophers, when smitten with the specious logic of the *laissez faire* school, can close their eyes to the most obtrusive fact that civilisation presents. In spite of the influence of philosophy, all forms of which have thus far been negative and nihilistic, the human animal, with his growing intellect, has still ever realised the power that is vouchsafed through mind, and has ever exercised that power. Philosophy would have long since robbed him of it and caused his early extermination from the earth but for the persistence, through heredity, of the impulse to exercise in self-preservation every power in his possession; by which practice alone he first gained his ascendancy ages before philosophy began.

The great fact, then, to which I allude is that, in spite of all philosophy, whether mythologic, metaphysical, or naturalistic, declaring that man must and can do nothing, he *has*, from the very dawn of his intelligence, been transforming the entire surface of the planet he inhabits. No other animal performs anything comparable to what man performs. This is solely because no other possesses the developed psychic faculty.

If we analyze mind into its two departments, sense and intellect, we shall see that it is through this latter faculty that these results are accomplished. If we inquire more closely into the mode by which intellect operates, we find that it serves as a guiding power to those natural forces with which it is acquainted (and no others), directing them into channels of human advantage. If we seek for a single term by which to characterize with precision the nature of this process, we find this in *Invention*. This essential characteristic of all intellectual action is invention.

Glancing now at the *ensemble* of human achievement, which may be collectively called civilization, we readily see that it is all the result of this inventive process. All practical art is merely the product of successful invention, and it requires no undue expansion of the term, nor extraordinary power of generalisation, to see in all human institutions only modified forms of arts, and true products of the intellectual, or inventive, faculty.

But what is the general result of all this? An entirely new dispensation has been given to the world. All the materials and forces of nature have been thus placed completely under the control of one of the otherwise least powerful of the creatures inhabiting the earth. He has only to know them in order to become their master. Nature has thus been made the servant of man. Thus only has man succeeded in peopling the entire globe while all other animals are restricted to narrow faunal areas. He has also peopled certain portions far more densely than any other species could have done, and he seems destined to continue multiplying his numbers for a long time yet in the future. But this quantitative proof is even less telling than the qualitative. When we confine our attention to the *élite* of mankind we do not need to have the ways specified in detail by which the powers of mind have exalted the intellectual being above all other products of creation. At the present moment the most dense and the most enlightened populations of the globe occupy what are termed temperate latitudes, which means latitudes in which for from three to five months each year vegetation ceases entirely, the waters are locked in ice, and the temperature frequently sinks far below the zero of the Fahrenheit thermometer. Imagine the thin-skinned, furless animal man subsisting in such a climate. Extinguish his fires, banish his clothing, blot out the habitations that deck the civilised landscape. How long would the puny race survive? But these are not products of nature, they are products of *art,* the wages of thought—fruits of the intellect.

When a well-clothed philosopher on a bitter winter's night sits in a warm room well lighted for his purpose and writes on paper with pen and ink in the arbitrary characters of a highly developed language the statement that civilisation is the result of natural laws, and that man's duty is to let nature alone so that untrammeled it may work out a higher civilisation, he simply ignores every circumstance of his existence and deliberately closes his eyes to every fact within the range of his faculties. If man had acted upon his theory there would have been no civilisation, and our philosopher would have remained a troglodyte.

But how shall we distinguish this human, or anthropic, method from the method of nature? Simply by reversing all the definitions. Art is the antithesis of nature. If we call one the natural method we must call the other the artificial method. If nature's process is rightly named natural selection, man's process is artificial selection. The survival of the fittest is simply the survival of the strong, which implies, and might as well be called, the destruction of the weak. And if nature progresses through the destruction of the weak, man progresses through the *protection* of the weak. This is the essential distinction.

In human society the psychic power has operated to secure the protection of the weak in two distinct ways: first, by increasing the supply of the necessities of life, and, secondly, by preventing the destruction of life through the enemies of man. The immediate instrumentality through which the first of these processes is carried on is art, the product of invention. The second process takes place through the establishment of positive institutions.

It is difficult to say which of these agencies has been most effective. Both were always indispensable, and therefore all comparison is unprofitable.

Art operates to protect the weak against adverse surroundings. It is directed against natural forces, chiefly physical. By thus defeating the destructive influences of the elements and hostile forms of life, and by forcing nature to yield an unnatural supply of man's necessities, many who would have succumbed from inability to resist these adverse agencies— the feebler members of society—were able to survive, and population increased and expanded. While no one openly denies this, there is a tendency either to ignore it in politico-economic discussions, or to deny its application to them as an answer to naturalistic arguments.

If, on the other hand, we inquire into the nature of human institutions, we shall perceive that they are of three kinds, tending to protect the weak in three ways, or ascending degrees. These three successively higher means through which this end is attained are, first, Justice, second, Morality, and third, Charity. These forms of action have been reached through the development, respectively, of the three corresponding sentiments: Equity, Beneficence, and Benevolence.

All of these altruistic sentiments are wholly unknown, or known only in the merest embryo, to all animals below man, and therefore no such means of protection exist among them. They are strictly human, or anthropic. Many evolutionists fail to recognise this. Some sociologists refuse to admit it. They look about and see so much injustice, immorality and rapacity that they are led to suppose that only natural methods are in operation in society. This is a great mistake. In point of fact, the keener the sense of justice the more conspicuous the diminishing number of violations of it come to appear, and conversely, the obviousness of injustice proves the general prevalence of justice. It is the same with morality and philanthropy.

If we consider the effect of these three codes of human conduct in the direction of enabling the weaker one to survive we shall see that it has been immense. Out of the first has arisen government, the chief value and function of which has always been and still is such protection. Great systems of jurisprudence have been elaborated, engrossing the attention of a large portion of the population of enlightened as well as of barbaric states. To say that these have been failures because often weighted with grave defects is to misinterpret history and misunderstand society. No one could probably be found to gainsay that the moral law of society has exerted a salutary influence, yet its aim is strictly altruistic, opposed to the law of the survival of the fittest, and wholly in the direction of enabling those to survive who would not survive without its protection. Finally, the last sentiment to be developed, and doubtless the highest, is so universally recognized as peculiar to man that his very name has been given to it—the sentiment of *humanity*. Yet the mode of protecting the weak arising out of this sentiment is the one that has been most seriously called in question by the naturalistic school. It must be admitted that humanitarian institutions have done far less good than either juridical or ethical institutions. The sentiment itself is of recent origin, the produce only of highly developed and greatly refined mental organization. It exists to an appreciable degree only in a minute fraction of the most enlightened populations. It is rarely directed with judgment; no fixed, self-enforcing code of conduct, as in the other cases, having had time to take shape. The institutions established to enforce it are for the most part poorly supported, badly managed, and often founded on a total misconception of human nature and of the true mode of attaining the end in view. Hence they are specially open to attack. But if ever humanitarian sentiments become diffused throughout the body politic, become the object of deep study, as have those of justice and right, it may be confidently predicted that society will prove itself capable of caring for the most unfortunate of its members in a manner that shall not work demoralisation.

In all these ways man, through his intelligence, has laboured successfully to resist the law of nature. His success is conclusively demonstrated by a comparison of his condition with that of other species of animals. No other cause can be assigned for his superiority. How can the naturalistic philosophers shut their eyes to such obvious facts? Yet, what is their attitude? They condemn all attempts to protect the weak, whether by private or public methods. They claim that it deteriorates the race by enabling the unfit to survive and transmit their inferiority. This is true only in certain cases of hereditary diseases or mental deficiencies, which should be taken account of by man because they are not by nature.

Nothing is easier than to show that the unrestricted competition of nature does not secure the survival of the fittest possible, but only of the actually fittest, and in every attempt man makes to obtain something fitter than this actual fittest he succeeds, as witness improved breeds of animals and grafts of fruits. Now, the human method of protecting the weak deals in some such way with men. It not only increases the number but improves the quality.

But "government," at least, must *laissez faire*. It must not "meddle" with natural laws. The laws of trade, business, social intercourse, are natural laws, immutable and indestructible. All interference with them is vain. The fallacy here is a *non sequitur*. It may be readily granted that these laws are immutable and indestructible. Were this not the case it would certainly be hopeless to interfere with their action. But every mechanical invention proves that nothing is easier than to interfere successfully with the operation of these uniform natural forces. They have only to be first thoroughly understood and then they are easily *controlled*. To *destroy* a force is one thing, to control its action is quite another. Those who talk in this way involve themselves in the most palpable inconsistency. They must not be allowed to stop where they do. They must go on and carry their strictures to a logical conclusion. They must deny to government the right to protect its citizens from injustice. This is a clear interference with the natural laws of society. They must deny to society the right to enforce its code of morals. Nothing is more unnatural. They must suppress the healing art which keeps the sick from dying as they do among animals. Nor is this all. They must condemn all interference with physical laws and natural forces. To dam a stream must be characterised as a "vain" attempt to overcome a natural law. The wind must be left free to blow where it will, and not be forced against the fan of a windmill. The vapour of heated water must be allowed to float naturally into the air and not be pent up in a steam-boiler and thence conducted into the cylinder of a steam-engine. All these things and every other device of inventive man are so many attempts to "violate" the laws of nature, which is declared impossible.

What then remains of the *laissez faire* doctrine? Nothing but this: That it is useless, and may be dangerous, to attempt to control natural forces until their character is first well understood. This is a proposition which is true for every department of force, and does not involve the surrender of the whole domain of sociology after it has been demonstrated that society is a theatre of forces.

The truth thus comes forth from a rational study of nature and human society that social progress has been due only in very slight degree to natural evolution as accomplished through the survival of the fittest, and its chief success has resulted from the reduction of competition in the struggle for existence and the protection of the weaker members. Such competition, in so far as it has been permitted to operate, has tended to lower the standard of the fittest and to check advancement. It is not, of course, claimed that the natural method has ever been fully overcome. It has always operated, and still operates, powerfully in many ways. It has been chiefly in the simpler departments of physical and mechanical phenomena that the psychic, or anthropic, method has superseded it. The inventive arts have been the result. Vital forces have yielded to some extent to the influence of mind in bringing about improved stocks of animals and vegetables, and even certain social laws have come under rational control through the establishment of institutions. Still, every step in this progress has been contested. It was not enough that the intellect was feeble and ill-fitted to grapple with such problems. It was not enough that ignorance of nature's laws should cause unnumbered failures. A still stronger barrier was presented by the intellect itself in the form of positive error embodied in philosophy. As already remarked, philosophy has always been negative and nihilistic, and has steadily antagonised the common sense of mankind. It is only quite recently that there has come into existence anything like a truly *positive* philosophy, *i.e.*, a philosophy of *action*. The intellectual power of enlightened man has at length become sufficient to grasp the problems of social life. A large body of truth has been accumulated by which to be guided in their solution. Positive error in the drawing of false conclusions from established facts is now the chief obstacle. Rational interpretation has come to prevail in all the lower departments of phenomena. It is chiefly in the complex departments of psychic and social action that error still holds sway. Nothing remains to be done but to apply the established canons of science to these higher fields of activity. Here there is still competition. Here the weaker still go to the wall. Here the strong are still the fittest to survive. Here Nature still practises her costly selection which always involves the destruction of the defenceless. The demand is for still further reduction of competition, still greater interference with the operations of natural forces, still more complete control of the laws of nature, and still more absolute supremacy of the psychic over the natural method of evolution.

These ends will be secured in proportion as the true nature of mind is understood. When nature comes to be regarded as passive and man as active, instead of the reverse as now, when human action is recognized as the most important of all forms of action, and when the power of the human intellect over vital, psychic and social phenomena is practically conceded, then, and then only, can man justify claim to have risen out of the animal and fully to have entered the human stage of development.

10

MORAL AND MATERIAL

PROGRESS

1885

Ward originally called this essay "Two Forms of Social Progress"—in some ways a better title. The paper is shot through and through with Ward's particular kind of optimism, a highly impersonal optimism that found reassurance about the possibilities of progress through the use of the "Psychic Factors" of the mind and the spirit to overcome the inertia of nature. "No paper that I have ever published attracted more attention than this one," he wrote twenty-five years later, and he added that it contained ideas not to be found in DYNAMIC SOCIOLOGY.

One of the most obvious and frequently observed facts that lie upon the surface of modern society is the persistence of social evils in spite of the progress of discovery and invention brought about for the purpose of relieving them.

The actual removal of social evils constitutes moral progress; the discovery of principles and the invention of appliances calculated to remove them constitute material progress.

Transactions of the Anthropological Society of Washington, Vol. III, in *Glimpses of the Cosmos*, IV, 6–15.

It is these two forms of social progress which it is proposed to consider in this paper.

As to the degree to which moral progress has taken place and is taking place in society, there are wide differences of opinion. Some sanguine minds imagine it to be very rapid, but this is generally due to a confusion of unrelated phenomena. They either confound material with moral progress directly, or they confound predominance of cherished religious beliefs with that of morality, or the establishment of favorite forms of government with that of justice and liberty. Others, and this is much the larger class, deny that any moral progress has ever taken place or is now taking place, and maintain, on the contrary, that there has been moral degeneracy, and that the world is growing constantly worse. In so far as these are merely influenced by the survival of a tradition very prevalent among early races they may, perhaps, be left out of the account. Many of them, however, disclaim such influence and base their convictions on the facts of history and the condition of society as it is. But such also must be set down as extremists, incapable of duly weighing the evidence from all sides of the question.

A highly respectable class, embracing many of the finest minds of the present period, see no hope except in the gradual change of the constitution of the human mind, to be brought about through hereditary influences and the slow developmental laws by which man has been at length raised above the brute. They deny the power of intelligence to improve the moral condition of society, and regard the ethical faculty as entirely distinct from the intellectual. "It is," said Mr. Herbert Spencer to an American reporter, "essentially a question of character, and only in a secondary degree a question of knowledge. But for the universal delusion about education as a panacea for political evils, this would have been made sufficiently clear by the evidence daily disclosed in your papers." And in a private letter received after his return to England, relative to views which I had expressed, he re-asserts this doctrine, and says: "As you are probably aware and as, in fact, I said very emphatically when in America, I regard social progress as mainly a question of character and not of knowledge or enlightenment."

In the light of all these somewhat conflicting opinions, if we were to rest the case altogether upon authority, we should at least be compelled to admit that the real moral progress of the world has been extremely slow, and that it is imperceptible even in the highest stages of enlightenment. Such, too, seems to be the lesson of history and of observation. It is only when we contemplate long periods of history and contrast the present or the recent past with the remote past that an advance can be perceived in the moral condition of mankind. Yet, when such an historic parallax is once secured, the fact that moral progress actually has taken place is distinctly seen. To read the history of England and compare the acts committed a few centuries ago by men of our own race, with what any one can see would be done now under like circumstances, is sufficient to demonstrate that improvement has been going on in both individual and public morals. Making every possible allowance for all that is bad in the present social system, no one could probably be found candidly to maintain that it is inferior, from the moral point of view, to that of the middle ages or even of the sixteenth century. Modern kings, bad as they are, no longer put their sons to death to prevent them from usurping their thrones, and the sons of kings, however profligate they may be, do not seek to dethrone their fathers. When Rome was at its zenith, it was no more than every one expected that the great armies of Caesar and Pompey, on their triumphal return from victorious fields, would turn their arms upon each other for the mastery of the empire. And I have heard those familiar with Roman history predict, at the time when the vast armies of Grant and Sherman, far out-numbering the Roman legions, were marching victoriously through different parts of the South, that the last grand struggle of the war would be between the Army of the Cumberland and that of the Potomac—forgetting that since the age of the Caesars there had been moral progress sufficient to render both the leaders and the soldiers incapable of such an act.

Political opponents are no longer beheaded on the accession of a new party to power; neither are they thrust into dungeons nor exiled, as formerly. Persecution for opinion's sake has practically ceased. Scientific men are no longer burned at the stake, like Bruno and Servetus, nor made to recant, like Galileo and Buffon. Witchcraft has dwindled into innocent palmistry, and heresy is only punished in a few backward communities by a mild form of social ostracism. Imprisonment for debts has been abolished, and the Fleet and the galleys are things of the past. Primogeniture and entail have disappeared from most codes of law, and trial by jury has been instituted in the most influential states. The slave trade has been suppressed wherever European powers have acquired supremacy, and slavery has been abolished in all the most enlightened countries. Vast public and private charities have been instituted, and societies for the prevention of cruelty to children and to animals receive the sanction of law. And finally a great moral crusade, with a display of far more zeal than knowledge, is being preached against the admitted evils of intemperance.

There has, then, been some moral progress within the historic period, but, considering the amount of moral agitation, it has been slight.

It is the characteristic of moral progress that it takes place rhythmically. In the achievement of moral reforms there are always experienced partial and temporary failures, prolonged interruptions, serious reverses, and constantly recurring waves of reaction, so that at no time has it been possible for the candid observer to perceive that any certain advance was being made. The ground continually being lost is never appreciably less than the ground gained, and none but the ignorant, the blinded, or the oversanguine see much cause for congratulation. In the great ocean of moral action so nearly equal are the tidal ebbs and flows that only the stoical philosopher whose vision ranges back into the remotest past or forward unto the remotest future, with utter contempt for the transient present, can perceive the minute increments of secular change—much as the geologist, provided with his vast time-measures, perceives the changes that are slowly taking place on the coasts of continents washed by the tides and waves of the apparently changeless ocean of waters.

Such is moral progress in society. With it we may now compare, or rather contrast, the other form of social progress which we have distinguished as material.

Material progress results entirely from mental and manual labor laid out on invention and construction. Moral progress is a product of *feeling,* material progress one of *thought;* the action accompanying the former is called *conduct,* that accompanying the latter is called *labor.* Conduct is confined to the avoidance of interference with liberty of action in others. Labor is directed to the production and distribution of the objects of desire. Moral action aims at the restraint or control of the forces of society, of human desires, prejudices, and passions. Invention and labor aim at the control and utilization of physical and mechanical forces, and of such vital processes as underlie pastoral and agricultural pursuits.

The contrast in the essential nature of these two classes of social phenomena is thus seen to be very wide, but it is not greater than is the difference in their mode of operating. We have seen that moral progress always takes place by rhythmic action, and that its secular slowness is not due to its own inherent sluggishness, but to the fact that only the algebraic sum of its many fluxes and refluxes can be counted. In material development nothing of the kind is found. Every step is a permanent gain. Every mechanical invention is an inalienable contribution to the material prosperity of society. If the particular device first produced becomes at length obsolete, as is usually the case, it is only because from it as a basis better devices, involving additional principles and doing more efficient service, have grown up. And such, in fact, is the nature of all inventions.

But the machine is only the material embodiment of intellectual conceptions, and it is these that lie at the foundation of all material progress. Indeed, much of this progress has consisted of such conceptions without any definite materialization. Of this class is all real knowledge of nature, only part of which can be directly applied to man's material amelioration. Every natural truth acquired proves advantageous, and the progress of pure science, like the progress of invention, has been steady though not uniform, never intermittent nor rhythmical. The misguided forces of feeling which underlie the fluctuating moral activities of society have often resisted the progress of science, have seriously checked it, sometimes apparently arrested it during long periods, but they have never succeeded in forcing it backwards. The same is true of art, especially of practical or useful art. This fact is strikingly exemplified in the interest attaching to the few alleged "lost arts," as though it were next to impossible for a single art to be wholly lost. And so it is. Every age has known all that was known by the age that preceded it and has added something to this. Every age has possessed all the arts of the age that preceded it, and has added something to them. And this in spite of the most prolonged moral reactions, such, for example, as that of the middle ages.

If we examine the arts, implements, utensils, and weapons of any of the lower tribes, as, for example, the Esquimaux, of the extreme north, we shall find that they represented a high degree of skill, a large amount of inventive thought, and a considerable real knowledge of the laws of nature and of physical forces. A comparison of many such tribes also shows that these devices represent, like those of the most enlightened peoples, a series of steps in invention answering to our improvements. But a better implement is never abandoned for a poorer one, and here, as in the higher races, progress has been constant—always forward. We may therefore safely conclude that the present high state of material advancement in scientific nations is the result of a series of intellectual conceptions materially embodied in art, stretching back into that dim past when the club embodied the highest mechanical principles known to man.

Such is material progress, and such are the essential particulars in which it so widely differs in nature and method from moral progress. But, great as these differences seem and are, there is a point toward which they may be made, hypothetically at least, to converge. This point is where the human activities are conceived as natural phenomena, and their control through the normal inventive process is contemplated as a true art. If the power to do this shall ever be attained, there is no reason why morals may not progress in the same manner and at the same rate as material civilization. The true interpreters of human history now understand that it is to material progress, i. e., to science and art, that what moral progress has actually taken place is indirectly due. It is knowledge of the universe enlarging the mental horizon that has dispelled the bigotry of pre-scientific ages and thrown the mantle of charity over individual conduct and opinion. And it is the arts of intercommunication that have really civilized the modern world, as compared with the world before their introduction.

But since morals, from the point of view of social science, are concerned exclusively with the welfare of men, and since material progress, both physical and intellectual, is also directed exclusively toward this same end, the question naturally arises, why does not the welfare of men advance *pari passu* with the progress of science and art? As already remarked, no thoughtful person will maintain that it does so advance, some insisting that the two are wholly independent, and others claiming that the moral condition of society is degenerating in spite of the brilliant material civilization of these later times. After conceding all that is possible on the side of a real moral progress in society the case is bad enough, and the blunt comment of crude common sense naturally and properly is, of what use are science and art if they are incompetent to add anything to the general welfare of mankind? And to this question the response of the highest science is that if they cannot do this they are of *no* use. The welfare of mankind is the ultimate test of utility, and whatever fails to withstand that test stands condemned.

But admitting, as has already been done, that all the perceptible moral progress that has taken place has been due to that of intelligence in interaction with the practical arts which it necessarily creates, it may still be a question whether this trifling result is really worth the Titanic efforts which this teeming age puts forth. The attempt to answer this question would probably be attended with insuperable difficulties and need not be made. It will be more profitable to consider the far more important one whether, in the nature of things, this admitted slight influence of material upon moral progress could, even theoretically, be so far increased as to render them somewhat proportional in amount.

Moral progress may be defined as embracing all those changes in man's social condition which actually enhance his general well-being; material progress may be defined as embracing those changes which give him power, if judiciously employed, to improve his condition, without implying such employment. If these definitions are correct, it is evident that all that is needed to make moral progress depend quantitatively upon material progress is to secure the judicious employment of the modifications of crude nature which are produced by human thought and action. Knowledge, ingenu-

ity, skill, and industry need to be applied to moral ends and
directed to the attainment of the social well-being. At present
science and art are only potential factors in civilization. The
need is that they be converted into actual factors. They are
well nigh omnipotent in the accomplishment of anything
toward which they can be once fairly directed. The difficulty
is entirely that of securing for them the opportunity for free
action. The power, for example, to produce a large quantity
of a useful commodity may exist, but the conditions be wanting for placing the product in the hands of those who want
it. This checks the production without affecting the producing
power. That lies latent, and such latent power is simply
wasted. Nor is it altogether a discrepancy between production
and distribution. The power to distribute exists as well as the
power to produce, but the conditions are wanting which are
necessary to call that power into exercise. And this is the
actual industrial state of society.

What is true of art is true of science. Intelligence, far more
than necessity, is the mother of invention, and the influence of
knowledge as a social factor, like that of wealth, is proportional
to the extent of its distribution.

Society has always presented to the thoughtful student two
great inequalities as the adequate explanation of nearly all
its evils—inequality of knowledge and inequality of possession.
Moral progress, in so far as it has taken place at all, has
consisted in the slight diminution of one or both of these
inequalities. This is always accomplished by the adoption of
a better system of distribution. These two commodities, information and possession, differ in the essential particular
that the latter is and the former is not destroyed in consumption. The existence of a supply of knowledge for distribution is
therefore proved by the very fact of its inequality. But there
is a sense in which the supply of wealth for distribution is
also practically unlimited. Production never ceases from having
reached a limit to the power to produce. It always ceases

from having exceeded the power of the community to consume. But the limit of consumption is in turn never that of the desire to consume; it is always that of the power to obtain. The power of both production and consumption is limited only by that of distribution—not the mechanical means of distribution, for these, too, are unlimited, but the conditions to the performance of the sociological function of distribution. Could the distribution of knowledge and of physical necessities go on at a rate at all proportional to their possible creation, the moral progress of society, i. e., the increase in its aggregate well-being or enjoyment, would not only be as rapid, but would also be as uniform and steady as its material progress. If the knowledge now in possession of the few were in the possession of all, its benefits would be far more than proportional to its universality, since inequality itself often renders knowledge positively injurious. Although it be true that if the actual wealth of the world were equally distributed the share of each individual would be a very small fortune, yet if the limitations to possible distribution were removed production would so far increase that almost any desired portion might fall to each and all.

Wherein, then, consists this mysterious yet potent barrier to the distribution of wealth and wisdom; this practically prohibitory tariff upon the world's commerce in both thoughts and things?

The answer is rather deep than difficult. The two processes as they go on in society belong to antithetically opposite categories of social phenomena. We have in them the ultimate kernel of that broad contrast which has just been drawn between moral and material progress. It is the great distinction between natural and artificial processes, between genetic and teleologic activity, between growth and manufacture, between the method by which feeling works and that by which intellect works. The former is a method of direct effort, and fails in the great majority of cases to attain its end because of obstacles which are never taken into account. The latter is a method of indirect calculation by which the obstacles are foreseen, and in one way or another provided against before the advance is attempted. Hence it is always successful if the phenomena and laws to be dealt with are really understood. This is why science and art, as already stated, move ever forward, never backward. The discovery of truth on the one hand, and the invention of artificial appliances on the other, are always going on, multiplying the power of man to produce and distribute the objects of desire. Of the gain thus made nothing is ever lost. But when we come to the actual utilization of the products of discovery, invention, and handicraft, we find this under the control of the opposite class of forces. The power to produce either knowledge or wealth is controlled by man, exercised when it can serve his purpose, checked or arrested when it no longer does this. But the power to possess—the ability to obtain the truth discovered or the commodity wrought— is controlled by natural laws and depends upon the thousand accidents of life—the conflicting wills of men, the passions of avarice and ambition, the vicissitudes of fortune, the uncertainties of climate and seasons, the circumstances of birth and social station, the interests and caprices of nations and rulers. Of what use is discovered truth to the millions whose minds it can never reach? Why produce useful commodities which those who need them are unable to obtain? For while all producers are also consumers, and nearly all consumers are at the same time producers, yet few can satisfy their wants, however capable they may be of producing an equivalent in value of other forms. Inventions in the practical arts by which the power is acquired to multiply the products of labor, instead of working the rapid amelioration of the laboring classes, actually injure their prospects by throwing skilled artisans out of employment; and instead of resulting in greatly increased production they do not appreciably affect production, but reduce the amount of labor to the disadvantage of the laborer. The plea of over-production in periods of financial depression is the sheerest mockery, since it is just at such times that the greatest want is felt. It may be true that more is produced than the consumers can obtain, but far less is produced at all times than they actually need and are able to render a full equivalent for. The eager manner in which every demand for laborers is responded to sufficiently proves this. It proves also that the industrial system is out of order, and that we live in a pathological state of society. The vast accumulations of goods at the mills avail nothing to the half-clad men and women who are shivering by thousands in the streets while vainly watching for an opportunity to earn the wherewithal to be clothed. The storehouse of grain held by the speculators against a rise in prices has no value to the famished communities who would gladly pay for it in value of some form.

Yet in all this the fault cannot fairly be said to lie with individuals nor with corporations, with manufacturer nor merchant, with producer nor consumer. These do but act the nature with which they are endowed. This defective circulation of industrial products is the result of the state of society. It is in one sense normal, since it is due to the operation of natural laws governing social phenomena. The enormous inequalities of both the classes named and the evils resulting, constituting the major part of the woes of mankind, are simply due to the fact that the agencies for distributing knowledge and wealth are *free* in the politico-economic sense, i. e., not regulated nor controlled by intelligent foresight. The contrast between moral and material progress is the contrast between Nature and Art. Nature is free. Art is caged. The forces of Nature play unbridled among themselves, until choked by their mutual friction, they are equilibrated and come to rest. Art commands them with tones of authority to pursue paths selected by intelligence and thus indefinitely to continue to exert their power. Under the dominion of Science,

i. e., under the intelligent control of physical forces, man's power to create the objects of desire and to send them where he will, is practically unlimited. But under the dominion of Nature, i. e., under the free operation of the social forces, as yet beyond the reach of science, these objects of human necessity in seeking unaided their proper destination conflict perpetually in their passage, dashing against unseen obstructions, forcing themselves into inextricable entanglements, polarizing themselves around powerful centers of attraction, heaping themselves up in inaccessible "corners," or flying off on tangential lines to be lost forever.

This is what in modern phrase is very properly denominated the "waste of competition." But it is far more than the mere waste of the wealth produced. It is the paralysis of the strong hands of science and art as they cooperate with labor in the creation of value. It is the stubborn, the protracted resistance which the moral forces of society offer to its material as well as to its moral progress.

The statement of the problem is its theoretical solution, which can be nothing less than the conquest by science of the domain of the social as it has conquered that of the physical forces.

But alas! how wide is the difference between the theoretical and the practical solution of a problem to the bare statement of which the foremost thinkers of the age are as yet unwilling to listen.

The paper was discussed at length by Messrs. Powell, Welling, Thomas, Baker, Peters, Hart, and Ward. . . .

Mr. Ward, in reply to numerous inquiries and objections made during the discussion of the paper, explained that for the sake of brevity he had omitted any precise definition of the term Moral Progress as used in the paper. He said that the term was often employed in two quite different senses, and that much of the discussion had considered it in the other sense from that clearly implied in the paper. There is a subjective sense which relates to individual character and an objective sense which relates to collective well-being. The paper did not pretend to discuss the question whether human character had advanced, or how much it had advanced. It aimed only to consider the relation of material civilization to social well-being, the sole test of moral progress in this objective sense being the condition attained with respect to the enjoyment of life. This progress might be either positive, consisting in an increase in the pleasures of life; or it might be negative, and consist in the reduction of the pains of life. In fact this negative progress has been by far the most observable, the chief improvement in man's condition thus far being some slight mitigation of the evils of existence. In view of this criterion of moral progress as measured by the degree of collective happiness, all that had been said respecting higher standards of taste in literature and social life was irrelevant to the discussion, since it simply confounded refinement with enjoyment, which are two entirely distinct things. Admitting that finer sensibilities are capable of higher enjoyment, this is far from proving that they necessarily enjoy more, for they are also capable of more acute suffering, and the whole question originally was whether material civilization prevents more of the latter than it occasions. . . .

11

BROADENING THE WAY

TO SUCCESS

1886

All his life, Ward was self-conscious about his lack of formal education and formal training in the sciences. Perhaps the most variously learned man in America, he was in a very real sense self-taught: He taught himself Latin and Greek, he trained himself to the use of French by keeping a diary in that language, he taught himself botany, geology and paleontology, and during it all he taught himself and everybody else sociology. All his life, he was preoccupied—perhaps we can say obsessed—with the problem of education. Education was, to use the title he planned for his major work, "The Great Panacea," the instrument and the philosophy for the regeneration of mankind. Everywhere in his sociological writings, Ward addresses himself to the problem of the discovery of talent and of genius. We could easily make a separate volume of his observations on this fascinating theme but must content ourselves here and later with some representative passages.

"Broadening the Way to Success," *The Forum,* II (November 1886), 345–350.

. . . There is no need to search for talent. It exists already, and everywhere. The thing that is rare is opportunity, not ability. The fact that many do struggle up out of obscurity does not so much show that they possess superiority, as that they happen to be less inextricably bound down than others by the conventional bonds of society. And those who have succeeded in bursting these bonds have usually done so at such an immense cost in energy, that their future work is rendered crude and well-nigh valueless. Such is the character of most of the results accomplished by so-called self-made men. To attain to a position where they can labor in any great field, they must carry on a life-long battle against obstacles; they must display enormous individuality, amounting to conceit; they must become heated contestants and bitter partisans. All this narrows the mental horizon, and renders the results superficial and unenduring. There is no more vicious popular fallacy than that the powers of the mind are strengthened and improved by adversity. Every one who has accomplished anything, against adverse circumstances, would have accomplished proportionately more had such circumstances been removed. The talent that can fight against adversity is never of the highest and best quality. Between honest work and open warfare there is a certain incompatibility. True greatness is timid, and recoils before obstacles. The finest and most genuine of all qualities—those which, if allowed free scope, will produce the greatest and most enduring results—will not brook opposition, and shrink from the least sign of hostility. Far from implying cowardice, this is simply the characteristic modesty of true greatness. It is a paradox of daily observation, that those who are the nearest right are the least convinced of it; and hence those who possess the greatest truths are often deterred from uttering them against opposition, not from any fear of opposition, but from fear of the possibility that after all they may not be true. It is due to this principle that the greatest intrinsic merit never comes to the surface. True merit will not create its opportunities. It requires that opportunities be brought to it. If this is not done there is no result, and society is the loser. Nearly all the work of permanent value that has been done in the world has emanated from men possessing these qualities, and left undisturbed in their continuous exercise. The greatest blessing of the world has been leisure, for though it may sound paradoxical, it is in leisure that the grandest work has always been performed, while from toil no great progressive consequences have ever flowed. Leisure engenders thought, which toil never does, and the thought of a moment may project a mechanism that will perform the labor of hundreds of hands.

When we study history, and see who the true promoters of civilization have been, we perceive how these statements are sustained by examples. The men who have increased the world's stock of knowledge, and placed the race in possession of the secrets of nature and the keys to its control and utilization, are the true benefactors of mankind. A study of the personal history of such men shows that without exception they have been in possession of rare opportunities. They have either been entirely free from the distractions of want and the necessity of toil, or they have found themselves situated in the midst of those scenes and objects which are to constitute their special field of labor, and which furnish the incentive to the effort, however great, which they must put forth in order to achieve success. Examples would be superfluous, as they cannot fail to present themselves to the reader's mind; and as to the alleged exceptions, I doubt whether a single one of them will bear the light of candid biographical scrutiny.

Many persons of an optimistic turn of mind look benignantly over the history of man, and, seeing the great number of individuals who have distinguished themselves by the display of towering qualities, break out in admiration of the grandeur of the race. But the true philosopher, who correctly discerns the significance of these examples, sees in them only signs of the possibilities of the race. The grandeur that he sees is only a possible grandeur. For every actual great name in history he sees a hundred potential great names. The present corps of workers in every department of science and culture, and in every land, are viewed kaleidoscopically, and multiplied indefinitely.

Science is only just beginning to reveal the true extent of the latent energies of organic life. Ten years ago, treating of the local distribution of plants, I myself wrote:

There is no . . . necessary correspondence . . . between organism and habitat, no . . . necessary . . . harmony between species and environment. This need only exist so far as is necessary to render the life of the species possible. Beyond this the greatest inharmony and inadaptation may be conceived to reign in nature. Each plant may be regarded as a reservoir of vital force, as containing within it a potential energy far beyond and wholly out of consonance with the contracted conditions imposed upon it by its environment, and by which it is compelled to possess the comparatively imperfect organization with which we find it endowed. Each individual is where it is and what it is by reason of the combined forces which hedge it in and determine its very form.

Since these words were written this principle has been widely recognized by botanists. It is now known that the plants of every region possess the potency of a far higher life than they enjoy and that they are prevented from attaining that higher state by the adverse influences that surround them in their normal habitat. The singling out of certain species by man, and their development through his care into far higher and more perfect forms to supply his needs, both physical and aesthetic, further demonstrate this law. Man gives these plants a new and artificial environment favorable to their higher development, and they develop accordingly. In a word, he gives them opportunity to progress, and they progress by inherent powers with which all plants are endowed. Once,

when herborizing in a rather wild, neglected spot, I collected
a little depauperate grass that for a time greatly puzzled me,
but which upon analysis proved to be none other than genuine
wheat. It had been accidentally sown in this abandoned nook,
where it had been obliged to struggle for existence along
with the remaining vegetation. There it had grown up, and
sought to rise into that majesty and beauty that is seen in a
field of waving grain. But at every step it had felt the resistance of an environment no longer regulated by intelligence.
It missed the fostering care of man, who destroys competition,
removes enemies, and creates conditions favorable to the
highest development. This is called cultivation, and the difference between my little starveling grass and the wheat of
the well-tilled field is a difference of cultivation only, and
not at all of capacity. I could adduce any number of similar
examples from the vegetable kingdom; and the zoologist, the
stock-breeder, and the fancier could furnish equally pointed
illustrations from the animal world. But the laws of life are
the same in all departments, and even man is no exception
to them. Man has developed thus far as the wild animal has
developed, as the wild grasses have developed. He has come
up slowly, as these have, under a natural environment, under
the influence of adverse agencies and of competition. And if as
an individual he has at last learned to exercise control over the
lower kingdoms of nature, as a social being he has never yet
consciously attempted his own liberation from the retarding
influence of his natural environment. He has never yet taken
measures for the removal of competition and other obstacles
to social progress.

There is a school of philosophers, never more strongly intrenched than at the present time, who not only deny the possibility of such action on the part of society, and insist that to
attempt it would entail great evil, but who go further, and
maintain that competition and adversity are the most effective
aids to social progress. They point to the development that

has taken place among animals and plants under the laws of natural selection, and deprecate in the strongest terms any attempt on the part of man to interfere with the operation of these laws in society. They forget entirely that civilization itself has been the result of successful interference with these very laws. The cereals, the fruit-trees, and the finest breeds of animals are not the results of natural but of artificial and intelligent selection, and they might as well maintain that these would have produced themselves, as that man can ever attain his highest development without conscious, intelligent, and systematic culture.

The central truth which I have sought to enforce is that, like plants and animals, men possess latent capacities which for their development simply require opportunity. Heredity will surely do its part, and therefore need not be specially attended to, but without opportunity, however great the native powers, nothing can result. I look upon existing humanity as I look upon a pristine vegetation. The whole struggling mass is held by the relentless laws of competition in a condition far below its possibilities. Just as what might be grain is mere grass, just as the potential greening is a diminutive crab-apple, so the potential giants of the intellectual world may now be the hewers of wood and drawers of water. On the theory of equality, which I would defend, the number of individuals of exceptional usefulness will be proportional to the number possessing the opportunity to develop their powers; and this regardless of any of the class distinctions that now exist. This number, in the present condition of society, is not a fixed percentage of the total population; it is a fixed percentage only of those who possess opportunity. This class is very small in proportion to the whole, but is capable of being indefinitely extended. But if, with the relative handful who at present possess opportunities, we have such results as we now see, what may we not expect when this favored class is made co-extensive with the entire population?

To the intelligent reader it need scarcely be explained that there is a legitimate and fairly practical way of enlarging this favored class. It consists in arbitrarily placing them under a changed environment favorable to the development of all their faculties. To this process the term education is usually applied, but it must be understood in that comprehensive sense which embraces this complex and fundamental conception. It is so rarely used in this sense, that, to prevent the necessity of explanation and the danger of misconstruction, I have purposely avoided its use. And yet, so great is the progress now being made in the direction of truer and broader ideas of education, that I doubt not many will readily recognize its appropriateness in the present discussion.

In conclusion, I may add that, while I am far from being over-sanguine as to the early realization of such far-reaching reform, I do not regard such a glimpse into the future as in the least utopian. In a country like ours, where all power resides in the opinions of the people, we have only to suppose them to possess a clear conception of their interests and of the measures necessary to secure them, in order to see such measures adopted and enforced. And while I agree with the *noli-tangere* philosophers and the hereditarians, that legislation cannot be successfully applied to the alteration of the great laws of nature, such, for example, as those of heredity, I regard the work of creating opportunities, by which gifted individuals can utilize their powers, as simply in the nature of police regulation, capable of being conducted by any body politic.

12

FALSE NOTIONS

OF GOVERNMENT

1887

Like President Eisenhower, Lester Ward worked most of his lifetime for the national government; unlike Eisenhower, he drew from that experience the conclusion that in the United States at least, government was not a necessary evil but a positive good, and that government could be trusted to do well whatever it undertook to do. This was to be increasingly the burden of Ward's social and political philosophy. It is not without interest that this essay on the paradox of the distrust of government was published just at the time of the enactment of the Interstate Commerce Act, a law that may be taken to mark the beginning of federal centralization in the United States.

There is perhaps no more unfortunate term in the language than the word "government." Besides having a harsh sound it has a harsh meaning. In its primary sense, to govern is to

---

"False Notions of Government," *The Forum*, III (June 1887), 364–372; in *Glimpses of the Cosmos*, IV, 64–71.

interfere with the liberty of action. It is to command and to prohibit, to exact and to refuse. Nothing is more unpleasant than this, and hence everybody naturally objects to being governed.

Whatever may have been the origin of the word as applied to the central authority in a state, it must be admitted that, until a comparatively recent date in human history, the governments of the world had always done so much of this kind of governing that it had come to be looked upon as almost their only function. However constituted, when once in existence they had considered it their privilege to govern in this objectionable sense. From this have arisen most of the great struggles that peoples have had to make for liberty, i. e., for relief from this kind of government. And when one government had been overthrown another was immediately organized, which soon proved as oppressive as the first. Hence there gradually grew up a wide-spread popular distrust of all government, amounting often to positive hatred.

This deep-seated dread and detestation of government has been salutary in the extreme. It has resulted within the last two centuries in abolishing, throughout all the most enlightened states of the world, all real governmental oppression. The so-called monarchies of Europe that survive (Russia excepted) are monarchies only in name, and some of them, as for example, Sweden, are more representative than some countries that style themselves republican. The royal prerogatives are pared down to a minimum, ministers perform all executive duties, and the legislators are chosen by the people to make laws which neither crown nor ministry dare violate.

Both in the monarchies and in the republics, as now constituted, the old forms of governmental abuse are impossible. The only oppression practicable in them is that which the people themselves sanction. The power of majorities to oppress minorities still exists, but in practice it is inoperative. For such is the popular sense of justice that if a majority undertakes to practice any real wrong upon a minority, enough voters will speedily go over to the minority to convert it into a majority, and secure the redress of the wrong. Knowing this, and wishing to remain in power, the government, i. e., the officers of any given administration, is careful to refrain from shocking this public sense of justice, and no serious attempts to wrong the minority are made.

There is another reason why none of the objectionable methods of government are any longer possible. Everything must now be done according to law. There is scarcely any discretionary power. The laws are made by representatives chosen by the people, and these do nothing but carry out to the best of their ability the will of their constituents, who, in turn, constantly watch them and scrutinize their vote on every measure. The executive branch can do nothing but execute these laws, and this it does with great fidelity and exactness. Rarely, indeed, do we hear of cases in which an executive officer has exceeded his authority as expressly given in some statutory enactment, and nearly as rare are the cases in which such enactments are not faithfully executed. Such officers may at first imagine that they are going into places where they can exercise some discretionary power, but they soon find that every duty is specifically prescribed, and that all they can do is to perform it as they must swear that they will do. Very few ever have the least desire to overstep their authority. Those who are intrusted with funds are powerless to appropriate them to their own uses. The crude popular notion that the officers of government have nothing to do but help themselves to the people's money is disproved at every change of administration. A treasurer of any modern state finds himself, on admission to office, in the midst of the system of checks which renders any attempt at fraud unsuccessful, and which is itself an almost infallible detective of any irregularities on the part of officers and subordinates.

In fact, throughout the entire system of a modern representative government, the limitations that exist to the violation of law, the perpetration of fraud, or the abuse of power, are so great and so effective that it is only at rare intervals that such things are practiced or attempted. This statement is no less true because of the prevailing popular impression to the contrary, and the persistent attempts of a certain class of journals to inculcate the belief that wide-spread corruption and constant malfeasance in office are the characteristics of public life. It has been shown over and over again that losses through dishonesty are very much less in public than in private financial transactions, and scarcely a case can be named in which an officer has undertaken any high-handed proceedings in excess of his prescribed duties.

It thus appears that government now is a very different thing from what it formerly was. The so-called "rulers" are the most innocent of men, having neither power nor desire to do evil. If evil is done it is because they have been instructed to do it by those who choose them. This, as a general proposition, is perfectly true, and only needs such special qualification as arises from the imperfection of human nature and human institutions. I have brought it prominently into view in order to point out a fundamental fallacy in most of the current reasoning about government.

So deep-seated had become the fear of governmental oppression, and so firmly had this sentiment taken root in the constitution of man, that not even the complete revolution which it wrought throughout the civilized world has sufficed to eradicate it. It still exists, and permeates the entire body politic. The most representative forms of government are still feared, watched, and suspected as if they were self-constituted despotisms.

Most persons regard this as a healthy state of things, and one calculated to prevent abuses and forestall dangers. This is by no means the case. On the contrary, its effects are extremely injurious in a variety of ways. In the first place, good men will not subject themselves to this unjust censorship, and will have nothing to do with government, and thus the tone of government is greatly lowered. Again, this feeling tends to produce a thoroughly false and perverted idea of what government really is. In consequence of it the voter imagines he is conferring vastly more power upon his candidate than it is possible to confer. He looks upon the public officer as a sort of lord, capable of exercising arbitrary power, and thus a glamour is thrown over government which completely obscures its true and simple character. This intensifies party spirit and the strife to gain control of the government, which is regarded in the light of booty to be captured. A corollary to this reasoning is the notion that public offices are merely spoils belonging to the victor. And here it should be remarked that, contrary to popular belief so often reiterated, this system of frequent rotation in office, due to political vicissitudes, is in no sense a democratic idea, but is a relic of past ages of abuse of power, when kings and despots made and unmade the fortunes of men. The test of progress toward true democracy is the constantly diminishing power of the ruling class and the adoption by government of business principles in conducting the affairs of the people. From this the so-called spoils system is the farthest remove conceivable.

The old idea of government was that it was a power essentially hostile to the people, but fastened upon them by fate. The modern survival of this idea contemplates government as a "necessary evil." No matter how representative it may be it is still looked upon to a great extent as an arbitrary personality, with great power and evil intent, requiring the exercise of "eternal vigilance" to prevent it from destroying all liberty. Many who know better are unable to divest themselves of this view, and entertain it as a mere hereditary instinct. In fact, it is one of those late social instincts of self-preservation, which persist, as all instincts do, long after the conditions under which they were developed have passed away.

This irrational distrust of government not only makes it worse than it otherwise would be, but, so far as this is possible, it tends to give it the character it is accused of possessing. When any one knows that he is believed to possess great power he will try to exercise more power than he legitimately has. Whenever modern governments do exercise power not vested in them by the people it is because they are conscious of this false sentiment, which ascribes to them more power than they have any claim to. The occasional instances of municipal mismanagement and malfeasance are doubtless attributable to this cause.

But, bad as all these consequences are, they are trivial compared to that which we will now consider. The most disastrous effect of this false public sentiment is that it deprives government itself of its chief element of usefulness to the people, viz., its power to protect society.

Without going back over the history and reputed origin of government, it will not be disputed that its primary purpose is protection. In the earlier and more primitive types of society the chief protection required was that against the crude physical elements of human nature that perpetually conflicted and destroyed all peace. These still exist, perhaps undiminished, and it is not denied that they are fairly and effectually held in check by government. But besides these, in the modern epoch of vast undertakings and complicated civilization, there has grown up another class of social evils against which protection should be secured, which is far more dangerous than that of brute force, sporadic passion, and low animal cunning. I refer to the evils of organized aggrandizement, the abuse of wealth, and the subtle processes by which the producer of wealth is deprived of his share in it. These evils have grown up with civilization, and are simply the organized expression of human acquisitiveness. They are the natural products of an advancing intelligence without moral restraint. In short, they represent the rule of mind, which is no more moral than is the rule of muscle. Without government the latter would have prevailed; the weaker would have gone to the wall; the "fittest," in the same sense that zoologists use that term, would have survived; but what society would have been no one dare conjecture. But in the unregulated rule of mind we are able to see some of the results. Yet it has, as it were, but just begun, and no one can predict its ultimate consequences. They are so bad now that the leading question must soon be, How shall society be protected? Under the system as it now exists the wealth of the world, however created, and irrespective of the claims of the producer, is made to flow toward certain centers of accumulation, to be enjoyed by those holding the keys to such situations. The world appears to be approaching a stage at which the laborer, no matter how skilled, how industrious, or how frugal, will receive, according to an oft-quoted law of political economy, only so much for his services as will enable him to "live and reproduce." The rest finds its way into the hands of a comparatively few, usually non-producing, individuals, whom the usages and laws of all countries permit to claim that they own the very sources of all wealth and the right to allow or to forbid its production.

These are great and serious evils, compared with which all the crimes, recognized as such, that would be committed if no government existed would be as trifles. The underpaid labor, the prolonged and groveling drudgery, the wasted strength, the misery and squalor, the diseases resulting, and the premature deaths that would be prevented by a just distribution of the products of labor, would in a single year outweigh all the so-called "crime" of a century. This vast theater of woe is regarded as wholly outside the jurisdiction of government, while the most strenuous efforts are put forth to detect and punish the perpetrators of the least of the ordinary recognized crimes. This ignoring of great evils while so violently striking at small ones is the mark of an effete civilization, and warns us of the approaching dotage of the race.

Again the legitimate action of government in the protection of society from these worst of its evils the instinctive hostility to government, or "misarchy," above described, powerfully militates. In the face of it the government hesitates to take action, however clear the right or the method. But it is proper to point out that this groundless over-caution against an impossible occurrence would not in and of itself have sufficed to prevent government from redressing such palpable wrongs. It has been nursed and kept alive for a specific purpose. It has formed the chief argument of those whose interests require the maintenance of the existing social order in relation to the distribution of wealth. Indeed, it is doubtful whether, without the incessant reiteration given to it by this class, it could have persisted to the present time. This inequitable economic system has itself been the product of centuries of astute management on the part of the shrewdest heads, with a view to securing by legal devices that undue share of the world's products which was formerly the reward of superior physical strength. It is clear to this class that their interests require a policy of strict non-interference on the part of government in what they call the natural laws of political economy, and they are quick to see that the old odium that still lingers among the people can be made a bulwark of strength for their position. They, therefore, never lose an opportunity to appeal to it in the most effective manner. Through the constant use of this *argumentum ad populum* the anti-government sentiment, which would naturally have smoldered and died out after its cause ceased to exist, is perpetually fanned into life.

In view of all this, it becomes clear that nothing is so much needed at the present time as the removal of the popular error on this point. It is the duty of all those who have the true reform of society at heart to point out in the most convincing manner that the people are no longer in any danger from governmental oppression, that their present danger lies in an entirely different direction, that what they really need is more government in its primary sense, greater protection of the exposed masses from the rapacity of the favored few, and that, instead of distrusting and crippling government, they should greatly enlarge its power to grapple with these evils. Let it be insisted upon that this is nothing but the re-clothing of government with its original power to protect society. It was for this that it was instituted, and unless it does this it has no right to exist. Originally it undertook to make protection complete. It extended it to all cases of social abuse. It recognized the natural inequalities of citizens, and had no other object than to see to it that none should thereby be debarred from their rights. But then the inequalities were chiefly individual and personal. They were therefore natural, and hence governmental protection certainly must have counteracted to some extent the law of the survival of the fittest. With the progress of civilization all this has been changed. Social inequalities are now the result of circumstances, of accident. They are artificial. The strongest are no longer the best physically or mentally. They are merely the favored, often the pampered and degenerate. How much more, then, should protection be vouchsafed to the victims of such inequality! Yet for such there is no protection in law or government.

The great evils under which society now labors have grown up during the progress of intellectual supremacy. They have crept in stealthily during the gradual encroachment of organized cunning upon the domain of brute force. Over that vanishing domain government retains its power, but it is still powerless in the expanding and now all-embracing field of psychic influence. No one ever claimed that in the trial of physical strength the booty should fall to the strongest. In all such cases the arm of government is stretched out and justice enforced. But in those manifold and far more unequal struggles now going on between mind and mind, or rather, between the individual and an organized system, the product of ages of thought, it is customary to say that such matters must be left to regulate themselves, and that the fittest must be allowed to survive. Writers of a certain school are fond of appealing to Malthus, Darwin, and Herbert Spencer, and strongly deprecate the bolstering up of the weaker elements of society. They picture the degeneracy that must follow all attempts to oppose the "immutable laws of nature." Yet, to any one who will candidly consider the matter, it must be clear that the first and principal acts of government openly and avowedly opposed these same laws in preventing, through forcible interference, the natural results of all trials of physical strength. These laws of nature are violated now every time the highway robber is arrested and sent to jail.

Primitive government, when only brute force was employed, was strong enough to secure the just and equitable distribution of wealth. To-day, when mental force is everything and physical force nothing, it is powerless to accomplish this. This alone proves that government needs to be strengthened in its primary quality—the protection of society. There is no reasoning that applies to one kind of protection that does not apply equally to another. The only question that need be asked is, whether justice is done. If justice is not done it should be enforced by the state against any and all opposing interests. It is utterly illogical to say that aggrandizement by physical force should be forbidden, while aggrandizement by mental force or legal fiction should be permitted. It is absurd to claim that injustice committed by muscle should be regulated, while that committed by brains should be unrestrained.

I am aware that in expressing these views I do but utter the thought of a considerable number of able and active writers and thinkers upon current social and political questions. They constitute the nucleus of a practical social philosophy which must sooner or later solve all the knotty questions of the time. For this they need only to become the property of the general public and to be so firmly grasped by the great mass as to form an intelligible code of political action. Above all, the working people should realize that the government is their own and will be just what they make it. They should learn to look upon it as a creature of their will. They should cease to fear and distrust it, and should seek to mold and shape it. They should turn a deaf ear to those who seek to use it as a scarecrow to frighten them into inaction. If they are to secure from government that protection which forms its only claim to exist, they must throw off all party allegiance, and demand of all candidates the strongest pledges of fidelity to their interests, and sustain none who do not honestly and earnestly fulfill those pledges. They need no revolutionary schemes of socialism, communism, or anarchy. The present machinery of government, especially in this country, is all they could wish. They have only to take possession of it and operate it in their own interest.

The true solution of the great social problem of this age is to be found in the ultimate establishment of a genuine people's government, with ample power to protect society against all forms of injustice, from whatever source, coupled with a warm and dutiful regard for the true interests of each and all, the poor as well as the rich. If this be what is meant by the oft-repeated phrase "paternal government," then were this certainly a consummation devoutly to be wished. But in this conception of government there is nothing paternal. It gets rid entirely of the paternal, the patriarchial, the personal element, and becomes nothing more nor less than the effective expression of the public will, the active agency by which society consciously and intelligently governs its own conduct.

13

SOME SOCIAL

AND ECONOMIC PARADOXES

1889

*This tour de force, which anticipates in some ways the argu-
ments of Kenneth Galbraith, was first read to the Anthropological Society of Washington in 1888 and printed the following
year. The argument and the illustrations were elaborated in*
Psychic Factors *some four years later.*

. . . I propose in this paper to point out a few of the maxims of
social science, and especially of political economy, which appear to be on trial and to indicate what, as it seems to me, will
probably be the verdict of time as to their acceptance or rejection. But in this I do not arrogate to myself any gift of proph-
ecy or infallibility, for most of these problems are knotty and
obscure, and it is of the utmost importance to recognize how
much of what seems to be true is false and how much of what
seems to be false is merely paradoxical.

I shall speak chiefly of certain statements of a few modern

The American Anthropologist, II (1889), in *Glimpses of the Cosmos*, IV,
155–158, 160–165.

economic writers which are so much at variance with the current doctrines of political economy that, if true, they are certainly paradoxic, but before coming to these, and as a sort of preparation for them, I will first mention a few other propositions of a much broader character, which, assuming their correctness, may properly be called social or sociologic paradoxes.

I have preferred to state these apparently false propositions for the sake of defending them rather than to state the opposite and apparently true ones for the sake of combatting them, because it is less important to lay stress upon the error contained in the latter than upon the truth contained in the former, and also because the method of explaining paradoxes possesses a certain novelty which that of exposing fallacies does not, and this of itself may add some zest to a subject which at its best, will be regarded as dry, even if it be less "dismal" than the old-time political economy.

Perhaps the broadest of the paradoxes which can be claimed as sociologic and which certainly applies to the next lower stage of biologic law, and still more obviously to physical phenomena, is embodied in the theorem that

The artificial is superior to the natural.

Certainly this proposition does not seem true, but, on the contrary, seems to contravene all our common instincts and intuitions; but when subjected to the proper tests it is found to be true in all the simpler departments of knowledge. Man can make very little use of anything in its natural state. Value, *i.e.*, utility, is imparted to raw materials only by labor and skill. The products of labor and skill are artificial, and scarcely anything has *actual* value, i. e., capability of actual, immediate use, until it has been transformed from the natural into the artificial state. Therefore, if that which can be used is superior to that which cannot, the artificial is superior to the natural. Even those vegetable and animal products which have most value—the cereals, fruits, vegetables, superior breeds of cattle, horses, sheep, fowls, etc.—are the products of thought, intelligence, careful selection, and prolonged artificial culture and care, showing that the proposition holds true in the complex department of life as well as in the domain of mechanical law. It should and does hold true in the social world; but here, and here only, some of the highest authorities have disputed it. They decry all attempts at the artificial production of a higher social product, and call this interfering with natural laws. They base their opposition upon the idea, either expressed or implied, that the natural is superior to the artificial. This from our present standpoint is a *petitio principii*. It has usually been regarded as conclusive because no one seems to have questioned the major premise. This itself is now seen to be false when applied to the better-known departments of natural law. To deny of social forces what is admitted of physical and vital forces is to deny the existence of a social science. But our proposition does apply to society, for if it were true that the natural is here superior to the artificial then would anarchy be preferable to government.

Limiting the subject to this department, the strictly sociological paradox may be put in this form:

> *Social activities may be artificially regulated*
> *to the advantage of society.*

Political economists maintain that the normal action of the laws that govern the social and industrial world are not only economical, but the best possible, and cannot be disturbed with impunity. The philosophers of the individualist school take the same view. They sometimes go so far as to deny the expediency of sanitary regulation in cities, and maintain that the disease and mortality due to bad drainage will secure the improvement of the drainage by stimulating individual effort. They would have the lighting and paving of streets accomplished in the same way. Thus Mr. Herbert Spencer, who is admitted by all to be the leading sociologist of the world, says that

either by general government or by local government the levying of compulsory rates for draining and for paving and lighting is inadmissible as indirectly making legislative protection more costly than necessary, or, in other words, turning it into aggression. * * * Respecting sewerage there would be no difficulty. Houses might rightly be drained on the same mercantile principle that they are now supplied with water. It is highly probable that, in the hands of a private company, the resulting manure would not only pay the cost of collection, but would also yield a considerable profit. But if not, the return on the invested capital would be made up of charges to those whose houses were drained, the alternative of having the connection with the main sewer stopped being as good a security for payment as the analogous one possessed by gas and water companies. Paving and lighting would properly fall to the management of house-owners. Were there no public provision for such conveniences house-owners would quickly find it to their interest to furnish them. Some speculative building society having set the example of improvement in this direction, competition would do the rest. Dwellings without public footways before them and with no lamps to show the tenants to their doors would stand empty when better accommodation was offered; and good paving and lighting having thus become essential, landlords would combine for the more economical supply of them.

This is merely an example of the absurd lengths to which this favorite theory leads such writers. In the light of the sanitary progress of the nineteenth century, due entirely to organized social effort, such statements scarcely seem to emanate from a sane mind.

Starting from such extremes, it would not be difficult to show that the general doctrine of *laissez faire* is unsound when contemplated as a universal principle of sociology, and so much has latterly been said upon this point that many good writers, even in England, who still desire to hold on to the doctrine, such as Cairnes, Sidgwick, and Lefevre, are giving up its universal applicability and only contending for it in many cases on the ground of expediency. No one asks more than this, as no fair-minded person will deny that it is often better to allow the most absolute free play to the natural agencies, not merely of society, but of physical nature as well.

Not to dwell longer upon such broad generalizations, and coming now nearer to the domain of economics, I will state, at the risk of some apparent abruptness, another paradox in the following words:

> *Reforms are chiefly advocated by those*
> *who have no personal interest in them.*

I do not claim that this is universal, and there usually comes a time in the history of every reform when the victims of the evil to be reformed join in the work and help to secure its consummation. But in some cases, such as the abolition of slavery, even this does not take place. Associations that are organized for charitable, benevolent, and reformatory objects are composed almost exclusively of persons who are actuated by purely altruistic motives and have nothing to gain beyond the approbation of their fellows. Labor-reform movements are usually instigated and largely prosecuted by persons who are only interested in their success from some high moral point of view. Sometimes they are the employers of labor, and working-men's parties are often officered by lawyers, clergymen, professors in colleges, or writers on social topics. Selfish designs and personal ambition they doubtless often have, but very rarely are they men who would be pecuniarily affected by the success or failure of the cause.

I have introduced this principle chiefly in order to lay more special stress upon an important corollary to it, viz., that

> *Discontent increases with the improvement*
> *of the social condition.*

No one will deny to this proposition, provided it can be proved true, the character of a social paradox. The mind naturally reasons that as the causes for complaint are removed the discontent should diminish. But such has not been the history of past progress; it is not the condition of the present progress of society. The reason for this, like the reasons for all natural truths, which seem false when first stated, is clear when the explanation is furnished. We saw that in the case of emancipation the entire reform must be accomplished by others than the victims of slavery. We even hear of slaves who do not want their freedom. But however much they may want it, they are powerless to obtain it. And it is largely so with the industrial classes, who are not slaves in the accepted sense of the word. But up to a certain point they are, as truly as real slaves, both incapable of realizing the need of reform and powerless to act in improving their condition. Discontent is proportioned to the degree in which an oppressed class realizes its condition, and increases with the knowledge that relief is attainable by action. But this stage is not reached until external influences have already wrought an important change for the better. The French revolution did not come until the comparatively liberal king, Louis XVI, had called Turgot, a friend of the third estate, to his court and a great mitigation of popular grievances had taken place. Women did not begin to demand legal rights till most of the discriminations of the common law against them had been removed by statute. And, as we shall see, the workingmen did not become an element in politics until a great amelioration had taken place in their general condition.

This is the meaning of the paradox that discontent increases with improvement, but it should be noted that this presupposes the existence of hardship, and would be no longer true if entire justice could be attained.

The special importance of this law arises from the fact that one of the leading arguments against all attempts at industrial reform has been that the condition of the laboring classes is really improving. Mr. Henry George has greatly injured his case by denying this. His "Progress and Poverty" is little else than an elaboration of this denial—a systematic attempt to establish an untruth. This book has proved useful in stimulating honest inquiry into this question. It is now admitted at all hands that the condition of the working classes has improved and greatly improved in nearly all civilized countries. And it is claimed that on this account the discontent of labor is without good reason. But those who take this view do not understand that this discontent is wholly on account of the improvement that has taken place in the workingman's condition. It does prove, however, that the reform is not yet complete, and a movement that has reached the stage of arousing wide-spread discontent can never be arrested until all just grounds of discontent have been removed. . . .

Capital does more than labor towards the
production of wealth.

In view of the popular belief that labor creates all wealth, this, if true, must certainly rank as a paradox. To perceive its truth we must consider what constitutes capital, and to do this successfully we must, for the time being, cut loose entirely from all the current definitions, however true they may be, and look at the problem from one special point of view. It is a common thing to hear it said that in the modern industrial world it is not human power that produces most of the wealth, but natural forces. This is true, and is one way of looking at it. It is equally common to hear it said that it is not muscle, but brain, that accomplishes the chief results. This is also true, and is another way of viewing the question. Brain—i. e., intelligence—organizes and directs natural forces and the latter do the work. Still a third point of view is taken when it is said that it is machinery that performs most of the service. Machinery is that material embodiment of this intelligent direction of natural forces. But there is a fourth possible way of contemplating this superhuman production of wealth, if I may be allowed such an expression, which few, I imagine, have employed, and that is to ascribe it to capital. Yet it is clearly

correct to do this. The other explanations I have given are all
partial and incomplete. The term "machinery" is too narrow.
Even when it comprehends all kinds of implements and utensils it still fails to cover all forms of productive industry.
"Natural forces" is an expression which requires the subtle
explanation that it includes the properties of material substances to render it complete. "Intelligence" or "brain" is still
more vague and difficult to reduce to economic language. But
"capital" includes all these and every other possible agency or
factor, and it is really to this that all production beyond what
could have resulted from the exercise of naked human muscle
is due. I need not attempt to explain how small a part of
human wealth this latter would be. But this view of the subject
brings out with especial force the truth of the original proposition with which we set out, that the artificial is superior to
the natural.

Passing over the proposition that

Wages are drawn from products, not from capital,

which would have sounded paradoxical a short time ago, but
is now accepted by most advanced economists, I now come to
what I regard as the most important, as it is perhaps the most
debatable, of all economic paradoxes. It may be expressed in
the following form:

Profits rise with wages,

or in the stronger form:

Increase of wages results in increased profits.

Surely this proposition would stagger an old-time political
economist, and very few employers, with the aid of the alleged
unerring mercantile sagacity, could be brought to accept it. In
fact, not only is the exact opposite theory the only one taught
in the books, but the business of the whole world has always
been conducted upon it, and to the normal mind the statement

that profits will diminish as wages increase seems to be self-evident. How, then, can the opposite be maintained? . . .

The manner of proof is something like the arguments advanced in favor of non-resistance. Any one who understands it must admit its soundness, and yet if any small number were to attempt to practice it they would surely fail. It may be briefly stated somewhat in the following form:

Political economy, as expounded in all the books, teaches that industrial society is divided into two great classes—producers and consumers. In this classification the wage-receivers are uniformly regarded as producers. The consumers are a class who go into the market and purchase the products wrought by the wage-receivers. They are vaguely conceived, illy defined, never distinctly located, and, except that they do actually buy the goods and consume them, they are a sort of economic myth. The question, then, naturally arises, Who are these consumers? where are they? what are they? And when fairly looked at the answer is not difficult. A consumer is a human being. He is part of the population. Somewhere in the population he is to be found. But who is there that is not a consumer? Clearly, no one. The consumers are the whole population. The wage-receivers must, therefore, be both producers and consumers, and when we consult the census we find that they, with their dependents, constitute the great majority. Therefore, in all calculations based upon the nature of the market, not only must they not be ignored, but they must be regarded as the prime factor. It may be said that they consume much less proportionally than other classes. Their humble rank and simple wants make them scanty consumers, and therefore it is necessary to bid for the custom of the middle and upper classes and ignore the laboring classes. No one will claim that they consume as much *per capita* as the rich, and of many products they consume none. But here again we may properly ask, why is this so? The obvious answer is, because they have not the means. But will any one claim that the working classes consume all they would if they had the means? Surely not. There may be some so low that they could make no use of anything more than they have, but this is scarcely conceivable. With hardly an exception they want much which they cannot have because they have not the means to purchase it. But their means consist wholly in their wages. To increase their wages is to supply their wants. The laborer wants increased wages only that he may supply his needs, i. e., that he may become a larger consumer. The employer is apt to look at the question as though all that were paid for labor beyond the absolute minimum would be hoarded and lost to industry. This view, tacitly shared by the economist, is obviously false. What to the laborer is the supplying of his wants is to the manufacturer and the farmer expanding the market. The vast number of laborers and the certainty that all increase of wages will be expended and not hoarded make even the smallest general rise in wages an important stimulus to production. It enlarges the market for all classes of products. Statistics show that periods of high wages have uniformly been periods of increased production, and increased production means prosperity to the manufacturer—i. e., profits rise as wages rise.

From this, as the fundamental law, a large number of new and striking results, most of them in the nature of paradoxes, arise. Only a few of these can be considered here. One of them is that

Prices fall as wages rise.

. . . Surely, one would suppose that the cost of production would be greater if the cost of labor were increased. Just here lies the paradox. Doubtless this would be true for an isolated case, but it would not be true where the rise in wages was on a large scale. The reason is that with the increase in wages the market is enlarged and production must be correspondingly increased. But as production was at the maximum for existing methods before, the increased production must now be brought

about by an improvement in the methods—i. e., by the introduction of improved machinery. This always lessens the cost
of production, and as prices depend upon the cost of production they will necessarily fall. . . .

But perhaps the most important of the conclusions to which
such an inquiry leads are those relating to the hours of labor.
Two of these may be briefly considered. The first is that

A reduction of hours tends to increase production.

This perhaps sounds more paradoxical than any of the foregoing propositions. It seems absurd to say that more will be
produced in eight hours than in ten. But let us see: The laborer
remains a consumer the same after as before the reduction.
Unless more machinery be introduced the same amount of
manual labor will be required after as before to supply an
unchanged demand. Hence a larger number of laborers must
be employed. These, in the present state of industry, are always to be had. The average number of able-bodied workmen
constantly out of and seeking employment is estimated to be
one-fifth of the whole. As many of these as it required to balance the decrease of hours would at once find employment.
While unemployed the amount consumed by them is at an
absolute minimum. As soon as they begin to receive wages
they begin to consume more, and thus the demand for various
commodities is increased. This demand is sure to be met by
increased production, which will be secured by the introduction of improved machinery if it cannot be done otherwise.

But this is not the only way in which a reduction of the
hours of labor works an increase of production. By affording
a little leisure to the workingman it gives him a taste, or rather
an opportunity to indulge a taste already possessed, for certain
elements of culture and certain social refinements which he
will then begin to demand and which will be accordingly supplied, still further increasing the quantity and varying the
quality of production.

But assuming that the workingman's earnings were previously all expended on necessities, this last consequence would be impossible, and hence arises the final paradox, that

The reduction of hours tends to increase wages.

But for the foregoing explanations this would sound strangely enough. Whenever there is an appeal for a reduction of hours it is always met by the reply that in the state of business it can only be granted on condition that wages be correspondingly reduced. Business competition is supposed to render profits impossible under any such change, and this doubtless would be the case with isolated industries, at least at the outset. A reduction of hours is considered equivalent to an increase of pay. But even on this view we have seen that, in the long run, profits rise with wages, and they may, therefore, be expected to rise with a reduction of hours. If the reduction is made general and continued long enough to produce its natural and final effect upon industry and upon society, it will certainly create an increased demand for all classes of commodities, requiring the introduction of improved machinery and methods in their production, cheapening the cost of their production, and thus so far increasing the profits of the manufacturer as to enable him to pay higher wages. In fact, he will be left no choice of his own in the matter, but under the laws of business competition he will be compelled to do so to prevent a reduction in his profits.

Without dwelling longer upon these several propositions I will close this paper with a single comment. If any considerable part of what is claimed is true it proves in a most conclusive manner what I have so often insisted upon, that to the power of production there is practically no limit, and that all that is needed to place in the possession of every member of society every object of his desire is the power to purchase it. Very few indeed are there who possess or can possess every purchasable object of desire. The present production of industrial society would not be equal to a tenth, probably not a hundredth, of what would be consumed if every one could supply at will every proper and legitimate want of his nature. It is, therefore, useless to talk of increasing production except by the increase of the power to consume. The problem is, therefore, no longer how to increase production, but how to increase consumption—not the desire to consume, for that already exists, nor the ability to render an equivalent, which is also abundantly possessed, but the chances to exercise that ability in the gratification of that desire; in a word, *the opportunity to earn.* That the reduction of the hours of labor is one of the means to that end is certainly clear. The discovery of other means and of the best way to put every means into practice seems to me to constitute the chief economic problem of our times.

14

PSYCHIC FACTORS

OF CIVILIZATION

1893

After DYNAMIC SOCIOLOGY, *Ward "dropped philosophy" for a time and concentrated on his professional work, which was ever more demanding. Alas, he discovered, to his dismay, that* DYNAMIC SOCIOLOGY *was not understood and, what was worse, that it was considered by many "an abstruse speculation" rather than "a practical system." Meantime Ward had discovered Schopenhauer, "whose philosophy gave a subjective trend to human thought." With his mind turning increasingly to the study of psychic factors, Ward gave a lecture in 1891 on "Subjective Psychology or the Philosophy of Feelings."*

The crisis of the early nineties served as a kind of catalytic agent for bringing all these ideas together and creating out of them a new compound; and on the first day of 1892, Ward set himself to synthesize the ideas that had been stirring in his mind for some years. The plan of the new work was clear, and Ward filled in the details of the argument with greatest ease. Within three months he had written most of the book. Very much aware of its significance and hopeful of its influence, Ward wrote that to "America, the experimental ground of civilization, this book, written wholly within the quadricentennial

year of its discovery and published (issued) in that of the great
Columbian Exposition, is dedicated, and consecrated to the
cause of social progress and mental enlightenment on Ameri-
can soil." Unfortunately, Ward decided in the end not to in-
clude this dedication.

Though Ward persisted in thinking that all his seminal ideas
were to be found in that storehouse of sociological thought,
Dynamic Sociology, Psychic Factors *is generally recognized*
to be his best and most important book. Certainly more fully
than any other, and more clearly too, it sums up Ward's social
and political philosophy. Nowhere else, either in his own writ-
ings or in the writings of his disciples, can be found so forceful
and persuasive an argument for the role of the "psychic factor"
in counterbalancing and controlling nature, and nowhere else
can be found so cogently argued a case for the role of govern-
ment in the process.

Ward tells us that quite the ablest review of this book came
from the pen of John Dewey, then just on the threshold of his
distinguished career, "who clearly sees how the psychologic
treatment of social and economic questions reverses the old
method and opens up new vistas in all the sciences." Perhaps
Psychic Factors *did not quite do that, but it did mark one of*
the climacterics in the history of the philosophy of the welfare
state.

A. SOCIAL ACTION

The history of man, if it should ever be written, would be an
account of what man has done. The numerous changes that
have been made in the position of certain imaginary lines on
the earth's surface, called political boundaries, and the events
that have given rise to such changes, would be recorded, but

Psychic Factors of Civilization (Boston: Ginn and Co., 1893), pp. 97–
101.

instead of making the bulk of human annals as they now do, they would occupy a very subordinate place. Such changes and their conditioning events are temporary, superficial, and unimportant. They leave no lasting impress and are soon swept by time completely from the real record of man's achievements. The major part of a true history of man would be devoted to the reproduction of this real record. Although it is written on the face of nature by the events themselves, very much as the cosmical history of the earth is written in the rocks, still the history of man needs to be studied from these natural records, interpreted by the facts there observed, and described in writing and by graphic representation as much as the history of the earth needs to be thus treated by the geologist. Human phenomena, or, as they are popularly called, social phenomena, differ in these respects from geological and other phenomena only in the nature of the forces which produce them. In these it is the psychic forces. . . . Man is the instrument through which these forces operate, and the immediate cause of the phenomena is human action. As man has been a social being during the greater part of his history, and as the principal results of his activities have been brought about by some form of social coöperation, it is customary and proper to designate such action as social action. The laws and principles of such action belong to social science, or sociology, and it thus becomes clear that sociology rests directly upon psychology, and especially upon subjective psychology.

Subjective psychology is a philosophy of action. Looked at retrospectively and from the standpoint of natural history it is seen that all the changes that have taken place either in the organism or the environment have been due to the action of the former under the influence of the psychic or vital forces, and that from the time that conscious desires began to determine action great transformations have taken place and are still going on. Not dwelling on the subhuman stage, it is obvious that man is the being that has most notably displayed this transforming power. An animal of rather inferior physical strength, endowed with few natural weapons of either offence or defence, lacking the powers of nocturnal vision, keen scent, fleetness in pursuit or escape, flight, or special skill in swimming, by which to aid him in migration, he has nevertheless almost completely changed the appearance and character of everything above ground over half the land surface of the earth and established himself supreme over all else in all the habitable parts of the globe. All this is commonly and properly attributed to mind. . . . But the present point of view is that of insisting that the motive power of mind has been his multiplied and ever-increasing wants, to supply which perpetual effort has been put forth and ceaseless activity has taken place. This purposeful activity is the middle term of the threefold psychologic succession, mediating between desire and feeling and the necessary condition to the satisfaction of the former in attaining the latter. Here more than anywhere else pleasure or happiness has been made an end, though only intended by nature as a means. But neither did the transformations wrought by man's activity constitute in any sense the purpose of that activity. The sum total of these transformations constitute what is meant by material civilization, but man never made civilization an end of his efforts. In so far as this has been a gain the sole beneficiary of that gain has been society. . . .

There are those who maintain that civilization can only be achieved through the action of the individual, unconscious of the end, doing that which will conduce to the end. The present state of progress is adduced as proof that this is the necessary result. But while it is admitted that this has resulted in some parts of the world and in past history, it must be denied that the effect has been beneficial in all parts of the world or wholly so in any part, and also that any guaranty exists that it will continue indefinitely to be so, even where the actual benefits have been greatest. It can also be legitimately argued that much greater benefits might be secured if so-

ciety were the conscious agent and had its improvement for
its clearly perceived end. But this is an anticipation. This much
needs however to be said, that in predicting action as the
object of society the time has not yet come when it can be
said to be conscious of its end. Society has not yet begun to
seek its end. It has not reached the stage of psychic development attained by the Cretaceous insect, the Eocene bird, the
Miocene mammal, of the Quaternary man, when conscious
desire began to inspire activity in securing its satisfaction.
The soul of society is not yet born. Yet none the less is society
the beneficiary of the direct results of human action in so far
as they are beneficial, albeit that action is directed solely
toward the attainment of the object of the individual man,
viz., happiness.

It is the essence of the doctrine of individualism that what
is good for the individual must be good for society. This is
based on the admitted fact that society exists only for the
individual. Society is only an ideal—a Platonic idea, like
species, genus, order, etc., in natural history. The only real
thing is the individual. And it is argued: Why strive to benefit
that which has no feeling and therefore is incapable of being
benefited? The argument is plausible. Only it proceeds from
a misconception of what social reformers really mean when
they talk of improving society. There are none so simple as
literally to personify society and conceive it endowed with
wants and passions. By the improvement of society they only
mean such modification in its constitution and structure as
will in their opinion result in ameliorating the conditions of its
individual members. Therefore there is nothing illogical in
their claim, and to answer them it must be shown in each case
that the particular supposed reform that they are advocating
will not as a matter of fact result in the alleged amelioration of
the individual members of society. Arguments of this class are
legitimate.

It would also be legitimate to argue that no possible alteration in the existing status of society can produce beneficial
effects as thus defined, but I am not aware that anyone has
ever taken that position. It is too obvious on the most superficial view that the evils that individuals suffer are often due
to the constitution of society which entails them. This results
from the constant changes that are going on in every direction
through the activities of individuals seeking their ends, and
from time to time causing the needs of the mass to outgrow
the restrictions which society under very different previous
circumstances was obliged to impose. So that if a state of
perfect adaptation of the individual to society could be at any
given moment conceived to exist it would not remain so very
long, and new internal transformations would soon again throw
the individual units out of harmony with the social aggregate.
It is this inertia of society and its inability to keep pace with
the growth of the living mass within it that gives rise to social
reformers who are legitimate and necessary, nay, natural products of every country and age, and the ignoring of this fact
by conservative writers who lay so great stress on the word
natural, is one of the amusing absurdities of the present period.

So long, therefore, as society remains the unconscious product of the individual demands of each age, so long will the
organized social state continue to be found out of accord with
and lagging behind the real spirit of the age, often so intoler-
ably so as to require more or less violent convulsions and social revolutions. But if ever an ideal social organization shall
come to be a clearly defined conscious individual want, it will
be possible to establish one that will have elements of flex-
ibility sufficient to render it more or less permanent. But here,
as everywhere else under the dominion of the psychic forces,
the end of the individual or object of man, happiness, or some
improvement in his personal condition, must be put vividly
before him as the loadstone of desire and motive to action.

B. CONVENTIONAL ETHICS

That unthinking persons, theological writers, and authors of sentimental homilies should extol morals and regard it as the chief end of life is not perhaps to be wondered at; but that philosophers of breadth and penetration should have so uniformly failed to assign it its proper and natural place in their systems, will always remain one of the curiosities of the human mind. It would at least be supposed that where one of these latter was also a professed teacher of social science, and as such to have been forced to make the most careful study and analysis of all the different kinds of social action, he could not help seeing the subordinate rank and incidental character of those negative phenomena which alone belong to ethics. It is all the more surprising, therefore, to find Mr. Herbert Spencer making this subject to form the cap-sheaf and crown of his great system of synthetic philosophy, and speaking of that part of his system as the one to which he regards "all the preceding parts as subsidiary."

While sociology deals with all human actions and, therefore, includes ethics, the latter deals only with the limited class of actions which are properly included under the word *conduct,* and which, as said above, constitute the conflicts that occur in normal action. They are not only unimportant from their limited scope, but from their essentially negative character. Their tendency, as in mechanical friction, is to impede, and to their full extent, to prevent the regular operations of society. They are therefore wholly non-progressive. Any one who from moral considerations acts in any respect differently from what the psychic forces within him normally impel him to act, to that extent lessens the effect of his action. Of course this is far from saying that it is not very frequently necessary and in all respects best to do this, it is merely to insist that there is nothing so wonderful and exalted about moral acts as is com-

Psychic Factors of Civilization, pp. 104–111.

monly supposed, when viewed from the broadest philosophical standpoint. If one sees the question only from the standpoint of social progress, which consists in producing the maximum permanent improvements in man's material surroundings, all hindrances to this consummation are bad, and those acts which are morally good are in most instances socially bad.

It may be admitted that the subject of interferences among human actions and of their avoidance is a complex and difficult one, nevertheless it has been so long and exhaustively studied that it seems impossible to add anything of value. All the great moral precepts are as old as human records. The "golden rule" of Christ was laid down independently by Hillel and Confucius and never practised by any one. Among the best maxims are those of the Brahmins, while Antoninus and the Stoics have furnished as pure and lofty conceptions of duty as any modern moral science writer could wish. Mr. Spencer laid claim to finding a "scientific basis" for ethics. One volume of his *Principles of Ethics* is now out and I am unable to see that he has sustained that claim if by "scientific basis" he means anything else than the old basis. What he says that is new is no part of ethics. The doctrine that pleasure is the good and pain the bad, and that happiness is the end of action, while "scientific," is not ethical. It is a corollary dimly seen by Spinoza and others, . . . which is a principle of psychology, or, one may say, of biology. And as to his "Justice" the subject does not belong to ethics, but to jurisprudence. As treated by him it is a partisan defence of extreme individualism, amounting to practical anarchism.

However important moral conduct may be in itself, and there is no difference of opinion on this point, there are many reasons, in its overdone condition already referred to, why it should not be made to absorb so large a share of the attention of thinking persons. The moral precepts observed at any time and in any country are the effect and not the cause of the moral condition of those who observe them. If there is any mutual interaction between ethical teaching and moral conduct by which each influences the other and tends to cause the advance of both it is very slight. Certain it is that the former can be and frequently is pushed so far that the moral sense is more or less blunted and deadened by the iteration of moral injunctions. It would probably be better for personal morality if ethics were only taught historically and philosophically.

Another serious evil results from the erroneous belief that moral character can be improved by ethical teaching. Many persons, and especially teachers, habitually labor under such a load of responsibility for the moral character of those who come within the circle of their influence that they become paralyzed for usefulness in life. No one dares to say what he thinks. All originality is screened out of whatever is produced. Teaching, that noblest of all vocations, degenerates into pedantry. This has now reached such a stage that the utterances of professors in colleges have assumed a stereotyped form and the sagacious student knows in advance what is going to be said. Or, if any one of these should chance to say anything original, he feels obliged immediately to recant it, or to add a saving clause to the effect that he meant something else. And it is getting to be the practice in set papers, orations, and scholastic addresses in which the mind has been allowed some freedom to expand, to close with a "protest," as the Catholic writers call it, namely a disclaimer of everything that could be construed to be injurious to morals. Frequently, after stating an important scientific truth, it is deemed necessary to explain to the reader, as the judge does to the jury, how much of it will do to believe and what conclusions it will not do to draw from it. University lectures become infected with this true moral cowardice, until the lecture-room style can be recognized and readily distinguished from the independent exposition of the original investigator. The same difference is seen in the books produced by the two classes, in the cringing fear that animates the one, contrasted with the manly courage characterizing the other.

Along with the dwarfing effect of this state of things, there goes the further demoralizing influence of egotism and conceit. For the idea of continually guarding the character of others begets an inordinate conception of personal importance, and this is always seen grotesquely mixing itself with pretended humility. A form of this sometimes takes possession even of truly great minds, and unless checked by wholesome influences from without they are apt to merge into a state in which they vastly overestimate the effect their labors are to produce. It was so with Auguste Comte, after long practising his *"hygiène cérébrale"* of reading nothing and conversing with no one, but evolving his system out of his inner consciousness, until he fancied himself the high priest of a new dispensation and even fixed the time for its universal acceptance. And do we not see some trace of this enlarged personality in Mr. Herbert Spencer when, in the preface to his Data of Ethics, he explains his haste to lay before the world his ethical system before any serious evils should result from its delay? For it is in this connection that he says: "Few things can happen more disastrous than the decay and death of a regulative system no longer fit, before another and fitter regulative system has grown up to replace it." Under such a weight of responsibility he ought at least to be consoled by the view expressed in this chapter and to congratulate himself that the morals of the world may still be safe even if he should not live to complete his Principles of Ethics.

To all this may now be added the further law that the moral state is a product of social evolution and a condition to the existence of society. The moral code only differs from the legal code in taking cognizance of cases that society will adjudicate without the aid of the courts. Society will not tolerate an incorrigibly immoral member. To be in society at all and out of jail he must practice the moral virtues of his age and country. Great latitude there no doubt is in these matters, but his treatment by his fellow men will depend upon the degree to which he conforms to popular conceptions of right, and though he may keep within legal rules, if he persists in violating moral rules he will be ostracized and deprived of the means of gaining a livelihood, and ultimately made to perish and make room for those who will conform. Therefore there is no need to preach morality. It is self-regulating. Society literally compels its members to observe its moral laws.

To the statement that ethics merely represents the social friction it may be objected that this is to take too narrow a view of the subject, that there are departments of ethics that are not covered by this definition. I have tried to discover such and thus far failed, although there are some cases in which this is apparently true. It may be said that ethics need not necessarily relate to others, but may relate wholly to self. One may do an immoral act to himself wholly irrespective of any other individual. For example he may be intemperate and thus abuse his own nature. To this it may be replied that if he were alone in some vast wilderness and his act were unknown to any other human being this would be a case in point. But it is merely a hypothetical case which could practically never occur, and if it should occur it would have no importance, because such a life would be socially useless. But the moment he is brought into society his immoral practises begin to react on others and in various ways to increase the friction of the social machinery.

It is also true that this view relates primarily to normal or egoistic conduct and only secondarily to supra-normal or altruistic, better named *supererogatory* conduct. At least beneficence, benevolence, philanthropy, charity, etc., do not directly result from conflicts in normal action. But we have only to analyze the motives to these to perceive that they are at least the indirect consequences of such conflicts. Taking charitable acts as the generic type of the whole supererogatory class, it is obvious that they presuppose the prior existence in society of serious obstructions to the normal course of action. They exist only because there is a class in society who are in some way more or less deprived of the means of subsistence. How came such a class to exist? Clearly through some form of interference with their normal actions. There is an abundance of food. The benevolent class possess a large enough surplus to sustain the indigent class, and they are but a handful compared with the non-benevolent class who possess a surplus. Those who have nothing, were they free to act, would proceed to supply themselves with the surplus. Something prevents them from doing so. It is not to the purpose to inquire here what the nature of these barriers is, it is only necessary to point out that they exist. But this is only to say that action has been interfered with, arrested, clogged, choked, and hence objects of charity exist in society. An act of charity is, therefore, from our present standpoint, simply a mode, usually only a temporary one, of relieving pressure upon this class, of clearing away the obstructions to life, in a word, of overcoming the social friction.

The above is independent of the ethical nature of this kind of social friction and also of that of charitable action in general. It is fashionable now-a-days to animadvert upon all charitable work from the supposed fundamental and scientific standpoint that it interferes with the law of the survival of the fittest in society. The argument proceeds from a superficial analogy between animal life and human life, and is neither scientific nor sound. But this much is true and is the basis of the popular error, namely that under the law of parsimony, i. e., that an individual will always seek the greatest gain for the least effort, it is easy to create a pauper class by injudicious charity. This class then becomes in society the strict homologue of the degenerate parasite so well known in almost every department of biology.

There is, however, a really fundamental and scientific objection to charity, but this I have never seen stated. It is that charity is really the giving by the benevolent class, not to the indigent class, but to the non-benevolent class. To illustrate this let us take the case of waiters' "tips" and porters' fees. All who have ever given the subject a moment's thought know that to tip a waiter or fee a porter is simply to give so much money to a hotel keeper or a railroad company. Its effect is to encourage these to continue to keep down the wages of these employés to the point of dependence upon the public, and the more generous the public the lower will be the wages. If all would resolve to cease tipping and feeing altogether, these employés would be paid regular wages like other employés. Charity and alms-giving do not differ in principle from this giving of tips and fees. It is true that in the latter case it is definitely known from whom the money should be taken as an act of justice, while in the former case the ones who should pay it are a large ill-defined class. But there is no doubt that the ones who have the wealth of the world have included in it the share of those who have none. The only escape from this conclusion is to say, as many are ready to do, that those who have nothing have no right to exist in society. If the indigent class were coextensive and identical with the criminal class there would be some ground for this position. But those who assume it generally argue that the poor are more moral than the rich, and it is probably true that the percentage of criminals from the wealthy classes is greater than that from the indigent classes. The only argument remaining is that poverty is due to idleness and profligacy. Yet if the percentage of idle and profligate rich could be compared with that of the idle and profligate poor, it would make a far worse showing for the former than that of the comparative criminality of these two classes. The conclusion therefore remains unassailable that the means of subsistence is justly due to the indigent class from the opulent class, and no amount of patchwork on the part of a few benevolent persons can ever balance this great account with society. Its effect is to increase the surplus of the non-benevolent in the sums contributed by the benevolent.

The several considerations above brought forward are merely samples of the short-sighted and superficial character of nearly everything that is said or done with relation to ethics. This is because in the nature of things there cannot be any logical and fundamental treatment of that subject. The moment logic and scientific principles are applied the problem ceases to be an ethical one and becomes a sociological one. The ethical and sociological standpoints are the opposites of each other. The former looks to the curbing, the latter to the freeing of social energy. Any philosophy that has for its object the hemming and cribbing of a great natural force can have no permanence. As well try to dam the waters of a river and hope for final success.

This thought introduces the fundamental truth with which this treatment of social friction must conclude. It is that the whole subject of ethics is essentially provisional and the stage to which it belongs is a merely transitional stage. There are those who by devoting their whole lives to doing good conceive of the life of future blessedness as one in which there shall be no other occupation but that of doing good. They forget that they have been taught that in that life there will be no one to need their ministrations. Could they realize such a state it would appear a wretched one. The only thing they enjoy they would be deprived of. I have known saintly beings of this class who seemed so to long for an opportunity to do good, that they could not conceal a secret joy at the occurrence of an unfortunate accident which promised to furnish such an opportunity. Were all suffering abolished the occupation of such persons would be gone. And yet Mr. Spencer and other ethical writers do but reflect a wide-spread popular sentiment in regarding ethical conduct as the climax of human achievement and ethics as the goal of philosophy.

C. CAUSES OF ETHICAL PROGRESS

. . . The idea that there must always be a field for ethical action is only a part of the more general idea that all things must always be what they now are. And both of these ideas prevail in the face of the fact that the most radical changes have actually many times taken place within the narrow limits of human history. "The poor always ye have with you" is supposed to express a necessary social truth. It is doubtless as true now as it was two thousand years ago, but that is far from giving warrant for saying that it will continue to be true two thousand years hence. There are many who think that it will have ceased to be true two hundred years hence. But if it shall thus cease it will not be ethical teaching but improved social organization that will have produced the change. And so one might take up one by one all the social facts that make ethical conduct possible, and theoretically conceive of their elimination. It will, of course, be said that such an idea is visionary and utopian. Grant this and it still remains true that if any of the existing evils can be removed the domain of ethics is to that extent circumscribed. Deny that this is possible and the utility of all ethical work is given over. Admit that it is possible and there is no place to stop short of a reclamation of the whole field.

But is this claim wholly utopian? Has there been no moral progress? If not why continue to inculcate moral principles? As a matter of fact there has been great moral progress. Let any one read the history of England, even the meager account of its kings and their exploits which is called history, and compare the acts of the men of the 12th to the 16th centuries with those of the men occupying relatively the same national and social positions to-day, and see whether there has been any moral progress. Not even in Russia which we call despotic

---

Psychic Factors of Civilization, pp. 112–115.

is there anything to compare with the immorality that openly stalked abroad three hundred years ago over all Europe. The subject need not be enlarged upon. The other point to be noted is that none of this real moral progress has been due to the enforcement and inculcation of moral precepts. It has been wholly due to the march of events, such as the growth of scientific ideas, the spread of letters, the influence of commerce, the establishment of universities, the invention of printing, and the introduction of machinery and manufactures; in general to the progress of intelligence, laying bare the enormity of the abuses formerly practised and creating a new code of morals which society literally enforces. Men could not be as cruel and immoral as they once were if they would. The power of public sentiment crushes every display of it. In other words as already stated, the modern improved morality is a condition to the modern improved state of civilization and the latter is the cause of the former, not the reverse as ethical expounders teach.

The effect of social friction is always painful, therefore moral progress, which consists in reducing this friction, is restricted in its popular acceptation to the lessening of pain, i.e., to the mitigation of suffering, the decrease of misery, and the removal of unhappiness in general. In short it is negative in its character, and such it really is in the main. But there may be a positive moral progress consisting in the increase of pleasure, the heightening of enjoyment, and the broadening and deepening of human happiness. Just as social friction is painful so social action is pleasurable. All desire is for the exercise of some function, and the objects of desire are such only by virtue of making such exercise possible. Happiness therefore can only be increased by increasing either the number or the intensity of satisfiable desires. It has in fact been greatly increased in both these ways. Without elaborating this principle I will simply point to the very modern date of two of the highest sources of man's present enjoyment in civilized countries, the enjoyment of music and the enjoyment of what may be called beauty in the amorphous—in the landscape, the cloud, the sea, the rocks, and the mountains. No faculty for appreciating either of these sources of delight seemed to exist in what we call ancient times, and it is practically wanting in all but modern civilized races. At least it cannot be sufficiently developed elsewhere to make up any considerable part of their enjoyment of life, which is the present point of view. Yet its germs doubtless exist in all races and have existed at all times, capable of development through civilization.

The highest ideal of happiness, therefore, is the freest exercise of the greatest number and most energetic faculties. This must also be the highest ethical ideal. But it is clear that its realization would abolish moral conduct altogether and remove the very field of ethics from a scheme of philosophy. To remove the obstacles to free social activity is to abolish the so-called science of ethics. The avowed purpose of ethics is to abolish itself. The highest ethics is no ethics. Ideally moral conduct is wholly un-moral conduct. Or more correctly stated, the highest ideal of a moral state is one in which there will exist nothing that can be called moral.

Whether we look at the subject from the standpoint of social progress or from that of individual welfare the liberation of social energy is the desideratum. The sociologist demands it because it increases the progressive power of society. The moralist should demand it because it increases happiness. For activity means both, and therefore the more activity the better. True morality not less than true progress consists in the emancipation of social energy and the free exercise of power. Evil is merely the friction which is to be overcome or at least minimized. This cannot be done by exhortation. It must be done by perfecting the social mechanism. The tendencies that produce evil are not in themselves evil. There is no absolute evil. None of the propensities which now cause evil are essentially bad. They are all in themselves good, must necessarily be so, since they have been developed for the sole purpose of enabling man to exist, survive, and progress. All evil is relative. Any power may do harm. The forces of nature are good or bad according to where they are permitted to expend themselves. The wind is evil when it dashes the vessel on the rocks; it is good when it fills the sail and speeds it on its way. Fire is evil when it rages through a great city and destroys life and property; it is good when it warms human dwellings or creates the wondrous power of steam. Electricity is evil when in the thunderbolt it descends from the cloud and scatters death and destruction; it is good when it transmits messages of love to distant friends. And so it is with the passions of men as they surge through society. Left to themselves like the physical elements they find vent in all manner of ways and constantly dash against the interests of those who chance to be in their way. But like the elements they readily yield to the touch of true science, which directs them into harmless, nay, useful channels, and makes them instruments for good. In fact human desires, seeking their satisfaction through appropriate activity, constitute the only good from the standpoint of sociology. They are the *Social Forces*.

D. NATURE AND ART

. . . Man and society are not, except in a very limited sense, under the influence of the great dynamic laws that control the rest of the organic world. Dynamic biology is a department distinct from dynamic sociology. The dynamics of society is, in the main, the antithesis of the dynamics of animal life. The psychic element . . . supplants "nature" by *art*. If we call biologic processes natural, we must call social processes artificial. The fundamental principle of biology is

Psychic Factors of Civilization, pp. 134–137.

natural selection, that of sociology is artificial selection. The survival of the fittest is simply the survival of the strong, which implies and would better be called the destruction of the weak. If nature progresses through the destruction of the weak, man progresses through the protection of the weak. And so it is throughout. The terms are all reversed.

It would be wrong to say that modern scientific philosophers take no account of so important a matter as brain development and human intelligence. They only fail to see the radical change of base which these have effected. Imbued with usually safe uniformitarian principles they naturally shrink from sensational speculations about cataclysmic changes. But it is possible to carry this method too far. For while it is true that nature makes no leaps, while, so long as beginnings only are considered, all the great steps in evolution are due to minute increments repeated through vast periods, still, when we survey the whole field, as we must do to comprehend the scheme, and contrast the extremes, we find that nature has been making a series of enormous strides, and reaching from one plane of development to another. It is these independent achievements that the true philosopher must study. Not to mention the difference between a nebula and a solar system, or between a ball of fire and a habitable planet, the origin of life, through the development of a substance in which life inheres, was a *saltus* that finds no parallel. . . . [For] now we have to contemplate a third cosmic epoch in the history of life, the birth of the intellect, developed in obedience to the same laws and for the better attainment of the same purpose—the satisfaction of desire.

The current sociology, it may be safely said, fails to recognize the full import of this psychic factor. Just as metaphysicians lost their bearings by an empty worship of mind, so modern evolutionists have missed their mark by degrading mind to a level with mechanical force. They seem thus ready to fling away the grand results that the doctrine of evolution cannot otherwise fail to achieve. I freely admit that the theologians commit a fatal error in treating the soul as independent of the body, but this enormous fallacy is scarcely greater than that of the modern evolutionist, who ignores the magnitude of the step which was taken when the soul acquired a directing agent. The enthusiastic student who climbs the Alps may climb to little purpose or come to grief unless he employs a guide. The great ship may sail beautifully in mid-ocean, but when she approaches a harbor she needs a pilot. Enthusiasm cannot help the one nor fair winds save the other. The course of biologic evolution has been exceedingly irregular, the biologic policy is extravagantly wasteful, so that nothing but enormous fecundity could prevent utter failure. Progress in nature was exceedingly slow under the rule of simple forces. All this was for want of a guide. Indeed it is this which makes all the difference between the animal and the man. It is a superficial view to suppose that the human form is essential to a human being. Form may help or impede, but no particular form could have prevented the general result. It is easy to see defects as advantages in the actual human form. If we are thankful that man has a mouth and teeth instead of a toothless beak we may deplore his lack of wings. In either case and in any case the sapient brain would have made him the master creature.

But the temptation to descant upon the results of "brain development," upon the achievements of "mind," and upon the "rational faculties" has too often been yielded to and generally proves profitless because there is no attempt to show how it comes about that they are the causes of the observed effects, and it is not to be wondered at under such circumstances that the popular mind should as naturally ascribe these effects to the erect posture, the facial angle, the opposable thumb, and other anatomical differences that make the physical man, as to the more intangible qualities to which they are really and exclusively due. It still requires to be explained

in a clear and intelligible way what the particular attribute
of mind really is through which man's superiority has been
reached and by what steps it has been developed and the
vantage-ground gained. The study of the commonly accepted
faculties of the mind does not accomplish this object. The
processes of perception, cognition, conception, judgment,
reason, thought, however well understood, throw no light on
the problem. The facts of memory, imagination, creative
power, wonderful and fascinating though they may be, lead
us no nearer to its solution. The more we contemplate these
things the clearer it becomes that these are not what have
given man his advantage, and those who now possess them in
the highest degree have no advantage over the rest of mankind. . . .

E. INVENTIVE GENIUS

The important truth is that the development of inventive
genius in man ultimately resulted in the introduction of *art*.
It caused the raw materials of nature which had previously
constituted his only resources to be discarded and replaced
more and more, and at length almost exclusively, by artificial
products. So nearly is this transformation complete in modern
civilized countries that the fact is lost sight of even by political economists. That is, they find it so universal that they
come to regard it as the natural condition. This leads them
into the greatest absurdities. The biological school, which
may still be said to be the predominant one, is fond of treating civilization as the product of natural forces and of in-
veighing against everything that any one attempts to do to
modify or in any way interfere with those forces, forgetting
entirely that civilization in all its essential characteristics is an
exclusively artificial product, the product of the inventive

Psychic Factors of Civilization, pp. 199–201, 232–233.

genius of man in modifying and altering the course of nature. Every adjustment made at the behest of inventive genius is an interference with the course of natural law. Every object of art is such as nature never would have created. When one looks about and realizes how extremely seldom any other class of objects are ever used by man, some idea may be gained of the intensely artificial character of civilization. But this is as it should be, for everywhere the artificial is superior to the natural, and what is called progress consists in making everything more and more artificial, i. e., in putting more art into all products, discovering new and added utilities by calling into play still higher flights of inventive genius.

The great subjective factor of mind, the soul or will of nature, constitutes a transforming agency. . . . That factor is now under consideration. The great psychic, or as it now becomes, social force was undiminished and constituted the impelling factor, but it could accomplish little without the aid of the intellect in the form of an inventive faculty as a directive factor. With both factors at work the transformation became rapid and permanent. Nothing equal or at all comparable to it had ever before been accomplished. It could not await the slow methods of nature in bringing about after millions of generations the anatomical modifications that were referred to. It worked directly upon the environment radically changing it and rendering structural adaptations unnecessary. This may be why man has really undergone so few of the latter. Structural modifications can only go on under the influence of an environmental pressure in the given direction. But if the moment such a pressure is felt it is immediately relieved by an artificial device, the cause of the change is removed and the tendency to change ceases. This was practically done in the case of man, invention being constantly directed toward the relief of environmental pressure and along the line of free activity in the satisfaction of desire. . . .

The true secret of the efficacy of intellectual action is that *it makes nature do the work.* This is the fundamental principle underlying all invention. Man has a power within himself—the will—but this is extremely limited. He can accomplish very little of what he desires by the exercise of this power alone. But he finds himself surrounded by the unseen powers of nature over many of which he has no influence, but some of which, through the exercise of his intellect he has learned in a greater or less degree to control. He has learned that whenever he fully understands the nature of these forces it is possible to direct them into channels which will cause them to produce the effects that he desires. The phenomena of nature are uniform and take place according to invariable laws. When those laws are known it is usually possible to utilize them by simple adjustments. Great and irresistible as Nature seems to be, it is found that as a matter of fact she is easily managed. All that is required is to know her thoroughly and to know how to control her. The first is science, the second is art or invention. This is as true of the simplest tools as it is of the most complicated machinery. If it is desired to excavate a tunnel through a mountain the lowest class of labor performed in such an excavation involves this principle. The gang of workmen employed to do the digging could do comparatively nothing without their picks and shovels. These are products of art. Their adaptation to the work required to be done is a result of thought. All *labor* is something more than mere muscular exertion. The lowest class of laborers are *artisans* in a proper sense of the term. Political economists speak of production, but what is production but the work of natural forces directed by intelligence? Not only is the real labor chiefly done by nature but the product is wholly artificial. Man does little but direct. Machinery is simply an extension of the principle that was always employed. It diminishes the agency of muscle and increases the agency of physical force. . . .

F. THE ECONOMY OF NATURE AND MIND

. . . It is in rational man that the first application of anything worthy of the name of economy is made. Nature has no economy. Only through foresight and design can anything be done economically. Rivers thus constructed (canals, mill-races, irrigating ditches, etc.,) are straight, or as nearly so as true economy requires. . . . Everything that is done under the direction of the intellect is as economical as the degree of intelligence will permit. All failures to attain this maximum economy are due to ignorance—to lack of acquaintance with the conditions of the problem. The degree of economy therefore for the same degree of intellectual penetration will be exactly proportioned to the amount of knowledge possessed.

Nature's way of sowing seed is to leave it to the wind, the water, the birds and animals. . . . How different the economy of a rational being! He prepares the ground, clearing it of its vegetable competitors, then he carefully plants the seeds at the proper intervals so that they shall not crowd one another, and after they have sprouted he keeps off their enemies, whether vegetable or animal, supplies water if needed, even supplies the lacking chemical constituents of the soil, if he knows what they are, and thus secures, as nearly as possible, the vigorous growth and fruition of every seed planted. This is the economy of mind.

A closer analysis shows that the fundamental distinction between the animal and the human method is that *the environment transforms the animal, while man transforms the environment.* This proposition holds literally from whatever standpoint it be contemplated. It is, indeed, the full expression of the fact above stated, that the tools of animals are organic, while those of man are mechanical. But if we contrast these two methods from the present standpoint, which is that of

---

Psychic Factors of Civilization, pp. 256–261, 273–279.

economics, we see at once the immense superiority of the human, or psychological, over the animal or biological method. The economy is of two kinds, economy of time and economy of energy. It has taken much longer to develop any one of the organic appliances of animals, whether for supplying its wants or fighting its enemies, than the entire period during which man has possessed any arts, even the simplest. And yet such appliances, however complete or effective, have not sufficed to enable any species possessing them greatly to expand its territorial range, or to migrate far from the region to which it was originally adapted. Man, on the other hand, without acquiring any new organic adaptations, by the manufacture of tools, weapons, clothing, habitations, etc., by subjecting the animal and vegetable kingdoms to his service, and by the power of "looking before and after"—in short, by the aid of reason—has taken possession of the whole earth, and is the only animal whose habitat is not circumscribed. This, as just remarked, he has accomplished in a comparatively brief period, i. e., wholly since Tertiary time, and chiefly since the glacial epoch.

The economy of energy is fully as great as that of time, and may be regarded as the cause of the latter. It is the result of *art*. It has been seen that the mechanical products of rational design necessarily utilize some economic principle through which the muscular force necessary to be exerted is less for any given result accomplished than it would otherwise be. In the great majority of cases the result could not be produced at all without the aid of the proper implement or mechanism for producing it, and this becomes more and more the case as machinery gains upon hand labor. The sum total of all such devices forms the basis of the mechanic arts. Few realize how completely civilization depends upon art in this sense. The utter helplessness of man without the arts is well illustrated in DeFoe's Robinson Crusoe, but the author saw clearly that in order to enable his hero to survive at all, even in a tropical climate where nature's productions were exuberant, he must provide himself from stores of the wrecked vessel with a considerable supply of tools and other artificial appliances. What was true of Robinson Crusoe, thus circumstanced, is much more true of the great majority of mankind who inhabit what we call temperate climates, i. e., climates in which the temperature sometimes falls ten or twenty degrees below the freezing point, and where for several months each year all vegetative functions cease. One winter without art would suffice to sweep the entire population north or south of the thirtieth parallel off the face of the earth.

We are so much accustomed to the terms *labor* and *production* that we rarely stop to think what they really mean. Neither of these terms has any place in animal economics. All labor consists in an artificial transformation of man's environment. Nature *produces* nothing in the politico-economic sense of the word. Production consists in artificially altering the form of natural objects. The clothes we wear are derived chiefly from the sheep, the ox, the silk-worm, and a few other animals, the cotton plant, flax, hemp, and a few other plants; but between the latest stage at which nature leaves these latter and the final form in which they are ready for use there are many transformations requiring much art and great labor. The houses that man inhabits once consisted chiefly of trees, clay, and beds of solid rock. These, too, have been transformed by labor performed with tools and machinery. In like manner the entire cycle of human achievement might be gone through. It would be found everywhere the same.

The arts taken in their ensemble constitute material civilization, and it is this that chiefly distinguishes man from the rest of nature. It is due exclusively to his mind, to the rational or intellectual faculty. That is, it is an exclusively psychological distinction. Civilization, which is human development beyond the animal stage, goes forward under the economics of mind, while animal development takes place under the economics of life. The difference between these two kinds of economics is fundamental. They are not merely dissimilar, they are the direct opposites of each other. The psychologic law tends to reverse the biologic law. This latter law may be briefly defined as *the survival of the best adapted structures.* Those structures which yield most readily to changes in the environment persist. It has therefore been aptly called "survival of the plastic." The environment, though ever changing, does not change to conform to the structures but in the contrary direction, always rendering the partly adapted structures less adapted, and the only organic progress possible is that which accrues through changes of structure that tend to enable organic beings to cope with sterner and ever harder conditions. In any and every case it is the environment that works the changes and the organism that undergoes them. . . .

The prevailing idea is wholly false which claims that it is the fittest possible that survive in this struggle. The effect of competition is to prevent any form from attaining its maximum development, and to maintain a certain comparatively low level of development for all forms that succeed in surviving. This is a normal result of the rhythmic character of all purely natural, i.e., not rational or teleological, phenomena, as explained a few pages back. The greater part of what is gained in the flood tide is lost in the ebb. Wherever competition is wholly removed, as through the agency of man in the interest of any one form, great strides are immediately made by the form thus protected, and it soon outstrips all those that depend upon competition for their motive to advancement. Such has been the case with the cereals and fruit trees, and with domestic animals, in fact, with all the forms of life that man has excepted from the biologic law and subjected to the law of mind. The supposed tendency of such forms to revert to their original wild state, about which so much has been said, is simply their inability when remanded to their pristine competitive struggle to maintain the high position which they had acquired during their halcyon days of exemption from that struggle, which they can no more do than they can attain that position while subjected to it. Competition, therefore, not only involves the enormous waste which has been described, but it prevents the maximum development, since the best that can be attained under its influence is far inferior to that which is easily attained by the artificial, i.e., the rational and intelligent, removal of that influence.

Hard as it seems to be for modern philosophers to understand this, it was one of the first truths that dawned upon the human intellect. Consciously or unconsciously it was felt from the very outset that the mission of mind was to grapple with the law of competition and as far as possible to resist and defeat it. This iron law of nature, as it may be appropriately called (Ricardo's "iron law of wages" is only one manifestation of it), was everywhere found to lie athwart the path of human progress, and the whole upward struggle of rational man, whether physical, social or moral, has been with this tyrant of nature—the law of competition. And in so far as he has progressed at all beyond the purely animal stage he has done so through triumphing little by little over this law and gaining somewhat the mastery in this struggle. In the physical world he has accomplished this so far as he has been able through invention, from which have resulted the arts and material civilization. Every implement or utensil, every mechanical device, every object of design, skill, and labor, every artificial thing that serves a human purpose, is a triumph of mind over the physical forces of nature in ceaseless and aimless competition. The cultivation and improvement of economic plants and the domestication of useful animals involve the direct control of biologic forces and the exemption of these forms of life from the operation of the laws of nature. . . .

. . . The law of nature quickly succumbs to the law of mind, and whether it continues for a time, or whether, as it sooner or later must, it defeats itself and results in monopoly, the general effect on society is the same. If it be regarded as a sad commentary upon the operations of a rational being that there is no escape from the necessity of paying the highest price for everything that will be paid rather than do without, and irrespective of the cost of production, it must be remembered that it is only the individual that is as yet in any proper sense rational. If society itself were rational this would indeed seem absurd, and if it shall ever become so no such absurdity will be tolerated for a moment. Those who compare society to an organism have failed to observe that in this respect it resembles only some of the very lowest Metazoa, such as the hydra, which possesses no proper presiding and coördinating nerve ganglia, or still more closely some of those lower colonies of cells, each of which, like the individual members of society, is practically independent of the general mass except that by the simple fact of coherence a certain degree of protection is secured to both the individual cells and the aggregated mass. And yet many advocate a still greater independence of the individual, and deprecate all steps in the direction of integration, which they know to be the only way in which organic beings can make any progress in organization. So little have the principles of biology impressed themselves upon the students of sociology, even those who profess a synthetic grasp of both fields!

The reader cannot have failed to perceive the fundamental difference between the social phenomena above reviewed and those that take place everywhere in nature below the level of man's rational faculty, and hence, even when dealing with the universal law of competition, an entirely different set of principles must be applied to man from those which can be applied to irrational life. There competition is free, or rather it is pure. It continues as long as the weaker can survive it, and when these at last go to the wall and the better adapted structures survive and triumph, it is the triumph of a real superiority, and the strong and robust alone are left to recruit the earth. But when mind enters into the contest the character of competition is at first completely changed, and later competition itself is altogether crushed out, and while it is still the strong that survive it is a strength which comes from indirection, from deception, artfulness, cunning, and shrewdness, necessarily coupled with stunted moral qualities, and largely aided by the accident of position. In no proper sense is it true that the fittest survive. If this were their only function it is evident that brains would be a positive detriment to society. Pure animal competition would be far better. It is probably the contemplation of the hopelessness of this state of things which has given the gloomy cast to Oriental philosophy, and it is no wonder that those moderns who consider the present order unalterable should maintain that we live in the worst possible universe. Those who can see a surplus of good in things as they are, or can hope for their improvement under the laws of evolution unaided by social intelligence, must be set down as hopelessly blinded by the great optimistic illusion of all life.

While competition is not to be looked upon as a social desideratum, even in its pure animal form, much less in its aggressive human form, free individual activity under the full play of all natural motives is of the utmost importance. Among these motives those of friendly rivalry and honest emulation are legitimate, harmless, and powerful. These competition suppresses; it tends to choke individual freedom and clog the wheels of social progress. How can this true individualism be secured and complete freedom of individual action be vouchsafed? Herein lies a social paradox. It is clear from what has been said that this will never bring itself about. The tendencies are strongly in the opposite direction. Competition is growing more and more aggressive, heated, and ephemeral. Combination is growing more and more universal, powerful and permanent. This is the result of the most complete *laissez faire* policy. The paradox therefore is that *individual freedom can*

only come through social regulation. The coöperative effects of
the rule of mind which annihilate competition can only be
overcome by that still higher form of coöperation which shall
stay the lower form and set free the normal faculties of man.
Free competition that shall be both innocent and beneficial
may be secured to a limited extent in this way and in no other
way. . . .

A new and revised political economy will doubtless be
largely devoted to showing, not so much the glories of competition, which society does not enjoy, as how society may conduct itself in order to secure whatever benefits competition
can offer, and also how the competition that cannot be prevented can be shorn of its wasteful and aggressive features.
Neither should the higher attributes of reason and intelligence
be discouraged. They represent the true elements of civilization and progress. But these, too, should be deprived of their
fangs. The way to counteract the evil effects of mind operating
in the individual is to infuse a larger share of the same mind
element into the controlling power of society. Such a powerful
weapon as reason is unsafe in the hands of one individual
when wielded against another. It is still more dangerous in
the hands of corporations, which proverbially have no souls.[1]
It is most baneful of all in the hands of compound corporations which seek to control the wealth of the world. It is only
safe when employed by the social ego, emanating from the
collective brain of society, and directed toward securing the
common interests of the social organism.

But the object of this chapter was not to point out remedies
for social evils. It was . . . to show that any system of economics which is to deal with rational man must rest upon a
psychologic and not upon a biologic basis. In full view of all
the facts that have been set forth, facts that are for the most

---

[1] "They cannot commit treason, nor be outlawed, nor excommunicate,
for they have no souls."—Sir Edward Coke: Reports, Vol. V, Part X,
32 b, London, 1826, p. 303 (Case of Sutton's Hospital).

part obtrusive and have always been available to all, it is certainly remarkable that there should be any necessity for calling attention to this truth; but the only system of social economics that we possess, and the only social philosophy, other than the one referred to early in this chapter, that has been promulgated, completely ignore it and treat the human animal only as an animal. Not the economic writers alone, but the great philosophers as well, persistently cling to the law of nature and disregard the law of mind. A system of so-called "political economy," in which the *political* aspect, i. e., the relation of the state to society, is for the most part ignored, has grown up and been reduced to a series of dogmatic canons which until recently it was considered next thing to sacrilege to question or criticise. But partly with the increase of general intelligence, whereby the mind element is more clearly seen in industrial and social phenomena, and partly with the increase of critical independence on the part of economic students, the truth has at last begun to emerge that the greater part of these supposed economic axioms are not only open to criticism but positively untrue. So thoroughly current had most of them become that any fact established in opposition to them might appropriately be called a paradox, like some phenomenon that seemed to counteract the law of gravitation. . . . I will introduce here quite a list of the more important cases, preserving the form previously adopted and presenting the propositions which the industrial history of the world has established, although for the most part in direct opposition to the hitherto accepted tenets of political economy. They may therefore continue to go by the name of Economic Paradoxes.

1. Subsistence increases instead of diminishing with population (reversal of the Malthusian dictum).

2. The interest of the individual is rarely the same as that of society.

3. Owing to ignorance of the remote effects of actions men do not always do what is for their own interests.

4. Cheapness is a stronger inducement than quality, and the consumer cannot be depended upon to encourage the better producer.

5. Competition raises prices and rates.

6. Combination often lowers prices and rates.

7. Free competition is only possible under social regulation.

8. Private monopoly can only be prevented by public monopoly.

9. The hope of gain is not always the best motive to industry.

10. Public service will secure better talent than private enterprise for the same outlay.

11. Market values and social values are not identical.

12. The prosperity of a community depends as much upon the mode of consumption as upon the quantity produced.

13. Private enterprise taxes the people more heavily than government does.

14. The social effects of taxation are more important than its fiscal effects.

15. The producer cannot always shift the burden of taxation upon the consumer, e.g., under monopoly and aggressive competition.

16. Protection may reduce the price of the commodity protected, not only in the protecting but even in the importing country.

17. Capital, as embodied in machinery, contributes more than labor to the production of wealth.

18. Wages are drawn from products and not from capital, and the "wage-fund" is a myth.

19. Increase of wages is attended with increase of profits.

20. Prices fall as wages rise.

21. Diminished hours of labor bring increased production.

22. Reduction of the time worked enhances the wages received.

23. A man working alone earns the same as when his wife and children also work.

24. Lowering the rate of interest may lead to increased savings.

G. GOVERNMENT AND THE SOCIAL WILL

It is . . . in the highest degree illogical to argue that the state can never extend its powers. It is the organ of social consciousness and must ever seek to obey the will of society. Whatever society demands it must and always will endeavor to supply. If it fails at first it will continue to try until success at last crowns its efforts. If it is ignorant it will educate itself, if in no other way by the method of trial and error. Higher and higher types of statesmanship will follow the advancing intelligence of mankind, until one by one the difficult social problems will be solved. It is useless to maintain that the functions of government are necessarily limited to the few that have thus far been undertaken. The only limit is that of the good of society, and as long as there is any additional way in which that object can be secured through governmental action such action will be taken.

It seems scarcely worth while to notice the exceedingly narrow attitude of a certain class of persons who habitually speak of government as if it were something foreign to the people and hostile to the true interests of society. If there have been cases in which the ruling class wholly mistook their relations to society and seemed for brief periods and in certain countries to justify such a view, events have soon taught them better; and even where a king has imagined that he was the state he was at that moment only a servant of the social will, refusal to obey which would cost him and his descendants their title to power or their lives. But such views are especially meaningless in modern times when governments have become so extremely sensitive to the social will that a single adverse vote will overthrow a cabinet, and where appeals are every year taken to the suffrage of the people. . . . This country is to-day fully ripe for a series of important national reforms which cannot be made because a comparatively small number of influential citizens oppose them. Conservatism, fear of disapproval, and general timidity before the people, who are recognized as the real government, characterize the legislation of all modern nations. In order to the introduction and adoption of any reform measure it is necessary that the public will shall have been positively and emphatically made known. But when this is done in an unmistakable manner, such measures are often pushed through with much too great alacrity. Government is becoming more and more the organ of social consciousness, and more and more the servant of the social will. Our declaration of independence which recites that government derives its just powers from the "consent" of the governed has already been outgrown. It is no longer the consent but the positively known will of the governed from which government now derives its powers. . . . The social intellect should . . . first and foremost, grapple with the whole problem of reducing the social friction. Every wheel in the entire social machinery should be carefully scrutinized with the practiced eye of the skilled artisan, with a view to discovering the true nature of the friction and of removing all that is not required by a perfect system.

With regard to the method by which all this may be made practicable a final word may be indulged in. Before any such sweeping social regeneration as that which is here hinted at can be inaugurated a great change must be wrought in the whole theory of legislation. It must be recognized that the legislator is essentially an inventor and a scientific discoverer. His duty is to be thoroughly versed in the whole theory and practice of social physics. He is called upon to devise "ways and means" for securing the true interests and improvements of the people for whom he is to legislate. This obviously cannot be done by existing methods. A public assembly governed by parliamentary rules is as inadequate a method as could well be conceived of for anything like scientific legislation. Imagine all the inventors in the country assembled in a hall acting under the gavel of a presiding officer to devise the machines of the future and adopt the best by a majority vote! Or think of trying to advance scientific discovery by a general convention! Scientific associations there are, usually for the reading of papers setting forth the discoveries made by the members in their laboratories, and there would be no objection to this class of legislative assemblies. But in the latter case as in the former, the real work, the thought, research, observation, experimentation, and discovery of laws and principles of nature must be done elsewhere, under appropriate conditions, in the great field or in the private cabinet.

It may at first glance seem absurd to propose that legislation be done in any such way, but a little reflection will show that it is not only not absurd, but that there is at this moment a strong tendency in all enlightened countries toward its adoption. It is a well known fact that at the present time the greater part of the real legislation is done by committees. The members of legislative committees are carefully chosen with reference to their known fitness for the different subjects intrusted to them. These committees really *deliberate*. They investigate the questions before them, hear testimony and petitions, and weigh evidence for and against every proposed measure. This is truly scientific and leads to the discovery of the principles involved. Unless biased by partisan leanings they are very likely to reach the truth and report practical and useful measures. The body to which these committees belong respect their decisions and usually adopt their recommendations. The other members usually know very little about the merits of the questions, or at least, not having studied them, they defer to the superior judgment of those who have. Committee work is, therefore, the nearest approach we have to the scientific investigation of social questions. It is on the increase, and is destined to play an ever increasing rôle in national legislation.

There is one other important way in which the social intellect is being applied to human affairs. The theory is that the executive branch of government merely administers national affairs. This is a great mistake. A very large part of the real legislation of a country is done by the executive branch. The various bureaus of government are in position to feel the popular pulse more sensitively than the legislature. The officers charged with their administration become identified with certain industries and are appealed to by the public to adopt needed reforms. After stepping to the verge of their legal authority in response to such demands, whereby much real legislation is done not contemplated by those who framed the laws under which these bureaus were established, they finish by making recommendations of the rest to the law-making power. This latter usually recognizes the wisdom of such recommendations and enacts them into laws, thus ever enlarging the administrative jurisdiction of government. Such legislation is in a true sense scientific. It is based on a knowledge both of the needs of the public and of the best means of supplying them. It has been subjected to thoughtful consideration and mature judgment. It is a method that is being every year more and more employed, and its results are usually successful and permanent.

History furnishes the statesman an additional basis for legislation. It is now possible to acquire a knowledge of the industrial history of nations, not complete, it is true, because so much was lost during the period when history was supposed to relate exclusively to the operations of the state and those who stood at its head, but sufficiently full to serve as a valuable guide to the legislator. No man should consider himself qualified to legislate for a people who is not conversant with the history of modern nations at least, with their various systems of finance, revenue, taxation, public works, education, land surveying, patent and copyright law, military and naval equipment, general jurisprudence and constitutional, statute, and unwritten law. It will, of course, be said that very few legislators are thus informed, and this is true, but these few will be the ones who will do most to shape the action of the state and will furnish examples to all who aspire to play a leading part in the political drama.

Again there is the statistical method. No one will deny that this is rapidly becoming a leading factor in legislation. Statistics are simply the facts that underlie the science of government. They are to the legislator what the results of observation and experiment are to the man of science. They are in fact the inductions of political science, and the inductive method in that science is of the same value that it is to science in general, its only true foundation. There is no great state at this day that does not make an effort to collect statistics; in most of the leading nations of the world this is now done on an extensive scale. A census, which a short time ago was merely an enumeration of the population of a state, now means an exhaustive inquiry into its entire vital, industrial, and commercial condition. In this and many other ways governments furnish to their legislators the most important facts required to guide them in the adoption of the measures needful for the prosperity of the people.

There are many . . . ways in which the tendency toward scientific legislation is steadily growing, and, without indulging in any undue optimism on the subject, the fact may be considered established that no revolution is necessary in the character of society in order to bring about the gradual transformation required to realize all that has been foreshadowed in this chapter. The machinery already exists for the needed reformation and all that is necessary is that it be under the control of the developed social intellect. The quality of statesmanship is increasing. More thought is being devoted to the deeper questions of state and of society than ever before, and the signs of healthy progress are unmistakable. A modern Solon, paraphrasing the oft-quoted saying of the ancient one, has defined a statesman as "a successful politician who is dead." He doubtless intended to rebuke the tendency of every age to vilify public men while they are living and canonize them after they are dead. And it would be well if, not only those who stand at the helm of the ship of state at any given period, but also the achievements of this directive social intellect in guiding that ship into smoother waters, were looked at from the standpoint of some remote future date and estimated in the light of the history which is being made.

H. "THE INDIVIDUAL HAS REIGNED LONG ENOUGH"

. . . Physiocracy, as a habit of thought rather than a form of government, now goes by the name of individualism, and is carried so far by many as to amount to a practical anarchism, reducing all government to the action of so-called natural laws.

The general result is that the world, having passed through the stages of autocracy and aristocracy into the stage of democracy, has, by a natural reaction against personal power, so far minimized the governmental influence that the same spirit which formerly used government to advance self is now ushering in a fifth stage, viz., that of *plutocracy,* which thrives well in connection with a weak democracy or physiocracy, and aims to supersede it entirely. Its strongest hold is the widespread distrust of all government, and it leaves no stone unturned to fan the flame of misarchy. Instead of demanding more and stronger government it demands less and feebler. Shrewdly clamoring for individual liberty, it perpetually holds up the outrages committed by governments in their autocratic and aristocratic stages, and falsely insists that there is imminent danger of their reënactment. *Laissez faire* and the most extreme individualism, bordering on practical anarchy in all except the enforcement of existing proprietary rights, are loudly advocated, and the public mind is thus blinded to the real condition of things. The system of political economy that

---

Psychic Factors of Civilization, pp. 319–327.

sprang up in France and England at the close of the aristo-cratic stage in those countries is still taught in the higher insti-tutions of learning. It is highly favorable to the spread of plutocracy, and is pointed to by those who are to profit by that system of government as the invincible scientific foundation upon which it rests. Many honest political economists are still lured by the specious claims of this system and continue to uphold it, and at least one important treatise on social science, that of Herbert Spencer, defends it to the most extreme length. Thus firmly intrenched, it will require a titanic effort on the part of society to dislodge this baseless prejudice, and rescue itself once more from the rapacious jaws of human egoism under the crafty leadership of a developed and instructed rational faculty.

Under the system as it now exists the wealth of the world, however created, and irrespective of the claims of the pro-ducer, is made to flow toward certain centers of accumulation, to be enjoyed by those holding the keys to such situations. The world appears to be approaching a stage at which those who labor, no matter how skilled, how industrious, or how frugal, will receive, according to the "iron law" formulated by Ri-cardo, only so much for their services as will enable them "to subsist and to perpetuate their race." The rest finds its way into the hands of a comparatively few, usually non-producing, individuals, whom the usages and laws of all countries permit to claim that they own the very sources of all wealth and the right to allow or forbid its production.

These are great and serious evils, compared with which all the crimes, recognized as such, that would be committed if no government existed, would be as trifles. The underpaid labor, the prolonged and groveling drudgery, the wasted strength, the misery and squalor, the diseases resulting, and the prema-ture deaths that would be prevented by a just distribution of the products of labor, would in a single year outweigh all the so-called crime of a century, for the prevention of which, it is said, government alone exists. This vast theater of woe is regarded as wholly outside the jurisdiction of government, while the most strenuous efforts are put forth to detect and punish the perpetrators of the least of the ordinary recognized crimes. This ignoring of great evils while so violently striking at small ones is the mark of an effete civilization, and warns us of the approaching dotage of the race.

Against the legitimate action of government in the protection of society from these worst of its evils, the instinctive hostility to government, or misarchy, above described, powerfully militates. In the face of it the government hesitates to take action, however clear the right or the method. But, as already remarked, this groundless over-caution against an impossible occurrence would not, in and of itself, have sufficed to prevent government from redressing such palpable wrongs. It has been nursed and kept alive for a specific purpose. It has formed the chief argument of those whose interests require the maintenance of the existing social order in relation to the distribution of wealth. Indeed, it is doubtful whether, without the incessant reiteration given to it by this class, it could have persisted to the present time. This inequitable economic system has itself been the product of centuries of astute management on the part of the shrewdest heads, with a view to securing by legal devices that undue share of the world's products which was formerly the reward of superior physical strength. It is clear to this class that their interests require a policy of strict non-interference on the part of government in what they call the natural laws of political economy, and they are quick to see that the old odium that still lingers among the people can be made a bulwark of strength for their position. They therefore never lose an opportunity to appeal to it in the most effective manner. Through the constant use of this *argumentum ad populum* the anti-government sentiment, which would naturally have smoldered and died out after its cause ceased to exist, is kept perpetually alive.

The great evils under which society now labors have grown up during the progress of intellectual supremacy. They have crept in stealthily during the gradual encroachment or organized cunning upon the domain of brute force. Over that vanishing domain, government retains its power, but it is still powerless in the expanding and now all-embracing field of psychic influence. No one ever claimed that in the trial of physical strength the booty should fall to the strongest. In all such cases the arm of government is stretched out and justice is enforced. But in those manifold, and far more unequal struggles now going on between mind and mind, or rather between the individual and an organized system, the product of ages of thought, it is customary to say that such matters must be left to regulate themselves, and that the fittest must be allowed to survive. Yet, to anyone who will candidly consider the matter, it must be clear that the first and principal acts of government openly and avowedly prevented, through forcible interference, the natural results of all trials of physical strength. These much-talked-of laws of nature are violated every time the highway robber is arrested and sent to jail.

Primitive government, when only brute force was employed, was strong enough to secure the just and equitable distribution of wealth. To-day, when mental force is everything, and physical force is nothing, it is powerless to accomplish this. This alone proves that government needs to be strengthened in its primary quality—the protection of society. There is no reasoning that applies to one kind of protection that does not apply equally to the other. It is utterly illogical to say that aggrandizement by physical force should be forbidden while aggrandizement by mental force or legal fiction should be permitted. It is absurd to claim that injustice committed by muscle should be regulated, while that committed by brain should be unrestrained.

While the modern plutocracy is not a form of government in the same sense that the other forms mentioned are, it is, nevertheless, easy to see that its power is as great as any government has ever wielded. The test of governmental power is usually the manner in which it taxes the people, and the strongest indictments ever drawn up against the worst forms of tyranny have been those which recited their oppressive methods of extorting tribute. But tithes are regarded as oppressive, and a fourth part of the yield of any industry would justify a revolt. Yet to-day there are many commodities for which the people pay two and three times as much as would cover the cost of production, transportation, and exchange at fair wages and fair profits. The monopolies in many lines actually tax the consumer from 25 to 75 per cent of the real value of the goods. Imagine an excise tax that should approach these figures! . . . Under the operation of either monopoly or aggressive competition the price of everything is pushed up to the maximum limit that will be paid for the commodity in profitable quantities, and this wholly irrespective of the cost of production. No government in the world has now, or ever had, the power to enforce such an extortion as this. It is a governing power in the interest of favored individuals, which exceeds that of the most powerful monarch or despot that ever wielded a scepter.

What then is the remedy? How can society escape this last conquest of power by the egoistic intellect? It has overthrown the rule of brute force by the establishment of government. It has supplanted autocracy by aristocracy and this by democracy, and now it finds itself in the coils of plutocracy. Can it escape? Must it go back to autocracy for a power sufficient to cope with plutocracy? No autocrat ever had a tithe of that power. Shall it then let itself be crushed? It need not. There is one power and only one that is greater than that which now chiefly rules society. That power is society itself. There is one form of government that is stronger than autocracy or aristocracy or democracy, or even plutocracy, and that is *sociocracy.*

The individual has reigned long enough. The day has come for society to take its affairs into its own hands and shape its own destinies. The individual has acted as best he could. He has acted in the only way he could. With a consciousness, will, and intellect of his own he could do nothing else than pursue his natural ends. He should not be denounced nor called any names. He should not even be blamed. Nay, he should be praised, and even *imitated.* Society should learn its great lesson from him, should follow the path he has so clearly laid out that leads to success. It should imagine itself an individual, with all the interests of an individual, and becoming fully *conscious* of these interests it should pursue them with the same indomitable *will* with which the individual pursues his interests. Not only this, it must be guided, as he is guided, by the social *intellect,* armed with all the knowledge that all individuals combined, with so great labor, zeal, and talent have placed in its possession, constituting the social intelligence.

Sociocracy will differ from all other forms of government that have been devised, and yet that difference will not be so radical as to require a revolution. Just as absolute monarchy passed imperceptibly into limited monarchy, and this, in many states without even a change of name has passed into more or less pure democracy, so democracy is capable of passing as smoothly into sociocracy, and without taking on this unfamiliar name or changing that by which it is now known. For, though paradoxical, democracy, which is now the weakest of all forms of government, at least in the control of its own internal elements, is capable of becoming the strongest. Indeed, none of the other forms of government would be capable of passing directly into a government by society. Democracy is a phase through which they must first pass on any route that leads to the ultimate social stage which all governments must eventually attain if they persist.

How then, it may be asked, do democracy and sociocracy

differ? How does society differ from the people? If the phrase "the people" really meant the people, the difference would be less. But that shibboleth of democratic states, where it means anything at all that can be described or defined, stands simply for the majority of qualified electors, no matter how small that majority may be. There is a sense in which the action of a majority may be looked upon as the action of society. At least, there is no denying the right of the majority to act for society, for to do this would involve either the denial of the right of government to act at all, or the admission of the right of a minority to act for society. But a majority acting for society is a different thing from society acting for itself, even though, as must always be the case, it acts through an agency chosen by its members. All democratic governments are largely party governments. The electors range themselves on one side or the other of some party line, the winning side considers itself the state as much as Louis the Fourteenth did. The losing party usually then regards the government as something alien to it and hostile, like an invader, and thinks of nothing but to gain strength enough to overthrow it at the next opportunity. While various issues are always brought forward and defended or attacked, it is obvious to the looker-on that the contestants care nothing for these, and merely use them to gain an advantage and win an election.

From the standpoint of society this is child's play. A very slight awakening of the social consciousness will banish it and substitute something more business-like. Once get rid of this puerile gaming spirit and have attention drawn to the real interests of society, and it will be seen that upon nearly all important questions all parties and all citizens are agreed, and that there is no need of this partisan strain upon the public energies. This is clearly shown at every change in the party complexion of the government. The victorious party which has been denouncing the government merely because it was in the hands of its political opponents boasts that it is going to revolutionize the country in the interest of good government, but the moment it comes into power and feels the weight of national responsibility it finds that it has little to do but carry out the laws in the same way that its predecessors had been doing.

There is a vast difference between all this outward show of partisanship and advocacy of so-called principles, and attention to the real interests and necessary business of the nation, which latter is what the government must do. It is a social duty. The pressure which is brought to enforce it is the power of the social will. But in the factitious excitement of partisan struggles where professional politicians and demagogues on the one hand, and the agents of plutocracy on the other, are shouting discordantly in the ears of the people, the real interests of society are, temporarily at least, lost sight of, clouded and obscured, and men lose their grasp on the real issues, forget even their own best interests, which, however selfish, would be a far safer guide, and the general result usually is that these are neglected and nations continue in the hands of mere politicians who are easily managed by the shrewd representatives of wealth.

Sociocracy will change all this. Irrelevant issues will be laid aside. The important objects upon which all but an interested few are agreed will receive their proper degree of attention, and measures will be considered in a non-partisan spirit with the sole purpose of securing these objects. Take as an illustration the postal telegraph question. No one not a stockholder in an existing telegraph company would prefer to pay twenty-five cents for a message if he could send it for ten cents. Where is the room for discussing a question of this nature? What society wants is the cheapest possible system. It wants to know with certainty whether a national postal telegraph system would secure this universally desired object. It is to be expected that the agents of the present telegraph companies would try to show that it would not succeed. This is according to the known laws of psychology as set forth in this work. But why be influenced by the interests of such a small number of persons, however worthy, when all the rest of mankind are interested in the opposite solution? The investigation should be a disinterested and strictly scientific one, and should actually settle the question in one way or the other. If it was found to be a real benefit, the system should be adopted. There are to-day a great number of these strictly social questions before the American people, questions which concern every citizen in the country, and whose solution would doubtless profoundly affect the state of civilization attainable on this continent. Not only is it impossible to secure this, but it is impossible to secure an investigation of them on their real merits. The same is true of other countries, and in general the prevailing democracies of the world are incompetent to deal with problems of social welfare.

The more extreme and important case referred to a few pages back may make the distinction still more clear. It was shown, and is known to all political economists, that the prices of most of the staple commodities consumed by mankind have no necessary relation to the cost of producing them and placing them in the hands of the consumer. It is always the highest price that the consumer will pay rather than do without. Let us suppose that price to be on an average double what it would cost to produce, transport, exchange, and deliver the goods, allowing in each of these transactions a fair compensation for all services rendered. Is there any member of society who would prefer to pay two dollars for what is thus fairly worth only one? Is there any sane ground for arguing such a question? Certainly not. The individual cannot correct this state of things. No democracy can correct it. But a government that really represented the interests of society would no more tolerate it than an individual would tolerate a continual extortion of money on the part of another without an equivalent.

And so it would be throughout. Society would inquire in a

business way without fear, favor, or bias, into everything that concerned its welfare, and if it found obstacles it would remove them, and if it found opportunities it would improve them. In a word, society would do under the same circumstances just what an intelligent individual would do. It would further, in all possible ways, its own interests.

15

PLUTOCRACY

AND PATERNALISM

1895

Although Ward prided himself on his ability to remain aloof from the swirling currents of politics, he did from time to time lend aid and comfort to the forces of reform. Notwithstanding his protest of scholarly objectivity, there can be little doubt that this frontal attack upon the misdeeds of the American plutocracy was part of the larger campaign for social justice that we associate with Altgeld and La Follette, Henry George and Henry Demarest Lloyd. This article first appeared in THE FORUM, *then one of the more liberal American magazines.*

To judge from the tone of the popular press, the country would seem to be between the devil of state interference and the deep sea of gold. The two epithets, "plutocracy" and "paternalism," so freely applied, are intended to characterize the worst tendencies of the times in these two opposite directions, and are calculated to engender the bitterest feelings in

---

"Plutocracy and Paternalism," *The Forum,* XX (November 1895), in *Glimpses of the Cosmos,* V, 300–310.

the public mind. If such a thing were possible, it would certainly be useful, standing aloof from the contest, to make a cool, unbiassed analysis of the true meaning of these terms in their relation to the existing state of affairs. While it may be admitted that this is impossible, such an approximation to it as the conditions will allow can certainly do no harm.

On all subjects that interest mankind there are extremes of thought, and these form a sort of penumbra outside the general consensus of opinion among right-minded people. While most persons consider the possession of wealth a rightful condition and a laudable aim of life, there are some who accept Proudhon's dictum, "*la propriété c'est le vol*," and nearly all shades of opinion between these may be found. The average man desires to see the business interests of society left free and open to equal competition, but there are those who would have the state conduct all industry and make all citizens salaried employees. Between these views there are also many intermediate ones. This condition has always existed very much as it is to-day. On the whole there seems to be little danger that any of the extremes of popular opinion will ever prevail, but at the same time there is always a moderate, often rhythmic, drift in some direction, so that what were extremes are so no longer, and other unthought-of schemes occupy the van. It is this that constitutes social progress.

Justly or unjustly, society has made wealth a measure of worth. It is easy on general principles to prove that it is not such a measure. Every one is personally cognizant of numerous cases to the contrary. All will admit that, taken in the abstract, the principle is unsound, and yet all act upon it. Not rationally, not perhaps consciously, but still they do it. It is "human nature" to respect those who have, and to care little for those who have not. There is a sort of feeling that if one is destitute there must be a reason for it. It is inevitably ascribed to some personal deficit. In a word, absence of means is, in one form or another, made to stand for absence of merit. Its cause is looked for in character. This is most clearly seen in the marked contrast between the indisposition to help the unsuccessful, and the willingness to help the successful. Aside from the prospect of a *quid pro quo,* no one wants to waste time, energy, or money on what is worthless,—and possession is the primary test of worth.

It would be easy to work out the genesis of this sentiment, and to show how it is the natural result of the universal competition in society, where the fittest to survive is always the one who can gain possession of the greatest amount of this world's goods. It has therefore a rational basis, a substratum of truth on which to rest. We are chiefly concerned with it here as a fact. It is universal. Those who most thoroughly condemn it are influenced by it. The force that works against it in society is not the absence or weakness of the sentiment itself, but another and wholly dissimilar feeling, viz., sympathy. This sentiment is not rational, but illogical, as shown by the fact that men give alms to satisfy temporary want rather than opportunity to supply permanent needs. But of the other sentiment, which may be called "plutolatry,"—the worship of wealth,—even the victims show traces, and in denouncing the rich they unconsciously attribute to them a personal dignity proportional to their wealth.

Thus it comes about that wealth, in the existing state of society, is a tremendous power. It gives not only ease, plenty, luxury, but, what is infinitely more, the respect of all and the envy of the less favored. It gives, in a word, superiority; and the strongest craving of man's nature is, in one way or another, to be set over his fellows. When all this is considered, the futility of the proposal of certain reformers to eradicate the passion for proprietary acquisition becomes apparent. It may be assumed that this passion will continue for an indefinite period to be the ruling element of the industrial state. That it has done and is still doing incalculable service to society few will deny. That it may continue to be useful to the end of our present industrial era will probably be admitted by all but a small class.

If the accumulation of wealth, even for the benefit of individuals, were all that is involved in the term "plutocracy," the indictment would not be serious. If the governing power implied in the last component of the word were nothing more than the normal influence that wealth exerts, no great injury to society could accrue. Even the amassing of colossal fortunes is not an evil in itself, since the very activity which it requires stimulates industry and benefits a large number. There is, it is true, a danger—in the transmission of such fortunes to inactive and non-productive heirs—of creating a non-industrial class in perpetuity; but this could be remedied, without hardship to any worthy person, by a wise limitation of inheritance.

So much for plutocracy. Let us now turn to the other pole of public opinion and inquire into the meaning of "paternalism." Literally, of course, paternalism in government would be restricted to cases in which the governing power is vested in a single person, who may be regarded as well-disposed and seeking to rule his subjects for their own good, as a father governs his children. But a ruling family, or even a large ruling class, may be supposed to govern from similar motives. In either case the governed are not supposed to have any voice in the matter, but are cared for like children by the assumed wisdom of their rulers. How far from true paternalism is anything that exists in this or any other civilized country to-day may therefore be readily seen. No one will claim that there is any danger, in a representative government with universal suffrage, of any such state being brought about. This shows at the outset that the term is not used in its original and correct sense, but is merely borrowed and applied as a stigma to certain tendencies in republican governments which the users of it do not approve. What are these tendencies? In general it may be said that they are tendencies toward the assumption by the state of functions that are now entrusted to private enterprise.

On the one hand it is logically argued that the indefinite extension of such powers would eventuate in the most extreme socialistic system,—the conduct of all business by the state. On the other hand it is shown with equal logic that the entire relinquishment of the functions which the state has already assumed would be the abolition of government itself. The extremists of one party would land us in socialism; those of the other, in anarchy. But on one side it is said by the more moderate that the true function of government is the protection of society; to which it is replied by the other that such extension of governmental powers is in the interest of protection, viz., protection against the undue rapacity of private enterprise. Here, as almost everywhere else in the realm of politics, it is a question of quantity and not of quality. It is not a difference in principle, but in policy. It is the degree to which the fundamental principle of all government is to be carried out.

If we look for precedents and historical examples we find great diversity. If we take the question of government telegraphy we find that the United States is almost the only country in the civilized world that has not adopted it, while the reports from other countries are practically unanimous in its favor. That such a movement should be called paternalism is therefore quite gratuitous, and must spring from either pecuniary interest or unenlightened prejudice. From this on, up to the question of abolishing the private ownership of land, there is a multitude of problems presenting all shades of difference in the degree to which the principle of state action is to be applied in their solution. They need to be fearlessly investigated, coolly considered, and wisely decided in the true interests of the public. It was not the purpose of this article to discuss any of these questions, but simply to mention them in illustration of the popular use of the term "paternalism." It is clear that that term is employed solely to excite prejudice against the extension of the functions of the state, just as the term "plutocracy" is used to arouse antagonism to the wealthy classes. The words have in these senses no natural meaning, and, with intelligent persons, should have no argumentative weight.

Are there, then, no dangerous or deleterious tendencies in modern society? There certainly are such, and they may be said to be in the direction of both plutocracy and paternalism, giving to these terms not a literal, but a real or scientific meaning, as denoting respectively the too great power of wealth, and the too great solicitude for and fostering of certain interests on the part of government.

The first law of economics is that every one may be depended upon at all times to seek his greatest gain. It is both natural and right that the individual should be ever seeking to acquire for himself and his; and this rather irrespective of the rest of the world. It was so in the olden time, when physical strength was almost the only force. It is so to-day, when business shrewdness is practically supreme. Government was instituted to protect the weak from the strong in this universal struggle to possess; or, what is the same thing, to protect society at large. Originally it was occupied solely with abuses caused by brute force. It is still, so far as this primary function of enforcing justice is concerned, practically limited to this class of abuses, relatively trifling as they are. Crime still means this, as it did in the days of King Arthur, and as it does to-day in barbaric countries. Any advantage gained by force is promptly met by the law; but advantage gained by cunning, by superior knowledge,—if it be only of the technicalities of the law,—is not a crime, though its spirit be as bad as that of highway robbery and its consequences a thousand times worse.

From this point of view, then, modern society is suffering

from the very opposite of paternalism,—from under-government, from the failure of government to keep pace with the change which civilization has wrought in substituting intellectual for physical qualities as the workers of injustice. Government to-day is powerless to perform its primary and original function of protecting society. There was a time when brigandage stalked abroad throughout Europe and no one was safe in life or property. This was due to lack of adequate government. Man's nature has not changed, but brigandage has succumbed to the strong arm of the law. Human rapacity now works in subtler ways. Plutocracy is the modern brigandage and can be dislodged only by the same power,—the power of the state. All the evils of society are the result of the free flow of natural propensities. The purpose of government is, as far as may be, to prevent this from causing injustice. The physical passions of men are natural and healthy, but they cannot be allowed to go unbridled. Government was established, not to lessen or even to alter them. Exactly the same is needed to be done with the higher acquisitive faculty. It need not be condemned; it cannot be suppressed: but it can and should be directed into harmless ways and restricted to useful purposes. Properly viewed, too, this is to secure its maximum exercise and greatest freedom, for unrestrained license soon leads to conflict, chokes its own free operation, and puts an end to its activity. The true function of government is not to fetter but to liberate the forces of society, not to diminish but to increase their effectiveness. Unbridled competition destroys itself. The only competition that endures is that which goes on under judicious regulation.

If, then, the danger of plutocracy is so largely due to insufficient government, where is the tendency to paternalism in the sense of too much government? This opens up the last and most important aspect of the subject. If there were no influences at work in society but those of unaided nature; if we had a pure physiocracy or government of nature, such as prevails among wild animals, and the weak were thereby sacrificed that the strong might survive to beget the strong, and thus elevate the race along the lines of evolution,—however great the hardship, we might resign ourselves to it as part of the great cosmic scheme. But unfortunately this is not the case. Without stopping to show that, from the standpoint of a civilized society, the qualities which best fit men to gain advantage over their fellows are the ones least useful to society at large, it will be sufficient for the present purpose to point out that in the actual state of society it is not even those who, from this biological point of view, are the fittest, that become in fact the recipients of the greatest favors at the hands of society. This is due to the creation, by society itself, of artificial conditions that destroy the balance of forces and completely nullify all the beneficial effects that are secured by the operation of the natural law on the lower plane. Indeed, the effect is reversed, and instead of developing strength, either physical or mental, through activity incident to emulation, it tends to parasitic degeneracy through the pampered idleness of the favored classes.

What, in the last analysis, are these social conditions? They are at bottom integral parts of government. They are embodied in law. Largely they consist of statute law. Where this is wanting they rest on judicial decisions, often immemorial, and belonging to the *lex non scripta*. In a word, they constitute the great system of jurisprudence relating to property and business, gradually built up through the ages to make men secure in their possessions and safe in their business transactions, but which in our day, owing to entirely changed industrial conditions, has become the means of throwing unlimited opportunities in the way of some and of barring out the rest from all opportunities. This system of artificial props, bolsterings, and scaffoldings has grown so perfect as to make exertion needless for the protected class and hopeless for the neglected mass. In a word, it has become the bulwark of monopoly. Says Prof. John R. Commons in his "Distribution of Wealth":

"The heads of industries are no longer the independent Napoleons of finance; they find their sphere as high-salaried managers and legal advisers, while the successors of the *entrepreneurs* proper, the original organizers and promoters of enterprises, are simply the commonplace, idle recipients of the permanent profits and the mildly fluctuating temporary profits. . . . Instead of the profits being due to the powerful exertions and abilities of the captains of industry, they are due to certain fixed social relations and rights. The recipients of these incomes may with perfect security become idlers and drones. They abdicate their functions as *entrepreneurs* into the hands of salaried chiefs and advisers. They are no longer performing the services of society which were performed by their ancestors or predecessors, who organized and developed the business to which they have succeeded."

And thus we have the remarkable fact, so persistently overlooked in all the discussions of current questions, that government, which fails to protect the weak, is devoting all its energies to protecting the strong. It legalizes and promotes trusts and combinations; subsidizes corporations, and then absolves them from their obligations; sustains stock-watering schemes and all forms of speculation; grants without compensation the most valuable franchises, often in perpetuity; and in innumerable ways creates, defends, and protects a vast array of purely parasitic enterprises, calculated directly to foster the worst forms of municipal corruption. The proofs of each one of these counts lie about us on every hand. Only those who are blinded by interest or prejudice can fail to see them.

There is no greater danger to civilization than the threatened absorption by a few individuals of all the natural resources of the earth, so that they can literally extort tribute from the rest of mankind. If half a dozen persons could get possession of all the breadstuffs of a country, it would justify a revolution.

Fortunately, from the nature of this product, this is impossible, although long strides in that direction have from time to time been taken. But it is otherwise with some other products which, if less indispensable, are still among the modern necessaries of life. All the petroleum of this country is owned by a single trust. If men could not live without it there is no telling how high the price would be raised. Nothing limits it but the question of how much the public will pay rather than do without. That indispensable product, coal, has well-nigh reached the same stage through the several railroad combinations that now control it. That which costs sixty cents to mine, and as much more to transport, cannot be obtained by the consumer for less than five or six dollars. Does it speak well for the common sense of a great people that they should continue to submit to such things? There seems to be no remedy except in the power of the nation.

It is time, too, that the people began to look into the great question of transportation. If a thorough investigation should show that the hour is not yet come for the public management of the vast enterprises involved, it would at least show, as it has done in England, France, Germany, and nearly all the other countries of Europe, that they are in need of thorough and systematic regulation. Does any one, for example, suppose that there is any permanent advantage in the railroad rate-wars that are so frequently waged in this country? The low cut-rates are always of short duration, and the result is the ultimate combination of the interests involved, usually followed by higher rates than before. And why should several companies be allowed to build parallel lines between the same points, like the three between Philadelphia and Atlantic City, when one is abundantly sufficient to supply the traffic? Is it not clear that the public must pay this unnecessary expense? Would it be any infringement of human liberty for the state to forbid the construction of a railroad for the sole purpose of being sold to another that had no use for it except to get it out of its way? In France nothing of the kind is allowed, and the railroad system of that country is under strict and rational state regulation; yet no one complains of oppression.

One of the greatest needs of an industrious people is a safe and profitable investment of their surplus earnings. In the existing condition of things they are driven into the stock-market. In a few rare cases the stocks taken prove good. In still rarer cases—such as the first telephone shares—they become enormously productive. But in the great majority of cases they first fluctuate and finally fall below par, often to a mere nominal value. There seems to be nothing to prevent the directors of these concerns from manipulating the shares so as first to enrich themselves and then to leave the business a wreck. Witness the degeneracy of the great Thompson-Houston Electric Company, its absorption of other properties, its passage into the General Electric Company, the suspension of dividends, and the fall of the stock to thirty-five cents on a dollar. It may be said that those who choose to risk these losses should suffer for their folly. But there is nothing that is safe. Savings banks are even more precarious, for here failure results in total loss to the depositor. And there seems to be nothing to prevent the legal authorization of all kinds of investment schemes to tempt the public to entrust them with its money, until the organizers think they have all they want and can afford to "fail" and retire with it. If the state cannot really require a safe guaranty to investors, or prohibit such insecure organizations, it can at least offer, in the form of national savings banks, an opportunity for prudent people to make a safe disposition of their surplus funds; and this has been done in nearly every country except the United States.

One of the most crying evils of the times is the reckless manner in which the most important franchises are being given away. The following statement made by Mr. W. C. Dodge, President of the Associated Charities of the District of Columbia, in his annual address of December, 1891, has not, to my knowledge, been answered or denied. It is to be taken merely as a sample of what is going on throughout the country:

Here are seven street railroad companies, two gas companies, two telegraph companies, two telephone companies, and one electric-light company, not one of which gave a cent for their valuable franchises, and the whole amount of taxes paid by these fourteen corporations the past year is but $98,321.45,—a mere trifle as compared with the value of their franchises and the profits drawn by them from the public. Some have never paid in the full amount of their capital stock, and yet pay dividends and extend their works from their profits, while the stock of others is quoted on the market as from 100 to 400 per cent premium.

It is well known that in almost every country of Europe these franchises, based on "natural monopolies," are made to constitute one of the principal sources of revenue.

The "burning question" of our day is the reform of municipal government. The evils complained of all result from the same cause as the national evils already enumerated, which is at bottom the indifference of the citizen to what is being done by self-seeking individuals. Here, as everywhere, personal greed is laying the public under tribute. Individualism is supreme. Party politics are shrewdly brought in to obscure public interests, and behind this veil abuses go unperceived. The cities, as well as the nation at large, need to wake from the lethargy of *laissez faire,* and to take matters into their own hands. They would do well to begin with a study of the recent policy of the London County Council, and, if they doubted its efficacy, they would only need to pay a visit to the "Greater London." Some idea of what there is to be learned in this direction is given in a paper read by Mr. Sydney Webb, in August last, before the British Association for the Advancement of Science.

The very possession of wealth is only made possible by government. The safe conduct of all business depends upon the certain protection of law. The most powerful business combinations take place under legal forms. Even dishonest and swindling schemes, so long as they violate no penal statute, are protected by law. Speculation in the necessaries of life is legitimate business, and is upheld by the officers of the law though it result in famine; and even then bread riots are put down by the armed force of the state. Thus has society become the victim of its own system, against the natural effects of which it is powerless to protect itself. It has devised the best possible scheme for satisfying the rapacity of human nature.

And now, mark: The charge of paternalism is chiefly made by the class that enjoys the largest share of government protection. Those who denounce state interference are the ones who most frequently and successfully invoke it. The cry of *laissez faire* mainly goes up from the ones who, if really "let alone," would instantly lose their wealth-absorbing power.

A significant example of this is found in some of the provisions of the so-called Pooling Bill. In a paper read by the Hon. Carroll D. Wright before the American Economic Association in December last, he characterizes this as "state-socialistic," and says:

This pending legislation is demanded at the instance of the shippers and the railroads of the country, and its passage is being aided by a powerful lobby in their service. The railroads base their advocacy of the bill on the claim that it will be for the interest of the shippers to have such a law.

And he predicts that it will be followed by a demand that the government shall take charge of the roads and guarantee dividends to the stockholders. He further says:

All this will be at the demand and in the interest of the railroads and of the shippers, and not of the labor involved in carrying on the work of transportation, as the demand of to-day for the enactment of the pooling bill is alleged to be largely in the interest of the shippers and the public welfare.

Nothing is more obvious to-day than the signal inability of capital and private enterprise to take care of themselves un-aided by the state; and while they are incessantly denounc-ing "paternalism,"—by which they mean the claim of the defenceless laborer and artisan to a share in this lavish state protection,—they are all the while besieging legislatures for relief from their own incompetency, and "pleading the baby act" through a trained body of lawyers and lobbyists. The dispensing of national pap to this class should rather be called "maternalism," to which a square, open, and dignified paternal-ism would be infinitely preferable.

Still all these things must be regarded as perfectly natural, that is, inherent in the nature of man, and not as peculiar to any class. Therefore personalities and vituperation are entirely out of place. It is simply a question of whether they are going to be permitted to go on. The fault is altogether with the system. Nor should any one object to state protection of busi-ness interests. Even monopoly may be defended against ag-gressive competition on the ground of economy. The protection of the strong may not be too great, but there should be at the same time protection of the weak against the protected strong. It is not the purpose of this article to point out rem-edies, but tendencies, and it seems clear that right here are to be located the two greatest dangers to modern society. Here lies the only plutocracy, and here the only paternalism. The two are really one, and are embodied in the joint fact of state-protected monopoly.

The degree to which the citizen is protected in the secure enjoyment of his possessions is a fair measure of the state of civilization, but this protection must apply as rigidly to the poor man's possessions as to those of the rich man. In the present system the latter is not only encouraged, but actually tempted to exploit the former. Every trust, every monopoly, every carelessly granted franchise, has or may have this effect, and the time has arrived when a part at least of this paternal solicitude on the part of government should be diverted from the monopolistic element and bestowed upon the general public. If we must have paternalism, there should be no partiality shown in the family.

16

HERBERT SPENCER

1894   1909   1904

It is impossible to exaggerate the prestige and the admiration that Herbert Spencer commanded in the United States in Ward's generation. Of all earlier philosophers Newton's famous observation was true, that they were as children playing with pebbles on the beach, while all about them roared the great ocean of truth. To Spencer alone had been given to hear that roar and to reduce it to scientific harmony. Greater than Aristotle, more profound than Newton, he combined philosophy with science to prove what none had ever proved before: the inevitability of progress. His great "System of Synthetic Philosophy" demonstrated that man had evolved socially and psychologically as well as biologically from savagery to civilization, from chaos to order, from anarchy to law, and guaranteed continued progress toward perfection in harmony with the immutable workings of cosmic forces.

The Spencerian philosophy, as Ward was perhaps the first to make inescapably clear, called for a far-reaching policy of laissez faire—laissez faire not by government alone or in the political arena alone, but in what might be called the whole arena of civilization. The average American, to be sure, read Spencer merely to find support for his opposition to governmental intervention in the economic arena, but Ward saw that far more was involved than this, and that the issue was not governmental intervention versus laissez faire, but civilization versus nature.

Of Spencer it may truly be said that he was a sovereign of the sociological kingdom. We may be sure that Ward was familiar with the ancient adage that when you strike a king you strike to kill. Ward struck to kill.

We so far violate our chronological arrangement as to give here three interpretations of Spencer, separated by more than a decade. The first, written in 1894, was designed as a review of Spencer's data of ethics; it speedily broadened out to a general assault on the Spencerian social and political philosophy. The second, written toward the close of Ward's life, returned to the great issues of Spencer's sociology. The third, a memorial essay written in 1904, made few of the customary concessions to the elegiac, but surveyed no less critically than the others the faults and failings of Spencerian sociology.

A. THE POLITICAL ETHICS OF HERBERT SPENCER

1894

Mr. Spencer's sociology and political ethics rest upon *biology* and not upon *psychology*. If we seek a general term to express the fundamental principle that seems to underlie every statement of his works we shall perhaps find it in the word *self-adjustment*. With him everything that takes place properly is automatic. The following passage will serve as a sample of this biological ethics:

This principle of self-adjustment within each individual, is parallel to that principle of self-adjustment by which the species as a whole keeps itself fitted to its environment. For by the better nutrition and greater power of propagation which come to members of

Annals of the American Academy of Political and Social Science, IV (January 1894), in *Glimpses of the Cosmos*, V, 51–66.

the species that have faculties and consequent activities best adapted to the needs, joined with the lower sustentation of self and offspring which accompany less adapted faculties and activities, there is caused such special growth of the species as most conduces to its survival in face of surrounding conditions. This, then, is the law of sub-human justice, that each individual shall receive the benefits and the evils of its own nature and its consequent conduct.[1]

Or again:

Since this connection between conduct and consequence is held to be just, it follows that throughout the animal kingdom what we call justice, is the ethical aspect of this biological law in virtue of which life in general has been maintained and has evolved into higher forms; and which therefore possesses the highest possible authority.[2]

The importance of this aspect of the question will justify one further quotation:

The prosperity of a species is best subserved when among adults each experiences the good and evil results of his own nature and consequent conduct. In a gregarious species fulfillment of this need implies that the individuals shall not so interfere with one another as to prevent the receipt by each of the benefits which his actions naturally bring to him, or transfer to others the evils which his actions naturally bring. This, which is the ultimate law of species life as qualified by social conditions, it is the business of the social aggregate, or incorporated body of citizens, to maintain.[3]

In this passage it is made clear that the general self-adjusting law of nature is held to apply to society, and man is duly advised that nature is to be imitated. Other passages, however, put this much stronger:

The broad fact then, here to be noted, is that Nature's modes of treatment inside the family-group and outside the family-group are

---

[1] Herbert Spencer, *Justice*, p. 9.

[2] *Ibid.*, p. 150.

[3] *Ibid.*, p. 213.

diametrically opposed to one another; and that the intrusion of either mode into the sphere of the other, would be destructive either immediately or remotely. Does any one think that the like does not hold of the human species? He cannot deny that within the human family, as within any inferior family, it would be fatal to proportion benefits to merits. Can he assert that outside the family, among adults, there should not be, as throughout the animal world, a proportioning of benefits to merits? Will he contend that no mischief will result if the lowly endowed are enabled to thrive and multiply as much as, or more than, the highly endowed? . . . Society in its corporate capacity, cannot without immediate or remoter disaster interfere with the play of these opposed principles under which every species has reached such fitness for its mode of life as it possesses, and under which it maintains that fitness.[4]

It is clear from this that Mr. Spencer is utterly blind to the most conspicuous fact in society, that under an unregulated or "competitive" *régime* there is very little relation between "benefits" and "merits" or "fitness." It is partially to enforce such a correspondence that the state exists, and the essence of the idea of "justice," in the human sense, is the proportioning of benefits to merits, which "Nature's methods" do not secure. A typical example is the gradual substitution of trial by law for trial by battle, which formerly prevailed. In the complications of modern society "conduct" has little to do with this proportioning, and bad conduct is fully as successful as good. The "accident of position" is a much more potent factor. The State is now at work upon this difficult problem, still striving, as ever it has striven, to proportion benefits to merits, i.e., to enforce justice against nature's methods. But let us hear Mr. Spencer further:

Pervading all Nature we may see at work a stern discipline which is a little cruel that it may be very kind. That state of universal warfare maintained throughout the lower creation, to the great per-

---

4 "The Man *versus* the State," p. 361.

plexity of many worthy people, is at bottom the most merciful provision which the circumstances admit of. It is much better that the ruminant animal, when deprived by age of the vigor which made its existence a pleasure, should be killed by some beast of prey, than that it should linger out a life made painful by infirmities, and eventually die of starvation. By the destruction of all such, not only is existence ended before it becomes burdensome, but room is made for a younger generation capable of the fullest enjoyment; and, moreover, out of the very act of substitution happiness is derived for a tribe of predatory creatures.[5]

No one, of course, objects to this phase of purely animal ethics for animals, but when prescribed for men, as in the following passage, the dose becomes excessive:

A sad population of imbeciles would our schemers fill the world with, could their plans last. A sorry kind of human constitution would they make for us—a constitution continually going wrong, and needing to be set right again—a constitution ever tending to self-destruction. Why, the whole effort of Nature is to get rid of such—to clear the world of them, and make room for better. Mark how the diseased are dealt with. Consumptive patients, with lungs incompetent to perform the duties of lungs, people with digestive organs that will not take up enough nutriment, people with defective hearts which break down under effort, people with any constitutional flaw preventing due fulfillment of the conditions of life, are continually dying out, and leaving behind those fit for the climate, food, and habits to which they are born.[6]

This last, and much more in the same vein, is said under the head of "Sanitary Supervision" by municipalities and other governing agencies, as in argument against it, and against all public acts arising out of sympathy for the unfortunate, which action, he declares, "defeats its own end. It favors the multiplication of those worst fitted for existence, and, by consequence,

---

[5] "Social Statics, Abridged and Revised," p. 149.
[6] *Ibid.*, p. 205

hinders the multiplication of those best fitted for existence—leaving, as it does, less room for them."[7]

This doctrine, laid down in his "Social Statics," in 1850, he retains in the abridgment and reaffirms in his later writings. After quoting extensively from the early work and reapplying the doctrine of natural selection to society, he adds:

And yet, strange to say, now that this truth is recognized by most cultivated people—now that the beneficent working of the survival of the fittest has been so impressed on them that, much more than people in past times, they might be expected to hesitate before neutralizing its action—now more than ever before in the history of the world, are they doing all they can to further survival of the unfittest![8]

These citations ought to satisfy the most incredulous that the political ethics of Herbert Spencer, as well as his sociology, rests directly upon biology and completely ignores the influence of both feeling and thought in rendering human conduct and social life a field distinct from that in which the irrational animal acts and lives. He carries his general principle through a great number of departments of social action, applying everywhere his law of equal freedom. He recognizes that society is the theatre of natural laws, but to him these are only the laws of life, or of the universe in general. He sees that the organic world is governed in much the same way as is the inorganic, the laws of cosmic evolution becoming those of natural selection and the survival of the fittest in the struggle for existence. In a word the law of nature is the law of force both above and below the level of vital activities. He sees no other law in society, and seems irritated and annoyed at any attempt on the part of society to "interfere" with this law. Like some religious partisans who declare the absolute inde-

---

[7] *Ibid.,* p. 207.

[8] "The Man *versus* the State," p. 365.

structibility of their faith, while at the same time manifesting unconcealed concern for its safety, Spencer, while quoting the maxim, *jura naturæ sunt immutabilia,* betrays a lively apprehension lest something be done to change them, and defends them valiantly against the schemes of ignorant "meddlers" (this word with its derivatives probably occurs a hundred times in the two volumes).

The arch offender in this line is, of course, government, which to him is scarcely a natural product. While recognizing it as such in his cooler moments, his *animus* against it is so strong as to make him treat it as something apart from the general scheme of society, a sort of interloper or parasite, that has foisted itself upon society and is using it for its own ends. In his eyes government consists of a group of ill-disposed individuals, "politicians," who have in one way or another worked themselves into power, and whose object is to deprive the people of their liberty, property, or happiness. This is expressed in such passages as this:

> "Thus much of your work shall be devoted, not to your own purposes, but to our purposes," say the authorities to the citizens; and to whatever extent this is carried, to that extent the citizens become slaves of the government.[9]

Or, again:

> Public departments, all of them regimented after the militant fashion, all supported by taxes forcibly taken, and severally responsible to their heads, mostly appointed for party reasons, are not immediately dependent for their means of living and growing on those whom they are designed to benefit.[10]

These utterances clearly show that in his mind there is no bond of mutuality between the government and the citizen;

---

9 "Justice," p. 223.
10 *Ibid.,* p. 231.

that with him the former is an outside power working against the latter and for itself alone, and he declares that:

> Government, begotten of aggression and by aggression, ever continues to betray its original nature by its aggressiveness.[11]

As already remarked, what seems chiefly to trouble him is the attempt on the part of government to "interfere," "meddle," and "tamper" with the laws of nature, which he variously designates as "the normal working of things," "the constitution of things," "the order of Nature," "causal relations," etc., laying, of course, great stress on the law of supply and demand and the laws of trade and commerce in general. Whenever he speaks of the natural forces of society it is in this sense, for, adhering to the biological point of view, he can, of course, perceive no other social force than the struggle for existence, that is, the mere life-force. The true social forces are psychic and therefore ignored. Indeed, had he recognized them his entire course of reasoning would have been reversed, for they operate directly against the vital force, and tend to defeat the law of nature as manifested in the struggle for existence. He dimly perceives this, it is true, but mistakes the normal operations of the law of mind, antagonizing the law of life, for an abnormal element intruding upon the domain of natural law. If he could rise to a position from which he could see the whole field of both life and mind he would see that society is itself a product of the latter and could not result from the former. The same is true to an increased degree of government. It is the result of the "interference" of the psychic with the vital law. All human institutions are in the same case. Animals have no institutions. Looking deeper we perceive that it is this that characterizes all art. Everything artificial is a product of the psychic force and results from interference with "the constitution of things." "The normal working of things" would

---

[11] "The Man *versus* the State," p. 369.

never produce tools, weapons, clothing, or shelter. It is the essence of invention and artificial construction to "meddle" with "causal relations." But all this is just as "natural" and "normal" as are the purely physical or vital processes. It simply takes place in a different department of natural forces. It is the psychic process, the work of mental agencies.

As has been intimated, Mr. Spencer recognizes the *efficacy* of these interferences with nature, as he is pleased to call them. He is right in denying that there is any power that can take from, or add to, the actual force in the universe. To a great degree, too, the organic force of the world is incapable of increase or diminution, and even that part of it that belongs to society is practically a fixed quantity. Only by commuting it into some other form of force can its volume be changed. But all this is beside the point. The interferences of which he complains are not attempts to create or destroy the forces of society. They are attempts to *direct* them. This is easily done. The arts are all the result of the intelligent direction of natural forces and the properties of substances into ways and shapes that are useful to man. In the domestication of animals and the cultivation of vegetables the same is done for the higher class of forces displayed by living things. Government and all other social institutions apply the same principles to the laws of human action. They are all successful in proportion to the degree of intelligence, i.e., of the understanding of those forces and properties, with which they are conducted. Mr. Spencer would not discourage art, he would not decry agriculture, he does not attack any other human institution except government.

His reason for this seems to be that many of the acts of government have resulted in failure. This no one denies. But so have a large percentage of all other human schemes been failures. All social operations are primarily empirical. All have been products of multiplied experiments, and have attained success only after failure has taught wisdom. Not to speak of the abortive machines and worthless inventions that flood the patent offices of all countries, we need only to consider the business failures of modern times to see that the method of psychic progress is that of trial and error, at least in the earlier stages of every department of social life. If permitted to go on success is ultimately achieved and progress is made. It has been so in all the lower efforts, and it has been so in that highest effort, that of society to govern itself. Mr. Spencer's sociology, therefore, which would minimize government to the utmost, and even hints at its ultimate elimination, is an essentially destructive, and in no sense a constructive system. His political ethics which denies the right of society to adopt ways and means for its own improvement and advancement, is a censure of the whole course of human history.

A large part of the matter of the works now under consideration consists of enumerations of cases of governmental failure. Most of these cases are drawn from the history of European nations a century or more ago: the laws and ordinances interfering with trade and commerce, class legislation, sumptuary laws and laws fixing prices, wages, etc., mischievous and meddlesome legislation, laws that missed their purpose, produced unexpected effects, or the opposite effect from the one intended, laws that have had to be repealed, etc., etc. He has accumulated a mass of facts of this class that are highly interesting, often amusing, and certainly valuable as historical knowledge if not as guides to future lawmakers. But the fact that there is no longer any such legislation shows that these methods, however successful once, are not valued now and would not be tolerated. The failures, in so far as they were such, have taught their lesson and served their purpose in the great school of political experience. His claim that there is danger of reverting to such methods is simply puerile. The cases that he adduces of more modern legislation are of a very different class, and while some of the acts he enumerates are doubtless unwise and short-sighted, and will be repealed, the general body of legislation that he condemns is not only approved but demanded by the moral sense of Europe and America. Such is the anti-child-labor legislation, short-hour legislation, factory legislation, sanitary legislation, appropriations for public works, regulation of railways, public management of the telegraph system, the parcels post, and above all public instruction or national education. All of these and many other measures, some of them long since adopted on the Continent, now popular in England or America or both, he condemns in the most unmeasured terms as mischievous and pernicious, and as contrary to his canon of justice, the law of equal freedom. If anything further were needed to prove that canon unsound this fact would do so: that it stands in the way of the accomplishment of an urgent social demand.

Aside from the one glaring omission of Mr. Spencer's system, already pointed out—the omission of the psychic factor—and aside from many minor ones which cannot be noticed here, there are two other important omissions which call for special mention. The first of these is the failure to perceive that modern governments are all, to a greater or less degree, representative, and that their acts are consequently not wholly those of the individuals that make up the governing body at any given time, but are in a certain correct sense the acts of society. He has himself admitted that all governments, even the rudest, reflect the state of society over which they hold sway. But in an enlightened social state, such as that of England, Western Europe, and the United States, there is a close bond of union between society and the government. Whether they call themselves monarchies or republics, they are all in fact impure democracies, and the legislators and principal administrative officers are chosen by the people, or change with the changes in the popular voice. Such governments are controlled, after their selection as much as in their selection, by the wishes of their constituents. They are watched and warned and urged and petitioned, and their continuance depends upon their obedience. Rarely, indeed, do they dare to disobey the known will of the people. This being so, the anathemas of Herbert Spencer upon the *personnel* of government are misdirected. "The sins of legislators" are the sins of voters, and his plea should have been made to the wider tribunal. His counsel of "resistance"[12] is based on the assumption that the government is doing some great wrong, but those who are advised to resist are themselves the wrong-doers, and are not likely to resist their own acts. His denial of the right of majorities to legislate for minorities might be discussed in this connection, but it scarcely seems worth while to go over such well-beaten ground.

The second of the omissions under consideration is even more serious than the first. It is the failure to observe that the evils from which modern governments are called upon to protect society are of a very different nature from those with which the earlier governments of the world had to contend. A great change in the groundwork of society, due to various obscure causes working together during long periods, is always difficult to perceive, and the new evils thus insidiously introduced are hard to eradicate because they require the application of new and unaccustomed remedies. Such is the present state of society in the most advanced nations. Protection, which is the only governmental function that Mr. Spencer will recognize as legitimate, formerly meant the redress of private wrongs to persons and property, chiefly through physical causes. Under autocratic governments with limited industrial operations these were the chief internal evils of society, except those caused by the rapacity of the governing class. Competition prevailed almost exclusively in all branches of business, causing its share of the individual crime which it was the duty of government to prevent or punish. But a great revolution took place in Western Europe, and the character of governments underwent a complete change, often

---

12 "Social Statics, Abridged and Revised," p. 184.

without change of name. Power passed from the hands of the ruling class into those of the people, and the most intense jealousy of all government interference in private business became general. The laws of trade were respected by the State and were allowed to operate untrammeled. This was an immense relief, and an era of unexampled industrial prosperity ensued. Wealth was rapidly accumulated, but in this reign of natural law in society it was drawn toward the strongest centers of attraction. The only justice respected in the distribution of wealth was the kind that Mr. Spencer alone recognizes. Under this crude form of justice the distribution was correspondingly unequal. Then came the era of machinery and the breaking up of guilds and trades, unsettling the status of the artisan, and turning him adrift to take his chances in the universal competition. These facts are familiar to all economists and students of real history. The industrial condition of the world has completely changed. The evils to be dealt with now are of an entirely different class from those of former industrial epochs. States have recognized this, and whatever differences may exist as to methods, all governments have felt called upon to take some action for the protection of society from these new dangers. The workingman has a voice in government, and its acts are largely his doings. Mr. Spencer, often as he condemns the "great man theory" of history, seems not to have correctly read the real history of his own age. He still thinks that the natural forces of society can be safely left to take care of themselves. And when he sees the State moving steadily forward and grappling one by one with these new evils, he sees in it the ghost of bygone despotism, and imagines a return to sumptuary laws, to the corn laws, and the *corvée*. He thinks the world gone mad, and works himself up into something like a frenzy. Because people will have public schools he cries out:

We have fallen upon evil times, in which it has come to be an accepted doctrine that part of the responsibilities are to be discharged not by parents but by the public—a part which is gradually becoming a larger part and threatens to become the whole. Agitators and legislators have united in spreading a theory which, logically followed out, ends in the monstrous conclusion that it is for parents to beget children and for society to take care of them. The political ethics now in fashion makes the unhesitating assumption that while each man, as parent, is not responsible for the mental culture of his own offspring, he is, as citizen, along with other citizens, responsible for the mental culture of all other men's offspring! And this absurd doctrine has now become so well established that people raise their eyebrows in astonishment if you deny it. A self-evident falsehood has been transformed into a self-evident truth![13] . . .

In his "Coming Slavery" he completes this dire picture in a way that even Edward Bellamy ought to be satisfied with:

Already exclusive letter-carrier, exclusive transmitter of telegrams, and on the way to become exclusive carrier of parcels, the State will not only be exclusive carrier of passengers, goods, and minerals, but will add to its present various trades many other trades. Even now, besides erecting its naval and military establishments and building harbors, docks, breakwaters, etc., it does the work of ship-builder, cannon-founder, small-arms maker, manufacturer of ammunition, army-clothier and boot-maker; and when the railways have been appropriated 'with or without compensation,' as the Democratic Federationists say, it will have to become locomotive-engine-builder, carriagemaker, tarpaulin and grease manufacturer, passenger-vessel owner, coalminer, stone-quarrier, omnibus proprietor, etc. Meanwhile its local lieutenants, the municipal governments, already in many places suppliers of water, gas-makers, owners and workers of tramways, proprietors of baths, will doubtless have undertaken various other businesses. And when the State, directly or by proxy, has thus come into possession of, or has established, numerous concerns for wholesale production and for wholesale distribution, there will be good precedents for extending its

---

[13] "Principles of Ethics," I, p. 545.

function to retail distribution: following such an example, say, as is offered by the French Government, which has long been a retail tobacconist.[14]

Finally, in his "Postscript" to this same work, he abandons hope in the following language:

"Do I expect this doctrine to meet with any considerable acceptance?" I wish I could say, yes; but unhappily various reasons oblige me to conclude that only here and there a solitary citizen may have his political creed modified.

And no wonder, when we consider what the adoption of his "political creed" would involve. Not only would it involve the repeal of all the humane and industrial legislation to which reference has been made, but it would abolish all public works, including lighthouses and harbors; it would necessitate a return to a private postal system which the whole world has outgrown; would reëstablish the monopoly telegraph in those countries which have replaced it by a national telegraph, always found to possess advantages similar to those of a national mail system; the parcels post of England and equivalent systems of the Continent would give way to our express monopolies, which Mr. Spencer extols because he does not understand them; it would turn over cities to private water companies and private fire companies, both types of the "natural monopoly;" there would be a reversion to a system of strictly private, or "wildcat" banking; public schools would be abolished, probably the last thing next to liberty that any enlightened nation would surrender; and all forms of sanitary regulation, including quarantine precautions against great epidemics, would be left to the wisdom of individual citizens. As this last seems to cap the climax of *laissez faire* absurdity, it may be well to listen to his statement of the case, although

---

[14] "The Man *versus* the State," p. 327.

the reader may require to be assured that the following passage is not intended as a burlesque:

Respecting sewage there would be no difficulty. Houses might readily be drained on the same mercantile principle that they are now supplied with water. It is probable that in the hands of a private company, the resulting manure would not only pay the cost of collection, but would yield a considerable profit. But if not, the return on the invested capital would be made up by charges to those whose houses were drained: the alternative of having their connections with the main sewer stopped, being as good a security for payment as the analogous ones possessed by water and gas companies.[15]

According to Mr. Spencer's political ethics the State has no right to prevent the adulteration of food or the deterioration of fabrics, and he says that "the interest of the consumer is not only an efficient guarantee for the goodness of the things consumed, but the best guarantee." . . .[16]

But there is a still more serious charge against the political ethics of Herbert Spencer. "In a popularly governed nation," he says, "the government is simply a committee of management;"[17] yet he denies to that "committee of management" the right to manage the business of society. This would be a singular state of things in any corporate enterprise conducted by business men. And why, forsooth, has not that great corporation, society, the same right to choose its directors and instruct them to manage its business that smaller corporations have? . . .

Notwithstanding the vulnerable character of so large a part of Mr. Spencer's reasoning, he argues with such an air of confidence that only critical readers are likely to suspect the *ex parte* nature of his statements. The following example reminds one strongly of the oracular responses from Delphi,

---

[15] "Social Statics, Abridged and Revised," p. 218.

[16] *Ibid.,* p. 163.

[17] *Ibid.,* p. 410.

and may be commended to him as quite as likely to apply to his own opinions as to the opinions of others:

Men of the past quite misunderstood the institutions they lived under. They pertinaciously adhered to the most vicious principles, and were bitter in their opposition to right ones, at the dictates of their attachments and antipathies. So difficult is it for man to emancipate himself from the invisible fetters which habit and education cast over his intellect; and so palpable is the consequent incompetency of a people to judge rightly of itself and its deeds or opinions, that the fact has been embodied in the aphorism—'No age can write its own history.' If we act wisely, we shall assume that the reasonings of modern society are subject to the like disturbing influences. We shall conclude that, even now, as in times gone by, opinion is but the counterpart of condition. We shall suspect that many of those convictions which seem the results of dispassionate thinking, have been nurtured in us by circumstances. We shall confess that, as heretofore, fanatical opposition to this doctrine and bigoted adhesion to that, have been no tests of the truth or falsity of the said doctrines; so neither is the strength of attachment nor dislike which a nation now exhibits toward certain principles, any proof of their correctness or their fallacy.[18]

Upon the whole, it may be considered as in the highest degree unfortunate and discouraging that almost the first prominent system of sociology, as distinct from political economy, should proceed from so low and so narrow a standpoint as virtually to constitute a protest against all attempts to deal scientifically with the subject. It is simply a wet blanket on the enthusiasm of all who would follow social science. It throws over it the dismal pall that fell on political economy, and it stamps it with the words: No future! If this is all that Herbert Spencer can make of it, what can lesser lights hope to accomplish?

It is simply astonishing that the great exponent of the law of evolution in all other departments should so signally fail to grasp that law in this highest department. And it furnishes

---

[18] "Social Statics, Abridged and Revised," pp. 80–81.

a curious parallel that, just as he failed to perceive the fundamental difference between cosmic and organic evolution, and
the coöperation in the latter of the radiant with the gravitant
forces[19] in the production of the phenomena of life, so he has
likewise failed to perceive the equally fundamental difference
between vital and psychic evolution, in the latter of which the
power of feeling under the direction of thought has furnished
to the evolutionary process an entirely new dispensation. In
seeking to bring all the products of evolution—worlds, plants,
animals, man, society—under one uniform law, adequate only
to the lowest, and ignoring the new and powerful principles
that came forward at the several successive cosmical epochs,
he has dwarfed the later of these into relative insignificance,
and instead of carrying his system up symmetrically and
crowning it with the science of man, he has tapered it off
and flattened it out at the summit, degrading that noblest department to the level of political controversy and wholesale
personal censure. The name of "administrative nihilism," by
which Professor Huxley long ago so happily characterized
this, is likely to abide, and the extreme *noli tangere* individualism with which the entire social philosophy of Herbert Spencer is permeated, must, in spite of all disclaimers,[20] impart to
it the character of a gospel of inaction.

B. CAREER OF HERBERT SPENCER

1909

. . . Coming now to the "Principles of Sociology," we find
that the work was not hampered by any previous work, and,
as in the "Biology," the field was clear for a new start in a

---

The Popular Science Monthly, LXXXIV (January 1909), in *Glimpses of
the Cosmos*, VI, 312–316.

[19] *Popular Science Monthly*, XI (October 1877).
[20] "The Man *versus* the State," p. 418.

most alluring direction. If the order in which the volumes of the "Synthetic Philosophy" stand is the order of nature, marking the course of evolution, we should expect to find the "Sociology" opening with a chapter or an introductory part setting forth the causal connection between sociology and psychology. But, just as no causal connection was shown between biology and psychology, so none appears binding psychology and sociology together. . . . What we do find, however, is a rather definite intimation that it is biology rather than psychology that forms the natural basis of sociology. How could anyone be expected to doubt this when nothing is said in the first volume of the "Sociology" about its relation to psychology, while, after the long treatise on the beliefs, customs, and ideas of primitive races, belonging rather to anthropology, we find in part II. that "a society is an organism," and that social growth, social structures, social functions, and social organs are treated from the strictly biological point of view. Mr. Spencer denied that he based sociology upon biology and censured two American authors for intimating that he seemed to do so, but the comparison that he used is not at all apposite.[21]

The other two volumes of the "Principles of Sociology," based as they are on his great compilation, "Descriptive Sociology," are above criticism in their comprehensive sweep as a vast induction. Some of his facts will, of course, be denied, but he admitted that the reports of travelers must be taken with many grains of allowance. Yet these are almost the only sources from which an author who is not himself a traveler must rely. For those therefore who consider such a work to constitute "Sociology" the only vulnerable part is the terminology, classification, and arrangement of the subject-matter. The phrase "ecclesiastical institutions" may be justly objected to as seeming to predicate something like a church

---

[21] "Life and Letters," II, p. 357.

of the religious structures of primitive man. The word "eccles-iastical" might be stretched sufficiently to justify this were there no better term, but it is universally admitted that the priesthood was practically coeval with human society, and we possess an adjective corresponding to this noun which is more euphonious and more expressive than the one used. By all means, then, should the phrase *sacerdotal institutions* be substituted for "ecclesiastical institutions." The introduc-tion of "political institutions" between the "ceremonial" and the sacerdotal is a forced arrangement. The ceremonial are largely sacerdotal, and their separation is difficult. The sacer-dotal should probably stand first, and the "professional," beginning with the "medicine man," so similar to a priest, should follow. "Political institutions" would then be in order, to be followed by "industrial institutions." But Mr. Spencer had no conception of gentile society and the fundamental distinction between it and political society, so clearly set forth by Morgan. This classification shows how late the latter class of institutions have always been in the historical development of society. Still less was he acquainted with that other most important of all transformations which is undergone by every advanced society at the proper stage in its history, viz., union and amalgamation of groups, whether through war or peace, by which a third and higher group results from the blending of two lower groups, constituting what is appropriately called the cross-fertilization of cultures. It is only through this that all the higher political, industrial, economic, and professional institutions arise.

After thus threading the mazes of cosmic, organic, psychic, and social phenomena, we come at last to the "Principles of Ethics," which Mr. Spencer regarded as the crown of his system. One can not but be struck by the resemblance in this respect of Herbert Spencer's career to that of Auguste Comte. Both began with a lively interest in what may be called po-litical ethics, an interest which they both continued to feel through life. But both saw, after their early survey of the field, that the world was not ready for their final achievement, and therefore both stopped and devoted twelve or fifteen years of arduous labor to laying a scientific foundation for the *magnum opus* which was to reform the world. Comte laid special stress on this, and placed as a motto at the head of the first volume of his "Politique Positive" the lines of Alfred de Vigny:

Qu'est-ce qu'une grande vie?
Une pensée de la jeunesse, exécutée par l'age mur.

Spencer could not even wait to complete the last of the preparatory works, and stopped in the middle of it to write the final work. So strongly was he impressed by the importance of this last work, and so apprehensive that he might not live to complete it, that he said in the preface to the first part ("Data of Ethics" issued separately):

I am the more anxious to indicate in outline, if I can not complete, this final work, because the establishment of rules of right conduct on a scientific basis is a pressing need. Now that moral injunctions are losing the authority given by their supposed sacred origin, the secularization of morals is becoming imperative. Few things can happen more disastrous than the decay and death of a regulative system no longer fit, before another and fitter regulative system has grown up to replace it.

The implication of course is that Herbert Spencer's "Principles of Ethics" will henceforth constitute the Koran of moral doctrine to the exclusion of all other codes! Comte has been pronounced an egotist and a fanatic for proclaiming himself the high priest of the religion of humanity, but he never assumed to be an infallible pope in the domain of moral conduct. The parallelism, however, does not end here. The world has passed judgment upon Comte's career, and while his final work for which he had lived and labored, viz., his "Positive Polity," has been declared a mistaken dream, the preparatory work, his "Positive Philosophy," which he intended to be only the pedestal upon which the monument was to stand, is looked upon by most men as a path-breaking, by many as an epoch-making achievement, and as marking the beginning of scientific philosophy. In Spencer's case it is too early to speak thus definitely, but all things point to the complete rejection of his political ethics as outlined in "Social Statics" and perfected in his "Principles of Ethics" and "Man Versus the State," while his cosmic philosophy, which he regarded as little more than a foundation for the other, grows more solid with time, and is clearly seen to be too massive for the flimsy superstructure that he sought to erect upon it.

In Spencer's system ethics is placed last in the series of subjects or sciences, as if it were the highest evolutionary product. Although he laid no stress on the serial arrangement of the sciences, and in his little book on the "Classification of the Sciences," written to refute Comte's "hierarchy," he practically ignores it, still he could not answer the charge of arranging his volumes in practically the same order as Comte arranged the sciences. Nor did he deny that he regarded this as the order of evolution. As Comte did the same for his "Morale," the implication is that they both regarded ethics as a science of the same type as the others, only higher in the scale, and, in fact, the highest of them all. It would thus grow out of and be affiliated upon sociology. The treatment of it does not in either case sustain this claim. In Spencer's case this is much more marked than in Comte's, because they had quite different ideas of what constitutes a moral science. Spencer, as we have seen, regarded it simply as a "regulative system," which is not a science at all. His treatment of it virtually carries out this idea, and his "Principles of Ethics" scarcely differs from the traditional moral teaching of other writers, except that it is "secular" and recognizes no religious or "ultra-rational" sanction. After he had abandoned his "absolute ethics," as set forth in his "Social Statics" (expunged from the last edition), but shown to be false by a study of the widely divergent moral ideas of the races of men, the last claim to the title of a science had been withdrawn from ethics, and it stood at the head of the system having no organic connection with the other sciences of that system. What, then, is his ethics? It is simply an attempt to make a practical application of the true sciences, especially of sociology, to human needs. In so far as it is a science in any sense, it is an applied science, and the greater part of it may be denominated applied sociology.[22]

The subject of Spencer's relations with Comte and the similarity of their ideas has been purposely avoided in this article, because it presents the least attractive side of a great man's mind. His overweening affection for what he called "the progeny of the brain,"[23] his intense love of originality, which often seems to exceed his love of truth, and his morbid sensitiveness to any apparent appropriation of his ideas, blinded him to the merits of others and often led him to refine upon a distinction without a difference. Jealousy as well as envy may be a compliment. This can alone explain Spencer's attitude toward Comte. He must have felt, and been oppressed by the fact that there was a man on the other side of the Channel who, like himself, was striving to give the world a philosophy of science. And in fact, from this point of view, Auguste Comte was to the first half of the nineteenth century what Herbert Spencer was to the second half. . . .

C. HERBERT SPENCER'S SOCIOLOGY
1904

"Nihil de mortuis nisi bonum." In these days, when science mourns, no one covets the task of pointing out defects. If Her-

---

The Independent, LVI, No. 2887 (March 31, 1904), in *Glimpses of the Cosmos*, VI, 171–177.

[22] See "Applied Sociology," pp. 317–318.
[23] "Life and Letters," I, 254.

bert Spencer did not create sociology, he at least raised it into life and started it on its grand career. It required courage to do this and to embody it in a great scientific system on an equal footing with biology, psychology and ethics at a time when others passed it by and disdained to speak its name. This brave act will always be regarded as more than atoning for any shortcomings that the most critical will ever find in Herbert Spencer's sociology. As one of those who have freely criticised that part of his vast scheme during his lifetime, the present writer feels it incumbent frankly to avow that nothing he could say in disparagement of certain aspects of Spencer's treatment of the subject appreciably diminishes the debt of gratitude which he, in common with all lovers of truth, acknowledges to Herbert Spencer for the three monumental volumes in which he has unfolded that science.

But the saying is too trite to need repeating that there is always danger of resting any case upon authority, however great, and that the only condition to progress in any science or in any field of inquiry is fearless and independent scrutiny of the basic doctrines of even the greatest masters. It is, therefore, no derogation from the magnitude of Spencer's achievement to say that, like all things human, it has its defects. In the present case it is perhaps better to say, that it has one defect, for by the side of this one all the others are dwarfed into insignificance. And but for the weighty and vital character of this defect it would be unworthy of any one at a time like the present to point it out, and thus break the even flow of just and sincere praise for one who has made an epoch and has now laid down his pen.

How shall we formulate this one salient deficiency in Herbert Spencer's sociology? It may sound too dramatic to say that it consists in ignoring the human mind as a factor in sociology. True, his system embraces two volumes on psychology. Nevertheless I make bold to affirm not only that he did not base his sociology upon his psychology, but that his psychology is of a kind such that sociology could not be based upon it. Written before the biology and transferred to a position between that and the sociology, where, of course, it should stand, it is, nevertheless, as completely isolated as if it formed no part of the Synthetic Philosophy. The sociology, great as are its intrinsic merits, does not represent a science like other sciences, upon which man can lay hold and use as an instrument for his own advancement. Every other science rests upon a body of uniform laws which have been discovered by investigation, and which, as soon and as fast as discovered, can be put to immediate use in furthering the interests of life and ameliorating the condition of mankind. The science of sociology as taught by Spencer is a complete exception in this respect. Its laws are not pointed out, and there is not only no intimation that if there are social laws they may be utilized to human advantage, but there is a distinct implication, repeatedly expressed, that no such use can be made of them.

In Spencer's psychology spare allusion is made to the most fundamental and essential of the intellectual faculties, the faculty of invention. This is the faculty that has the chief value in sociology. It is the one that has produced nearly all the effects that distinguish man from an animal. But for it he could never have migrated and peopled the earth. It is the basis of all the arts. It underlies all discovery in science. It has accomplished the whole of what is called material civilization. It has done this by applying the known laws of nature to the uses of man. The various sciences, one after another, as fast as established by the discovery of their laws, have thus been put to practical service. There is no law of nature which cannot be made available for such purposes to a greater or less extent. It is the essence of a science that it shall explain certain invariable laws governing the phenomena with which it deals. All true sciences are of that character. If sociology is really a science it must also possess this character. And as man has been able to make practical use of every other science, it must follow that when social laws are really known and a social science is established he will be able to make a practical use of it. This in Spencer's sociology is at least impliedly denied, and in his other works it is expressly and vehemently denied.

To every science there corresponds an art. If there is a social science there must be a social art. That there is such an art no one can doubt, but thus far, it must be frankly confessed, it has remained chiefly an empirical art. In this respect it does not differ from all other arts. All have their empirical stage before they reach their scientific stage. But the empirical arts have all been useful, and the social art, even in its empirical stage, has been the most useful of all, since it has been the condition to the development of all the other arts—nay, to the very existence of society itself. But just as the usefulness of all other arts has been enormously increased by scientific discovery, so the usefulness of the social art will be increased, and in quite as great proportion, by the discovery and application of the laws and principles underlying social phenomena. It is not necessary to point out what all this is to consist in. I have attempted this on numerous occasions and gone as far as possible with the light we possess. But the essential thing is to recognize social phenomena as a field for scientific discovery and for the exercise of the inventive faculty precisely as in other departments of science and art. This class of scientific research once recognized and entered upon, the possible directions that it shall take, the methods and the technic will soon reveal themselves. If there are social laws and social forces, work in the social field will differ from that in other fields only in the nature of these laws and forces. Just as invention in the physical world consists in directing physical forces into channels of human advantage, so invention in the social world must consist in directing the social forces into such channels. The empirical social art seeks to drive men to do what is supposed to be for the interest of society. The inventor never seeks to coerce natural forces. By means of appropriate apparatus de-

vised by his ingenuity, he causes or *induces* them spontaneously to flow in the desired channels. It must be so with the
social inventor, and social invention, once seriously undertaken, will speedily do away with all mandatory, prohibitory
and penal legislation, and inaugurate an era of scientific, or
attractive legislation, which will make obedience to law the
form of action that the individual most desires, thus rendering
the operations of society automatic and spontaneous.

Of all this we find absolutely nothing in any of the writings
of Herbert Spencer.

There is another point of view from which we may contemplate Herbert Spencer's sociology. In his biology we are taught
that organic evolution takes place through the joint action of
differentiation and integration. Organic progress is measured
by the degree to which organs and structures are multiplied
to serve the various ends of higher and higher life, and by the
degree to which these multiplied structures and organs are
then subordinated to the directive influence of a more and
more perfect nervous system, and ultimately to the absolute
control of one supreme directive organ, the perfected brain.
It is these two conditions which constitute respectively organic
differentiation and organic integration.

Mr. Spencer early espoused the doctrine that human society
constitutes an organism analogous in many respects to the
organisms of which the world of life is composed. He pointed
out these analogies in great numbers and supplied the most
convincing arguments for the doctrine that have yet been adduced. But it is noteworthy that he generally, and no doubt
intentionally, avoided, as far as possible, those analogies that
relate to the nervous system, altho it is here that the most
important ones are to be found. He did, however, say that the
function of Parliament was analogous to that of the brain of
animals, and it is the prevailing view of those who defend
the social organism theory that government is the sociological
homolog of the brain.

Certain it is that organic integration is effected solely through the nervous system, and, in the higher organisms, through the brain. The various organs and structures would never spontaneously co-operate in the interest of the whole organism and work together in that perfect harmony necessary to carry on the functions of life without an organized nervous system to give and execute the commands of the creature. Mr. Spencer laid great stress on social differentiation, but was almost silent as to social integration. But what is social integration? Evidently it is some co-ordinating system that regulates the manifold organs of society and requires them to work in harmony for the good of the whole. And what can this be but the power, however constituted and by whatever name called, that every society, however undeveloped, possesses, and which is the agent and exponent of the society? Sociologists prefer to speak of collective action, or of the action of society itself, rather than to use the narrower, less correct, and more or less objectionable word government. That term is apt to be taken to mean the particular persons whom society at any given time has selected as its agents to execute its will and conduct its affairs. These persons are nothing but instruments and of no significance from the sociological point of view. The action taken in any case is that of society acting as an integrated unit, in the same sense as the acts of an animal or a man are those of the complete organism under the control of a nervous system presided over by a supreme central ganglion or brain.

Is the analogy, then, to stop with differentiation only? Is the social organism nothing but a complex mass of highly differentiated organs and structures without any co-ordinating and controlling system capable of making them work to some prescribed end and co-operate in carrying on the functions of society? Such is the conclusion to be drawn from Herbert Spencer's sociology.

Mr. Spencer started out in his great career as an avowed and extreme individualist, thoroughly imbued with the doctrines of the economists of his day. Individualism was then and is still taken to mean the opposite of collectivism. But, properly viewed, it is nothing of the kind. It can be successfully shown that there is nothing contradictory in the two doctrines, and that true individualism is not only consistent with true collectivism, but can, in fact, only be attained by means of it. This may seem paradoxical, but it will seem still more so when I say that the proof of it has been chiefly supplied by Mr. Spencer himself.

In defending the doctrine of the social organism he introduced certain qualifications. He enumerated first the respects in which a society resembles an organism, and, secondly, those in which it differs from one. Altho he reduced these latter to a minimum, and often showed that they were more apparent than real, there remained one which he saw to be fundamental. He said:

The last and perhaps the most important distinction is that while in the body of an animal only a special tissue is endowed with feeling, in society all the members are endowed with feeling. . . . It is well that the lives of all parts of an animal should be merged in the life of the whole, because the whole has a corporate consciousness capable of happiness or misery. But it is not so with a society, since its living units do not and cannot lose individual consciousness, and since the community, as a whole, has no corporate consciousness. And this is the everlasting reason why the welfare of citizens cannot rightly be sacrificed to some supposed benefit of the state, but why, on the other hand, the state is to be maintained for the benefit of citizens. The corporate life must here be subservient to the lives of the parts, instead of the lives of the parts being subservient to the corporate life.

Thus we see that it was upon this one important respect in which society differs from an organism that Mr. Spencer justified his individualism and maintained that his attitude of hostility to collective action was in harmony with his general scheme of philosophy. In this he was certainly mistaken, and, what is more, it is this undeniable fact that the individual alone is capable of enjoyment and suffering that constitutes the chief argument for striving to attain the maximum social integration.

According to the Lamarckian law, which Mr. Spencer fully accepted, it is function that creates organs. Whatever organs, structures or parts an organism acquires, they have all been developed in response to a demand growing out of the needs of the organism. The consequence is that all development, whether organic or social, always is and must necessarily be in the direction of some specific advantage to be derived therefrom. And, conversely, whatever is demanded as such an advantage will ultimately be supplied by the development of the structure, organ, or part that is adapted to secure it. Now, as he says, it was manifestly to the advantage of the organism that the manifold parts should come under the complete dominion of the whole organism. Any individual liberty on the part of the various organs and structures would quickly entail the destruction of the organism with all its parts. And all because it is the organism that is sensitive and conscious, while the parts may be regarded as, relatively at least, insensible and unconscious.

All this is reversed in a society, and for the very reason that Mr. Spencer gives—viz., that here it is the parts that are sensitive and conscious, while the society as such is unconscious and incapable of either enjoyment or suffering. This it is that explains the difference between social integration and organic integration. The former, according to the Lamarckian law, is directed exclusively toward securing the interests of the parts —i. e., of individuals. It is, and must necessarily be, introduced for this purpose. Nothing can originate, either in the organic or the superorganic world, which is not advantageous. To conceive of the origin of a disadvantageous organ, or structure, or institution, is to misunderstand the first principle of evolution. The end is the cause of the means, which arises solely for the sake of the end. The end is always the *good* of something. The idea of a good involves that of the capacity to feel. In a word, it implies a sentient being. An organism is such a being, but a cell or a gland is not. An individual man is such a being, but a state or a society is not. It follows that organic development must be in the direction of securing the interest of the organism and not of its parts, while social development must be in the direction of securing the interest of the individual and not of society as such. The general means employed in both cases has been integration but organic and social integration are unlike in this respect.

Just as in the organic world structures have been the means employed in securing the end—the good of the organism—so in the superorganic world society has been the means employed in securing the end—the good of the individual. This social integration, which is the scientific expression for collectivism, is the only means by which the freedom and happiness of the individual can be secured. Primarily it was the only means by which the human race could protect itself from hostile influences and continue to exist. And now, as always, it is the only means of protecting individuals from the egoistic domination of other individuals. Without a co-ordinating and restraining power to regulate the conduct of individuals toward one another and prevent the wholesale exploitation of the weak by the strong, liberty and happiness would be impossible. The highest aim of true individualism is the maximum individual liberty. Social integration restricts the individual's freedom, but this restriction is as nothing compared to that which other individuals would cause in its absence. Even Mr. Spencer's "equal freedom" can only be attained through such collective restraint as shall forbid one individual to interfere with the liberty of another. Within these limits the more complete the social integration the greater the real and legitimate liberty of every individual.

The existing "social unrest," of which we are hearing so much, is due in the main to the imperfect state of social integration at which the world has arrived, and its sole remedy must be through more and more complete integration. The present social movement is wholly in this direction. Mr. Spencer saw the movement, but he misinterpreted it. He saw in it "the coming of slavery," instead of the coming liberation of mankind. He imagined that it was morbid, abnormal and temporary, whereas it is perfectly healthy, normal, and destined to continue. He did not perceive that the fundamental distinction which he so clearly pointed out between the animal and the social organism necessarily reverses the direction of social evolution and causes it to work for the good of the individual.

The movement toward collectivism, which no one with his eyes open can fail to see taking place in spite of all that the philosophers may say, is really a true social evolution, proceeding on natural principles, and aiming at the same end as all other forms of social progress—the good of mankind. It differs from organic evolution only in the fact that it seeks the good of the parts instead of the whole, of individuals instead of society considered as something to be benefited. If Mr. Spencer had seen this he might have made his sociology not only symmetrical in itself but harmonious with his entire scheme of philosophy, of which it would have become the natural culmination and the true crown.

17

SOCIAL GENESIS

1895 1897

In 1894 and 1895, Ward gave a series of lectures to the Hart-
ford (Connecticut) Society for Education; these were subse-
quently published in the newly established American Journal
of Sociology, *and finally in book form, as* OUTLINES OF SOCIOL-
OGY. *"Social Genesis" is an amalgam of the Hartford lectures*
and a lecture given at the Columbian University in Washing-
ton, D.C., the following year. We give here only the concluding
pages.

. . . Genetic progress, the blind, unconscious working of the
social forces making for human perfectionment in the collective state, is what is generally understood by social evolution.
Every stage of ethnic culture, from savagery to enlightenment,
is a product of this genetic, unconscious social evolution. For
most writers on social science this is the only kind of social
progress recognized. Long before sociology was named there
were many such writers. With the habits of abstract reasoning
which all that passed for philosophy had encouraged, it was
the practice of such writers to make use of the few facts that

---

"Social Genesis," *American Journal of Sociology*, II (January 1897),
539–546.

their education, observation, and experience had given them to work out by logical deduction from these facts the most general laws that they were capable of formulating. Much of this reasoning was sound, nearly all of it was logical, i. e., did not violate the canons of logic, and many of the conclusions reached were correct, but so narrow was the induction, and so many and important were the unknown or neglected premises that the general fabric of their philosophy was worthless. Such was the greater part of the so-called political economy which the present age has inherited from the age that went before it. Most of the pre-Comtean sociology comes under this head. A few publicists, like Montesquieu, wrote rather from the standpoint of jurisprudence. Hobbes was the panegyrist of political power, and Malthus, although really following the same lines as Adam Smith and Ricardo, put his work into the form of a sort of philosophy.

All this, as well as the French physiocracy that preceded it and largely inspired it, had the merit at least of regarding society as a domain of law, and its chief defect was in failing to recognize a sufficient number of factors and in omitting some of the most effective ones. These men saw in human society a theater of wide general activity which proceeds from the inherent nature of man. They perceived that if men were left quite to themselves they would, in seeking their personal ends, spontaneously initiate and carry on all the industries of society. Owing to the manifest abuses of power by the ruling classes in seeking to raise revenues for their own uses, conquer other nations for their own glory, and otherwise satisfy their own greed and ambition, whereby the free flow of these natural activities was checked, industry and commerce were stifled or misdirected, and the general prosperity was interfered with and diminished, they felt called upon to counteract these tendencies and advocate the liberation of the natural forces of society. In taking this course at such a time they accomplished a worthy purpose and inaugurated a wholesome reform.

No one denies that the unrestrained activities of the human race would work out some sort of social development. The analogy with organic evolution in the subhuman sphere is also a true one. Though qualified in its details by the differences between men and animals, even by the immense difference between the human mind and the animal mind, with a corresponding difference in the results, the principle according to which these results are accomplished is essentially the same. Those reformers who maintain that the monopolistic tendencies so prevalent in society under the apparent absence of external restraint or collective influence are peculiar to human affairs, and wanting in the lower domains of life and mind, simply betray their lack of acquaintance with those domains. In fact, the fundamental condition to biological development is monopoly. Natural selection operates on this principle exclusively. What is called the survival of the fittest is simply the monopoly of the strongest. It does not work here either in the mild manner characteristic of human society, viz., that of allowing the weaker to exist, only under conditions of reduced activity and stunted growth, but it is thoroughgoing and crushes out the unsuccessful competitors completely. It is only paralleled in human society in those rare cases where a superior race overflows the domain of an inferior one and utterly eradicates it—does not enslave it and allow it to lead a life of subjugation, much less, as is the more frequent case, partially commingle with it and ultimately absorb it, but destroys its roots and branch so that it utterly ceases to exist. This is the method of nature in the animal and vegetable kingdoms, and thus is organic evolution brought about. At least such is the tendency and frequent result, but of course the competitors are often so nearly balanced in this monopolistic power that they coexist for long periods or indefinitely.

The expressions natural selection and survival of the fittest give only the positive side of this general law. There is a negative side which brings out the nature of the law even more clearly. Selection implies rejection, and survival suggests extinction. It may be looked at as a process of *elimination*. The survival of the fit means the failure of the unfit. The selection of the strong is the destruction of the weak. The rejected vastly outnumber the selected. Throughout nature this is the law, and the result is, or has thus far chiefly been, progressive development or structural perfectionment. Up to a certain point this law must have operated on man as on the animal; the only men with whom we are now acquainted have gone beyond it, or at least greatly reduced its effects.

As already stated, sociology has nothing to do with structural changes in man, and social development consists in modifying the environment. But even here the law of natural evolution may and does apply. Monopolistic tendencies are apparent in all social operations. They assume a great variety of forms. The self-aggrandizement of rulers is one of those forms. One of the principal mistakes of the social philosophy under discussion, and one still largely prevalent, is that of assuming that the desire to rule differs in some generic way from other desires, that it is not *natural*, and does not belong to the class of natural laws. It certainly admits of no such monopolistic tendencies. And it cannot be doubted that the efforts put forth to satisfy this desire have resulted in some of the most effective steps in social evolution. To this influence is largely due the founding of great nations, and there is probably no one factor in the progress of society more potent than the crystallizing and humanizing effect of bringing great areas and vast populations under a single set of regulative agencies.

But taking for the moment the standpoint of the physiocratic school of writers referred to, and separating the natural forces of society into the two classes, which may be called industrial and governmental, let us endeavor to form an idea of what the result would be if the former alone existed. In the face of the obvious fact that if the latter class were at any moment wholly in abeyance it would immediately resume operations and soon restore the existing duality of conditions, let us make a complete abstraction of all this and seek to represent ourselves the normal result of the industrial forces working alone. Some such attitude has always been tacitly assumed by those who habitually condemn the governments of the world and conceive them to be hostile to society. These misarchists see the beneficent influences of natural law in the industrial world interfered with by what seems to them an extraneous power, which most candid persons will probably admit to be in itself, at least as commonly defined, non-progressive or only negatively progressive. But the class I refer to take a part and declare it repressive and obstructive of progress. The celebrated "parable of Saint Simon" gives perhaps the most extreme expression to this view that has thus far been uttered, but Mr. Herbert Spencer, although he would not abolish government, is unquestionably its severest modern critic, so much so that anarchistic organs openly claim him as their philosopher.

Now if we could imagine that no single member of society would for a moment think of such a thing as the formation of a governing body, and conceive of each of its members as simply pursuing his individual ends in a private way; taking possession, each as best he might, of some portion of the soil, cultivating it for his own use, exchanging his surplus products with others who, choosing as now other occupations, should produce other useful things; making contracts, not indeed legal, but moral, conditioned ultimately on each one's individual power to enforce them; building cities and entering into mercantile and other kinds of business; adopting a mutually accepted medium of exchange, or carrying on a banking system based on the much-praised principle of credit and trust; establishing manufactures of all kinds and disposing of the products; building railroads and operating them without any other restrictions than those imposed by the laws of business and the conditions favorable to the maximum profits; conducting educational institutions wholly on "business principles;" each one worshiping as now in the manner he prefers; and in all other respects acting individually and without collective restraint—if we could conceive, I say, of such a state of things, we might gain a clear idea of society distinct from government. The two things are not essential to each other, at least in thought, and it would be a great gain to the sociologist to be able to separate them. Even if it be admitted that government is a necessary part of human association, it would be an advantage temporarily to abstract it just as we can abstract any other one element of association. Some, of course, will say that the things specified could not be done in such a state; that government is a condition to conducting the normal operations of society, and that the hypothesis involves the assumption of higher moral attributes than humanity possesses. Such an assumption would render the hypothesis worthless. This, therefore, is precisely the question to be asked and answered. If it is held that without government society would defeat itself and succumb and the race disappear or lapse into a purely animal or non-social condition, then the inquiry is ended. But given the mental powers possessed by man, few will go so far. The real question therefore is: What would have been the condition of society had no government ever been framed? How many and which ones of the existing institutions and operations of society would exist, and what other ones would have been developed? These are difficult questions, but they are legitimate ones for the sociologist to raise and, as far as possible, to settle. This is especially the case at a time like the present, when able philosophers are calling in question the very *raison d'être* of government. Unquestionably these are the ones upon whom it devolves to answer these questions, but aside from all controversy it is profitable to consider them.

Assuming that society would have survived a pure state of anarchy from the beginning, it is obvious that there must have been some kind of organization. This is implied in the idea of association. Gregarious animals have no rulers or laws, but they still have a social organization. There are social forces that hold them together. So it would be with men. It is claimed with much truth that government is never the result of a desire to be governed, but always of a desire to govern. Peoples never clamor for a ruler, but rulers rise up spontaneously and assume gubernatorial powers. If there were no ambition to rule, no desire to hold office, no love of glory, and no expectation of emolument beyond what private life affords, would the members of society ever take steps to have a government established? Perhaps not, and yet there is no doubt that many institutions would arise under such circumstances. In fact we may regard all the institutions of society except those that form a part of government as having arisen in this spontaneous way. The multitudinous forms of association that prevail belong to this class. These are all limited as to membership, which is more or less voluntary. They exist for a great variety of widely different purposes, and the same person may belong to any number of them at the same time. It is clear that these would exist even if no government existed, and the various objects of these associations would be accomplished. The primary social forces would be in full activity in a state of anarchy the same as under any form of government, and men would put forth the normal efforts to preserve, continue, and mitigate life. If, as has been assumed, human nature was what it is, the egoistic propensities would exist as now, and even if no one wanted to undertake their control society would certainly adopt some means of holding them in check. This is proved by the way in which the citizens of frontier districts, in the absence of adequate governmental protection, deal with adventurers and desperadoes who disturb the peace. Vigilance committees may be regarded as incipient spontaneous governments, without any motive of ambition or emolument. So far as mere protection from anti-social tendencies is concerned, they seem to prove that government would always originate itself spontaneously. How far it would go if these motives were permanently absent seems, then, to be the real question.

It is therefore clear that society would not only exist without other government than that which would originate spontaneously from other causes than the desire to rule, but also that it would progress in some degree. This progress might be regarded as typically genetic, and the exclusive product of the normal action of the social forces directly modifying the environment in the interest of society.

I have stated this hypothetical case in order to draw the distinction as clearly as possible between genetic progress and telic progress. So large a part of even past social progress has been telic that it is extremely difficult to separate the two. Still, from a certain point of view, nearly all the progress thus far attained may be regarded as genetic. In the sense of being the result of the normal action of natural laws all of it must be so regarded.

There is a sense, then, in which society makes itself, is a genetic product, and its progress takes place under the general law of evolution that prevails in all departments of natural phenomena. In organic development new principles are constantly coming in, but none of these exempts the resultant phenomena from the action of the law of evolution. That law applied to plants after each of the successive steps, sexuality, exogeny, phanerogamy, gymnospermy, angiospermy, apetaly, polypetaly, gamopetaly, insect agency, etc., had been taken, the same as before. In the animal kingdom it was not affected by the successive appearance of the several higher types of structure from moners to mammals and to man. Even the psychic faculty, the gradual growth of which resulted in an almost complete reversal, from birds upward, of the conditions that governed all creatures below and including the Reptilia, did not visibly check the onward march of organic progress, and the appearance of man with his rational faculty, while it has not wholly arrested physical development, had the effect of transferring the evolutionary forces to the social field to go on at an accelerated pace. No more has social telesis interfered with social genesis, and the telic progress which individual men have secured to society becomes an integral part of the natural evolution of the human race. We may even rise to a higher plane and take into the cosmic conception the past, present, and prospective conscious and intentional social modification, and thus bring the whole into one great scheme of social evolution.

18

COLLECTIVE TELESIS

1895 1897

"Collective Telesis" was the final lecture in the Hartford series and the final chapter in a book that grew out of that series, OUTLINES OF SOCIOLOGY. *As Ward wrote in his preface, he addressed himself not to social philosophy but to social science. By "telic"—one of his favorite words—Ward meant "the law of mind" as distinct from "the law of nature." The triumph of the law of mind, he observed, "inaugurated a whole new order of things."*

. . . As government is an application of what society knows about the nature of the social forces, it is a true art, but the condition in which we now find this art corresponds to that in which all other arts are prior to the application to them of the wider principles of systematic science, and society may be considered to occupy the place, relatively to what it will ultimately attain, that are occupied before the era of science.

This brings us to the kernel of our subject. It may be called *the social art.* The science of society must produce the art of society. *True legislation is invention.* Government is the art

"Collective Telesis," *American Journal of Sociology,* II (May 1897), 807–815.

234

that results from the science of society through the legislative application of sociological principles. In every domain of natural forces there are four steps: First, the discovery of the laws governing phenomena; second, perception of the utilities (modes in which the phenomena can be modified to serve man); third, the necessary adjustments to secure the useful end; and, fourth, the application of all this in producing the result. The first of these steps is that of pure science; the second and third are involved in invention, and properly constitute applied science; the fourth is art in its proper sense. In taking these successive steps there has usually been considerable division of labor. Scientific discoverers are not often inventors, and inventors rarely make the products they invent. Still, two or more of the steps are often taken by the same individual.

Now, looking at society as a domain of natural forces, we may see how readily it admits of being subjected to this series of processes. Discovery of the laws of society is the natural province of the sociologist. He should also be looked to for the detection of utilities, but this work also belongs in a still higher degree to the legislator. Adjustment is the exclusive province of legislation, and laws, when framed according to these principles, would be such adjustments and nothing else. The execution of the laws is the resultant social art. It requires no great stretch of the imagination to see how widely this scheme would differ from the corresponding features of the present régime. It is still easier to see its immense superiority. As was shown in the last paper, the essence of telic action consists at bottom in making natural forces do the desired work instead of doing it ourselves. This is exactly what is needed in society. The desires, passions, and propensities of men are bad only in the sense that fire and lightning are bad. They are perennial natural forces, and, whether good or bad, they exist, cannot be removed, and must be reckoned with. But if society only knew how, it could utilize these forces, and their very strength would be the measure of their power for good. Society is now spending vast energies and incalculable treasure in trying to check and curb these forces without receiving any benefit from them in return. The greater part of this could be saved, and a much larger amount transferred to the other side of the account.

The principle that underlies all this is what I have called "attractive legislation." But it is nothing new or peculiar to society. It is nothing else than the universal method of science, invention, and art that has always been used and must be used to attain telic results. No one tries to drive back, arrest, curb, and suppress the physical forces. The discoverer tells the inventor what their laws are; the inventor sees how they may be made useful and contrives the appropriate apparatus; the man of business organizes the machinery on a gigantic scale, and what was a hostile element becomes an agent of civilization. The effort is not to diminish the force, but usually to bring the maximum amount to bear on a given point. This is true direction and control of natural powers. So it should be in society. The healthy affections and emotions of men should not be curbed but should be directed into useful channels. Zeal and ardor are precious gifts if only they tend in the right direction, and society may profit by every human attribute if only it has the wisdom to utilize it.

The principle involved in attraction, when applied to social affairs, is simply that of *inducing* men to act for the good of society. It is that of harmonizing the interests of the individual with those of society, of making it advantageous to the individual to do that which is socially beneficial; not merely in a negative form, as an alternative of two evils, as is done when a penalty is attached to an action, but positively, in such a manner that he will exert himself to do those things that society most needs to have done. The sociologist and the statesman should coöperate in discovering the laws of society and the methods of utilizing them so as to let the social forces flow freely and strongly, untrammeled by penal statutes, mandatory laws, irritating prohibitions, and annoying obstacles. And here it is important to draw the line sharply between sociology and ethics; between social action and social friction.

All desire is for the exercise of some function, and the objects of desire are such only by virtue of making such exercise possible. Happiness therefore can only be increased by increasing either the number or the intensity of satisfiable desires . . . The highest ideal of happiness, therefore, is the freest exercise of the greatest number and most energetic faculties. This must also be the highest ethical ideal. But it is clear that its realization would abolish moral conduct altogether and remove the very field of ethics from a scheme of philosophy. To remove the obstacles to free social activity is to abolish the so-called science of ethics. Ideally moral conduct is wholly unmoral conduct. Or more correctly stated, the highest ideal of a moral state is one in which there will exist nothing that can be called moral.

Whether we look at the subject from the standpoint of social progress or from that of individual welfare the liberation of social energy is the desideratum. The sociologist demands it because it increases the progressive power of society. The moralist should demand it because it increases happiness. For activity means both, and therefore the more activity the better. True morality not less than true progress consists in the emancipation of social energy and the free exercise of power. Evil is merely the friction which is to be overcome or at least minimized . . . . The tendencies that produce evil are not in themselves evil. There is no absolute evil. None of the propensities which now cause evil are essentially bad. They are all in themselves good, must necessarily be so, since they have been developed for the sole purpose of enabling man to exist, survive, and progress. All evil is relative. Any power may do harm. The forces of nature are good or bad according to where they are permitted to expend themselves. The wind is evil when it dashes the vessel on the rocks; it is good when it fills the sail and speeds it on its way. Fire is evil when it rages through a great city and destroys life and property; it is good when it warms human dwellings or creates the wondrous power of steam. Electricity is evil when in the thunderbolt it descends from the cloud and scatters death and destruction; it is good when it transmits messages of love to distant friends. And so it is with the passions of men as they surge through society. Left to themselves, like the physical elements, they find vent in all manner of ways and constantly dash against the interests of those who chance to be in their way. But, like the elements, they readily yield to the touch of true science, which directs them into harmless, nay, useful channels, and makes them instruments for good. In fact, human desires, seeking their satisfaction through appropriate activity, constitute the only good from the standpoint of sociology.[1]

Few, of course, will be satisfied with these generalities, and many will doubtless ask for some concrete illustrations of scientific legislation. Even those who accept the general conclusions that thus logically flow from the facts of genetic and telic progress will still find themselves at a loss to conceive what definite steps can be taken to accelerate the latter, or how the central ganglion of society can inaugurate a system of social machinery that will produce the required results. This is quite natural, and the only answer that can be made is that, owing to the undeveloped state of the social intellect, very few examples of true ingenuity on the part of legislators exist. Society, as I have shown, if comparable to an organism at all, must take rank among creatures of a very low order. The brain of society has scarcely reached the stage of development at which in the animal world the germs of an intellectual faculty are perceptible. Only when spurred on by the most intense egoistic impulses have nations exhibited any marked indications of the telic power. This has developed in proportion to the extent to which the national will has coincided with the will of some influential individual. Great generals in war, inspired by personal ambition, have often expressed the social will of their own country by brilliant feats of strategy and generalship, and famous statesmen like Richelieu have represented a whole

---

[1] *Psychic Factors*, pp. 113–115.

nation by strokes of diplomacy that called out the same class of talents in a high degree. Even monarchs like Peter the Great, Frederick the Great, and Charles XII, not to mention Cæsar and Alexander, have made their own genius in a sense the genius of their country. In fact a ruling class in times when the people were supposed to exist for them, when a king could say "I am the state," and when revenues were collected for their personal use, often devised very cunning schemes of a national application for their own aggrandizement. But as the world threw off these yokes, and nations grew more and more democratic, the telic element declined, and the most democratic governments have proved the most stupid. They have to rely upon brute force. They are shortsighted and only know how to lock the door after the horse is stolen. They are swayed by impulse. They swarm and "enthuse," and then lapse into a state of torpor, losing all that was gained, and again surge in another direction, wasting their energies. In fact they act precisely like animals devoid of intelligence.

All this is what we ought to expect if the principles I have enunciated are sound, and is, indeed, one of the clearest proofs of their soundness. And yet republics have not proved wholly devoid of a directive agent. Under exceptional circumstances they have displayed signs of collective intelligence. But most of the cases that can be cited have either concerned their national independence or the equally vital question of raising revenue. Nearly all the examples cited in *Dynamic Sociology* and *Psychic Factors* belong to these classes in which, in a literal sense, necessity has been the mother of invention. Anyone who watches the inane flounderings of a large "deliberative" (!) body like the American House of Representatives, working at cross purposes and swayed by a thousand conflicting motives, can see how little reason has to do with democratic legislation. But for the committee system by which, to a certain extent, the various public questions become the subject of scientific investigation, it is doubtful whether the business of the country could be transacted at all. And it is only by a much greater extension of this system, perhaps to the extent of dispensing entirely with the often disgraceful, and always stupid, "deliberations" of the full House, that scientific legislation can ever be realized.

The other important direction in which there is hope of similar results is the gradual assumption of legislative powers, at least advisory, by the administrative branch, which always feels the popular pulse much more sensitively than the legislature, and to which is entrusted not merely the execution of the public will (the art of government), but also in the main the devising of means to accomplish this—the strictly inventive function of government. If the legislature will enact the measures that the administrative branch recommends as the result of direct experience with the business world it will rarely go astray.

The examples given, in which military chieftains, diplomats, monarchs, and ruling families have employed design in national affairs, do not indicate the growth of the social intelligence or the integration of the social program. They are merely instances of the usurpation of the powers of society by individual members. On the other hand, the tendencies in the direction of democratic government do mark progress in social integration, however feeble may be the telic power displayed. Crude and imperfect as such governments may be, they are better than the wisest of autocracies. Stupidity joined with benevolence is better than brilliancy joined with rapacity, and not only is autocracy always rapacious, but democracy is always benevolent. The first of these propositions can be disputed only by citing isolated exceptions. The second may not be so clear, yet it admits of ready demonstration. It is not necessary to postulate a different nature for the democratic legislator from that of the autocratic ruler. However self-seeking the former may be, social service turns his egoism to the good of society. It is an example of the truth that what are called bad motives are only relatively so, and that the social forces only need to be directed to render them all good. For in seeking his own interests the representative of the people must obey their will. The will of the people must be good, at least for them. Constituencies have the same nature as representatives or kings, but whatever they will must be right from their standpoint. The good consists in the satisfaction of desire, and this can only become bad when it is secured at the expense of others. But where a constituency is in question this is not possible except in very sectional questions which cannot be discussed here. *A fortiori* must obedience to the will of a whole people be right, and therefore the representative of the people, whatever may be his personal character, is constrained by his office to do only what is right. If he fails another is put in his place. It is thus that it comes about that representative governments are essentially benevolent, i. e., they always *wish well* for the people, or, as the more common phrase expresses it, they *mean well*. And anyone not prejudiced against government must see that, whatever their faults of the head, they are right at heart.

Democracy has therefore been a great step forward, and has practically solved the moral side of the question of government. Reform in the future must come from the mind side, and surely there is great need of it. How can it be brought about? This is the problem of sociology. I have wrestled with it for many years, not in the hope of doing anything in this direction myself, but with the object of discovering, if possible, a theoretical solution to propose to the world for its consideration. The result of my reflections on this subject is given in the second volume of *Dynamic Sociology,* and although I have not ceased to revolve these matters in my mind during the fourteen years that have elapsed since the first edition of that work appeared, I cannot say that my conclusions have undergone any essential modification. I would now lay more stress upon certain parts of the general argument, and somewhat less on others, but the argument as a whole still stands as worked out in that volume. As democratic governments must be representative I see no way to increase their intellectual status except by increasing that of constituencies, and I still regard this as the one great desideratum. If the social consciousness can be so far quickened as to awake to the full realization of this truth in such vivid manner as to induce general action in the direction of devising means for the universal equalization of intelligence, all other social problems will be put in the way of gradual but certain solution.

But there are some who will say that if this little is all there is to sustain the claim that society is one day destined to take its affairs into its own hands and conduct its business like a rational being, it would be as well to abandon it. If the long period of human history has shown so little advance in the direction of a social intelligence we might better leave matters entirely to the two spontaneous methods described in the two preceding papers. The first answer to this is that the sociologist does not profess to be a reformer, and is not advocating any course of social action. All he feels called upon to do is to point out what the effect of a certain course of action would be as deduced from the fundamental principles of the science, and to state what he conceives the tendencies to be as judged from the history of development.

The second answer to this objection is that it is the one that is always raised whenever anything is mentioned which is different from that which now exists, that it is based on the natural error that things are stationary because they seem to be so, and grows out of the difficulty of conceiving a state of things widely different from the actual state. If we were to indulge in fable, a lump of inert matter would be laughed at by the other lumps if it should assert that it would one day become a graceful tree-fern, and shade the earth with its feathery foliage; a plant that should declare its intention to break away from its attachments to the soil and move about in space on four legs, feeding on other plants instead of air, would be called a vain boaster by the surrounding vegetation; a barnacle that should insist that it would one day have a backbone would be utterly discredited by other barnacles; a bat that should fly into a dark corner of a room and escape through an opening known to be there would be called a fool by the bee that was vainly buzzing against a pane of glass in the hope of accomplishing the same object. It is the "impossible" that happens. We can look backward more easily than we can look forward. Science teaches us that something has happened. Evolution proves that immense changes have taken place, and now that we can see what they were and according to what principles they were brought about there is nothing so startling in the facts. It is only when we try to imagine ourselves as present before an event and striving to forecast it that we realize the folly of raising such objections as we are considering. Yet this is our real attitude with respect to future events. It may be logical, admitting that progress is to go on and that great changes are to take place, to question whether any particular change that anyone may describe is to be the one that will actually occur. There is no probability that anyone can foretell what the real condition of society is to be in the future. But it is illogical, in the light of the past, of history, and especially of natural history, and of what we actually know of evolution, cosmic, organic, and social, to say that any condition to which this knowledge points as a normal result of the continued action of the laws of evolution is impossible.

19

ETHICAL ASPECTS

OF SOCIAL SCIENCE

1896

Ward gave this paper originally as a lecture at George Washington University in November 1895. When he sent it to the International Journal of Ethics, *the editor, Doctor Burns Weston, observed that "it certainly was heterodox ethics" but agreed to publish it. It must indeed have startled the readers of that orthodox academic journal to read that "the so-called science of ethics is essentially negative"; happily, Ward concluded that "all science is essentially ethical."*

. . . We have seen that the so-called science of ethics is essentially negative, that it aims at restraint, that its tendency is to curb, repress, and ultimately destroy the alleged evil propensities of mankind. But all true science is essentially constructive. Where, then, is the fundamental fallacy which must lurk somewhere in the current moral philosophy? It lies in the very assumption of evil propensities. Such supposed

---

International Journal of Ethics (July 1896), 441ff., in *Glimpses of the Cosmos*, V, 275–281.

propensities form an integral part of the natural forces that underlie the social world. They belong to the nature of man. They would never have been planted there if they had not been necessary to his development. They are evil only in so far as they conflict with individual or social interests. They do not differ in this respect from any other element of power in the world. If man only knew fire as something that destroys, that would be classed as an evil agency. Man may have passed through such a stage in his history. Certainly, this was his attitude towards electricity until within less than a century. The attitude changes in proportion as the knowledge of the nature of the agent increases. Strange as it may seem, the natural forces about which man knows least are those that reside within him. The latest sciences to be developed are those of mind and society,—psychology and sociology. But when man shall attain to an acquaintance with the laws governing these fields at all proportional to that which he has now acquired in the fields of physics and mechanics, the practical value of this knowledge will probably be as much greater than the other, as it is more difficult to acquire.

This knowledge of the psychic and social forces constitutes the basis of the new ethics. But it seems folly to call it ethics. The real science to which all these ethical considerations belong is *social science*. This is a true science. It is constructive. Like every other true science, it aims to utilize the forces operating within its domain. These are the social forces, and included in them are all the supposed evil propensities of human nature. Instead of condemning these, it recognizes them, and, after the manner in which science deals with all natural powers, it seeks first to render them harmless and then to make them useful. This is always possible so soon as their nature is known. Such has been the history of science in every other field. Such will be its history in the social field.

The method of science is not that of checking the flow of natural forces. It aims not to diminish, but to increase their effect. It restrains only where they are doing harm. But this is done by directing them into new courses where they no longer do harm. It seeks to find useful directions, and thus brings good out of evil. More than this. It unites many currents into one, and multiplies the power which it is desirable to have applied to any useful purpose. It assists nature to store its energy that it may expend it economically. Thus it secures far greater results than nature would achieve unaided, and renders these results beneficial, instead of indifferent or injurious.

All this social science aims to accomplish in the domain of the social forces. Its field is not restricted to conduct, but extends to all action. Its object is not to limit activity, but to increase it. It uses restraint only in order to direct it into useful avenues. But this results in the greatest freedom and the maximum activity. Man has already learned that liberty is not secured through anarchy, but through government. What is true in the political world is true in the social world. The new ethics, which is social science, seeks the utmost individual liberty. But, like every science, it aims at results. Its true object, to use the forcible expression of Mr. Benjamin Kidd, is *social efficiency*. The social forces, once in their proper grooves, may all exert their utmost energy, as their friction is thus reduced to the minimum. Enthusiasm and zeal are beneficent powers when directed to useful ends. The emotions and even the passions of men are precious gifts to society, because they represent vast powers for the accomplishment of results. These results constitute social progress, which follows necessarily upon the liberation of the dynamic agencies of society.

It cannot, of course, be denied that there are catabolic elements in man's nature, elements productive of evil results. There are criminal impulses, often congenital, in dealing with which moral suasion is powerless, and which are therefore beyond the reach of the ethical code. Most of these are survivals from an antecedent state, savage or even animal. They were once useful, but are now mere vestiges, like the tonsils or the vermiform appendage—sources of social, as these are of physical disease. Where this is not the case, and the destructive elements are not atavistic but normal, such as anger, hate, jealousy, envy, and the rest, they are the products of a cramped social environment. They only appear when the free play of the healthy, harmless, anabolic sentiments is impeded or prevented. In the ancestral state these impulses passed into action and caused battles between rivals, the destruction of the weaker, and the ultimate restoration to the conquerors of liberty to pursue harmless pleasures. In society they result in immoral conduct or crime.

Now, it is precisely the function of social science to do away with this state of things, not by allowing free vent to catabolic impulses, but by removing the conditions under which they arise. As they are due to the constraint of the harmless impulses, the liberation of these latter prevents the former from manifesting themselves. This constitutes one of the best illustrations of the theory of the social forces and of social friction. Rage is the true homologue of the heat generated by friction. Remove the friction and the heat will not exist. It is only a "mode" of the general force employed. The social forces are identical with all other natural forces, even to the extent of conforming to the law of the transmutation of forces. The catabolic impulses are only modes of manifestation of the general psychic force; they are the forms which the natural or anabolic sentiments assume under frictional restraint.

The sociological point of view is thus seen to be precisely the opposite of the ethical point of view. It is that of the liberation instead of the restraint of human activity. In short, it is positive, not negative, and on this the whole distinction turns. It is not necessary to abandon the good as the end of action. Indeed, however insignificant the domain of feeling may be (and it is certainly an exceedingly restricted field relatively to the whole universe of matter, space, and time), we are so circumstanced that we are compelled to regard it as everything to us. Therefore a positive even more than a negative ethics will make the good its end. But there is this manifest difference. Negative ethics sets bounds to its own scope and tends to consume itself. When all preventable evil shall disappear its course is run. As this is only theoretical and cannot probably be actualized, it can only be regarded as a logically fatal objection, but the practical objection is that the method of negative ethics would repress the normal activities of society which form the condition of positive ethics.

Is there, then, no limit to the extent to which the good may be increased? At first view it would seem that there must be such a limit. Reduced to its simplest expression, the good consists in the exercise of the faculties. To go into the physiology of this proposition would carry me too far, but I believe it can be sustained. Even an unexpected physical pleasure, such as that derived from a delicious morsel or a fragrant bouquet, presupposes a specialization of the nerves of taste or smell which has made the flavor or the odor agreeable, and the fact of experiencing such a pleasure is simply the exercise of a faculty which it has required untold ages to develop. The human body is a reservoir of a vast number of such capacities for enjoyment, and when we include the psychic faculties, aesthetic, intellectual, social, there is scarcely any limit even now to the wants which men possess to be satisfied. The good is nothing more nor less than the satisfaction of these wants.

But can we say of good as we may say of evil that its range is limited? Can all desires be conceived as gratified just as all pains may be conceived as removed? Not in the *élite* of the human race, certainly. In the animal, with only physical and a few social wants, this might be possible, but in man, with all his spiritual aspirations, it is inconceivable. Certain individuals with coarse organizations might perhaps be placed in the same class with animals in this respect, but the finer organizations cannot be so placed. It is not, however, with individuals that the question chiefly deals, but with the race as a whole. It is not a question of satisfying present as much as future wants. History furnishes plenty of examples of the creation of new wants.

In the domain of aesthetics this is very manifest. Music is a comparatively modern art. This is not altogether nor chiefly because musical notation, instruments, and methods were unknown to the ancients. It is principally because the love of music had not yet been created in the physical mechanism of the men of that time. There are still not only races but individuals of our own race, in whom it does not exist.

The Greeks and Romans were far advanced in architecture and sculpture, and they had the art of painting men and animals, plants and buildings, all symmetrical objects. But there appears to be no evidence that they painted landscapes. They had not yet acquired the power of admiring the landscape. Caesar marched his armies over the Alps and wrote much of his Commentaries on their summits, but he was utterly oblivious of their beauties. The love of nature as a whole, especially in its amorphous aspects,—mountains, waters, clouds, etc.,—is a recent acquirement, like the love of music.

In the domain of social life, the more refined sexual sentiments furnish a striking example of the power of man to acquire new wants. It is only in the European race that these have assumed any marked prominence, and even in this race they have been developed within comparatively recent times. Brilliant as were the intellectual achievements of the Greeks and Romans, and refined as were many of their moral and aesthetic perceptions, nothing in their literature conclusively proves that love with them meant more than the natural demands of the sexual instinct under the control of strong character and high intelligence. The romantic element of man's nature had not yet been developed. This constitutes a distinctly modern need. It is rooted in the lower passion and has grown out of it, but it is distinguished from it by the fact that the presence alone of the object is its satisfaction. This step is an exceedingly long one, and was gradually taken during the Middle Ages, assuming its developed proportions under the knights-errant and the troubadours from the eleventh to the thirteenth century. To-day it prevails throughout Europe, America, and other countries that have been settled by Europeans, and nowhere else. It has completely revolutionized the social life of these peoples and has purified their literature. This is why the older literature requires to be expurgated before it is fit for modern ears. It was too erotic. Modern literature, although it deals with love to a far greater extent than ancient, is chaste, because love means something entirely different from what it formerly meant. The needs of modern peoples growing out of it are much more numerous and imperative than before, but they are so pure and elevated that it is possible to treat them with the utmost freedom without causing the least shock to the finest sensibilities.

Again, true conjugal affection, as it exists to-day in enlightened communities, and which is a different thing from the spiritualized sexual sentiment last considered, although an outgrowth from it as that is an outgrowth from the sexual instinct, constitutes another and still more modern source of social enjoyment developed by civilization. Nor is it less important, for it has done more than all other influences combined to cement and solidify the most important of all social structures, the family. The monogamic sentiment is gaining strength and becoming more and more the bulwark of society. Those who see in the prevailing unrest relative to marriage only signs of degeneracy fail to interpret these signs correctly. It is in reality due to the very strengthening that I have mentioned of the true bonds of conjugal affection, coupled with a rational and altogether proper determination on the part of individuals to accept, in so important a matter, nothing less than the genuine article.

I might go on and enumerate the proofs that the race is constantly acquiring new powers of enjoyment in the aesthetic, moral, social, and intellectual world, but these examples must suffice. Nor is there to be found the slightest evidence that its capacity for such acquisition will ever be exhausted. This, then, is the basis for a positive ethics which cannot consume itself. It stands on the same footing with every other science and is in all essential respects a true science. These higher aspirations, which are the spiritual representatives of the lower wants, sublimated by intelligence and culture, are, like the bodily cravings out of which they have evolved, *faculties* —i. e., powers, and contribute to the full extent of their intensity to the motor strength of society. The new ethics aims not only to liberate all these social forces, but to utilize them in propelling the machinery of society.

I have thus far only spoken of the dynamic agencies of society. These would, indeed, be unmanageable without the aid of a directive agency. This is the *intellect*, which serves as a guide to the social forces. And right here lies the explanation of the sterility of the old or negative ethics. It does not recognize the reason as a factor. It does not attempt to guide or direct the destructive elements of social activity. It treats them as only baneful, and wages a crusade against them. It invents such epithets as sin, vice, immorality, and seeks to stamp these out. It denounces, anathematizes, condemns, or else it pleads, expostulates, and exhorts. All this, if separated from the influence of example and personal magnetism, is without effect—mere *brutum fulmen*. As well might King Canute command the sea to retire, or Pope Calixtus III. drive Halley's comet from the skies.

The method of science under the guidance of intelligence is to attract the natural forces, not to drive them; to free them, not to fetter them. There is no more misleading expression than the one so commonly used to the effect that Franklin "chained the lightning." So far from his chaining it, he found for it an unobstructed path, albeit one in following which it not only could do no harm, but could do and has done incalculable good. And all subsequent dealings on the part of science with this wonderful agent have only served to increase its power. The most violent thunderbolt that ever rent the clouds was not equal to the great Baltimore dynamo that recently forced a train through the tunnel against the power of the strongest locomotive.

And so it will be with the social forces when once we learn how to control and utilize them. This is social science in its applied stage. Its purpose is to find unobstructed paths along which they may operate to their full extent. It will minimize the social friction and utilize the social energy. It will devise the requisite social apparatus to this end. Just as material progress under science consists in the development of the practical arts of which machinery is the highest expression, so social progress will consist in the development of the supreme social art of which social machinery will constitute the highest manifestation.

This is not, of course, the place, even if it were advisable, to offer any hints as to the character which this social machinery is likely to assume. As well might our ancestors have sought to predict the machinery of to-day. But on numerous previous occasions I have attempted to indicate some of the initial steps in social invention. My chief purpose, however, has been to emphasize the fact that sociology is a science, that it is a domain of natural forces of which man may take advantage precisely as he has taken advantage of the physical forces of nature. Until this truth can be perceived and vividly brought home, not only to philosophers, but especially to men of affairs, statesmen, and legislators, it is vain to speculate upon methods and details.

It is only within the scope of the present paper to deal with the ethical aspects of the question, and I must end as I began by repeating that all science is essentially ethical. Social science is more so than other sciences only because it deals more directly and exclusively with the collective welfare of mankind. It seeks not merely to reduce the social friction and thus accomplish all that the old ethics has so vainly striven to secure, viz., negative moral progress, but also and chiefly to put the manifold existing and prospective wants of mankind in the way of satisfaction, and thus to bring about a progressive and unlimited train of benefits and a truly scientific or positive moral progress.

I have called these ethical aspects. In this I may be mistaken, but it is only a question of the meaning of words. As I said at the outset, I have never entered the field of ethics, and if the universal betterment of man's estate does not belong to ethics, it is a field into which I do not care to enter.

20

UTILITARIAN ECONOMICS

1896 1898

This essay grew out of some extemporaneous remarks by Ward on a paper on the "Formulation of Normal Laws" by Professor Simon Patten, at the 1895 meeting of the American Economic Association. Thereafter, Ward got a good deal of mileage out of it: a lecture (in French) at the Congress of the Institut International de Sociologie, a lecture at the University of Chicago, and a contribution to the American Journal of Sociology.

. . . The "riddle of the universe" is: What are we here for? or as Humboldt expressed it: "Wüssten wir nur wenigstens, warum wir auf dieser Welt sind?"[1] Many besides Kidd have admitted that "there is no rational sanction for the conditions of progress."[2] The fact that we are here, and the fact that we constantly make sacrifices to secure our remaining here, become, therefore, to the thoughtful, troublesome puzzles. The great mass of mankind give no thought to the subject. Even

---

"Utilitarian Economics," *American Journal of Sociology,* VIII (January 1898), 520–536.

---

[1] *Memoiren,* I, 367.
[2] *Social Evolution,* p. 59.

the intelligent are for the most part content to feel that there is something within them that makes them cling to life irrespective of whether life is gain or a loss.

Hitherto the subject has been approached either from the religious, the ethical, or the philosophical point of view, but quite recently for the first time it has been approached from the economic point of view. Dr. Simon N. Patten has pointed out that society presents us with two very different kinds of economy—a pain economy and a pleasure economy.[3] This puts the whole question in an entirely new light, and opens up novel and promising lines of discussion looking to its solution. It is not that the truth itself is an altogether new one, but chiefly that it furnishes a new standpoint from which to contemplate the old truth.

I have been for many years engaged in trying to solve this problem. I have shown that it has as its basis the fact called feeling, i. e., pleasure and pain. I have endeavored to demonstrate that feeling has had an objective and not a subjective origin, that it is simply a condition to the existence of the beings that possess it, and that the phenomena of good and evil are purely incidental, unintended, and apart from the general scheme of nature. I have further shown that this mere incident has been made the end of the creature, an end wholly distinct from the end of nature, producing activities that sometimes coincide with those involved in evolution, sometimes run parallel with and independent of them, sometimes deviate widely from them, and sometimes more or less directly conflict with them. I have traced many of these abnormal influences and shown what remarkable aberrations they have wrought in the world. Indeed, I have gone much farther than this. In carefully defining the nature of the social forces, I have shown

---

[3] *The Theory of Social Forces.* Supplement to the Annals of the American Academy of Political and Social Science, VII, No. 1 (January 1896), 75ff.

that they consist in social wants, and have classified these. My primary classification was into essential and non-essential, and the former of these great classes was further subdivided into those relating respectively to the preservation and the perpetuation of life. It is clear that the economic view does not specially embrace the non-essential social forces, and it is equally clear that of the essential forces it is chiefly or wholly centered on those of preservation. What especially bears on the present question is the fact that my subdivision of the preservative social forces was into positive and negative, the former seeking pleasure, the latter avoiding pain.[4] . . .

In our western civilization, as already remarked, the great majority even of the well-informed, and practically all of the lower classes, are optimistic. The former do not reflect upon their condition, and the latter simply struggle to exist. Neither ask what existence means. A few of both classes find it unbearable and try, often successfully, to put an end to it, but these only incur the contempt of the rest. A number even smaller than that of the suicides do reflect, not so much upon their own condition as upon that of others, and, finding it generally bad, declare that there is no rational ground for existence. These are called "pessimists" and are held in still greater execration than the suicides.

But this state of things is not universal. It is peculiar to western peoples, and quite a different one prevails in the East. At least the bulk of the teachings of oriental nations is pessimistic, and even the lower classes are represented as generally regarding life as an evil and annihilation as a blessing which they hope to attain. It is true that it is difficult to ascertain the real state of things in those countries, compelled, as we mostly are, to depend upon the interpretations of men of the West, who show by their conflicting reports that they are incapable of thoroughly assimilating the oriental spirit. I am, therefore,

---

[4] *Dynamic Sociology*, I, 472.

prepared to believe that, in the lower ranks at least, there is also a preponderance of optimism in the East.

But to show that there is everywhere a basis for pessimism it is only necessary to point to the wide prevalence of asceticism throughout Christendom. Christianity may have simply averted a universal pessimism by introducing the conception of a future compensation for present evils. Mohammedanism does the same, and wherever these faiths prevail asceticism takes the place of pessimism. Asceticism in all its forms recognizes the same truth that pessimism asserts, viz., that affairs, in this world at least, are bad. Christianity openly teaches this, and the burden of its texts, its hymns, and its sermons is the worthlessness of mundane things. All its austerities are based on this idea, and the self-denial, mortification, penance, and puritanism, so prevalent in Christian countries, are only so many expressions of the universal undercurrent of asceticism.

Moreover, the ethical code of the West is not only tinctured with this same spirit, but is virtually based upon it, as I hope to make clear later, so that, after all, there is not so much difference in the two great philosophies of the world as might be supposed from a superficial view of the question.

Aside, therefore, from pessimism, which declares that matters are the worst possible, and is therefore a sort of licensed hyperbole, and aside even from *pejorism*, which assumes to decide the question whether the good or the bad predominates, and declares for the latter, there is throughout the world, and especially among all peoples whose rationality is at all marked, a universal recognition, though largely unconscious, of what may be called *malism*, which only vaguely declares that things are bad. It is the basis of this feeling that I now propose to examine, in order, if possible, to determine whether it is an objective reality or an illusion.

It is just here that biology lends its aid. What is the condition of the animal? Darwin has shown that there is a "struggle for existence." I am not disposed to exaggerate the meaning of this phrase. I admit that animals are largely unconscious of any "struggle," and that it may not greatly lessen their enjoyment of life. They do not suffer from imaginary evils, they do not anticipate those of the future, and they may not vividly remember the pains previously experienced. In fact, as is well known, they fear the ones they have never experienced as much as those they have actually suffered. Their mental states are chiefly controlled by instincts made up of the inherited experiences of their ancestors. But turn it as you may, the fact remains that in nearly every natural race of creatures, in order to hold their own against the buffets of the world, somewhere from ten to a thousand individuals have to be born for every one that lives out its normal period of existence. In every case the great majority succumb, before the age of reproduction, to enemies, to disease, to starvation, or to the elements, and the survivors, throughout their entire lives, are incessantly threatened with the same fate. It is, therefore, no wonder that animals are "wild." They seem to resort to every conceivable device to escape these dangers, and nature through innumerable instincts seems to aid them in their efforts. Some are fleet of foot or swift of wing; others have delicate senses of hearing, sight, or smell; others have wonderful powers of concealment; and still others are endowed with numberless arts of imitation, feigning, and deception. All this is independent of the countless organic devices for protection—shells, armors, spines, bristles, musk sacs, ink bags, and all the forms of imitative coloring.

Nearly all animals are always on the alert. Some, as hares, sleep with their eyes open. Thousands are nocturnal in order to evade diurnal enemies, and are thus denied all the enjoyments of a life in the open daylight and sunshine. All are constantly ready to fly at the least sign of danger, and even those that prey upon others must themselves watch lest stronger or more cunning ones deprive them of their spoils. Even if there were no other animal to fear, there would remain the fear of

men, "ces monstres nos éternels ennemis."[5] This fact, that one
half of the animal world lives by devouring the other half, has
perhaps been too frequently dwelt upon, but it still stands in
all its sullen hideousness before the defenders of a moral order.
In this subworld of animal life the primary motive is fear.

But if the human race cannot realize its condition, the animal races cannot be expected to do so. Their sole thought is to
escape from danger. It is not to be supposed that they have
any idea of preserving life. What they seek to avoid is simply
pain, not death. Dr. Patten is therefore perfectly right when
he says that animal existence (in the wild state) represents a
"pain economy." When we realize that it is pain only that
animals fear and fly from, we can understand what is meant by
the instinct of self-preservation. As pain leads to death, to
escape it is to escape death and to preserve life. For thus was
it ordered in the primary adaptation which brought feeling and
mind into the world. This shows us the great value that the
biological aspect of the subject possesses for psychology, for
economics, and for sociology. It explains the meaning of the
law of self-preservation in man. What is this meaning?

"Self-preservation is the first law of nature." So runs the
adage. And it is true. It is true quite independently of the
quality of the life that so much effort is made to preserve.
Whether it is worth preserving or not has no bearing upon
the result. This is so because man was himself once an animal
and knew nothing about death. He then fled from pain as
animals do. After his brain had so far developed that he was
capable of mentally connecting pain with death and of realizing that to escape pain was to preserve life, the instinct which
had brought him through to that state was ineradicably implanted in his nature, and no amount of knowledge or force of
reason has ever sufficed to disturb it. By the time he was able
to express ideas by oral language so completely had the deriva-

---

[5] Voltaire, "Le Chapon et la Poularde," *Dialogues,* etc., p. 100.

tive conception of preserving life supplanted the original conception of escaping pain that the latter was lost sight of, and it would be to many today a new thought, while some might even be found to question it.

Here, too, is to be found the true explanation of *optimism*. It is simply the instinct of self-preservation, a survival of the instinct of pain avoidance, and forms the negative aspect of the primordial psychic factor *feeling*, which was the essential condition to the origin and development of the entire class of beings that possess it. It is not, therefore, to be expected that anything so deeply rooted in the constitution of organic nature should be affected by the cold calculations of latter-day philosophers who may balance up the debits and credits of life and figure out a deficit. Whether there be such a deficit in animal life, and whether there has been any such in human life thus far, or in any stage or portion of it, it may be impossible exactly to decide, but in any case it is certain that the instinct to escape danger has been successful in tiding man over the prolonged period of his prehistoric existence and in buoying him on into his present more or less civilized state.

During all the early portion of this period, however long it may have been, there was nothing to interrupt the steady and persistent action of this psychic force working in complete harmony with cosmic law toward the primary end of organic evolution. But as the cerebral hemispheres grew and the thinking powers increased, and especially after society, art, and industry had become fixed institutions, and after priesthoods had been established, forming a sedentary class, philosophy took root and the thought of man turned to the study and analysis of his condition. Then began, by little and little, that slow transformation which has ultimately brought about the pessimism of the East and the asceticism of the West, to which reference has been made. It has never been sufficiently pronounced to resist the powerful tide of optimism, but it has created a manifest ripple on the surface and here and there an eddy in the stream itself.

While orientalism would seem to be more favorable than asceticism to the growth of this anti-optimistic tendency, the indications are that it is in the West that we must look for its greatest development. This is not because Christianity is more favorable to it, but because it is here that a true knowledge of nature is being acquired through the revelations of science and the unavoidable philosophy that is growing out of them. The most enlightened western races are letting in the dry light of investigation and reason upon every domain of nature and are fearlessly formulating the resultant logic, leaving consequences to take care of themselves. Latterly these researches have been more and more directed to the higher social conditions, and they have not only confirmed the widespread belief in malism, but have penetrated to its causes and conditions and somewhat stripped it of the sanctity that has hitherto surrounded it. In the present state of the world there may be danger that these influences will antagonize the normal laws of development and tend to bring the hitherto rapid growth of population to a standstill.

I long ago pointed out that reason often works at cross purposes with natural law, and may have brought about the extinction of races. This, however, related to the effect of error, which only a rational being can commit, and the remedy lies in the discovery of truth and the diffusion of knowledge. This stage is probably past by the leading races of the world. But there is another way in which reason may conflict with law, and this is the case before us. There is a great dualism in the organic world. There are two wholly independent forces at work which may coöperate, or may follow parallel lines without affecting each other, or may conflict in any and all degrees. The only check upon this last is the fact that direct conflict, if sufficiently prolonged, leads to extinction, and only such races have survived as have avoided such conflict, at least to the extent of maintaining their existence.

These two forces are the ones which I have on numerous occasions described as those, on the one hand, which secure the performance of *function,* and those, on the other, that proceed from *feeling.* The first are *normal,* and constitute the primary law of evolution as it operates in the organic world. The second are *supra-normal,* and constitute an entirely new departure from that primary law. They are, so to speak, wholly incidental and unintended, not having been, as it were, contemplated by nature when the psychic element was introduced. That element was developed for a totally different purpose, viz., as already stated, in order to enable a certain class of evolutionary products to exist which could not have existed without it, to wit: plastic organisms. These must possess some means of escaping destructive tendencies and of replenishing organic waste through metabolism of their substance. The only such means that we can conceive of is feeling, i. e., sensitiveness to pain and capacity for pleasure. In order to secure the end these subjective states must constitute the motives to all the so-called spontaneous activity of this class of beings. As a matter of fact, they do constitute such motives. Their *normal* operation secures the ends of nature in a most admirable manner, and this adaptation of means to ends is one of the most striking and wonderful in the whole range of nature's operations. So long as the psychic element remained at this lowest stage of pure feeling, it was a perfectly safe ally of the other cosmic forces. The struggle might go on, and no matter how great the havoc among the animated and sensitive molecules and cells, they would all prove true to their original purpose and survive or perish as fate might decide.

But the same agencies that created the primary psychic element worked for its development. The more intense it was, the more certain were its effects in securing the preservation and multiplication of life. A stage was at length reached at which a second element, derivative, indeed, but distinct in its mode of action, made its appearance and was slowly developed. This was the *reason,* dimly apparent in some very lowly creatures, and plainly manifest in the highest animal races. . . .

Born of the cosmic law and created to be the servant of the primary element, it may be described in one phrase as a device for securing indirectly those ends which could not be secured directly. It is easy to see that, so far at least as the ends of the creature were concerned, this step represented a great gain.

The profound bio-psychic dualism under consideration demands still further elucidation. . . . Function is essentially static, while feeling alone is dynamic. The former rests on the law of heredity, the latter underlies the phenomena of variation. But throughout the animal series these two factors coöperate with sufficient exactness to be in the main safe. They are self-regulating, and natural selection may be trusted to correct any dangerous tendency toward an undue deviation from the type. Near the end of that series there have occurred, it is true, enormous aberrations, in certain respects almost completely reversing the normal condition of things, but none of these have seriously interfered with the law of heredity, and in some the power of structural advancement has been manifestly increased. These aberrations have all been due to the growth of an inchoate rational faculty which, in exact proportion to its strength, has made feeling more and more an end. The necessary effect of the reason is to increase the tendency to vary, and a stage was at length reached at which this tendency began to threaten the safety of the type.

Early in the human period this stage was reached, and but for certain countervailing agencies the race must have been prematurely extinguished. The law of self-preservation would not alone have sufficed to save it, and if there is any distinction between that law and the remedial optimism that supervened, this is what we are now seeking. Viewed from this standpoint, optimism may be characterized as the law of *social* self-preservation. We find everywhere in savage, barbaric, semi-civilized, and even civilized races a certain class of ideas in common which make for race preservation, in more or less direct conflict with individual interest. These are embodied in customs, institutions, religious observances, and moral precepts. They are sometimes referred to as the "collective wisdom" of mankind, a wisdom far greater than that of any individual, since they seem to involve foresight and to constitute a sort of social clairvoyance. They form the various codes of action—legal, moral, conventional, and social—of all races, and are rigidly enforced against the recognized anti-social propensities of individuals. Most of them are aimed directly at race preservation, but there are some, as, for example, the severe penalties imposed for the violation of the law of exogamy, which look to the preservation of the vigor of the race. They rest on a universal consensus respecting those things which, however pleasing to the individual, are injurious to the race and in any way threaten to reduce its numbers or weaken its strength. In one sense they are not rational, and in many respects they strikingly resemble the instincts of animals. Indeed, they may be regarded as the true homologues of these instincts. If they do not rest on reason, they at least embody the highest wisdom. They almost always have the powerful sanction of religion, and for this reason some have confounded them with religion itself. Others believe them to be of divine origin and not explainable on natural principles. In fact, they are difficult to explain, as, for example, how the lowest savages find out that close interbreeding deteriorates the stock. I am myself disposed to call in the law of natural selection and to assume that existing races represent the survivors in a prolonged struggle in which those not possessing these saving qualities have succumbed. This places them squarely in line with animal instincts, and the current of modern opinion runs in the direction of basing all instincts primarily upon some germ of reason.

Feeling may be said to have been developed as a means to the ends of nature, which are preservation and multiplication. But to the creature, which knew nothing of these ends, the means must be itself an end, and throughout the sentient world the subjective states described have always been, and must always continue to be, the ends of the feeling creature. But reason is a form of knowing, and step by step the knowing powers increased. The only purpose they could have for their possessors was that of better and better realizing the subjective states. It thus becomes easy to see how the pursuit of the creature's ends might often be quite a different thing from that of the ends of nature, and this, in fact, has been the case to a marked extent, which explains the dualism. It is this truth that lies at the bottom of the problem before us; indeed, it lies at the bottom of the whole philosophy of man and society.

In man reason has become a powerful element, and he has always used it, and will always continue to use it, for its primary purpose of better securing his only end, the satisfaction of the demands of his nature. As the eminent ethnologist, M. Paul Topinard, has recently said:

"His sensorium is the focus in which all is gathered. He is perforce subjective. He is by sensibility and by logic egocentric. *I* first, *others* afterwards. . . . The thinkers that exercise their ingenuity in adapting him to the conditions of existence, in creating for him a world of his own, in laying down the rules for his conduct, and in seeking foundations for it least open to attack, must not forget that his only cherished aim is his own happiness."[6]

The happiness that man has always sought and is still seeking is, however, more or less relative. I have shown what is the condition of the animal in the wild state and how far short it falls of a state of ideal happiness. While man through his reason has undoubtedly improved upon that state, has reduced the enormous death rate, and has both lessened his pains and increased his pleasures, he has, to offset these gains, the evils of an intensified memory, the new powers of imagination and of anticipation, and a swarm of delicate mental capacities for feeling unknown to humbler creatures. And what has been his

---

[6] *The Monist*, VI, No. 1 (Chicago, October 1895), 46, 49.

real condition from this point of view? A single glance into the lower strata of society even today is sufficient to show that it represents a pain economy. The leading motive still is fear, and the chief effort is not to enjoy, but simply to live. With all due allowance made for the superior "contentment" of the lower classes, and of their incapacity to enjoy the things that the more favored chiefly value, it must still be admitted that the great mass even in civilized countries lead a negative rather than a positive existence.

While it may not be possible to draw any line, it is evident that there exists somewhere a line that separates the negative from the positive state of existence—the pain from the pleasure economy. If we call all pains *minus* and all pleasures *plus*, that line will fall at the point where the algebraic sum of pains and pleasures is equal to zero. Any society below that line represents a pain economy, and only those societies that lie above that line represent a pleasure economy. There are certain tests which may be applied in trying to decide on which side of the zero line a given society should be placed. One is the economic test. The old economics doubtless reflected a large amount of truth and was more or less adapted to the time in which it was formulated. That science was almost exclusively based on the consideration of man as an animal, or, at best, as a "covetous animal," i. e., an animal with some idea of the value of property. The fact that the Malthusian law has proved to hold throughout animal life shows that the man at least about whom Malthus was talking was only an advanced kind of animal. And it seems probable that the modern revolt against the old political economy is due as much to the fact that there has been a change in man himself as to any discovery by recent writers that the older writers were wrong. Certainly the old economics was wholly adapted to a pain economy, or a general state of society in which fear was the principal motive and life, not happiness, the principal aim. We may, therefore, infer that such was the state of society in Europe down to the close of the eighteenth century. *A fortiori*, all antecedent history must belong to a pain economy.

Another test is the ethical code. Almost the only ethics we have is what may properly be called negative. It is based on restraint and condemns nearly all activities that have happiness, and especially pleasure, for their object. It is safe to infer that there is good reason for this. In a pain economy the ethical code must necessarily be negative. It must lay chief emphasis upon those things which must be done. All but two of the ten commandments are negative in form in both Exodus and Deuteronomy, showing that it was then regarded as dangerous to pursue pleasure for its own sake. For where every energy is taxed to its utmost to maintain existence, any relaxation is unsafe. All must be perpetually on guard, and there must be no sleeping on one's post. Pursuit of pleasure means neglect of duty, and the terms pleasure and duty are the later homologues of the primary equivalents, feeling and function. It is the antithesis between the creature and the cosmos, between the individual and the race, or, expressed in the language of theology, between man and God. In a pain economy a state of happiness at all prolonged is incompatible with safety. This is the true explanation of the austere ethical code under which we live, which, like every other structure, whether anatomical or social, tends to persist long after the causes that brought it forth have ceased to act.

The preservation, perpetuation, and increase of the human family, as well as the general development and perfectionment of our race and of all organic forms, which constitute what I have called the ends of nature, form, it is true, an inspiring theme, and an object well worthy of the tremendous sacrifices that have been made to secure it, yet, properly viewed, it has nothing whatever to do with economics. That science is based exclusively on the idea of utility in the narrower sense of good to the individual, and, however paradoxical it may sound, these grand objects are, in and of themselves, absolutely of no *use*.

That is to say, utility relates solely and exclusively to what I have called the ends of the sentient creature, or, in the human sphere, the ends of man, and this notwithstanding that, as I have shown, the pursuit of such ends is purely incidental and unintended, and forms no part of the general scheme of nature.

But inasmuch as we have this dualism as one of the most remarkable facts of existence, it is the part of wisdom to recognize it and try to understand its significance. Instead of a mere temporary episode in the history of the world, it is a permanent condition. It has come to stay, and already its effects in every department upon which it has exerted an influence have been most sweeping. It has completely revolutionized some of these departments, even below the human plane, and its power over human and social affairs is stronger than anywhere else. This assertion of the claims of feeling, this *Bejahung des Willens zum Leben,* this soul of nature, is what I have elsewhere characterized as the "transforming agency," and I have indicated some of the fields in which its activity has been greatest, and enumerated certain of its achievements.

These facts are sufficient to show that this new cosmic and social agency is a growing power. I am now endeavoring to trace its history, and I propose to characterize the movement in its later social aspects as the subjective trend of modern philosophy. There has been going on along a number of more or less independent lines a continuous, though somewhat rhythmic, movement in the direction of the fuller realization of the ends of man as distinguished from those of nature, a subordination of the latter to the former, or an ignoring of the latter when they conflict with the former. This movement is nothing more nor less than a gradual transition from a pain economy to, or at least toward, a pleasure economy. It represents, in the fullest sense of the phrase, the progress of utilitarianism. It has been wholly due and strictly proportional to the growth of the rational faculty, the increase of knowledge, and the march of science. Without these it could only lead to disaster. The great danger has been that of running counter to the law of natural evolution and of bringing about racial degeneration and extinction. Reason has acted as a pilot to keep the ship of life off these bars and to guide it safely on in the current of natural law. This movement embodies all that is meant by the progress of the world, and underlies every problem of history, government, and society. Many have been alarmed at its encroachments, and the moral and religious teachers of every age have antagonized it and stigmatized it as hedonism and sensuality. Those who early scented it and voiced it—the Cumberlands, Shaftesburys, Hutchesons, Priestleys, Beccarias, and Benthams—have been attacked, denounced, and discredited as Utopian dreamers. But its greatest strides have been taken since their day, due far less to their influence than to the agencies which they sagaciously presaged. The opposition still continues, but grows weak and half-hearted. The latest warning voice has been that of Mr. Benjamin Kidd, who, while sympathizing with the movement, which he profoundly misunderstands, bases his plea upon the doctrine that acquired characteristics are not transmissible, a doctrine which Weismann has himself virtually abandoned, confounds optimism with religion, and makes the increase of population constitute the whole of "social evolution."

It is too late now to stem this tide. The claims of a feeling world have come before the bar of rational judgment and been admitted. Those of a cold, unconscious Cosmos must give way except in so far as they may prove helpful in adjusting the others. A pain economy may be tolerated by non-rational beings. The savage and barbaric tribes of men may remain below the zero line. The lowest strata of so-called civilized society will doubtless long continue to vegetate with no hope beyond the preservation of existence under the operation of the ancestral optimism. Pessimism and asceticism will continue to attest the condemnation of reason for the condition of the world. In spite of all this, under science which makes for *meliorism*, the leveling process will go on, greater and greater numbers will rise above the economic *Nullpunkt*, and the field of pain economy will shrink as that of pleasure economy expands.

21

THE GOSPEL

OF ACTION

1899

This was, in effect, a review of Huxley's Romanes Lecture on "Evolution and Ethics," which expressed ideas that Ward thought he had anticipated some years earlier.

There is always danger that an important principle once established may be saddled with unwarrantable assumptions or supposed corollaries and pass into a sort of popular creed, unfavorably influencing men's activities and largely neutralizing the advantages of the general truth arrived at. It was so with the wholesome doctrine of noninterference with private enterprise—the *laissez faire, laissez passer* principle—put forth at a time when government was in the hands of a small ruling class bent on their own aggrandizement, and always true for many kinds of social activity, but which under democracy has become the bulwark of the so-called money power and the only hope of the classes in their effort to exploit the masses.

The Independent (New York), Vol. LI, No. 2641 (July 13, 1899), in *Glimpses of the Cosmos*, VI, 58–63.

There are many analogous cases, but we are just now concerned with a great scientific principle, the one that has produced the most radical change that human thought has ever undergone—the principle of evolution—which the whole scientific world, with only minor individual qualifications, now accepts. This profound and far-reaching truth has given rise to an entirely new philosophy, much of it thoroughly sound, consisting of legitimate deductions from the facts of nature that have taught the world this principle, but other parts of it false, as, resulting from departures from the strictly scientific method, the introduction of illegitimate elements, and the elaboration of a mass of assumptions with which the facts are not at all in harmony. They are the products of the old propensity of the human mind to speculate far beyond the strict boundaries of concrete things and to construct systems largely independent of the real world.

I have in mind one of these deviations from the teachings of science manifested in the writings of certain truly great philosophers of our time who have taken the trouble to acquaint themselves with all the essential truths that modern science has unfolded. The particular fallacy embodied in this philosophy, which is fast becoming the basis of all the popular thinking of our day, is what, in analogy to one of the phases of theological thought, may be appropriately characterized as the modern *nature-worship*. The great lesson that science first taught to man was the lesson of nature. The truth embodied in it was stirringly shadowed forth even by Wordsworth:

> *To the solid ground*
> *Of Nature trusts the mind which builds for aye.*

It became clear that nature was the chief object of study. From her bosom were being drawn all the rich blessings that science was showering upon the world. With this as a datum-point the speculative reason began to draw inferences. The first resulted in the injunction: Observe nature. Nothing could be more sound or wholesome. The second brought forth another injunction: Imitate nature. Nothing could be more false or pernicious.

While it cannot be complained that the first dictate of this proposed philosophy of science has not been obeyed, it is equally clear that the second has also been generally recognized and widely acted upon, and the result is that we are confronted with another huge error of the speculative faculty lying athwart the track of human progress, sullenly refusing to move, and powerfully obstructing the march of ideas and the advancement of the material interests of humanity.

The discoveries in astronomy, physics, and chemistry had made it clear that the physical universe was a domain of law, and not of the caprice of gods and demons. The vegetable and animal kingdoms had come to be studied also from this point of view, and the study of man had begun to take the form of a natural history science. Both the science of races, ethnology, and of industrial activities, political economy, acquired this character, and the idea of improving the condition of society was as little entertained as that of modifying the species of plants and animals that Linnaeus and Cuvier had declared fixed and immutable. That natural history should pass through this statical phase is not to be wondered at, but even after Lamarck and Darwin had established the science of dynamic biology and shown the possibility of artificially improving the races of plants and animals, this idea still remained wholly foreign to the science of the human races and of society. Political economy still remained the same hopeless science that Malthus had made it; and down to the present closing years of the nineteenth century we find the leading philosopher of evolution, Mr. Herbert Spencer, treating sociology as a natural history science, and tho recognizing a secular genetic progress in human affairs, not only denying the power of man to accelerate that progress but deprecating as harmful all attempts in that direction on the part of society. His extreme views on this question have been aptly characterized by Prof. Ludwig Stein as the doctrine of a social nirvana.

The whole drift of modern philosophy relative to human affairs is to the effect that they are subject to natural laws that must not be interfered or "meddled" with. It is insisted that somehow this can do much harm, but that under no circumstances can it do any good; and the philosophers forget that the first of these declarations destroys their claim for the immutability of these laws and involves the admission of the possibility at least of affecting events favorably as well as unfavorably. I pointed out this flaw in the logic as long ago as 1883, and undertook to show that the effort to control the course of natural phenomena in the interest of man and society embodied nothing inconsistent with the general teachings of science. I did not then go deeply into this question, but contented myself with demonstrating that in so far as science had really benefited man it had been through such modification and alteration of the course which natural phenomena would have otherwise taken, and that this is the principle underlying all useful art. It was clear to me even much earlier (and this it was which inspired my first work) that the current interpretation of the law of evolution amounted to a gospel of inaction and was as fatal to all initiative as had been either the optimism which asserts that there is nothing to do or the pessimism which declares that nothing can be done. It threatens to plunge the world into a lethargy as complete as that of the Middle Ages. The synthesis of the two half truths, optimism and pessimism, is meliorism. What there is true of both freedom and determinism is that every act is a cause which will produce its legitimate effect, and that this effect will not be produced unless the act is performed. Mr. John Morley has admirably expressed this idea in the following language:

"It would be odd if the theory which makes progress depend on modification forbade us to attempt to modify. When it is said that the various successive changes in thought and institution present and consummate themselves spontaneously no one means by spontaneity that they come to pass independently of human effort and volition. On the contrary, this energy of the members of the society is one of the spontaneous elements. It is quite as indispensable as any other of them, if, indeed, it be not more so. Progress depends upon tendencies and forces in a community. But of these tendencies and forces, the organs and representatives must plainly be found among the men and women of the community, and cannot possibly be found anywhere else. Progress is not automatic, in the sense that if we were all cast into a deep slumber for the space of a generation, we should awake to find ourselves in a greatly improved social state. The world only grows better, even in the moderate degree in which it does grow better, because people wish that it should, and take the right steps to make it better. Evolution is not a force, but a process; not a cause, but a law. It explains the source and marks the immovable limitations of social energy. But social energy itself can never be superseded either by evolution or by anything else."[1]

Professor Huxley was almost the only prominent man of science who saw the evil to which the kind of philosophy above described was leading, and in his lecture on "Administrative Nihilism," 1871, he dealt it some very heavy blows, but he did not there enter deeply into the argument, and contented himself with pointing out some of its logical absurdities. This had little effect in stemming the tide of thought in the direction of a thoroughly sterile philosophy, and no one seemed to wake up to a realizing sense of the true situation.

So deeply was I impressed with this state of things that in 1884 I formulated a protest against it as strong as I was then able to make it, and with a view to landing it as nearly as possible into the heart of the philosophical camp I published it in the English psychological journal, *Mind*. In this paper I showed that the gradual growth of the rational faculty had

---

[1] John Morley "On Compromise." I find this extract in that excellent little collection entitled "Voices of Doubt and Trust," selected by Volney Streamer [George Iles]. New York, 1897, pp. 124, 125.

introduced an entirely new element into all economic operations, to a great extent reversing the conditions that obtain
in the animal world and in the unthinking masses of mankind,
and rendering most of the laws of political economy that had
been laid down by the earlier economists wholly inapplicable
to the modern social state.

During the eight years that followed this scarcely a voice
was raised against the current tendencies. Mr. Spencer's philosophy was gaining ground as volume after volume emerged
from the press and was devoured by the reading public. Its
inadequacy to meet the changing conditions of social life was
more and more apparent to my mind, and I at last made a
renewed effort, not so much to refute it as to probe the question to the bottom, and to arrive if possible at a theoretical
basis for the opposite class of views which were being freely
expressed by a large class of social reformers who possessed
few of the scientific qualifications for answering the argument,
and from whom there was almost as much to be feared as from
the philosophers themselves. It was clear that there were two
principles at work, both psychic in a broad sense, but the one
which had been alone previously attended to, based on the
ever-recurring wants of man, prompting him to seek satisfaction through direct efforts to attain his ends, and therefore
relatively simple and easily reducible to economic laws, and
the other based on his intelligence, calculation, foresight, and
cunning, which are subtle elements and difficult to deal with
scientifically, and the increasing prominence of which was
constantly baffling the economists and throwing their schemes
into confusion.

All this I elaborated into what seemed to be a somewhat
complete philosophy of mind, individual and collective. It is
embodied in my "Psychic Factors of Civilization," which appeared in the autumn of 1893, but more than a year earlier I
presented to the public the general conclusions arrived at in
the form of an address as vice-president of the Section of
Economic Science and Statistics of the American Association

for the Advancement of Science at its meeting in Rochester in August, 1892, and it appeared in the "Proceedings" of the Association for that year under the title: "The Psychologic Basis of Social Economics." To give these conclusions as wide a vogue as possible I also published this address, slightly condensed but under the same title, in the "Annals of the Academy of Political and Social Science" for January, 1893. In a much expanded form it constitutes Chapter XXXIII of the "Psychic Factors," which is entitled "The Economy of Nature and the Economy of Mind."

These papers contain, so far as I am aware, the only attempt that has been made to formulate what I call "the law of biologic economics," and to contrast this with "the law of mind," or the method by which intelligence works in human affairs. The total failure of all economists to note this fundamental distinction is the sufficient cause of the glaring discrepancies between economic theory and historical fact, and it is this which has not only brought political economy into disrepute, requiring its very name to be changed to *economics*, but has caused the rise of an entirely new school of economists, whose teachings are to large extent diametrically opposed to those of half a century ago.

It was in 1893 that Professor Huxley delivered his famous Romanes Lecture on "Evolution and Ethics," in which he struck the same key-note, and it was in 1894 that he wrote the still more remarkable "Prolegomena" to that lecture, which precedes it in the ninth volume of his "Collected Essays." These masterly documents have been the subject of almost unnumbered criticisms in the public press, often from the pens of shallow and flippant reviewers, but sometimes of able and responsible thinkers; and altho there has usually been an attempt to qualify or even overthrow Huxley's position, this always seems faint and feeble when placed by the side of the terse and vigorous utterances of that "prince of debaters," as Matthew Arnold called him.

But Professor Huxley, besides the weight of his name in

giving currency to his views, had the tact to connect the subject with that of ethics, with which it really has nothing to do, doubtless perceiving that this catchword in the title would commend it to many who would never read a purely scientific article.

These papers by Professor Huxley have undoubtedly done more than anything else that has been written to set the world thinking in the right direction upon the true teachings of science relative to human and social affairs. They show that to the influence of intelligence in artificially modifying the environment of man in his own interest there is scarcely any limit, and that all that the world stands in need of is vigorous action in this direction. Nature is indeed first to be observed, but, having been learned, the laws of nature become the property and servants of man, and he is not to imitate the methods by which nature accomplishes results, but must direct the forces of nature into channels of his own advantage, and utilize for his own good all the powers of the universe. It is not the doctrine of inactivity, of the folding of the arms, of *noli me tangere*, of *laissez faire*, that naturally and legitimately flows from a full comprehension of the law of evolution, but a gospel of action, a recognition of the law of causation and of man as a great and potent cause in the world. The true crown of a system of scientific philosophy is not an Ethics which seeks to restrain and circumscribe activity, but a Sociology which aims at the liberation of action through the directive agency of intelligence.

22

THE THEORY OF
THE LEISURE CLASS
1900

It is not an exaggeration to say that Thorstein Veblen was to economics what Ward was to social thought. Both challenged the assumptions and preconceptions that had for so long comforted the business and political communities—and the academic community as well; both insisted upon looking behind form to function, behind theory to reality. They had other things in common as well. They were both in a sense outsiders —if not alienated from the respectable academic community, at least not welcomed into it. They were both rebels, but philosophically rather than politically. They were both men of deep learning and wide culture. Both were, in the end, among that company of movers and shakers who "trampled the kingdom down."

Ward had been writing and indirectly teaching for almost twenty years when Veblen—already forty-two—published his first and, as it proved, his most influential book, THE THEORY OF THE LEISURE CLASS. Most of the reviews were hostile or be-

---

"A Review of *The Theory of the Leisure Class*, by Thorstein Veblen," *American Journal of Sociology*, V (May 1900), 829–837.

wildered, but two celebrated the explosion of new ideas in economics—those by William Dean Howells, who could always be trusted to discover merit, and by Ward. Of this review Ward later said that "of all the reviews I have ever written, this is the best one from nearly every point of view."

The Theory of the Leisure Class. An Economic Study in the Evolution of Institutions. By THORSTEIN VEBLEN. New York: The Macmillan Co., 1899.

A late critic of a book has the same advantage as the critic of an old painting. He need not have any ideas of his own. He has learned what the proper thing to say is, and he has nothing to do but to say it. In the present case the proper thing to do is to condemn the book and call it pessimistic, even "cynical." Pessimism now means: looking facts in the face; seeing things as they are; calling a spade a spade. Anyone who does this is deserving of censure as disturbing the order of things. If there is one thing that the world does not want, it is truth. Truth is a medicine that must be administered in sugar-coated pills. A very little of it reacts upon the public system and will not go down. This is no modern fact. It has always been so. It is what they used to burn folks for. Nowadays they merely put their books on a sort of moral *index librorum expurgandorum.*

The trouble with this book is that it contains too much truth. It also suggests a great deal of truth that it does not contain, and this is quite as bad as to tell the truth outright. Galileo and Servetus were not persecuted for what they said, but for the deductions that their persecutors made from what they said. The reviewers of this book base their criticisms almost entirely on the conclusions they themselves draw from what is said in it, and scarcely at all on what it actually says. They forget entirely that it is, as its secondary title states, "an economic study in the evolution of institutions," and they assume in all gratuity that it is an attack on existing institutions. That is a pure deduction, but one for which there is no warrant in the book. Someone has said that the law of gravitation would be attacked if it was suspected of jeopardizing human interests. The history of man is exactly paralleled in the history of plants and animals, but no one has inveighed against the facts of biology, because they concern subhuman creatures. Darwin was soundly belabored for supposed consequences to man of his facts, but only for such.

Now, no truth has come more clearly forth from the most thorough study of organic evolution than that its whole method is essentially wasteful. Darwin showed this; Huxley multiplied examples of it; and even Herbert Spencer, who would have man imitate nature in all things, has supplied some of the most striking examples of the prodigality of nature. In describing this prodigality naturalists have not been suspected of condemning the habits and instincts of the birds and animals, of the fishes of the sea and the infusorians of the pool. But when an economist of a strictly scientific habit of mind investigates the history of the human species, discovers that human evolution, like organic evolution, is the outcome of the rhythmic action of great cosmic forces, one set of which is centrifugal and destructive, and tells us how these wasteful processes go on in society in coöperation with the conservative ones, he arouses hostility and is regarded as dangerous. And all because the specimens he has to investigate are men. In fact, the book is a mirror in which we can all see ourselves. It is more. It is a telescope through which we can see our ancestors, and when, all at one view, we see all the generations of our pedigree down to and including ourselves, we perceive how little difference there is, and the image takes on a rather ugly aspect. That is why it offends. This tracing back institutions, customs, habits, ideas, beliefs, and feelings to their primitive sources in barbarism and savagery, and showing what is the real basis of them, is not pleasant occupation for people who are proud of their ancestors, for many such have nothing but ancestors to be proud of.

It is perfectly legitimate to endeavor to show that the facts are not as stated, but a critic who does this must proceed scientifically. He must not waste his efforts in showing that there are other facts that have an opposite tendency. He must remember what the author of the book has set himself as a task: and in this case it must be admitted that he has clung tenaciously to this one field, resisting the temptation, which, as anyone can see, must have been strong, to go out of that field and deal with the opposite class of facts. There is no doubt that he could write as strong and able a book on the "instinct of workmanship" as he has written on the "instinct of sportsmanship," and it is to be hoped that he may do so. But in dealing with this book the critic has no right to complain that it is not a book on some other subject than the one chosen. As a matter of fact, there is much gained in dealing with one aspect of human evolution at a time. Very few writers are able to keep the different factors distinct. It requires a clear head. Nearly all the treatment we find of such highly complex subjects is vitiated by the perpetual mixing up of the fields of inquiry, until all is muddle and *Wirrwarr.* Here for once we have a single subject clearly handled and consistently adhered to, at the risk even of giving offense to those whose suggestibility is so strong that they cannot keep other subjects out of view.

It may be said that the author ought at least to have shown how this very leisure class, and solely by virtue of its leisure, has made the greater part certainly of the earlier scientific discoveries, and worked out some of the most important problems; that even modern science owes as much to this class as to all other classes combined, as shown by de Candolle in his *Histoire des Sciences et des Savants;* that all the important "institutions," including the learned professions and the sciences, have, as Spencer has shown, developed out of "ecclesiastical institutions," and owe their existence and advanced modern character to that typical "leisure class," the priesthood, given over to "vicarious leisure" and "devout observances;" that no class and no human being, as the labor reformers so justly insist, can do any high intellectual work, or even cultivate the mind, without a certain amount of leisure and respite from incessant toil. Our author might, it would seem to some, have at least dwelt upon these well-known and universally admitted facts relating directly to the leisure class. But, in the first place, he is not engaged in explaining the intellectual and moral progress of the world, and, in the second place, these facts are too well known to need restatement, and he seems to have no taste for hackneyed topics. Such facts are not opposed to anything he says, but are simply also true. They are patent, while what he tells us is latent, and he chose between the two classes of subjects, telling us a good many things we did not know before instead of telling us so much that we did know. In the third place, and principally, his point of view is strictly economic, and he deals with a subject within his own specialty, and has not seen fit to branch out into wider fields, as economic writers are so much in the habit of doing. *Ne sutor ultra crepidam.*

In a word, our author is dealing with the question of wealth, and his whole treatise is confined to the "pecuniary" aspect. He finds that everything has a pecuniary value, which has little to do with its intrinsic or rational value; that this pecuniary value has grown out of a long series of events in human history leading back to the age of barbarism. It is a typical case of conventional ideas as distinguished from rational ideas. It can only be made to seem rational when we know and can trace its history, and see how, under all the circumstances, it could not have been otherwise. Pecuniary value is the result of natural causation, like everything else, but the series of terms consists of a long winding labyrinth of causes and effects that have ultimately produced something which, looked at directly, appears irrational and absurd. In this it is no exception to the general law of survivals in ethnology. Every lawyer knows what a legal fiction is, but most of them are mistaken in imagining that only advanced races are capable of creating such fictions. The study of ethnology shows that early institutions are a mass of fictions. The savage is more logical than the civilized man. Analyze the *couvade,* considered as the fiction by which the matriarchal was transformed into the patriarchal system without a break in the chain of logic.

Pecuniary value, as distinguished from intrinsic value, is a survival, and it has probably never before been so well traced out. Here are a few of the steps, but the book must be read to see them all and how they are connected: As soon as property became recognized as the thing that chiefly insures the satisfaction of desire, the "law of acquisition" went into effect, and thenceforth the problem was how to *acquire* the most with the least effort—not how to *produce* the most. The "least effort" part of the formula lies at the foundation of the author's distinction between "industry and exploit." Exploit is comparatively easy. Industry becomes synonymous with drudgery. The love of activity, i. e., the actual pleasure in the exercise of the faculties, which is the essence of the "instinct of workmanship," could scarcely be eliminated, and "leisure" is by no means incompatible with activity. But excessive activity—the prolonged and laborious exertion required for the constant reproduction of the objects of consumption—is essentially irksome and has always been avoided when possible. But these objects must be produced in order that their consumption may be enjoyed, and the only way to possess them without producing them is to make others produce them. Any power to do this is immediately exercised, and as things have been constituted in the history of mankind, this has taken the form of creating a dependent industrial class and an independent leisure class. The simplest form of this was slavery, and as the author shows, the first slaves were women; afterward captives were made slaves; and finally all were enslaved but the few having privilege and power. Extensive modification of this normal state, of course, took place with time.

Now, the most natural thing in the world is that these two sets of persons should form two great classes totally unlike in almost every respect. The dependent class is low, debased, degraded. The independent class is high, noble, exalted. This is not merely the judgment of the higher class, but also that of the lower. It is the universally recognized relation and constitutes what is called the *régime of status*. All the occupations of the dependent class are, in our author's happy phrase, "humilific," and all the occupations in which the independent class can engage must be "honorific." These occupations must not cross each other. They must be wholly different. The humilific occupations are all industrial, productive. Therefore the leisure class must pursue no industrial or productive occupations under pain of being suspected of dependence. The humilific occupations are the only ones that are "useful" in the economic sense. Therefore no member of the leisure class may do anything useful. The leisure class derive pleasure from the exercise of their faculties, but such exercise must involve no "utility," and must be characterized by "futility." There are certain directions in which the pleasures of activity may be indulged without the suspicion of dependence or necessity. Among these purely futile occupations we find war, the chase, gaming, politics, ruling, religious observances, etc. Then there are many incidental ways in which the leisure class, when in full power, are able to enjoy themselves. Thus it is said that a common amusement of the Roman nobles was to knock down a plebeian and then hand over a sesterce, which was the amount of the fine fixed by law for such offenses; and the idea of "fun" that the young British gentry entertained in the sixteenth century was to disfigure the faces of the poor they met in the streets by means of a sharp-pointed cane that they carried for such purposes. Everything done must be in the nature of sport, nothing must have the character of work. The surplus energy must express itself in wholly non-industrial and absolutely parasitic ways, otherwise there is loss of caste.

The above may give some idea of the general nature of the fundamental antithesis that sprang up naturally, as shown, and has persisted even down to our own times. The distinction has been characterized as "invidious," and this word has been criticised as imputing blameworthy motives. But it is used in a literal sense, as that which has *envy* at its root, for not only does the industrial class envy the leisure class, but every member of the leisure class is perpetually striving to gain the envy of others of that class. Though all the members of the leisure class are exempt from drudgery, they are by no means all equal in their "ability to pay," and, as there is no limit to the possibility of conspicuous futile consumption, no one ever has as much as he wants in order to outdo and eclipse his rivals. There is thus brought about, not only a hierarchy of wealth, but a perpetual scramble to excel one another. Wealth becomes the basis of esteem. The standard is wholly pecuniary. Not only must wealth be possessed, but there must be a show of its possession. It must be made obvious to all that there is an inexhaustible reserve. Hence leisure must be made conspicuous by "conspicuous consumption" and "conspicuous waste." If only enough persons and the right persons could see it and know it, it would be highly honorific to light a cigar occasionally with a thousand-dollar bill. A man must not limit his consumption to himself and his family. He must live in a palace many times larger than he can possibly fill, and have a large retinue of servants and retainers, ostensibly to minister to his wants, but really to make clear his ability to pay.

From this arises the important principle of "vicarious leisure" and "vicarious consumption." Most of these servants must also be exempt from any productive work, and the women of his household must be absolutely non-productive and inactive. In the modern system of semi-industrial and quasi-predatory exploitation by the bourgeoisie the "captain of industry" must manage his business, and therefore seem to be doing something, mayhap something useful, but appearances must be kept up as in the feudal manor, and upon his wife devolves the "performance of leisure" and the display of her husband's ability to pay for useless things. He confers on her a vicarious leisure, and in dress and social appointments she is able to show his ability to consume and to waste to any required extent.

It will be seen that it is throughout the application of the fundamental maxim of "political economy"—the greatest gain for the least effort. But as effort is itself agreeable, the effort meant is only industrial, productive, useful effort. Primarily war and the chase were the principal honorific employments, growing out of the antecedent state in which both were more or less productive. War for booty gave way to war for captives, i. e., slaves to do the productive work, and ultimately the chase entirely lost its productive value and was indulged in merely for sport. Witness the contempt in our day for the poacher and the "pot-hunter." At first all exploit was predatory; it has now become what our author aptly calls "quasi-predatory." There is no more regard for real justice or right now than then, but the exploitation must conform to laws made by the exploiting class, and so have a show of justice. The purpose is to acquire at all hazards, but it is not enough to say that this must be done irrespective of whether anything is produced or not. All acquisition must be non-productive under pain of falling out of the leisure class.

No biologist can fail to observe parallels in the organic world to many of the facts set forth in this book. Space forbids their enumeration, but one can scarcely refrain from noting among nature's many wasteful ways the phenomena of secondary sexual characters, typified by the antlers of the stag and the gaudy tail of the peacock. These may be compared to wasteful human fashions, such as are enumerated in the chapter on "Pecuniary Canons of Taste." The principal difference is that nature, in producing these useless and cumbersome organs, has really given them a high degree of intrinsic beauty, even as judged by human tastes, while the products of human fashion, based on the canon of "pecuniary beauty," or costliness, are useless impediments to activity without the slightest claim upon any rational standard of taste.

The author's theory of why fashions change is ingenious, and must be largely true. The ugliness caused by their superfluous cost renders them intolerable to behold for any great length of time, so that a change is demanded by the aesthetic sense even of the leisure class; but the new ones can be no better, because they, too, must have these marks of "reputable futility" and "conspicuous waste," that are necessarily offensive to taste, which is based on the instinct of workmanship. They must therefore also soon give way to others no better than they, and so on indefinitely. It is perpetual conflict between pecuniary beauty and rational beauty, which are incompatible, but in which the former always prevails, and all the latter can do is to condemn the product and compel the victor to bring on another.

The genesis of a great number of institutions, customs, practices, and beliefs is worked out in the book, and their barbaric origin clearly shown. It would be useless to attempt their enumeration here, and only a few of the most curious can be named, such as the exemption of women from labor (vicarious leisure); inebriacy and dissipation; costly and unaesthetic decoration; the non-punishment of crime when on a large scale; religious ceremonial evolutions recalling the terpischorean stage or dance; the higher learning, or "classicism;" preference for inferior hand-made over superior machine-made goods; love of archaism in general; the respectability of conservatism; the conservatism and degeneracy of the higher institutions of learning; patriotism, dueling, snobbery; English saddles, walking sticks; athletic sports, college fraternities, the "cap and gown," etc., etc.

The author has certainly handled the English language with consummate skill, and, notwithstanding his indictment of "classicism," he displays no mean acquaintance with the classics. The book abounds in terse expressions, sharp antitheses, and quaint, but happy phrases. Some of these have been interpreted as irony and satire, but, as said above, this is the work of the critics themselves. The language is plain and unmistakable, as it should be, but the style is the farthest removed possible from either advocacy or vituperation, and the language, to use the author's own words, is "morally colorless." Some of it, if it is not classical, is likely to become so. His general terminology has already been used to a considerable extent in this review, the peculiar terms and expressions being put in quotation marks. Many others might be given if space permitted, such, for example, as "reputably wasteful expenditure," or "reputable waste," "reputable futility," and "pecuniary reputability;" and he speaks of certain things that have "advantages in the way of usefulness." On the other hand, we have such expressions as "vulgarly useful occupations," "vulgar effectiveness," and the "taint of usefulness." Then we have the "predatory animus," "quasi-predatory methods," "predatory fraud," "predatory parasitism," and "parasitic predation." Many incidental expressions are noteworthy, such as the "skilled and graded inebriety and perfunctory dueling" of the German students, and his statement that the "higher learning" chiefly confers a "knowledge of the unknowable." He says that the "exaltation of the defective" and admiration for "painstaking crudeness" and "elaborate ineptitude" are characteristics of "pecuniary standards of taste." And anyone who has noted how all athletic sports degenerate and become restricted to a few professionals will appreciate his remark that "the relation of football to physical culture is much the same as that of the bull fight to agriculture."

As has already been seen, the two great social classes are characterized by an assortment of sharply contrasted words and phrases, and not only their occupations, but their underlying instincts, are clearly marked off by such expressions as the "instinct of sportsmanship" and the "instinct of workmanship;" "exploit and industry," or "exploit and drudgery;" "honorific and humilific" occupations, and "perfunctory and proficuous" activities, all forming the primary contrast between "futility and utility." In each of these pairs the first belongs to the leisure class and represents the superior fitness to survive in human society. The leisure class constitutes the biologically fittest, the socially best, the aristocracy.

Of the general make-up of the book, as of all that issue from that well-known house, there is nothing to be said but praise, unless it be to note the retention of the superfluous *u* in such words as "honour," "favour," "colour," etc. To speak of our American "Labour Day" is a clear case of "archaism" and "conspicuous waste," and might be cited in defense of the main thesis of the book.

23

SOCIAL MECHANICS

1900

Nineteen hundred was a busy year for Ward. That year he was asked by his old friend William Harris, then United States Commissioner of Education, to attend the Paris Exposition as an official representative of the United States and to prepare a report on Sociology at the exposition. A number of other Congresses were associated with the exposition, and Ward planned to attend them all: the International Institute of Sociology, the International Institute of Geologists, and the International Association for the Advancement of Science, Art, and Education.

Ward sailed for Europe in May, spent a month in England, and then headed for his Congresses in Paris. In August he gave a lecture on "The Dependence of Social Science on Physical Science," another on "The Place of Sociology in the Curriculum," and to the Institute of Sociology he read a paper on LA MÉCANIQUE SOCIALE. *On his return to the United States Ward prepared an elaborate report of one hundred and fifty-some pages on "Sociology at the Paris Exposition," which was*

"Sociology at the Paris Exposition of 1900," in Report of the Commissioner of Education, *Annual Reports of the Department of the Interior, 1900–1901*, Washington, D.C., 1901, 56th Congress, 2nd session, Document #5, pp. 1590–1593.

duly buried in the annual report of the Commissioner of Education.

It must be constantly borne in mind that the activities of men are the effects of the social forces as causes. Most of these activities are purely statical. They come under M. Tarde's law of imitation, and are mere repetitions. But there are some, and the frequency of these increases with the increase in human intelligence, that break over this rule, and, to however small an extent, depart from the normal, add some little to what has gone before, and improve upon the old way. This is what M. Tarde calls invention. The term innovation seems preferable, as more generic. All this is little more than the simple statement of the observed facts. The principle underlying it remains to be sought. It is to be found in the psychology of human action.

We will suppose a given action to be dynamic and not merely static, to be an innovation and not a simple repetition. If we analyze such an action we shall find that it has three distinct effects: 1, to satisfy desire; 2, to perform a function; 3, to modify the environment. Only the first of these effects is consciously sought. The individual as an organism is impelled to action by the motives that are in his nature, and he can only act in obedience to these motives. They are the psychic, and become, when taken collectively, the social forces. The generalized formula to which all such motives can be reduced is the satisfaction of desire, and when this phrase is comprehended with sufficient breadth it is seen to be true that no action ever is or can be performed except for the purpose of satisfying desire. The action is supposed to accomplish this end, but whether it does so or not, it must be intended to do so, otherwise there would be no motive, and we should have an effect without a cause. But whether an action does in fact satisfy the desire for which it was performed has, as we shall soon see, no bearing upon its dynamic character. It may fail entirely in its primary purpose and still be a dynamic action.

The second effect of the action, viz, the performance of function, is primarily a wholly unconscious one. The agent is not normally concerned at all with it. It is the result of ages of cosmic adaptation so complete that the individual has no need to know that his action will produce this effect. Throughout the entire animal kingdom below man it is not probable that the functional effect is ever considered, or that it is known to the agent that a given action, such as eating, will have a functional effect, such as to nourish the body. The sole motive is desire (hunger, etc.). Even in the lowest races of men, as M. Letourneau has pointed out, it is doubtful whether the reproductive act is known to be the cause of reproduction, and in the most civilized communities of the world the cases in which it is performed for that purpose are extremely rare. The fundamental effect is altogether statical, and merely results in the repetition of cells (nutrition, growth) or of individuals (reproduction, multiplication), and adds nothing in the direction of modifying the type of social structure.

Let us now consider the third effect, which was characterized as modification of the environment. Social progress, as I have so often pointed out, differs from organic evolution in the important particular that, whereas in the latter the environment transforms the organism, in the former man transforms the environment. This third effect is in chronologic sequence the first. The end of the individual is the satisfaction of desire, but except in the very simplest cases this end is not the immediate effect of the action. The end must usually be attained through means. The action is expended directly and immediately upon some means which secures the end. The extent to which this is true depends upon the position of the agent in the scale of organic development. The lowest of all creatures are simply bathed in a nutrient medium which penetrates and nourishes their bodies. A little higher, as in Vorticella, they draw the nutritive particles to themselves by the vortical action of cilia. At still higher stages they seek their food with increasing conscious effort, until, in the highest animals, such as the Carnivora, the pursuit and capture of their prey involves great effort and exertion. But here, as throughout the entire animal kingdom below man, the effect is to strengthen and adapt the organism by virtue of the Lamarckian principle of increase by use, supplemented by the Darwinian principle of natural selection. The extent to which the environment is modified is comparatively trifling. It is true that through certain instincts some changes are occasionally wrought in the environment. Birds build nests and beavers dams, and some rodents, such as the prairie dog, make subterranean homes that are more or less permanent. On the other hand, the effect is often destructive instead of constructive, as where all the food animals of a predatory species are destroyed, or where all the grass and herbage of a herbivorous species are eaten up. Instincts rarely produce any enduring results. Birds abandon their old nests every year and build new ones even in the same tree. It is clear that we can not say of any animal that its action tends to transform the environment in which it lives to its own permanent advantage.

But with man this is just what occurs. His efforts have very little effect in modifying or perfecting his own physical powers. Up to a certain point in the course of his slow emergence out of the animal state the biologic law doubtless applied to him, and in various ways, unlike those of the other animals, it modified his physical nature, giving him the erect posture, the plantigrade foot, the high facial angle, and the massive brain. But this process gradually diminished until for all the races now known to inhabit the earth it is inappreciable, and for all the developed races it is nil. In fact, a reverse process, at least in part, seems to have set in, and instead of physical advancement there is a tendency toward physical degeneracy.

On the other hand, even the most primitive types of men accomplish something in the direction of transforming the environment and adapting it to themselves, while everything that is included in the phrase material civilization consists in just this and nothing else. The general truth is vaguely recognized, but it is commonly supposed that it is the result of conscious and intentional action on the part of men. A careful analysis of the conditions shows that such is not the case, but that it is merely incidental and unintended, an unsought and undesired result of the effort to satisfy desire. If desire could always be satisfied without effort, without causing any modification of the materials which are in contact with man, there would be no human progress. No effort would be put forth for this purpose alone. The environment would remain as little changed as it is by the birds and animals that inhabit the forests and the plains.

The only reason for this difference is human intelligence. Man is the only animal whose mental powers are strong enough to enable him to see that his end, the satisfaction of his desires, can be attained through certain material means, through transformations in his environment. And the higher his intelligence the more of these means he perceives, but the more subtle and recondite the means the more difficult they become. The more remote the end the more laborious the means, and the employment of such means involves prolonged effort. But the more severe and protracted the effort the larger will be the incidental results, i. e., the greater will be the transformation wrought in the environment. The individual end is the only thing that is desired, but it is perceived by the reason that the end can only be attained through effort applied to the means.

Now the attainment of the end—the satisfaction of the desire of the individual—has no social importance. It may be set down as wholly statical. So also must be considered statical the indirect functional effect of satisfying desire—sustenance, nutrition, growth, reproduction, multiplication. The only consequence of the action that has any social value is the incidental alteration in the surrounding material conditions that had to be made before the other effects could be secured.

The most obvious form of transformation, and the one that still continues to be the most important, consists in the artificial shaping of raw materials to man's needs. The animal finds a world with such and such objects in it. It knows no other way than to utilize these objects nearly as they are. Man finds the same world, but he knows how to adapt the objects to his use, and he proceeds to do so in proportion to that knowledge. The result is that in a civilized race nearly everything that is said to have value in the economic sense has been transformed. Let anyone look about him and try to discover a wholly untransformed object of which he ever makes any use and he will find it a difficult matter to do so. Even light, heat, earth, air, and water are more or less modified to man's advantage.

This transformation of raw materials into objects of human use is accomplished by means of two processes—invention and labor. Every perception of the possibility of modifying the environment or any part of it in such a way as to secure the fuller satisfaction of desire is an invention. All the effort put forth in producing this modification is labor. The result, i. e., the actual modification brought about, is production in the economic sense of that term, and all production is of this kind and can be nothing else.

These products of invention and labor, i. e., of art, are therefore merely means to the individual end, which alone is a conscious and purposive effect. The second effect, viz, the functional end, or end of nature, of preserving and continuing life, is unconscious, and is the result of adaptation brought about by natural laws. Both these effects are statical in the scientific sense. The third effect, viz, that of modifying the environment, also unconscious, unthought of, and undesired, is the dynamic effect, and the only one that has any social value. Or, to express it in language that is teleological in form but not in fact, the end of the individual is the satisfaction of desire, i. e., human happiness; the end of nature is the preservation of the individual and the race; the end of society is the amelioration of the conditions of existence.

It remains to connect these conclusions with the primary definition of social dynamics, viz, that it deals with the modification of the types of social structures. So far as industrial structures are concerned this is clear enough, but for other structures than industrial it is not so clear. It should apply to all human institutions whatsoever. It does so apply as soon as we give sufficient latitude to the terms employed. Every human institution is constantly undergoing modification, and every increment of modification is the result of the operation of this dynamic principle. We must give to the term invention all the breadth that M. Tarde gives to it. The labor involved in realizing and perpetuating the invention is either a part of the act of invention or else it is simply imitation and repetition in manifolding the objects wrought.

But the objects need not belong to the industrial world. The product need not be a material product at all. The institution may be any of those immaterial social products that were dealt with under social statics. One of these which seems the least tangible, one about which there seemed to be doubt as to whether it should be classed as an institution at all, is language. No more difficult one could be selected by which to illustrate the principle under consideration. If our dynamic principle proves applicable to language it surely can be applied to any other human institution.

In this case the end desired is intercommunication between

men. The means employed is speech or gesture or some form of significant action. The change or modification of this immaterial social structure, or primitive human institution, takes place in the direction of improving and perfecting the symbols employed in the conveyance of thought from one individual to another. Every step in this direction is an invention in the proper sense of the term, and the increments gained are preserved by imitation and repetition, which may be characterized as labor or human effort. If we were to trace the whole history of the science of *semantics* we should find that it consisted entirely in a continuous application of this process from the rudest forms of language to the highest flights of oratory or literary expression.

The only difficulty with this illustration is that language is such a primitive institution that it can not be called exclusively human. It shades off into an animal instinct, and in tracing it backward the dynamic principle here set forth applies in diminishing degrees until it is lost or merges into the principle of natural selection, which is its biological homologue. The same would be found true of many other primitive institutions, such as religion, marriage, and even government. But this does not prevent the principle from coming gradually into full force with the progress of human society and constituting the basis of social dynamics in all departments. It is that which brings about all modifications in the types of social structures, and introduces new and more efficient structures that gradually succeed the old and obsolescent ones. Changes may of course be retrogressive, and we have in society forms of local and restricted catabolism corresponding to atrophy, reversion, atavism, parasitic degeneracy, and even extinction, in biology. These would form interesting subjects for discussion, and could be shown to come under the same law as the anabolic transformations, but this would carry me too far.

While the science of social dynamics is thus much broader than the simple question of social progress, still it is the science that deals with social progress, and it is the only science that can adequately explain the nature of progress. It not merely asserts, as did Auguste Comte, that progress depends upon order as its essential basis, but it shows, as he did not, just how this is so. For if progress consists exclusively in the advantageous modification of social structures, it is clear that the existence of such structures is presupposed. But order, as we saw, consists in the formation and coordination of social structures under the principle of social synergy, which is the principle of social statics. Without such structures there is no society, and society consists of social structures. Hence all social progress must grow out of social order, and be, as Comte said, "the development of order." It consists exclusively in the advantageous modifications of social structures, brought about unconsciously and unintentionally by the direct action of man upon his material and spiritual environment in his efforts to satisfy his wants. Both invention and labor come under this head of effort, which is the ultimate principle of social dynamics. We have endeavored to explain this principle rather than to name it. It corresponds to the Lamarckian principle of effort in changing the organic structures employed in securing the ends of the creature, such, for example, as the lengthening of the cervical vertebrae of the giraffe by the effort to browse on the boughs that are beyond the reach of other antelopes. In the other characteristic that the result is wholly unsought and even unknown to the individual there is also perfect parallelism in the biological and the sociological principle.

The only essential differences are, (1) that human effort is telic, in perceiving that the means will secure the desired end, and (2) that human effort affects the environment and not the organism. For convenience of distinction, therefore, between the purely automatic and reflex effort of the animal and the rational and teleological effort of man, we may apply to the latter the term *conation*.

The two great principles of the science of social mechanics are, therefore, social synergy, which controls the phenomena of social statics, and conation, which controls the phenomena of social dynamics.

24

CONTEMPORARY

SOCIOLOGY

1902

In the process of writing PURE SOCIOLOGY, *Ward prepared three long chapters surveying contemporary sociological thought. Concluding, wisely, that these had no place in* PURE SOCIOLOGY, *he published them instead as articles in the* AMERICAN JOURNAL OF SOCIOLOGY *of 1902. The articles were bound together as a pamphlet and were translated and published in book form in Germany and Japan. We have omitted most of the historical and analytical sections and retained only some passages in the first two articles that appear to represent characteristic Wardian views or to suggest some of the social functions of sociology.*

. . . Properly I should confine the enumeration [of sociological systems] to scientific conceptions, but some of the most widespread and popular of these conceptions lie outside the pale of science. They belong to the pre-scientific

"Contemporary Sociology," *American Journal of Sociology*, VII (January and March 1902), 475–500 *passim*, 629–643 *passim*.

period. They are to sociology what astrology is to astronomy, alchemy to chemistry, and horuspicy to physiology. Such is the greater part, for example, of the so-called Christian sociology, and with this is to be classed all that well-meant treatment of social problems which looks only to immediate reform of social evils, and which is characterized by warmth of sentiment, usually accompanied by personal vituperation.

A distinction is also to be made between an -*ism* and an -*ology*. I do not, for example, question the legitimacy of socialism as a subject for study and a field of labor, but it relates to action and implies a purpose, which excludes it at least from any *pure* science. Its relations to applied sociology need not be discussed here.

In the following enumeration of the principal systems of sociology I shall endeavor to find some single word or expression for each of the leading ideas, conceptions, doctrines, subjects, or groups of social facts characterizing them, which must sometimes be taken in a somewhat broader sense than the one that is current for the term, but with such explanations as I shall make I do not think that any confusion or misunderstanding is likely to arise.

I. *Sociology as Philanthropy.*

It is probably safe to say that this conception of sociology is the prevailing one with the public today. The word now frequently occurs in the newspapers, but always in this sense. More than nine-tenths of the papers that are read before the American Social Science Association proceed from that idea of social science. It is the housing of the poor, charity work generally, slumming, reform work in the neglected quarters of cities, settlement work, etc. Sometimes it gets beyond the tenement house and sweating system and deals with consumers' leagues and co-operative stores. It includes such municipal reforms as public baths and lavatories, and the placing of public parks, gardens, and art galleries within the reach of the less well-to-do classes. This cannot be called a system of sociology, and it has no one leading advocate or exponent, but it is the common notion of what sociology or social science is, and is all the idea that the general public, the newspaper reporter or editor, or the average member of Parliament or of Congress has of it. Of course, it is not science at all, and therefore it cannot be sociology at all. No one will, however, be so illogical as to construe this into condemning it. It is social work, often of a high order, and for the most part very useful, but it is not sociology. Nor need it be denied that there are aspects of philanthropy that may and should be made scientific. Such are all attempts to grasp those principles of human nature which lead to methods of dealing with the poor and the unfortunate that will permanently elevate them and not make parasitic degenerates of them nor bring about the survival of the unfit. Such was most of the work of Professor Amos G. Warner. We may therefore heartily indorse the words of another professional philanthropist when he says:

I plead, therefore, here as everywhere chance gives me opportunity, for a more intimate association and fellowship between professional sociologists and professional philanthropists. I deplore the sociological teaching which is fragmentary, disjointed, a mere mosaic of quotations from the reports of actual observers of human life in its various aspects, arranged without regard to proportion or perspective, and which produces the effect upon the mind of a Chinese painting resembling nothing in heaven or earth.[1]

II. *Sociology as Anthropology.*

Among scientific men by far the most common conception of sociology is one that is essentially anthropological. The

---

[1] Frederick Howard Wines, in the *Annals of the Academy of Political and Social Science*, XII (July 1898), 57.

moment the subject of human society is presented, it brings
up the wider conception of man as the being whose association
constitutes it, and with the natural scientific habit of looking
for the origin and development of things, attention is at once
turned to primitive, uncivilized, barbaric, and savage man,
and this field proves so large and so attractive that it holds
the attention. It cannot be denied that anthropology, as the
science of man, has as one of its departments the laws and
forms of human association, and from this point of view sociology is a branch of anthropology. But there is another point
of view which treats sociology as an abstract science and not
as a branch of zoölogy, and thus viewed it stands as one of
the great co-ordinate independent sciences alongside of biology, chemistry, and physics. Most sociologists look at it from
this point of view; but even then many consider it necessary
to dwell mainly on the forms of association of primitive
peoples. This has the advantage of making it certain that the
foundations of sociology will be laid broad and deep.

There is one special school that call their science *anthroposociology,* which seeks primarily a classification of the western
European races based on physical and mental characteristics.
The facts collected by this school are highly interesting and
important, but they draw from them a train of conclusions
which are one-sided and largely false. So far as the application
of the facts is concerned, it is characterized by what may be
called *teutonolatry,* which is the more remarkable as the
school is headed by a Frenchman. The point of view is very
narrow, scarcely going beyond what the present state of things
seems to teach, and quite ignoring even early human history.
It would be unfortunate for them if it should ever be shown
that Socrates, Plato, and Aristotle were dark-haired and dark-
eyed brachybrunes, as seems very probable. Alexander the
Great and Julius Caesar may not have been blond beasts
at all, although they were the kind of beasts that are wor-
shiped by Ammon and Nietzsche. And has it ever been proved

that Napoleon Bonaparte, the Corsican, was not of the species *Homo mediterraneus* rather than *H. europaeus?* Certain it is that the theory formulated from the facts of anthroposociology utterly fails to account for all the early civilizations that rose around the Mediterranean and in the valleys of the Nile and the Euphrates.

III. *Sociology as Biology.*

If, among scientific sociologists, the anthropological school is the most widespread, the biological school is certainly just now the most earnest, vigorous, and aggressive. It takes the definite form of looking upon human society as an organism in strict analogy with an animal or vegetable organism. We are nowhere told to which of the three great "kingdoms of nature," mineral, vegetable, animal, this organism belongs. It can scarcely be mineral or vegetable, but is it animal? Or does it form a kingdom apart, not yet recognized by the books? Another question that troubles the specialists in biology is whether this organism is to be regarded as a species, a genus, a family, or some higher classificatory group. If a species, to what genus does it belong? If a genus, to what family, etc.? There are as many questions of this kind as there are classificatory groups, until we reach the primary subdivision of nature into kingdoms, and we have seen that even here the same question still confronts us, and, so far as I am aware, no one has attempted to answer any of these questions. . . .

The general idea of a social organism is very old. Aristotle expressed it quite clearly, not only in his much-quoted ζῶον πολιτικόν, but in passages in which he declares that society is a giant having hands, feet, sense, and intelligence. St. Paul is supposed to have virtually embodied it in Romans, chap. 12, and 1 Corinthians, chap. 12. Marcus Aurelius said something very similar, and other cases might be cited earlier than Hobbes, who made the state an artificial man of vast power,

and emphasized the organic conception in the name *Leviathan*
of his principal work. But no scientific or properly biologic
treatment of the subject was made prior to the nineteenth
century. Comte in 1838 seems to be the first to mention a
social organism. He said:

> One may form a philosophic idea, just in all respects, of the true
> essential nature of these real variations by comparing them espe-
> cially with analogous variations in the animal organism, which are
> exactly like them, as subject to similar conditions, whether static or
> dynamic, with this sole rational difference that social modifications
> may become more extensive and varied than simple biologic modifi-
> cations. . . . The essential principle, established especially by the
> labors of the illustrious Broussais, destined henceforth to character-
> ize the philosophic spirit of positive pathology, is, by its nature, as
> applicable to the social organism as to the individual organism.[2]

Mr. Herbert Spencer, in his *Social Statics,* published in 1850,
says:

> We commonly enough compare a nation to a living organism.
> We speak of "the body politic," of the functions of its parts, of its
> growth, and of its diseases, as though it were a creature. But we
> usually employ these expressions as metaphors, little suspecting
> how close is the analogy, and how far it will bear carrying out. So
> completely, however, is a society organized on the same system as
> an individual being, that we may perceive something more than
> analogy between them.

He then proceeds to give certain examples, and adds:

> Hence we are warranted in considering the body as a common-
> wealth of monads, each of which has independent powers of life,
> growth, and reproduction; each of which unites with a number of
> others to perform some function needful for supporting itself and
> all the rest; and each of which absorbs its share of nutriment from
> the blood. And when thus regarded, the analogy between an

---

[2] *Philosophie positive,* IV, 285, 311.

individual being and a human society, in which each man, while helping to subserve some public want, absorbs a portion of the circulating stock of commodities brought to his door, is palpable enough.[3]

The exhaustive treatment which Mr. Spencer subsequently gave the subject is well known,[4] yet, after Professor Huxley had so clearly shown in his "Administrative Nihilism"[5] that the doctrine necessarily leads to the most extreme form of socialism, he qualified it to such an extent that he is scarcely claimed by the organicists as a member of that school. . . .

The chief and only useful analogies are not properly biological, but psychological. This is because the same psychic qualities that belong to the animal organism are at work in society through the co-operation of its organic units, the minds of men. But although the mind of man is more highly organized than that of lower animals, so that individual men move on a higher psychic plane than individual animals, still the spontaneous activities generated in human society by the interaction of the psychic units in the resultant so-called social consciousness do not, as a matter of fact, produce a co-ordinating system of a high order, nothing approaching the perfect adjustment and subordination of the parts to the whole that we see in any of the developed animal organisms. To find any kind of parallel we are obliged to go down among the lowest organic forms, to the state known as the *cormus*. Here we find every degree of co-ordination, from the simple colony held together by invisible lines along which the internuncial currents are vaguely propagated, to mere chains of

---

[3] These passages occur on pp. 451–453 of the original edition of 1850, and on pp. 267, 268 of the abridged and revised edition published in 1892 in a volume which also contains his essays entitled "The Man *versus* the State."

[4] See especially "The Social Organism," *Westminster Review*, New Series, XVII (January 1860), 90–121.

[5] *Fortnightly Review*, New Series, X (November 1, 1871), 525–543.

cells with something corresponding to nerves connecting them, and thence on to the earliest segmented organisms. No one can have failed to notice that it is chiefly with such primitive creatures that Mr. Spencer makes his comparisons. He was so much impressed with this necessity that he was finally forced by his critics to say in a footnote that his comparisons were general, and that "if any specific comparison were made, which it cannot rationally be, it would be to some much lower vertebrate form than the human."[6]

It is a matter of common observation that the deliberations of public bodies of men are not marked by the degree of good sense and judgment that characterizes the best minds that compose them. Indeed, they fall below the average intelligence of the members, and probably below that of the least intelligent individuals in such bodies. Spencer remarks that "not only is the corporate conscience lower than the average individual conscience, but the corporate intelligence too."[7] Gabelli has reduced this to the formula that "the faculties of men working together obliterate each other and are not added together." Novicow admits that human societies should not be compared with animals as highly differentiated as the higher vertebrates, but with representatives of the Tunicata (barnacles), for example. This, of course, rather supports than opposes his favorite theory that the élite constitute the social consciousness, but that theory has the fatal objection that it leaves society without any central organ of control at all, for whatever may be the moral influence of the élite, it possesses no authority, and purposely keeps aloof from all interference with social events. It is wholly unorganized, and really exerts less power in society than is exercised by unorganized crowds

---

[6] *Essays, Scientific, Political and Speculative* (New York, 1891), p. 305.

[7] *Study of Sociology*, p. 289.

and mobs. These latter, as everybody knows, display the minimum intelligence, and represent the non-rational, animal state, where feeling reigns supreme.

We must therefore fall back upon the prevalent view that government or the state is the homologue of the brain and ganglionic hierarchy in the developed animal, and here, it must be confessed, there is a general parallel and quite an array of special parallels. The difficulty with it is that, as already remarked, and as has been perceived by a score of writers, neither the degree of differentiation nor of integration is equal to that of any such animals. We may perhaps be thankful that it is not, for anything approaching it would realize the wildest socialistic dreams. . . .

We will next glance, still more briefly, at the other side of the subject, and consider a few of the objections that have been raised to the organic theory of society, and especially endeavor to enumerate the principal respects in which society has been shown to differ from an organism. Merely mentioning the three principal distinctions pointed out by Spencer from the first—viz.: that societies are (1) discrete instead of concrete, (2) asymmetrical instead of symmetrical, and (3) sensitive in all their units, but insensible in their ensemble, in all of which cases the reverse is true of living organisms—we may enumerate, as among the structures, organs, and functions of society which have no proper counterparts in any organic being: language, religion, contract, symbolism, migration, and exportation; and as among those belonging to living organisms which have no proper counterparts in society: birth, death, reproduction. The analogies that have been pointed out in all these cases are admittedly weak and unsatisfactory. The following points that have been made against the organic theory may also be regarded as well taken:

1. Societies become more and more settled as they develop, which is the reverse of the process in biology. For example,

nomads represent the free swimming state of the lower animals, and the settled societies represent the fixed state, as
of polyps, sponges, etc.

2. The higher a society, the less it feels the loss of any
organ, the reverse being the case among living organisms.

3. There is nothing in human society to correspond to the
great sympathetic plexuses, which have with much truth been
called the physical basis of man's moral nature.

4. As regards the élite as the social sensorium, it is well
known that intelligence tends to divide men, just as interest
(feeling) unites them. The élite is therefore a centrifugal force
in society, working for disintegration.

All these points—and many more might be adduced—are
quite independent of the general biological and classificatory
considerations urged at the beginning of this section.

About all that is left of the doctrine of the social organism
is that society, like an animal or a plant, but also like language,
law, the state, art, and science, is something organized—an
organization. Organization is a universal or cosmical process,
and in its fundamental aspects is very uniform.

Society differs fundamentally from an organism in not being
a concrete object at all. We cannot properly say that it consists of men and women, nor of their material environment,
nor of both these together. Man is a species or a genus, according to the scope given to these terms, but society is neither
of these, nor any other classific group. It comes nearer to the
conception of a herd or flock, of which the individual members are imperfectly held together by a certain psychic force.
It is, however, much more like a corporation, voluntary organization, church or other association of men. In fact
association is its essence, and sociology is the science of
human association. But association is an act, and *an* association
is a product of the act of associating. It is a relation among
individuals. Now, a relation is not a concrete object. It is an
abstract conception. Nothing but the individual is concrete.

A species is not a material thing. A genus is only a mental conception. The social-organism theory is a sort of modern revival of the old scholastic realism. The truth is that society is a relation, but when we examine all forms of truth we shall find that most of it is of this class, and also that relations are the most important of all *things*.

IV. *Sociology as Political Economy.*

So large a part of social phenomena relates to material things that many economists decline to recognize sociology as a science distinct from economics. Of this class we need not speak. There is, however, another class of economists who clearly see that economics as commonly taught fails to include large fields of phenomena that are of the highest importance, especially phenomena relating to population in a broader sense than that usually given to the science of demography. These economists would enlarge the scope of economics to embrace these fields. This department they often designate as social economics or social economy. This latter expression was used by John Stuart Mill when he was trying to find a name for a great science which he clearly saw to exist, distinct from political economy.[8] He then said: "This science stands in the same relation to the social as anatomy and physiology to the physical body." The organicists have never, to my knowledge, made any use, as they might have done, of this significant passage, but it is broad enough to serve equally well in characterizing society as an organized body or social organization. But Mill was specially concerned in distinguishing his new-found science from political economy, and he proceeded to do so in a clearly worded paragraph. . . .

The truth of the matter is that two distinct sciences are here

---

[8] *London and Westminster Review,* XXVI (October 1836), 11; *Essays on Some Unsettled Questions of Political Economy* (1844), p. 135.

involved, and the fundamental distinction between them is confused. It is not merely that one deals with production and wealth, and the other with consumption and welfare, though this is true and clear enough; but the initial standpoint is the opposite in the one from what it is in the other. In political economy the point of departure is the producer, while in sociology it is the consumer. But by the producer is not meant the laborer or the artisan, but the undertaker or manager; the man interested in securing the maximum production. And by the consumer is meant all who consume, i. e., the public, society at large. Utility means the same in both, but its application is wholly different. Utility always means satisfaction, but in economics it is satisfaction to the entrepreneur, while in sociology it is satisfaction to all who use the product. . . .

Mention might perhaps be made of another very successful kind of business, though classed as a learned profession, viz., the practice of law; and closely associated with it are a thousand little businesses that require expert legal knowledge. The system of jurisprudence that has grown up in civilized societies, the purpose of which is to cause security of person and property, is one of the richest heritages of the past, but it has come to employ a much greater number of persons than are necessary. Probably all the law business of any country could be done by one-fourth of the present number. The rest are simply parasites. The way in which they maintain their hold on society is through that other business called politics. Most politicians are lawyers, and this is chiefly due to the faculty they acquire in public speaking by their practice before the bar. Business men (merchants, manufacturers, railroad officials, etc.) have no opportunity to speak in public, and therefore, however good their judgment may be on public questions, they cannot attract the attention of the people in such a way as to become prominent in political affairs and get themselves sent to legislatures, to parliament, to congress, etc. The result is that legislatures always consist chiefly of lawyers. Nothing more natural than that bodies of lawyers, having the framing of all laws in their hands, should so frame them as to increase the amount of their own business. This, in brief, explains the superfluous law business of the world, which not only produces nothing in any economic sense of the word, but becomes a great charge and expense, and actually diminishes the degree of security by all manner of fictions and useless technicalities.

Now, respecting these non-productive, parasitic, and even injurious employments, economics has nothing to say except simply to consider whether they are successful. All kinds of business are equally legitimate, and even those which the state condemns as dishonest or pernicious are never suppressed at the suggestion of the political economist. So long as they are tolerated they are proper subjects of economic study, and we know that there is great diversity among states as to what forms of business should be prohibited, as witness legislation relative to lotteries.

Sociology, on the other hand, in its applied stage, concerns itself primarily with the question of the public utility of enterprises. Its standpoint is the good of society. To that end the individual manager of a business may be sacrificed, or, at least, he may be constrained to direct his energies and abilities into some useful channel. The modern interest in sociology is chiefly due to the obvious sterility of political economy. The social world is in a somewhat troubled state. The era of machinofacture has culminated in such an array of labor-saving inventions that the possibilities of production are well-nigh unlimited, but the capital has become concentrated in relatively few hands, while the artisan class has not acquired the general intelligence necessary to enable them to participate in such a movement. Thus enormous relative inequalities have grown up in modern society. At the same time these very causes have accelerated rather than retarded the rise of the proletariat, and improved the absolute, though not the relative, material condition of the working class. In a word, they have engendered discontent, which is a state that can only exist above a certain stage of physical and mental advancement. Society, though not in a dangerous condition, is in a sort of ferment, and there has been made possible a social problem, or rather a crowd of social problems. At first appeal was made to the economist, who was supposed to be able to offer a scientific solution of some of these problems. But his answers, though sometimes oracular in form, were about as satisfactory as the opinions of a certain J. Bunsby. More frequently he grew impatient and reiterated the traditional economic injunction against presuming to meddle with the workings of natural law. Many anxious inquirers, wholly discouraged by these cold blasts from high seats of learning, turn to the state and demand a statutory solution of social problems, but the state usually declines to respond, or perhaps adopts measures that fail to accomplish the purpose sought, or even aggravate the difficulties.

It is under such a condition of affairs that there has been gradually struggling into existence a new science which seeks a true and fundamental acquaintance with, rather than an immediate solution of, social questions; which is content to wait for such solution until the conditions of these questions are better understood. It does not hold them in haughty disdain, nor does it pretend to possess any panacea for social evils, but it is open to inquiry, takes a true scientific interest in social events and phenomena for their own sake, and either inhibits its concern for the practical results, or has faith that these will be best subserved by first laying in a store of knowledge. This science is sociology, and there is enough of intellectual stimulus in the study of its pure stage, wholly disconnected from its consequences, to keep quite a corps of earnest investigators in the field working on different lines.

But it is obvious at a glance that this science is much broader than that of political economy, even when that is expanded to embrace what is called political science (finance, administration, diplomacy, national enterprises, consular affairs, colonial relations, etc., etc.). These are all related to it, in fact may be included in it, but they do not by any means constitute the whole of it. Relatively to the whole domain of sociology, these are really quite narrow, and it is only their vital character that causes them to appear so all-absorbing.

V. *Sociology as the Philosophy of History.*

It is maintained by some that there is nothing new in sociology; that it is simply a new name for that which has long been called the philosophy of history; that human events make up its basis of fact; and that the only scientific treatment possible is the co-ordination of those facts and the tracing of their dependence, their antecedence and sequence—in short, their causal relations. Some color is given to this view by Comte's masterly summing up, under the head of social dynamics, of the course of history through the celebrated *trois états* in the fifth and sixth volumes of his *Positive Philosophy.* . . .

Comte was deeply impressed with the necessity of connecting the events of history together into such a series that their future occurrence could be predicted from the past. He says:

It is undeniable . . . . that history has not yet ceased to possess an essentially literary or descriptive character, and has not acquired a true scientific character by finally establishing a rational filiation in the succession of social events, so as to permit, as in other departments of phenomena, and within the general limits imposed by their higher complexity, a certain systematic prevision of their further succession.[9]

He does not characterize as philosophy of history the fifth and sixth volumes of his *Positive Philosophy,* but on the title-

---

[9] *Philosophie positive,* IV, 206.

page, and also in the preface of the third volume, of his *Positive Polity,* "containing the social dynamics or general treatment of human progress," he adds the words: "Philosophie de l'histoire." But he does not imply that that one volume constitutes the whole of sociology. In fact, he always made sociology exactly synonymous with "social physics," which embraces social statics as well as social dynamics, and no one has attempted to identify social statics with the philosophy of history. Nevertheless, Barth, who is perfectly familiar with Comte, says that "a perfect sociology would be exactly coextensive with the philosophy of history; they differ at bottom only in name."[10] It is curious that Lilienfeld,[11] whose standpoint is so strictly biological, should accept this view of Barth, but he says that it can only be realized through the application of the organic method. He is probably alone in being able to see any rational connection between the two methods. Tarde, on the other hand, declares that "it was not sociology that Comte founded; it is a simple philosophy of history that he offers us under this name, but admirably drawn up; it is the last word of the philosophy of history."[12] And De Greef, much to the same effect, remarks that "the sociology of Comte does not, properly speaking, merit that title; it is rather a philosophy of the history of ideas."[13] All such statements result from the tendency to ignore everything else in Comte's sociology but his historical review of human thought through the three stages: theological, metaphysical, and positive. These writers forget that Comte insisted that sociology was simply the last of a series of affiliated sciences, and as such virtually embraced

---

[10] *Ibid.,* p. 10.

[11] *Zur Vertheidigung der organischen Methode in der Sociologie* (Berlin, 1898), p. 31.

[12] *Les lois sociales* (Paris, 1898), p. 123.

[13] *Introduction à la sociologie,* première partie (Brussels and Paris, 1886), p. 226.

them all. If they would read again the fourth volume of the *Positive Philosophy*, "containing the dogmatic part of social philosophy," they would discover how much broader Comte's sociology was than they seem to suppose. . . .

It is, of course, natural and proper that sociology should deal mainly with the line of leading civilizations and races, because they represent the last and highest stages of culture and civilization, and present the most complex and difficult phenomena for investigation. They also possess a far greater practical interest than the outlying and more backward races and civilizations. Comte laid stress upon this as the final goal of the science, and he did not treat uncivilized and savage races, leaving us to infer that his acquaintance with anthropology was limited. I regard this as one of the great merits of his work, because, as was remarked in the first paper of this series, the temptation is so strong to permit the treatment of the lower races to absorb all attention, and thus narrow sociology down to mere anthropology.

Dr. Georg Simmel has also attempted to draw the line between sociology and the philosophy of history. He says:

This special task of sociology must be separated strictly from the philosophy of history. The philosophy of history seeks to bring historical facts, external as well as physical, in their entirety, under general concepts, by virtue of which history may satisfy certain demands, ethical, metaphysical, religious, and artistic. In complete opposition to this, sociology as a special science, the eventual scope of which I have attempted here to determine, restricts itself entirely to the realm of phenomena and their immediate psychological explanation.[14] . . .

Finally might be cited the now somewhat classic reply of Sir John Lubbock (Lord Avebury) to the declaration of Fustel

---

[14] *Annals of the American Academy of Political and Social Science,* VI (Philadelphia, 1895), 419.

de Coulanges that sociology is the same thing as history, "the science of social arts":

I can scarcely think that these two words can be employed as synonyms. In some respects history means more than sociology. Accidents, successions, dynasties, can scarcely enter into sociology; while the discussion of questions concerning education, health, the condition of the poor, and many other circumstances that contribute in large measure to the prosperity and well-being of mankind, have not formed, so to speak, any part of history, at least down to the present time.

There are then portions of history that do not enter into the domain of sociology, and questions of sociology that do not enter into that of history. How sad it is that historians have so neglected the social side of history! We find pages and even chapters devoted to wars, battles, and struggles for power, while the social condition of the people is entirely omitted, or treated in a phrase or two.

It is said: "happy is the people that has no history." No history? There cannot be a people without a history. It may be that history will consist of the development and of the quiet and silent growth of a people; but that is none the less a history, and it is for this very reason the more instructive and the more interesting.[15] . . .

VI. *Sociology as the Special Social Sciences.*

It is maintained by some that sociology is not a science in the proper sense, but simply a term employed to embrace a large group of more or less cognate sciences or subjects that are separately referred to as special social sciences. On this view all of these sciences together constitute sociology, and each of them belongs to it, but there is no implication of any organic relation among the special social sciences, or of anything in sociology that is distinct from them or peculiar to itself. Although these various sciences or groups of phenomena

---

[15] *Annales de l'Institut international de Sociologie,* I, 2. Opening address of the first president of the institute.

are admitted to be interrelated in various ways and degrees, there is no special way in which they are conceived as related to sociology, which may be looked upon as merely a mechanical mixture of them all. . . .

It is obvious that there could be no sociology until the greater number of these fields had been cultivated. It may even be admitted—and I for one would strongly insist upon it—that sociology cannot be properly studied without a fundamental acquaintance with those more general sciences that I have put at the head of the list. And their utility for the sociologist increases as the fields grow more complex, until biology, anthropology, and psychology become absolutely indispensable.

What, then, is the relation of the special social sciences to sociology? Schaeffle calls them the building stones out of which sociology is constructed. But this is a very rough, if not entirely erroneous, comparison. Sociology is not exactly a structure built of these materials. It is rather a generalization from them all. It abstracts from each all that is common and forms a sort of head, to which they constitute, as it were, the body and limbs. In short, sociology is an integration or synthesis of the whole body of social sciences. Wundt has set forth this distinction very clearly, referring everything to the special social sciences, except the general conceptions and principles of social life.[16] For my own part I prefer to see in the special social sciences the *data* of sociology. They furnish the facts, and sociology co-ordinates them. Many of them furnish great coordinated groups of facts and special laws well established in their own domains. Sociology treats these as units, and groups these groups into higher and more general conceptions. Sociology furnishes the highest of all generalizations. It is an abstract science, dealing with the laws and principles of all the other sciences. It stands at the summit of the hierarchy of the

---

[16] *Logik*, zweite ʻuflage, Bd. II, Abth. II, pp. 438 (footnote), 447.

sciences, and derives its truths from the entire series with increasing directness from physics and chemistry to biology and psychology. It can be properly understood only when considered from this point of view, and it should not be taught until regularly reached in this natural order of the sciences. In teaching it, therefore, anthropology and history, psychology and biology, and *a fortiori* the simpler branches of a common education, should be assumed as the necessary preparation supposed to have been made. The teacher can then proceed direct to principles. Without such preparation he must stop at every step and actually teach these ancillary sciences before he can begin his instruction in sociology proper.

I would furthermore accept practically all the disciplines . . . as special social sciences, although their relation to sociology is of a widely varying character. There is, however, one which many regard as a science co-ordinate with sociology, and which the two leading sociologists of the world, Comte and Spencer, have actually placed above that science in the natural sequence of sciences. I refer, of course, to ethics. I have never been able to share this view, and I consider ethics rather a typical social science, in so far as it is a science at all. In the first place, the ethical idea is essentially and necessarily social. It always implies a feeling creature as the recipient of the action, whether good or bad. Its basis is sympathy or altruism, either of which terms requires at least a duality of persons so related or associated as to exert an influence upon each other. There can be no sympathy without someone to *feel with*. There can be no altruism without an *alter*. This seems effectually to dispose of Spencer's claim to a distinct science of ethics. In the second place, it is hard to make anyone see that Comte's *morale* was practically identical with sociability, and as such was simply an extension or special amplification of his general conception of sociology. But anyone who will carefully examine his *Politique positive* from this point of view cannot fail to be struck with this fact. Here we find no moralizing, no flourishing of ethical precepts, no hortatory appeals to the moral sense, no laudation of moral conduct; in fact, nothing that at all resembles the current treatises on ethics, or "moral science," as a code of action designed to restrain evil-doing and encourage well-doing. Instead of this we find a scientific treatise on the evolution of altruism through sociability. It is in its earliest stages that this is most clear, and with primitive man, as all know, the ethical sense was confined to the nearest of kin. We must come down to very advanced nations to find the recognition of any distinct moral obligation toward the members of other nations and races. The anthropologists have clearly seen this, and they have considerable difficulty in distinguishing the moral from the social.[17] M. E. de Roberty,[18] one of the most enlightened followers of Comte, has ably and fully elaborated this view. It is, in fact, the "social consensus" of Comte and the "solidarity" of current sociological literature, and it all rests on sociability, or a certain mutual interest which the members of society take in one another. This is the root of altruism and of all ethics, and is an exclusively social sentiment.

The conception of sociology as consisting of all the special social sciences unaccompanied by any idea of their relations is of course an extreme one, and could not be entertained by anyone who recognized as special social sciences all those enumerated in the above list. Those who thus think of sociology do so in a vague way and have in mind only a few of the related sciences. Nevertheless the number of such persons is very large, while the number of those who think closely and carefully on the subject is small. Hence it seemed worth while to devote a little space to this somewhat popular view. It may be well, before leaving the subject, to advert to the opposite extreme, which is also somewhat prevalent. When any one

---

[17] "Ces deux termes sont presque synonymes."—Ch. Letourneau, *Revue mensuelle de l'École d'Anthropologie de Paris*, XI (November 15, 1898), 339.

[18] *Le bien et le mal* (Paris, 1896), *passim*.

subject is allowed to engross the mind, it is apt to assume undue prominence and engender extreme views with regard to
it. Even sociology may become in some minds a sort of fetich.
This tendency is seen in what may be called the *objectivation*
of social phenomena. Too much is often made of the social
consciousness, and society itself seems to be conceived by some
as a sort of independent being or entity. Mr. Spencer did good
service in checking this tendency by laying special stress on
the fact that the fundamental distinction between society and
an organism is that the former is incapable of enjoyment or
suffering, and exists only for the good of its individual members, each of which is thus capable. Attacks on the social order
are to be deprecated, not because it is possible to hurt the
social order as a feeling creature, but because any disturbance
of the social order reacts upon the individual who is a feeling
creature. No one has ever, to my knowledge, questioned this
proposition, and it is really little more than a truism. . . .

VII. *Sociology as the Description of Social Facts.*

The idea that science consists in the description of facts, or
in the accumulation of a mass of facts, is a very common one,
not only as a popular notion, but also among specialists in
many branches, especially in the field of biology, formerly
called "natural history." In my early botanical experience I
was impressed with the fact that the botanists I knew cared
chiefly for collecting all the plants in any locality and making
a catalogue of them. That was their idea of botany as a science.
Things are changed now, and most botanists are more interested in the morphological and histological study of plants.
But in this they often become absorbed in the study of some
special organ or kind of tissue, and look upon the microscopic
observation of certain minute structures and their exhaustive
description as constituting the science. It is evidently the same

in zoölogy. I do not say that either of these methods is not scientific. Both are necessary to the progress of science, but neither in and of itself advances science. It is not until some competent investigator takes up the isolated results thus attained, and brings them together into some orderly connection and constructs some kind of system, that any scientific truth is established. For science does not consist in facts, but in their relations, and these can be made known only by reasoning about the facts first collected, observed, and described.

It is not, therefore, surprising that there should be sociologists who look upon the collection and description of facts as constituting sociology. This would result from the nature of the human mind, if there were no other cause. The two opposite types of mind, the analytic and the synthetic, have been described by many philosophers. Naturalists are divided by this principle into two opposing camps; for, although all must observe, describe, and classify, the one class, impressed by the differences in things and the multiplicity of facts in nature, tend to divide and subdivide and multiply species and groups, while the other, embarrassed by the resemblances and common characters that they see among all objects, tend to combine and merge their species and groups and reduce their number. The former are called "splitters" and the latter "lumpers," and these follow each other over every field of science, each undoing the work of the other in the matter of classification. To outsiders this seems to lead to utter confusion, but in practice it really causes little inconvenience.

Most of the "descriptive sociology" that has been done and of that which has been recommended properly belongs to anthropology, i. e., to ethnography. There it is of the highest value to the sociologist as furnishing the data for sociology. The plan of monographing the facts of family life of the lower classes in civilized society, as pursued by Le Play and his school, belongs to sociology, or perhaps to demography. The very thought of making it universal or sufficiently extensive to form a reliable guide to the sociologist is appalling, and I have yet to learn of any important use that sociologists have been able to make of the work that has been done thus far. Most of the rest of the materials available for sociology are derived from history. History is the sociologist's great storehouse, and it cannot be said that the resources are meager. Next to fiction, history probably forms the largest department of literature. It is, of course, justly charged that history does not furnish all that the sociologist demands and requires. This is no modern discovery. Condorcet, writing in 1795 or earlier, said:

Thus far political history, as well as that of philosophy and of science, has only been the history of a few men; that which really forms the human species, the mass of families who subsist almost entirely by their labor, has been forgotten.[19]

The note thus sounded has been re-echoed all through the nineteenth century, until the "great-man theory" and *histoire-bataille* have come to describe what has hitherto usually passed for history. But in its stead has arisen the "historical school" of economists, and no one can deny that this school is furnishing the real materials for sociology, so far as they can be gleaned from history and literature. Sociologists are already using them, and will use them more and more. I have sometimes thought that more could be extracted from literature than is commonly supposed. If sociologists would go about it in some such way as Mr. Spencer accomplished his *Descriptive Sociology,* important results could be attained. If the early literature, like that of Greece and Rome, of India, Egypt, Persia, Syria, and China, could be thoroughly sifted for social facts, the labor, though great, would be well repaid. Such writers did not intentionally inform the world as to the industrial,

---

[19] *Tableau historique des progrès de l'esprit humain* (Paris, 1900), p. 158.

economic, and social condition of the ages and countries in which they lived and wrote, but on every page occur words that are full of meaning for the sociologist who will carefully weigh them and learn what they imply. The same would be true of the sagas and numerous traditional poems that have come down to us, such as the *Nibelungen Lied,* the *Ossian Tales,* the *Kalevala,* and the *Heliand,* as well as the oriental *Mahabharata* and *Shah-Namah,* the Indian *Vedas,* the Persian *Avesta,* and other sacred books. . . .

The next great reservoir of social facts, after ethnography and history, is statistics. This branch is being pushed with great energy, and often has the resources of great states behind it. It only needs to be wisely directed, and it will prove of inestimable value to the sociologist.

But there is still another source of social facts, as yet without a name, but always taken into account, and which is perhaps of more value to the sociologist than any of the foregoing. This is the sociologist's own social environment. If he would only recognize it, the facts he is seeking lie all about him. From birth to death he is literally bathed in a social medium and breathes a social atmosphere. In some respects sociology is at a disadvantage in having men for its subjects. It has some difficulty in collecting specimens, and more in taking them to pieces for analysis, though even these things are accomplished; but it has this great advantage that it never lacks for material. It does not have to go in search of subjects for study. On every hand they are always present. Neither are they shy or wild, so that it is necessary to trap or shoot them in order to get near enough to them to make close observations. Ornithologists and other zoölogists often strive to conceal themselves and bait their birds and animals, so that they can be observed in their natural condition, or they employ the fieldglass to bring them nearer to them, but this is attended with great difficulties and requires patience and skill. But the sociologist can always observe men from as close range as he pleases, and see them acting naturally and without fear or constraint.

No sociologist realizes how much use he unconsciously makes of his social environment. He not only studies the objects and the facts and phenomena of society in this way, but he is able to study the laws and principles of social life, and work out the finest theories of social action in the highest domains of psychic and spiritual activity. Kant, who never quitted Königsberg, could probe to the bottom the deepest problems of thought and conduct. A sociologist scarcely need travel to prosecute his researches. With a library of books he can learn what men have done in the past. His newspaper tells him what they are doing at present in all parts of the world. In his family, neighborhood, town, or city he daily meets man, and he has learned that men are fundamentally alike the world over and in all ages. It is, of course, better that he travel, and the more the better, provided he does not subordinate his reflective to his perceptive faculties. But sociology may almost be made a closet study, and the sociologist may study society in narrow surroundings, just as some truly great naturalists have practically spent their lives in their cabinets.

Sociology, therefore, in its more restricted and proper sense, is of all sciences perhaps the least to be regarded as a descriptive science. This is not because it ignores facts. It uses far more facts than any other science. But it is because its facts are supplied by other ancillary special social sciences—ethnography, demography, history, statistics, and the ever-present social environment, which might be called *mesography* when it is observed, recorded, and utilized by the sociologist. It is the special province of the sociologist to *use* these multitudinous resources and materials, and to construct the social system. It is induction on a vast scale, accompanied, as all induction always is, by sound deduction, or reasoning and intepretation. . . . Sociology is an organizing, generalizing, coordinating science, calculated to extract social truths from social facts. . . .

25

EVOLUTION OF

SOCIAL STRUCTURE

1904

Ward was at first invited to give one of the two papers on the progress of sociology at the St. Louis Exposition of 1904. He had already dealt with this subject in his essays on "Contemporary Sociology" and refused to retread that ground. At the last moment the committee asked him to speak on social structure, and he literally dashed off this essay and read it, without revision, to the Congress.

. . . Social structures are identical in . . . fundamental aspects, with both inorganic and organic structures. They are the products of the interaction of antagonistic forces. They also pass from a primordial stage of great simplicity into a secondary, more complex stage, and these two stages are closely analogous to the protozoic and metazoic stages of biology. I call them the "protosocial" and "metasocial" stages, respectively.

If we set out with the simple propagating couple, we soon

"Evolution of Social Structures," *American Journal of Sociology*, X (March 1905), 589–605.

have the primitive family group consisting of the parents and children. The children are of both sexes, and they grow to maturity, pair off in one way or another, and produce families of the second order. These do the same, resulting in families of the third order, and so on. After a few generations the group assumes considerable size, and constitutes first a horde, and finally a clan. The clan at length becomes overgrown and splits up into several or many clans, separating more or less territorially, but usually adopting the rule of exogamy, and living on comparatively peaceful terms at no great distance from one another. Their mode of reproduction is exactly analogous to the process of reproduction by division in the Protozoa, and this is what I characterize as the protosocial stage in race-development.

But the multiplication of clans through continuous reproduction in a geometrical progression, coupled with the limits prescribed by the food-supply, results in the wider and wider separation of the clans, until at length certain clans or hordes will have become so far removed from the primary center of dispersion as to lose all connection with it. At the low stage of mental development necessary to such a race of beings scarcely as much as a tradition would ultimately remain of the existence of a primordial group from which all had descended. One clan would keep budding off from another, and moving out farther and farther along lines of least resistance, until a great area of the earth's surface would at last become thus sparsely inhabited by a multitude of clans, each knowing only the few that are located nearest to it. As the dispersion takes place in all directions from the original center, or as nearly so as the configuration of the country and the nature of the food-supply will permit, those migrating in opposite directions become, after a sufficient lapse of time, so widely separated from one another as to constitute wholly distinct peoples. They all have languages, but in time the local variations that they naturally undergo render them to all intents and purposes different languages, at least so much so that if individuals of these long-separated groups should chance to meet, they could not understand one another. It would be the same with their customs, beliefs, and religion. They would have become in all essential respects different races.

We will suppose that in the end a whole continent is thus peopled with these alien hordes and clans, which would now have become innumerable. The process by which this is brought about is what I have called "social differentiation." But it cannot always last. A new process supervenes, and the stage of social differentiation is succeeded by a stage of social integration. The protosocial stage closes, and the metasocial stage comes on. In the protosocial stage the social structure is the simplest possible. The horde or clan is composed altogether of similar elements. The multiplication of such groups can be nothing but a repetition of similar groups, and there can be no change or variation, and therefore no progress or structural advance. Throughout the protosocial, as throughout the protozoic, stage there is no structural development, no evolution. The differentiation consists simply in the multiplication of practically identical clans. Just as organic evolution began with the metazoic stage, so social evolution began with the metasocial stage. So, too, as the metazoic stage was brought about through the union of several or many unicellular organisms into a multicellular organism, so the metasocial stage was brought about by the union of two or more simple hordes or clans into a compound group of amalgamated hordes or clans. In the organic world the result was the formation of tissues, the multiplication of organs, and the integration of the parts thus united into complete organisms. In the social world the result was the formation of what may be properly called social tissues, the multiplication of social organs, and the integration of all the elements thus combined into peoples, states, and nations. The study of social structure properly begins here; but social structure would be wholly unintelligible without a clear idea of both the principle and the materials of social structure. The principle is the interaction of antagonistic forces, and the materials are the primitive hordes and clans brought into existence by the process of social differentiation. We have now to descend from generalities and inquire into the specific character of social integration. A great area has become inhabited by innumerable human groups, but there is no organic connection between them. Each group lays claim to a certain area of territory, but they begin to encroach upon one another. Two groups thus brought into proximity may be, and usually are, utterly unknown to each other. The mutual encroachment is certain to produce hostility. War is the result, and one of the two groups is almost certain to prove the superior warrior and to conquer the other. The first step in the whole process is the conquest of one race by another. This is the beginning of the struggle of races of which we have all heard so much. Most persons regard this struggle as the greatest of all human misfortunes. But the sociologist studies the effects of race-struggle and finds in it the basis of his science. The first effect is the subjugation of one race by another. The second effect is the establishment of a system of caste, the conquering race assuming the rôle of a superior or noble caste, and the conquered race being relegated to the position of an inferior or ignoble caste. The greater part of the conquered race is enslaved, and the institution of slavery begins here. The slaves are compelled to work, and labor in the economic sense begins here. The enslavement of the producers and the compelling them to work was the only way in which mankind could have been taught to labor, and therefore the whole industrial system of society begins here.

The conquerors parcel out the lands to the leading military chieftains, and the institution of private ownership of land has its origin at this stage. Success in war is attributed to the favor of the gods, and those who pretend to be in communication with the gods are the most favored of men. They are installed in high places and made the recipients of large emoluments. From the condition of sorcerers, soothsayers, and medicine-men they are raised to that of a powerful priesthood. Henceforth they constitute a leisure class, and this is the origin of that most important human institution. Mutual race-hatred results in perpetual uprisings, requiring constant suppression by the military power. This is costly, dangerous, and precarious, and wisdom soon dictates a form of systematic treatment for offenders. Personal regulation gradually gives way to general rules, and these ultimately take the form of laws. Government by law gradually succeeds government by arbitrary military commands. The effect of this is nothing less than the origin of the state. The state is the most important of all human institutions. There is no institution about which so much has been written, and even in our day volumes are yearly appearing vainly endeavoring to explain the origin and nature of the state. They all completely miss the mark, and flounder in a sea of vague and worthless speculation. The state is a spontaneous genetic product, resulting, like all other social structures, from the interaction of antagonistic forces, checking and restraining one another and evolving a great social structure destined to become the condition to all social progress. Under the state there are recognized both rights and duties. So long as the law is not violated there is liberty of action, and the foundations of human freedom are laid.

Another great institution takes its rise at this stage, viz., that of property. With the establishment of the state, with its recognition of rights under the law, it becomes possible, as never before, to enjoy undisturbed any object that has been rightfully acquired. Such an object then becomes property, and belongs to its owner even if not in his immediate possession. He need no longer fear that, unless it is constantly watched and forcibly defended, it will be wrested from him by others who have no other claim than that of superior strength. The immense sociological importance of this cannot be too strongly emphasized.

For a man's possessions need no longer be confined to what he can himself consume or enjoy; they may greatly exceed his wants, or consist of objects for which he has no need, but which are needed by others who have other things that he does want and for which he can exchange them. He can manufacture a single product many thousand times in excess of his needs, and exchange it for a great variety of other objects similarly produced in excess by others. We thus see that the institution of private property was the foundation at once of all trade and business and also of the division of labor. But property was not possible until the state was established, whose most important function was at the outset and still remains the protection of the citizen in his proprietary rights.

With the establishment of the state, or even before, there begins a differentiation of social tissues. The analogy with organic tissues is here particularly clear and useful in helping us to understand the process. All well-informed persons are now familiar with the fact that the tissues of all developed animals consist of an ectoderm, or outer layer, an endoderm, or inner layer, and a mesoderm, or intermediate layer, and that out of one or the other of these fundamental tissues all the organs of the body are formed. Now, the evolution of the meta-social body is exactly parallel to this. The conquering race, or superior class or caste, represents the social ectoderm; the conquered race, or inferior class or caste, represents the social endoderm. The social mesoderm is not so simple, but it is not less real. It is one of the most important consequences of race-amalgamation.

Within the social body, under the régime of law and the state, there is intense activity. Compelled by mutually restraining forces to remain in one place and not fly off on various tangents, the vigorous elements of the new complex society display a corresponding intensity in their inner life. Only a small part of the superior race can hold high places under the state, and the great majority of them are obliged to support themselves by their own efforts. Neither are all the members of the subject race held in bondage; a large percentage remain free, and must of course maintain themselves by some form of useful activity. These two classes are too nearly alike in their social standing to continue long socially and economically independent. It must be remembered that both races have descended from the same original stock, although they do not know it. There is therefore no essential difference in their general character. The superiority by which one was able to conquer the other may have been due to a variety of more or less accidental causes. It does not render them superior in other respects. The individuals of both races will differ greatly in character and ability, and members of the subject race will often excel those of the dominant race in certain respects. They are all struggling together for subsistence, and it is inevitable that their interests will often be the same. Race-prejudice will thus gradually give way, and in the general industrial strife there is a greater and greater commingling and co-operation. There thus arises a large industrial class made up of these two elements, and this class may be appropriately called the "social mesoderm." This industrial, commercial, or business class is the real life of the society. The ruling class becomes more and more dependent upon it for the supply of the resources of the state, and gradually the members of this class acquire more or less influence and power.

As time goes on, the situation is accepted by all, and race-prejudices give way. The interaction of all classes increases, and a general process of assimilation sets in, tending toward a complete blending of all classes into a single homogeneous group. Intermarriage among the members of the two races grows more and more frequent, until ultimately nearly or quite all the members of the society have the blood of both races in their veins. The final outcome of it all is the production of a people. The people thus evolved out of heterogeneous elements is different from either of the races producing it. It is a new creation, the social synthesis of the race-struggle, and is as homogeneous in its constitution as was either of its original components.

Only one more step in this process of evolution of social structures is possible on the simple plane on which we have been tracing it, and that is the making of a nation. The new people that has been developed now begin to acquire an attachment, not only for one another as members of the society, but also for the place of their birth and activity. They realize that they are a people and that they have a country, and there arises a love of both which crystallizes into the sentiment that we call patriotism. All are now ready to defend their country against outside powers, and all are filled with what we know as the national sentiment. In a word, out of the prolonged struggle of two primarily antagonistic and hostile races there has at last emerged a single cemented and homogeneous nation.

We thus have as the natural and necessary result of the conquest and subjugation of one primitive group by another no less than fourteen more or less distinct social structures or human institutions. These are in the order in which they are developed: (1) the system of caste; (2) the institution of slavery; (3) labor in the economic sense; (4) the industrial system; (5) landed property; (6) the priesthood; (7) a leisure class; (8) government by law; (9) the state; (10) political liberty; (11) property; (12) a business class; (13) a people; (14) a nation.

The first two of these social structures are not now regarded as useful, but they were useful when formed and, indeed, the essential conditions to all the subsequent ones. The priesthood and the leisure class are now no longer necessary to a high civilization, but they still exist, and under proper limitations they have an important function. All institutions undergo great modifications and some are completely transformed with time.

The case considered is that of the union of two primitive

groups which occupied at the outset the same social position, and that the lowest known. It may be called a case of simple social assimilation. That there have been many such cases there is no doubt, but no such could be observed by enlightened man, for the simple reason that no such primitive groups exist, or have existed since there have been enlightened men. This may sound strange when we constantly hear of existing hordes and clans. But I make bold to affirm that none of the hordes or clans now existing are at all primitive. Nay, I go farther and maintain that all hordes and clans, all tribes, and all races are equally old. The lowest race on the earth is as old as the most enlightened nation. There is no escape from this except in the old exploded theological doctrine of special creation. The theory of polygenism is a form of that doctrine applied to human races. To admit it involves the surrender of the whole doctrine of evolution. If man has evolved from a lower prehuman stage, he emerged as man at a given time, and all human races have descended from that one truly primitive type. All human races are therefore equally old. The differences among them are not at all due to the time it has required to reach their present state, because all have had the same time in which to do this. The differences are wholly due to the different conditions under which they have been placed and in conformity with which they have developed.

There has, of course, been a great variety of influences at work in determining the direction and degree of development of the races of men, but there is one element that has had more to do with this than any other, or perhaps than all others combined; that is the element with which we have been dealing, viz., the element of social assimilation. When we realize that all human races are equally old, we can readily see that all cases of simple assimilation, such as the one sketched, must have occurred far back in the early history of man. The period of social differentiation may have been very long. It may have occupied half of the two hundred thousand years that are commonly assigned to man on the earth. But whatever its length, that period is long past, and the period of social integration has been at least as long. All the cases of simple assimilation had run their course ages before there were any records of any kind, and human history acquaints us only with types of a far higher order.

In other words, the only cases of which we have any actual knowledge are cases of compound social assimilation. Compound assimilation results when peoples or nations that have already formed in the manner described out of lower social elements again amalgamate on a higher plane and repeat the process. When one perfectly integrated nation conquers and subjugates another, the same steps have to be taken as in the case of simple groups. The struggle is as much more intense as it is higher in the scale of social structure. But the new structures developed through it, although they have the same names and the same general character, become, when formed, more powerful and capable of accomplishing much more. The new society is of a higher grade and a more potent factor in the world. The new state, the new people, the new nation, are on a higher plane, and a long step is taken toward civilization.

But all the nations of which history tells us anything have undergone much more still than two social assimilations. Most of them have undergone many, and represent highly complex structures. With every fresh assimilation they rise in the scale of civilization. What they acquire is greater and greater social efficiency, and the principal differences between races, peoples, and nations are differences in the degree of social efficiency. Not only are the same social structures acquired in the first assimilation greatly increased and strengthened, but a large number of other, more or less derivative, but highly socializing, structures are added. The system of law, which was at first only a sort of police regulation, becomes a great system of jurisprudence. Government, which at first had but one branch, viz., the executive, acquires a judicial and finally a legislative branch. The state becomes a vast systematized organization. Industry, which at the beginning consisted wholly of slave labor under a master, and later included the simplest forms of trade, develops into a system of economic production, exchange, transportation, and general circulation. Property, which primarily meant only oxen, spears, bows and arrows, and primitive agricultural implements, now takes varied forms, the most important being those symbols of property which go by the name of money. Under the protection of the state, wealth becomes possible to a large number who possess the thrift to acquire it, and this takes the form of capital, which is the condition to all industrial progress and national wealth.

The existence of wealth—i. e., of a large number of wealthy citizens—creates another kind of leisure class, and many, freed from the trammels of toil, turn their attention to various higher pursuits. Art and literature arise, and civilizing and refining influences begin. Voluntary organizations of many kinds, all having different objects, are formed. Besides innumerable business combinations and corporations, there spring up associations for mutual aid, for intellectual improvement, for social intercourse, for amusement and pleasure, and also eventually for charitable and benevolent purposes. Educational systems are established, and the study of human history, of art and letters, and finally of nature, is undertaken. The era of science at last opens, invention and discovery are stimulated, and the conquest of nature and the mastery of the world begin.

Every one of these civilizing agencies is a social structure, and all of them are the products of the one universal process. They represent the products of that intensive activity which results from the primary clash and conflict of the social forces in the fierce grapple of hostile hordes and clans, and the far fiercer battles of developed nations bent on each other's conquest and subjugation. To see all this one has only to read the history of any of the great nations of the world that are leading the civilization of today. Everyone is familiar with the history of England, for example. No less than four typical social assimilations have taken place on English soil since the earliest recorded annals of that country began. Think of the animosities and hostilities, the bitter race-hatred, the desperate struggles, the prolonged wars, that characterize the history of England. What has become of all these warring elements? There is no country in the world where patriotism is higher than in England, and it is shared alike by Saxon and Celt, by Scot and Briton. Who now are the Normans that constituted the last conquering race? And do the Saxons, when they can be distinguished, any longer feel the chains that once manacled them? The equilibration is complete, and all class distinctions, at least those arising out of the race question, have totally disappeared. On the other hand, consider the achievements of England. Contemplate the wonderful social efficiency of that many times amalgamated people. The sociologist cannot shut his eyes to the fact that the social efficiency is mainly due to the repeated amalgamations and to the intensity of the resultant social struggles, developing, molding, and strengthening social structures.

France or Germany would show the same general truth, and those who are equally familiar with their history will find no difficulty in paralleling every step in the process of national development in all these countries. Austria seems to present an exception, but the only difference is that Austria is now in the midst of a new social assimilation. The equilibration is not yet complete. The Magyar and the Slav are still in the stage of resistance. It is said that, on account of the differences of language, they can never be assimilated. But in England there was the same diversity of language, and the languages of the Romans, of the Normans, of the Saxons, and of the Welsh and Scots had all to undergo a process of mutual concession, of giving and taking, and of ultimate blending, to form the new resultant language. It is not probable that just such a result will be attained in Austria, and no one is probably wise enough to foresee the end: but it seems probable that the time will come at last when all these race-elements will be fully conciliated and a great new race, people, and nation will emerge. The world regards the struggle sympathetically and unanimously echoes the sentiment: *Tu felix Austria nube.*

We know less of the great Asiatic peoples, and still less of the African; but, so far as their history is known it is shown to have been one of perpetual war. This means the repeated conquest and subjugation of one race or nation by another, and a long series of social assimilations, all similar to those described. That these countries have not attained the same stage of culture as have those of Europe is due to causes too subtle and obscure to be discussed here, even if I were competent to discuss them; but one truth seems to be growing more and more clear, viz., that the difference is due much less to the native abilities of these peoples than to the external conditions to which they have been subjected. Fifty years ago Japan and China were habitually classed together, and they were regarded as inferior races incapable of any such civilization as that of the western world. No one so classes them now, and it is all because Japan has resolutely set about adopting western methods. Should China ever do so, the result would be the same, and it is impossible to calculate what this might be.

But it is not necessary that the two races brought into conflict be of the same degree or order of assimilation. It is equally possible that they be of very different degrees in this respect. Of course, in such cases it is easy to see which will be the conquering race. The race having the greatest social efficiency will easily subdue the other, and the process of assimilation will be somewhat different. The new racial product will differ much less from the conquering race. That race will be prepotent and will virtually absorb the inferior race. If the difference is very great, as where a highly civilized race invades the territory occupied by a race of savages, the latter seems soon to disappear almost altogether, like the North American Indians, and to exert scarcely any influence upon the superior race. It is so in Australasia and in South Africa. But where there remains a great numerical disproportion of the native race, this latter being somewhat advanced in civilization, as in British India, other complications arise and new problems confront the student. In Mexico, and to a greater or less extent throughout Central and South America, there has been extensive blending of conquering and conquered races, giving rise to still other conditions and correspondingly varying the character of the resultant social structures.

This is not the place to dilate upon the remote effects of this vast process of universal social integration, but I cannot leave the subject without repeating what I have said before: that if we could but peer far enough into the great future, we should see this planet of ours ultimately peopled with a single homogeneous and completely assimilated race of men—the human race—in the composition of which could be detected all the great commanding qualities of every one of its racial components. And I will also add that to the subsequent duration of this final race on the earth there are no assignable limits.

But we are considering social structure and not social integration, although these are intimately bound up together. We have seen how social structures are formed. The spontaneous products of a great cosmical law, they could not be other than thoroughly organized, firm, compact, and durable mechanisms, comparable to organic structures—tissues, organs, organisms. This is the most important lesson taught by the science of sociology. If all the world could learn it, the greater part of all political and social failures would be prevented. It would dispel at one blow all the false notions so widely current relative to the alteration, abolition, or overthrow of any human institution. As human institutions are the products of evolution, they cannot be destroyed, and the only way they can be modified is through this same process of evolution. Universal acquaintance with the causes, the laws, and the natural history of social structures, and with their consequent durability, permanence, and indestructibility, would produce a complete change in all the prevailing ideas of reform, and the superficial reformers, however well-meaning, would forthwith abandon their chimerical schemes, and set about studying the science of society with a view to the adoption of legitimate means for the direction of the course of social evolution toward the real and possible modification and perfecting of social structures. For structures are easily modified by appropriate methods. They are of themselves always undergoing changes. It is in this that social progress wholly consists. But the integrity of the structures must not be disturbed. They must remain intact and be permitted, or even caused, to change in the desired direction, and to be ultimately transformed into the ideal human institutions that a progressive age demands. A condition of social statics may thus be converted into one of social dynamics. All social structures taken together constitute the social order. The problem is to inaugurate a condition of social progress. This cannot be done by disturbing the social order. Order is the condition to progress, and progress consists in setting up dynamic activities in the social structures themselves. A structure represents a state of equilibrium, but it is never a perfect equilibrium, and the conversion of this partial equilibrium into a moving equilibrium, provided it moves in the right direction, is social progress.

26

APPLIED SOCIOLOGY

1906

This was Ward's last book and the capstone of his sociological system. "This work," he wrote in his preface, "and its predecessor PURE SOCIOLOGY, *constitute together a system of sociology, and these with* DYNAMIC SOCIOLOGY, THE PSYCHIC FACTORS OF CIVILIZATION, *and* THE OUTLINES OF SOCIOLOGY, *make up a more comprehensive system of social philosophy."*

Elsewhere Ward wrote: "I seemed to have completed a cycle. Starting with applied sociology I had left it to wander through all the mazes of pure sociology, finally returning to my original starting point."

More than any of his other books, more even than THE PSYCHIC FACTORS, *this volume was frankly polemical. "It aims," wrote Ward, "to point out a remedy for the general paralysis that is creeping over the world, and which a too narrow conception of the law of cosmic evolution serves rather to increase than to diminish. It proclaims the efficacy of effort, provided it is guided by intelligence. It would remove the embargo laid upon human activity by a false interpretation of scientific determinism, and, without having recourse to the equally false conception of a power to will, it insists upon a power to act."*

Ward began writing this book in the summer of 1904 and

completed it by the next spring. By the time it was published, he had left the civil service and had embarked upon his short but immensely effective academic career at Brown University.

A. THE EFFICACY OF EFFORT

Progress is not automatic, in the sense that if we were all to be cast into a deep slumber for the space of a generation, we should arouse to find ourselves in a greatly improved social state. The world only grows better, even in the moderate degree in which it does grow better, because people wish that it should, and take the right steps to make it better.

JOHN MORLEY.

. . . The most important principle of social dynamics is effort. But its dynamic effect, from the standpoint of pure sociology, is unconscious, unintended, and undesired. The social development that results from it is spontaneous. Applied sociology assumes that effort is consciously and intentionally directed to the improvement of social conditions. A certain school maintains that all such effort is ineffectual; that it is in the nature of interfering with the forces that are causing natural or spontaneous social development, and is therefore detrimental. It is rarely stated in so general a form and is usually narrowed down to the question of interference by the state with the efforts of individuals. It then goes by the name of the doctrine of *laissez faire*. The usual form of stating this doctrine is that the interest of the individual is the same as that of the public, and therefore the public interest is only secured by the free activity of the individual. No one has gone to the extreme length, however, of defending criminal action under this rule, and therefore the qualification called the law of "equal freedom" is always made.

Applied Sociology (New York: Ginn and Co., 1906), pp. 13–17.

The defenders of this doctrine have not been content to limit it to the ordinary cases of interference with the activities of individuals, which would have little to do with applied sociology, but they extend it to include all collective action except that which is manifestly essential to the protection of society. All initiative on the part of society—or, as they usually say, the state, or the "government"—is condemned as involving interference with the activities of individuals. On the part of scientific men the study of evolution in general, and social evolution in particular, has given rise to a sort of scientific pessimism. The prolonged contemplation of purely spontaneous processes evolving highly developed products leads to complete distrust of all claims on the part of man to any power to accomplish similar results. It is so glaringly obvious that no human effort can create even the simplest form of organic life that the conclusion is at once drawn that all attempts to transform nature artificially are vain and visionary. The latest teachings of modern science have thus thrown a sort of pall over the human mind and introduced a new philosophy,—a philosophy of despair, it may be called, because it robs its adherents of all hope in any conscious alteration of the course of nature with respect to man, and denies the efficacy of effort.

Those who take the narrower view and condemn the efforts of society to ameliorate its condition do not content themselves with denying all efficacy in such efforts. This would at least be logical and would compel the advocates of social initiative to prove that such efforts may be successful. But the defenders of *laissez faire* almost uniformly take another step, fatal to their fundamental position, and insist that the interference which they condemn is injurious and pernicious in preventing in some way the successful operation of the benign tendencies of spontaneous natural law. This of course involves the admission of the efficacy of effort, and reduces them to demonstrating that the admitted effects must necessarily be injurious. The main and really difficult task of proving the efficacy of social effort is therefore already performed by the *laissez faire* school. It is not difficult to prove that social effort may have beneficial as well as injurious effects. To have simply maintained the futility, i.e., the complete inefficacy, of social action would have been hardly worth the trouble of condemning it. If it were always wholly without effect and things remained precisely the same after as before, the only rational attitude would be to smile at it as simply wasted effort on the part of deluded people, the same as we smile at the man who spends his whole life in trying to invent perpetual motion. But this has never been the attitude of the *laissez faire* school. They have always condemned social action with warmth and usually denounced it with vehemence as something calculated to do great harm. Indeed, a long list of its mischievous effects has been drawn up and is constantly appealed to. No better arguments could be desired by the defenders of social action. The fact is that the *laissez faire* doctrine is an *ex parte* doctrine. It looks at only one side of a two-sided fact. To a large extent it is arguing without an opponent. Most, though by no means all, of the counts of its indictment are admitted by those who believe in social action. The facts on the other side are almost too familiar to be enumerated and set off against the above-mentioned list. They are far more numerous and important, and their influence for good is immeasurably greater, than the sum total of evil that has resulted from the admittedly frequent mistakes that society has made in its attempts to control social phenomena in its interest. For it is such mistakes that constitute the whole indictment of the *laissez faire* school. I know of no one who has pointed this out or attempted to show as a part of the argument what the beneficial effects of social action have been.

From the great prominence which the individualistic philosophy has assumed, especially in France and England, since the time of the French physiocrats, it is commonly supposed that the general class of ideas upon which it rests has become the prevailing doctrine in these countries and America. There could be no greater mistake than this. While probably the great majority of intelligent persons either avowedly or tacitly subscribe to the doctrine in its main aspects, the fundamental, or as it may be called, subconscious, opinion is everywhere opposed to it. This is proved by the entire history of legislation during that period. The doctrine was undoubtedly salutary at the outset, and it is more or less useful still. It was primarily directed against the pretensions of a class. The action taken by that class can be called social action only in the sense that under all circumstances "the powers that be" actually represent society. That they do so represent it in one sense must be admitted, although, as everybody knows, in view of the general inertia and conservatism of mankind and of the advantage which long tenure and the command of national resources secures to the ruling class, that class may continue in power long after it has ceased to represent society in a more literal sense. The social action against which the new economy was aimed was largely the action of a relatively few individuals. It was egoistic and not social, and had become well-nigh intolerable. The new economy of *laissez faire, laissez passer* was much nearer to the social idea of the time, and it succeeded, though not without a violent revolution in France, in ultimately embodying itself in the state. From the date of this triumph of society over a class, state action in these countries and in all those that have grown out of them has approximated true social action as nearly as could well be expected.

The fundamental error of the modern *laissez faire* school has been that of confounding the present state of the world with the state of the world in the eighteenth century. The civilized world, by whatever name its governments may be called, is virtually democratic, and state action, in the long run at least, is social action in a nearly literal sense.

Now ever since society thus took the reins into its own hands, and far more than during the previous period when it placed them in the hands of a class, it has steadily been taking the initiative, assuming responsibilities, undertaking various enterprises, and taking over into its own control one after another a great array of industries and functions that had hitherto been intrusted to individuals. Economists who have been studying only the political economy of the close of the eighteenth century are alarmed at this, mistaking it for the usurpations of a ruling class, and overlooking the fact that it is true social action. Every step taken in this direction is in response to a public demand. Indeed, society is naturally conservative, and no such step is taken until the demand is practically unanimous and irresistible. The very ones who most strongly call for social action would probably admit the *laissez faire* doctrine in the abstract, but it has no influence on them when it conflicts with their interests.

Nor can it be said that all this social initiative has been fruitless. Scarcely a step taken in this direction, from the management of the public finances to the transmission of letters, packages, and messages, has ever been reversed, and the greater part of them have proved so obviously beneficial that they are looked upon as much in the light of social necessities as is the public administration of criminal law, once also left to "private enterprise." What the *laissez faire* economists have done is to go over the long series of these social achievements and cull out a relatively small number of relatively unimportant ones which they declare to have been failures or to be doing harm to society. These are held up as the sufficient proof of the evils of social initiative. Some of them are doubtless failures, and one of the supposed fatal blows against the movement is the number of laws that have actually been repealed, as not accomplishing their purpose.

Do not these rather show the wisdom of society in promptly correcting its mistakes when they are found to be such?

A full and candid survey of this field, however, shows that society has always been marching forward in the one irreversible direction, and that its achievements are already multitudinous and of the utmost importance. Social achievement has been the condition to individual achievement, and all forms of achievement are at once the product and the proofs of the efficacy of effort. The "miserable *laissez-faire*"[1] which seeks to check this natural flow of social energy has been appropriately called "moral curare"[2] and "social Nirvana."[3] Over against this doctrine of *laissez faire,* which is now only a doctrine, stands that of *faire marcher,*[4] which has always been a policy, and without the recognition of which there could be no science of applied sociology. . . .

B.　SOCIAL VERSUS POLITICAL JUSTICE

The justice of which we have been speaking, vast as its influence has been in securing man's moral advance, is after all only civil and political justice. It is a very different thing from social justice. The civil and political inequalities of men

Applied Sociology, pp. 24–25.

[1] Herbert Spencer, *Justice,* p. 44.

[2] Alfred Fouillée, *L'Évolutionnisme des idées-forces* (Paris, 1890), Introduction, p. lxxix.

[3] Ludwig Stein, *Wesen und Aufgabe der Sociologie* (Berlin, 1898), p. 26 (Abdruck a.d. Archiv f. syst. Philosophie, Bd. IV).

[4] This expression is probably as old as the *laissez faire* of De Gournay. I have met with it several times (see Guizot, *Histoire générale de la civilisation en Europe,* p. 27), not always in precisely the sense in which it is used here. It was revived in this sense by Dr. B. E. Fernow in his address as vice-president of Section I of the American Association for the Advancement of Science, Springfield meeting, 1895 (see the *Proceedings,* XLIV, 332, 334; *Science,* N.S., II [August 30, 1895], 257, 258).

have been fairly well removed by it. Person and property are tolerably safe under its rule. It was a great step in social achievement. But society must take another step in the same direction. It must establish social justice. The present social inequalities exist for the same reason that civil and political inequalities once existed. They can be removed by an extension of the same policy by which the former were removed. The attempt to do this will be attacked and denounced, as was the other, but the principle involved is the same. And after social justice shall have been attained and shall become the settled policy of society, no one will any more dare to question it than to question civil justice.

C. SOCIAL WELFARE

Let us look more closely into the nature of social justice. The welfare or happiness of mankind consists entirely in the freedom to exercise the natural faculties. The old idea that happiness is a negative state—a state of rest or repose—is completely exploded. It may have grown out of the enslaved and overworked condition of the mass of mankind during such a prolonged period of human history. But everybody knows that a state of inactivity, beyond that needed to recuperate from the effects of previous fatigue, becomes ennui, a state more intolerable than fatigue, and drives the sufferer to some form of activity, no matter what. The physiology of it is that the only source of pleasure is the exercise of some faculty. Conversely, the normal exercise of any faculty is always and necessarily attended with pleasure. Every desire is at bottom the result of some cause that temporarily prevents the normal exercise of a faculty. All want is deprivation, i.e, the withholding of whatever is necessary to set the system into healthy operation. Hunger is the deprivation of the stomach of the food upon which it expends its energy. Love, so long as unsatisfied, is the deprivation of the entire reproductive system of its normal functioning. These are the types of the whole list, and the same is true of all. Taking all the faculties together, physical, mental, spiritual, so far as these can be separated, and their joint normal exercise is what constitutes happiness, while the deprivation of such normal exercise is what constitutes misery. Complete deprivation would of course be immediately fatal, and the real misery of the world is due to the partial deprivation of the power of men to exercise the faculties by which nature has endowed them. On the other hand, whatever degree of happiness men enjoy is due to the power to exercise their faculties and to no other source.

The problem therefore manifestly is how to secure to the members of society the maximum power of exercising their natural faculties. It is a purely subjective problem and has nothing to do with the relative superiority or inferiority of men. It is wholly independent of the question of their intelligence or ability or social value. It is even independent of their capacity to enjoy or to suffer. It matters not how much satisfaction they are capable of deriving from the exercise of their faculties; it aims only to enable them to enjoy such faculties as they may happen to have.

D. INTELLECTUAL EGALITARIANISM

The proposition that the lower classes of society are the intellectual equals of the upper classes will probably shock most minds. At least it will be almost unanimously rejected as altogether false. Yet I do not hesitate to maintain and defend it as an abstract proposition. But of course we must understand what is meant by intellectual equality. I have taken some pains to show that the difference in the intelligence

---

Applied Sociology, pp. 95–98.

of the two classes is immense. What I insist upon is that this difference in intelligence is not due to any difference in intellect. It is due entirely to difference in mental equipment. It is chiefly due to difference in knowledge, if we include in knowledge a familiarity with the tools of the mind and an acquired ability to utilize the product of human achievement. . . . It is true that all the members of society have the use to a certain extent of the products of past achievement, but in no other sense do those members stand on the elevated platform who do not actually possess the heritage of the past. Now, as a matter of fact, it is only what I have called the intelligent class who really possess this heritage. They of course possess it in varying degrees, but most of them possess enough of it to give them dominion over those who do not possess it.

I have shown . . . that social heredity is not a process of organic transmission, that no part of the social germ-plasm passes from one individual to another, but that all knowledge must be separately acquired by every individual. The social organization must be such as to infuse it into the members of society as fast as they are capable of receiving it. This infusion of it is social transmission, and unless it is infused it is not transmitted. The only way in which products of past achievement have been preserved has been through such a degree of social organization as is sufficient to infuse them into a certain number of the members of society. This number has always, in the historical races, been large enough to prevent their being lost, and most or all human achievement has been preserved. But it is easy to imagine this great social duty to be neglected and all human achievement lost. There are parts of the world in which this has virtually happened, and this is the way in which races degenerate.

But society has never and nowhere been so organized as to transmit the products of achievement to more than a small fraction of its members. These constitute the intelligent class.

The rest are all intellectually disinherited, and while the intellectually disinherited always include and are nearly coextensive with the materially disinherited, the former is much the more serious condition. For the intellectual inheritance would bring with it the material inheritance and all the other advantages that are enjoyed by the intelligent class. Of all the problems of applied sociology that which towers above all others is the problem of the organization of society so that the heritage of the past shall be transmitted to all its members alike. Until this problem is solved there is scarcely any use in trying to solve other problems. Not only are most of them otherwise incapable of solution, but this primary problem once solved all others will solve themselves.

But here we encounter the great sullen, stubborn error, so universal and ingrained as to constitute a world view, that the difference between the upper and lower classes of society is due to a difference in their intellectual capacity, something existing in the nature of things, something preordained and inherently inevitable. Every form of sophistry is employed to uphold this view. We are told that there must be social classes, that they are a necessary part of the social order. There must be laborers and skilled workmen to do the drudgery work of the world. There must be menial servants to wait upon us. What would society do without the scavenger? All of which, while clearly showing that the persons who thus argue not only fear but believe that the lower classes are capable of being raised to their own level, reveals a lack of reflection and an incapacity for logical reasoning scarcely to be met with elsewhere. It recalls the remark of the Scotch engineer whom some fortune transported to the plains of Kansas before the days of Pacific railroads, that there could be no railroads in that country, for "where are the hills to put the tunnels through?"

As just remarked, only one man among all the thinkers of the world has ever thought or dared to combat this universal error. His position was stated and briefly discussed in *Pure Sociology*,[5] and certain qualifications of it were made, to which I would still adhere; but with these qualifications the doctrine of the equal intellectual capacity of all men is a perfectly sound doctrine, and is the doctrine upon which the applied sociologist must stand. It is true that this view has appearances against it, but, as I have often shown, there is no great truth in any department of science that did not at first have appearances against it. The whole march of truth has consisted in substituting the hidden and obscure reality for the falsely apparent. With this uniform trend of history before us, we ought by this time to have learned to suspect everything that seems on the face of it to be true. Let us glance at some of the evidence in favor of the Helvetian doctrine and against the current belief.

Rise of the Proletariat.—The history of social classes furnishes to the philosophical student of society the most convincing proof that the lower grades of mankind have never occupied those positions on account of any inherent incapacity to occupy higher ones. Throughout antiquity and well down through the Middle Ages the great mass of mankind were slaves. A little later they were serfs bound to the soil. Finally, with the abolition of slavery, the fall of the feudal system,

---

[5] I can scarcely refrain from quoting the following from a little book that it would harm no one to read: "I have seldom heard an argument or read an adverse letter or speech against the claims of justice in social matters, but our friend the scavenger played a prominent part therein. Truly this scavenger is a most important person. Yet one would not suppose that the whole cosmic scheme revolved on him as on an axis; one would not imagine him to be the keystone of European society—at least his appearance and his wages would not justify such an assumption. But I begin to believe that the fear of the scavenger is really the source and fountain head, the life and blood and breath of all conservatism. Good old scavenger. His ash-pan is the bulwark of capitalism, and his besom the standard around which rally the pride and the culture and the opulence of British society" (*Merrie England*, by Robert Blatchford (Nunquam), People's edition (London, 1894), pp. 187–188).

and the establishment of the industrial system, this great mass took the form of a proletariat, the fourth estate, considered of so little consequense that they are seldom mentioned by the great historians of Europe. Even at the close of the eighteenth century, when the greatest of all political revolutions occurred, it was only the third estate that was at all in evidence —the business class, bourgeoisie, or social mesoderm. This had been looked down upon and considered inferior, and only the lords spiritual and temporal were regarded as capable of controlling social and national affairs. This class is now at the top. It has furnished the world's brains for two centuries, and if there is any intellectual inferiority it is to be found in the poor remnant that still calls itself the nobility in some countries.

The movement that is now agitating society is different from any of the previous movements, but it differs from them only as they differed from one another. It is nothing less than the coming to consciousness of the proletariat. The class who for ages were slaves or serfs are now voters in an enlightened state. They have risen to where they can begin to see out, and they are rising still higher. . . .

E. THERE ARE NO CLASS DIFFERENCES

What has actually taken place in the history of the world has been a gradual upward movement of the mass from the condition of mere slaves to that of more or less skilled laborers with some general ideas about the land they live in and the world at large, until from a state in which at least nine tenths were submerged there is now in enlightened countries only a completely "submerged tenth." But there nevertheless exists in fact only a completely emerged tenth. The essential fact, however, is that there is no valid reason why not only the

---

Applied Sociology, pp. 100–101, 131.

other partially emerged eight tenths but the completely submerged tenth should not all completely emerge. They are all
equally capable of it. This does not at all imply that all men
are equal intellectually. It only insists that intellectual inequality is common to all classes, and is as great among the
members of the completely emerged tenth as it is between
that class and the completely submerged tenth. Or, to state
it more clearly, if the same individuals who constitute the
intelligent class at any time or place had been surrounded
from their birth by exactly the same conditions that have surrounded the lowest stratum of society, they would have inevitably found themselves in that stratum; and if an equal
number taken at random of the lowest stratum of society had
been surrounded from their birth by exactly the same conditions by which the intelligent class have been surrounded,
they would in fact have constituted the intelligent class instead
of the particular individuals who happen actually to constitute
it. In other words, class distinctions in society are wholly
artificial, depend entirely on environing conditions, and are
in no sense due to differences in native capacity. Differences
in native capacity exist and are as great as they have ever
been pictured, but they exist in all classes alike.

Capacity for Truth.—This brings us to the most important
of all the considerations involved in this problem, viz., the
fact that the difference in the native capacity of individuals
is never sufficient to exclude any person from the highest
social class. Nothing short of congenital mental imbecility,
feeble-mindness, or idiocy can take an individual out of the
social class to which his conditions of existence have assigned
him, and this, as we all know, does not remand him to a lower
social class, but only to the class of dependents or wards of
society; all of which proves that it does not require any great
or towering native abilities to enable an individual to maintain his place in the vanguard of society. The minimum
natural abilities above the stage of pathological imbecility

suffice for this. Herein lies the hope of the world, because it shows that the social heritage is no such burden as to require an Atlas to hold it up, but is readily adjusted to the feeblest shoulders and easily borne by all. It consists simply in the possession of the truth that has been brought into the world through the prolonged labors of thousands of zealous investigators, and which when possessed necessarily drives out the error which it replaces. The truth is no harder to carry than was the error; in many ways it is the lighter load. . . .

We are really here confronted with the problem of the efficacy of effort. It is the same "fool's puzzle," and if it was solved at that stage it remains solved for our present purpose. When we speak of civilization we refer to the human inhabitants of this planet. We do not mean the land and sea, the hills and valleys, the mountains and streams, the climate and seasons. These were here before man came, and however much they may have affected man, it is not these effects that constitute civilization. It is man's combined influence on his environment and on himself that chiefly constitutes civilization. In other words, it is his action, and without such action on his part there could be no civilization. To use Mr. Morley's illustration, if all men were to fall into a deep sleep for ages, and then awake, they would find that the environment had done nothing for them during that time. Whatever might have been the civilizing movements in process when they ceased action these would cease when their action ceased and could not be resumed until their action was resumed.

The rôle of the environment then is not to produce or to determine civilization. It is not an active agent but a passive condition. Indeed, as has already been said, it represents opposition. This opposition is not an active antagonism. It is in the nature of a passive obstruction to man's activities. It is man that is active. His will guided by his intellect is ever pressing against the environment. In proportion to the development of the guiding faculty man removes the obstruction presented by the environment. In the more advanced stages he transforms it, utilizes it, subjects it to his service, and compels the very powers that at first opposed his progress to serve his interests and supplement his own powers. It is this that constitutes civilization, and to the original natural environment there is now added an artificial environment of his own creation. This, as we shall soon see, is of far greater vital importance to him than his natural environment, the physical world into which he is born. Yet to this human action the environment opposes its *reaction,* and it is this interaction of man and his environment, or *synergy,* that accomplishes the results.

F. THE RESOURCES OF SOCIETY

. . . It is evident, . . . that education is absolutely indispensable at least to a literary career, and it is practically so to any career in a civilized community. This means that all who are without it are debarred at the outset from all hope of ever joining the forces of civilization. All the achievement of the world has been done by educated persons. Doubtless different kinds of achievement require different kinds and amounts of education, and the term must be given the broad meaning insisted upon from the first. It may, and in many cases does, consist almost wholly of experience, and still the cases of any great distinction having been attained under conditions of actual illiteracy are so rare as to be practically legendary.

But really, for all except the rarest cases, something more than the mere "common-school education" is required to insure success. A much broader view of the principal branches of learning is necessary to enable a person of talent or even of genius to select a career and pursue it successfully. The

Applied Sociology, pp. 229–233.

great men of all time have had this, however and whenever they may have acquired it. But when we consider how small the number is who have this privilege we see from what a limited group the efficient workers of the world have had to be selected. All outside of that group, whatever may be their native talents, are excluded even from candidacy to achievement. And yet, precisely as in the case of the inhabitants of backward provinces or districts, precisely as in the case of the poor and disinherited, precisely as in the case of the working-classes and proletariat, talent and genius are distributed throughout the ranks of the uneducated in the same numerical proportion as among the city-born, the opulent, the nobility, and the academicians. But we saw that centers of population, wealth, and social rank were conducive to greatness and achievement only in so far as they were substitutes for an educational environment. They make self-education possible. They furnish the education of experience, of intercourse with bright minds, of access to the treasures of learning stored up in libraries, of facilities for publication, of numerous readers of books written. It is all education, and it is, it may be admitted, education for much of which there is no substitute. Still, a well-organized system of public instruction in all the higher fields where genius delights to revel may and does constitute a basis for a genial career, and the recipients of such privileges are practically certain to seek out and find their appropriate local environment. They are certainly to a large extent a substitute for the economic and the social environment, and often result in the attainment of both.

At least, while it would be regarded as wholly utopian to propose to provide all with a high economic and social environment, and while it is in many ways undesirable that all should flock to the great educational centers, it is an entirely practical proposition to provide every member of society with such an education as will enable him to select and successfully pursue a career. If society could see this in its full meaning, it would perceive that it would be the most economical of all public measures. Even if there were no persons of talent or of genius among them, the superior public enlightenment that could not fail to result would repay a thousandfold all the effort and expense. But the certainty that potential genius does not exist everywhere in the same proportions as in the most favored classes insures the actual production of a great army of high-grade social agents, who without instruction could never make their talents effective and would remain forever unknown.

To sum up the general results of this inquiry, it may be safely stated that a well-organized system of universal education, using that term . . . as conferring "the maximum amount of the most important extant knowledge upon all the members of society," would increase the average fecundity in dynamic agents of society at least one hundred-fold. The fecundity is apparently about 2 to the 100,000 population. It can therefore be made at least 200 to the 100,000 or 1 to every 500.

One great factor, however, has been omitted by nearly all who have discussed these questions. This factor is nothing less than exactly one half of the human race, viz., womankind. Galton's point of view is of course exclusively androcentric. Woman is a wholly negligible factor in all his calculations. De Candolle devotes nearly two of the five hundred and seventy-six pages of his book to "Women and Scientific Progress," but no woman had ever been admitted to any of the great academies of which he treats. Jacoby's list may contain the names of some women. It would be profitless to search for them. M. Odin is the only one who has seen that the true cause of the small literary fecundity of women has been their almost complete lack of opportunity. He shows that where they have really enjoyed any opportunity they have done their share. Looking at the subject from the standpoint of the local environment alone, this is clearly brought out by the facts. The great superiority of Paris over all other cities in France has been sufficiently emphasized, even in the case of men. Paris produced 23.5 of the men of letters of France, but it produced 42.1 of the women of letters of France. This was because only there did woman find anything like a congenial environment. Only one other condition proved superior to Paris, and this was life in châteaux. The châteaux of France produced less than 2 per cent of the men of letters, but the produced over 5 per cent of the talented women.

The universal prevalence of the androcentric world view, shared by men and women alike, acts as a wet blanket on all the genial fire of the female sex. Let this be once removed and woman's true relation to society be generally perceived, and all this will be changed. We have no conception of the real amount of talent or of genius possessed by women. It is probably not greatly inferior to that of men even now, and a few generations of enlightened opinion on the subject, if shared by both sexes, would perhaps show that the difference is qualitative only. If this is so, the gain in developing it would be greater than that of merely doubling the number of social agents, for women will strike out according to their natural inclinations and cultivate fields that men would never have cultivated. They will thus add to the breadth, even if they do not add to the depth, of the world's progress. The estimates hitherto made of the resources of society have taken men only into consideration. We concluded that this amounted to 1 in every 500 of the population. How much can we add for women when they shall be fully recognized and taken into the fold? For the transition period it is not claimed that they would double the number of contributors to civilization, but very soon they would raise the proportion to 1 in 300, and ultimately they would contribute their full moiety.

There is, however, a certain crudeness, at least, if not positive error, in all these calculations of the number of geniuses, actual or potential, in the world. The fact is, that genius, like almost every other natural product, is entirely relative. There are gradations in everything, and here as everywhere *natura non facit saltus*. There are all conceivable degrees of genius, and the present irregularities among men in this respect are abnormal. They constitute in themselves a proof that something is preventing the full natural expression of this universally diffused social force. The different environments that we have been considering, local, economic, social, educational, as they actually exist in society, may be looked upon in two diametrically opposite ways. We have seemed to be considering them as so many sources of opportunity, and hence as generators of genius. But it is equally legitimate to consider them from their negative aspect. In every one of them the repressive influence is far greater than the liberative influence. Over against the metropolis stands the country, and for every Athens there is an Arcadia. The few rich are the antithesis of the many poor. The nobility is opposed to the proletariat. The intelligent class is immersed in the illiterate mass. We are looking only at the exceptions and ignoring the rule. In each environment the upper strata represent only what has succeeded in bursting through. To use the language of geology, they are extrusive materials. . . .

G. ETHICS DEMANDS THE SATISFACTION OF ALL NATURAL RIGHTS

As regards this whole subject of privative ethics, all that can be said is that when the problem of the equalization of intelligence shall have been solved and society awakes from its long and fitful sleep, it will all be over, like a horrid nightmare, and the world will be thankful that it was only a dream. Mankind want no eleemosynary schemes, no private

Applied Sociology, pp. 326–330.

nor public benefactions, no fatherly oversight of the privileged classes, nor any other form of patronizing hypocrisy. They only want power—the power that is theirs of right and which lies within their grasp. They have only to reach out and take it. The victims of private ethics are in the immense majority. They constitute society. They are the heirs of all the ages. They have only to rouse and enter upon their patrimony that the genius of all lands and of all time has generously bequeathed to them. . . .

. . . We may . . . at least consider a few of the modes in which, as it seems to us now, the positive improvement of the lot of man is likely to be effected. Some of these must necessarily be economic. The conditions of existence are such that human happiness depends in large degree upon the material surroundings of each individual. As has been consistently maintained, it consists entirely in the normal exercise of the faculties. But in order to that exercise there must be freedom from restraint. By faculties is meant the functions of nature. The bodily functions are imperative. The most vital of them all is the alimentary function. If the demands of the stomach are not regularly and adequately supplied life is jeopardized. Abundant nourishment for the body is therefore the first condition to liberty. But there are many other material wants that are also essential, some of them even to life. In cold climates clothing and shelter as well as such artificial heat as fuel can procure are conditions of existence. All these are furnished by money or its equivalent, and no person can live in society as it is now constituted without the wherewithal to purchase food, clothing, shelter, and fuel. There are thousands of other real wants the deprivation of which restrains the freedom to exercise the faculties. The means of supplying these are usually the same as those required to supply the primary wants. In general, up to a certain point, the more of these means an individual possesses the more wants he can supply, the more complete is the power to exercise all his faculties, and the greater is the volume of his life. In short, considering society as it actually is, and as it is likely to remain for a long time to come, within certain limits that may be approximately determined, the more any one possesses of this world's goods the greater may be the measure of his happiness.

The important corollary from all this is that, provided it can be equitably distributed among the members of society, the larger the amount of such goods in the world the better. But even in the richest countries the total wealth is only about one thousand dollars per capita. At five per cent this would yield fifty dollars per annum. At the very lowest estimate this would not feed, clothe, and house an average human being, including infants. Of course the male adult population is supposed to be earning something, but three fourths of the population earn nothing. Look at it any way we will, and assuming the most equitable distribution possible, the wealth of the world is lamentably deficient for the ordinary wants of mankind.

It follows from this that the prime desideratum is the *increase of production*. But some think that production cannot be increased. These are the ones who talk about over-production. Enough has been said on the latter point. There is no such thing as over-production in the sense of producing more than is needed. Ten, twenty, or even a hundred times as much is needed as is produced. The only question is, Can production be thus increased? It certainly can. There is scarcely any limit to the possible increase of production. This is especially true of artificial products. The world has scarcely commenced to use machinery. Rodbertus was right in believing "that natural wealth exists in practically unlimited quantities; that the mission of machinery is to centuple human productivity, and that the vice does not reside in the inability to produce, but in defective social organization.[6] Professor Clark says that

---

[6] See De Greef, *La Sociologie Économique* (Paris, 1904), p. 18.

"general over-production of qualitative increments is a theoretical and practical impossibility. . . . New motive powers, machines, and processes are multiplying, and promise to increase, beyond any discernible limit, the capacity of man to transform what nature places in his hand."[7]

Every little while the mills shut down because they cannot get rid of their product. This shows that much more could be produced by the existing plants if the market existed. Suppose the demand to increase tenfold, does any one suppose the market would be allowed to remain long unsupplied? If it should increase a hundredfold it would be supplied just as quickly as the machinery could be constructed. But in order really to satisfy all human wants it would undoubtedly increase a hundredfold. Suppose this actually to take place, what would it mean? It would mean that the satisfaction that mankind derives from the consumption of wealth would be a hundred times as great as now. Of course a large part of this would go to the negative side of the account. Suppose it to take half of it (and it could scarcely be less) to supply the privation entailed by present bad social conditions, there would remain the other half, or fifty times as much as now falls to the lot of the average man, to be set down on the positive side of the account. He would be carried as far over into a pleasure economy as he now is in a pain economy.

It may be said that no one could consume any such amount. The present millionaire consumes many times as much and still is not satisfied. Of course he wastes it,—indulges in ostentatious rivalry to display his wealth and surpass other millionaires. It is doubtful whether this affords him anything worthy to be called happiness. Positive ethics does not contemplate anything of this kind. But it demands the satisfaction of all natural wants, material and spiritual, the means of rearing a

---

[7] *The Philosophy of Wealth,* by John B. Clark (Boston, 1886), pp. 95, 100.

family free from all fear of want, of educating children to the limit of their capacities and tastes, of building attractive homes stocked with all enlightening agencies, of moving about in the world sufficiently to shake off all narrow provincialism, and of living in the great stream of human progress. For every member of society to be able to do this would take not less than a hundred times the means that now falls to the lot of the average human being. There would be no object in the increased production unless there were a correspondingly increased consumption. In the language of "political economy," positive ethics demands an enormous rise in the standard of living. It should go no further than the satisfaction of real wants, but every want satisfied adds to the fullness of life. Nor can we judge by existing wants. It demands the creation of new wants and the satisfaction of these. The whole object of the fine arts is to create new wants in order to satisfy them. This lifts the man so much higher in the scale of existence. But life itself is capable of being made a fine art. The human organization is susceptible of being attuned to a thousand refined and ennobling sentiments to which it is now a stranger, and every chord that is struck on this harp of a thousand strings creates a thrill that lifts the soul into a higher world.

Such is the mission of positive ethics, and it represents a state that contains within itself no limitations as to duration. . . .

H. ATTRACTIVE LEGISLATION

Attractive Legislation.—Although I have made frequent use of this expression and somewhat fully treated the topic in other works, still this has always been in an incidental way. It is here only that it finds its systematic place, and all that has been said of it in other places may be regarded as belonging here. It constitutes the most important application of the prin-

---

Applied Sociology, pp. 337–339.

ciple of attraction in general, and serves better than any other
example to illustrate the scientific character of sociology.
When we say that society does anything we mean of course
that it does it according to some settled method of social action. Society of course is an abstraction, but it is one of those
abstractions that are always doing something. Society always
possesses an organization, and it is this organization that acts.
It would be as reasonable to object to the statement that an
army does anything. An army is an abstraction in the same
sense that society is such. It is an organization capable of doing
much, and this is all that is meant by the action or the work
of society.

Social organizations differ greatly in their details, but they
all agree in acting through some regularly constituted authority. We Americans, accustomed to see all laws enacted by
representatives of the people chosen by their ballots and constantly watched by their constituents, are slow to acknowledge
that the so-called laws of the Russian government, for example,
which we know to be made by a few individuals without any
knowledge or coöperation on the part of the people, really
are laws, and we would fully justify the people in disobeying
and repudiating them if they had the power to do so. And yet
we must remember that representative government is of very
recent date, and is limited to a few of the most advanced countries. Society has, however, at all times and in all lands been
organized so that it could act. It was doubtless so to a certain
extent in the simplest hordes of the protosocial stage, though
here we may go back until the condition is reached in which
we find gregarious animals, which, nevertheless, possess a
sort of intuitive organization that serves their purpose. But
after the first conquest the constituted authority of the new
amalgamating society resides in the army with its chieftains,
and these rule with an iron hand. Later on . . . laws are made
and the state emerges. The action of the state is always that
of society, and it grows more and more intelligent with each
step in social assimilation. But for a great while the intelligence

of society is lodged in a few individuals who constitute its rulers. During all this period these constituted authorities are much more intelligent than the people at large. It is therefore more inventive, and while the ingenuity displayed is largely directed to securing the personal ends of these comparatively few persons, still a small share of it always tends to the amelioration of the whole mass. As I have previously stated, . . . autocracies are more intelligent, or rather, less stupid than democracies, and for the very reason that they are not representative. A people so low intellectually as to tolerate an autocracy could, if we conceive it to be democratically organized, do nothing in the way of social intervention. But autocratically organized it may do much, depending upon the mental character of its rulers. Nothing, however, worthy of the name of scientific legislation, i.e., legislative intervention in the interests of the people, is possible except in a democracy in which all the people are intelligent, so that the representatives of the people are persons of considerable mental development. When the people become so intelligent that they know how to choose as their representatives persons of decided ability, who know something of human nature, who recognize that there are social forces, and that their duty is to devise ways and means for scientifically controlling those forces on exactly the same principles that an experimenter or an inventor controls the forces of physical nature, then we may look for scientific legislation. And the fundamental principle that will be applied in all cases will be the principle of attraction. They will see that mandatory and prohibitory laws are highly expensive and largely ineffective, and that the only cheap and effective way to control the social forces and cause men to perform the acts beneficial to society is to offer such inducements as will in all cases make it to their advantage to perform such acts. It is probable that nearly or quite all the socially advantageous action could be secured through attractive legislation.

It must not be supposed that such legislation can be conducted to any considerable extent in the open sessions of legislative bodies. These will doubtless need to be maintained, and every new law should be finally adopted by a vote of such bodies, but more and more this will become a merely formal way of putting the final sanction of society on decisions that have been carefully worked out in what may be called the sociological laboratory. Legislation will consist in a series of exhaustive experiments on the part of true scientific sociologists and sociological inventors working on the problems of social physics from the practical point of view. It will undertake to solve not only questions of general interest to the state,—the maintenance of revenues without compulsion and without friction and the smooth and peaceful conduct of all the operations of a nation,—but questions of social improvement, the amelioration of the condition of all the people, the removal of whatever privations may still remain, and the adoption of means to the positive increase of the social welfare, in short the organization of human happiness. . . .

Attractive labor could never be fully secured without the aid of attractive legislation, and one of the leading problems always before the scientific legislator must be that of rendering labor more and more attractive and agreeable. The goal toward which all his efforts would tend would be a state of society in which no one should be obliged to do anything that is in any way distasteful to him, and in which every act should be so agreeable that he will do it from personal preference. The great economy of this is apparent at a glance, since all the negative terms of the equation would be eliminated and all energy conserved. This would increase in the same degree the productive power of society, and the increased production that would result, assuming, as in such a state of society it is safe to assume, that it was equitably distributed, would still further contribute to the general welfare. Thus all the varied streams of benefit would unite in securing the twofold end of increasing the sum total of social efficiency and social improvement.

27

THE ESTABLISHMENT

OF SOCIOLOGY

1906

In 1906 Ward was elected the first president of the newly organized American Sociological Society. This is his Presidential Address.

I do not propose on this occasion to enter into any defense of the claims of sociology to be called a science. I wish simply to show that its history, and the steps in its establishment, do not essentially differ from those of other sciences.

On a former somewhat similar occasion I took the same position, and as the words then spoken in a foreign tongue have never been reproduced in our own, they seem to form a fitting introduction to this address. This is what I said:

Certainly no member of the International Institute of Sociology doubts that there is a sociological science, but certain persons suppose that there is a difference between this and other sciences. The fact that the foundations of the science are still being discussed, and

"The Establishment of Sociology," *American Journal of Sociology,* **XII** (March 1907), 581–587.

that sociologists differ with regard to them, while the foundations of other sciences seem to be recognized by all, causes it to be imagined that sociology is a science different from the rest. But one needs only to study the history of other sciences to see that such is not the case. Without entering deeply into this study, it is sufficient to consider the most completely established sciences at a special epoch in their history. Everyone knows that astronomy is the most exact and the most perfectly established science that we have. Let us consider it, for example, in the seventeenth century. Descartes was acquainted with the theories of the ancients. He knew the Ptolemaic theory. That of Copernicus was familiar to him, as well as the modification of that theory proposed by Tycho Brahe. Modern astronomy is chiefly based on the theory of Copernicus, and its exactness depends entirely upon the law formulated by him of the revolutions of the planets. But was astronomical science established at that period? Certainly not. In the possession of all this knowledge the greatest genius of the seventeenth century rejected the true principle and elaborated a new hypothesis very different from all that had preceded it—a massive and complicated hypothesis which the modern world has almost entirely forgotten. Astronomy in the seventeeth century was, then, in a condition somewhat similar to that of sociology today.

It would be easy to show that the same was true of physics before the discovery of the law of gravitation, and also that it was true of chemistry before the discovery of the true nature of combustion. As regards chemistry . . . it is the glory of France and of the immortal Lavoisier to have made that great discovery which lifted chemistry out of the state of vague theories and false hypotheses, and placed it on the firm and secure basis on which it stands today.

But there is a difference between the modern theories of sociology and the theories which prevailed in the other sciences before their final establishment. The theories of Ptolemy and Descartes in astronomy were false, or they contained only a minute germ of truth. The theory of phlogiston in chemistry was almost entirely false. This is not the case with modern theories in sociology. The organicist theory is not false, nor is that of imitation, nor that of the struggle of races, nor that of social control, nor yet that of the consciousness of kind (these last two come from America, and I do not speak of principles laid down by myself). These hypotheses, and almost all others in sociology are true, or contain a considerable part of the grand sociological truth which is the final synthesis of them all.[1]

More recently a South American, Ernesto Quesada, professor of sociology in the University of Buenos Ayres, has uttered very similar words, going, however, much more fully into the subject.[2] He was practically driven to this course by a remark of the retiring dean, Miguel Cané, of the university, in a public address, reflecting severely upon the study of sociology. He said, among other things, that "sociology, far from being a science, was little more than empty verbiage," and added that

he would see with great satisfaction the abandonment of a word more pretentious than expressive of anything real, and more capricious than scientific. To study the various human groups, the causes that actuate them, and all the other determining elements of their respective activities, is to set forth principles of a general character, which, though accepted only provisionally, serve as a basis for further investigations. But from this to the erecting into a science, with fixed, immutable boundaries, of a mixture of hypotheses and empirical assertions, and calling it a science in the same sense as algebra or mechanics, seems to me an enormous stride. A science ought to be that impregnable region where alone reign truths and proved laws. If twenty professors, all working along the lines of the modern sociologists, were charged with the preparation of a program of the subject, I am certain that they would present twenty different programs, each conforming to the quality of mind, personal education, and peculiar method of the author; whereas, of twenty professors of geometry there would not be one who would dare to attack the hypothenuse and attribute to it properties that it does not possess.

---

[1] *Annales de l'Institut international de sociologie,* X (Paris, 1904), 50–52.

[2] Ernesto Quesada, "La sociología: Carácter científico de su enseñanza," *Revista de la Universidad de Buenos Aires* (1905), III. (Reprinted Buenos Aires, 1905.)

Professor Quesada replied to all this very fully and with great ability, but he failed to point out the complete irrelevancy of Dean Cané's attack, comparing sociology to mathematics, which is not a science of concrete things at all, but simply the norm by which all science is tested, and even referring to algebra, which is only an instrument, or tool, to be used in the solution of problems of quantity.

But Professor Quesada shows very clearly that no science is absolutely fixed. All are compelled to start with certain postulates—i. e., unproved propositions, or assumptions—and build upon these; and he enumerates the chief of them as defined by the masters in each science. He shows, moreover, that these postulates are often doubtful, and that several of them—as, for example, that of the atom of chemistry—are undergoing profound modification with the advance of our knowledge. He may be said to have made out a clear case that there is no "impregnable region where alone reign truths and proved laws," and that all the sciences are perpetually *in fieri*, in the same sense as is sociology. He does much more; for he proceeds to show, not only that sociology is already a science of great importance, but that it may be applied directly to practical affairs; and he promises in his lectures to show the legislators and statesmen of Argentina how they may utilize it in advancing the interests of their own country and people.

All attacks upon our science might easily be met in a similar way, and I have taken some pains to collect all the objections I could find and to ascertain the fallacy that underlies each one. I thought of presenting the result of this study; but not only would it require more time than can be devoted to it in this address, but, upon mature consideration, I conclude that it is not worth the while, as sociology is marching over all these stumbling-blocks, and nothing that its enemies can do will greatly check its sure and steady advance. What I propose to do, therefore, is simply to draw your attention to a few of the steps that sociology has taken, and endeavor to point out what has actually been done in the direction of its establishment as one of the great sciences.

Probably the most important result that sociology has accomplished is that of showing what society is; that, if it is not an "organism"—and few now would go that far—it is at least a great organization, bound together by organic ties in all its parts. To be more specific, sociology shows us that human institutions constitute the structures, organs, and organic parts of society, and that they are not independent, but are connected into one great system, which is society. It has not only done this as the result of a study of society in its finished form, but it has confirmed this truth by a study of the origin of human institutions. It has shown how they have arisen. It has traced them back to their primordial, undifferentiated forms, and studied their development from this state of homogeneity to their present state of heterogeneity. It has watched first their differentiation and then their integration.

The general result is that we have come to know what society really is. Sociology has enabled us to orient ourselves in this great maze of human life, to see what the human race is, how it came into existence, approximately when and where it began, in what ways it has developed and advanced, and how it has come to be what we find it. "Know thyself," said the old Greek philosophers; but man never did really know himself until these studies of origins had been undertaken and successfully carried out.

Involved in this we have the true genesis of all the most important human institutions—religion, language, marriage, custom, war, cannibalism, slavery, caste, law, jurisprudence, government, the state, property, industry, art, and science. Instead of a great bewildering maze, a vast meaningless chaos, society reveals itself as a true genetic product of uniform laws and forces, a product of social causation, and stands out in clear relief against the background of history.

But sociology has done more than this. It has not only dis-

covered the laws of society; it has discovered the principles
according to which social operations take place. It has gone
farther even than physics, which has thus far only discovered
the law of gravitation, but has not yet discovered its cause or
principle. Sociology has not only established the law of social
evolution, but it has found the principle underlying and explaining that law. Just as in biology the world was never satisfied with the law of organic evolution worked out by Goethe
and Lamarck until the principle of natural selection was
discovered which explained the workings of that law, so in
sociology it was not enough to formulate the law of social
evolution, however clear it may have been, and the next step
has been taken in bringing to light the sociological homologue
of natural selection which explains the process of social evolution. That principle is not the same as natural selection, but
it serves the same purpose. It also resembles the latter in
growing out of the life-struggle and in being a consequence
of it; but, instead of consisting in the hereditary selection of
the successful elements of that struggle, it consists in the
ultimate union of the opposing elements and their combination
and assimilation. Successively higher and higher social structures are thus created by a process of natural synthesis, and
society evolves from stage to stage. The struggling groups
infuse into each other the most vigorous qualities of each,
cross all the hereditary strains, double their social efficiency
at each cross, and place each new product on a higher plane
of existence. It is the cross-fertilization of cultures.

The place of sociology among the sciences has been definitely fixed. It stands at the summit of the scale of great
sciences arranged in the ascending order of speciality and
complexity according to the law of evolutionary progress. It
rests directly upon psychology, in which it has its roots, although it presents a great number of striking parallels with
biology, chemistry, physics, and even astronomy, showing that
there are universal laws operating in every domain of nature.

The motor principle of sociology is psychic, and the study of this principle has shown that social phenomena are produced by the action of true natural forces, which, when abstraction is made of all perturbing elements, are found to be as regular and reliable as are the forces of gravitation, chemical affinity, or organic growth.

As a result of this it has been possible to establish the sub-science of social mechanics and to work it out with something like the completeness that has been attained in the mechanics of physical nature. At least it has been possible to distinguish clearly between static and dynamic phenomena in society. This distinction, dimly seen by Comte, and still more dimly by Spencer, when fully and clearly apprehended, throws a flood of light over the whole field of social phenomena. Social statics is found to constitute the domain of social construction, and to explain the origin of all social structures and human institutions. It underlies the social order. Social dynamics, on the other hand, is the domain of social transformation, and explains all change in social structures and human institutions. It is the science of social progress. The laws of both these sciences have been to a large extent discovered and formulated, and their workings described.

All this has been accomplished by a careful study of the social energy alone. But sociology has not stopped here. It has plunged boldly into the far more difficult and recondite field of social control. The social energy is so powerful as to exceed its proper bounds and threaten the overthrow of the social order, and would do so but for some effective curb to its action. The motor power of society has to be guided into channels through which it can flow in harmony with the safety of society. This guidance has been furnished by the higher mind or intellect of man. This guiding or directing agent is a far more subtle element than the motor force itself, and one much more difficult to understand. But sociology has not shrunk from the task of studying it and unfolding its laws and operations, and these have been sufficiently mastered to be in large part formulated and described. This fairly complete mastery of the dynamic and directive agents of society has placed sociology in position to deal in a thoroughly scientific way with all the facts and phenomena of society—with its origin, its history, and its present condition.

Finally, with the light shed by social dynamics on the spontaneous modification of social structures and the consequent progress of society in the past, and further guided by the established law of social uniformitarianism, which enables us to judge the future by the past, sociology has now begun, not only in some degree to forecast the future of society, but to venture suggestions at least as to how the established principles of the science may be applied to the future advantageous modification of existing social structures. In other words, sociology, established as a pure science, is now entering upon its applied stage, which is the great practical object for which it exists.

28

ENDS BECOME MEANS

1907

Few scholars have had a wider range of interest than Ward, but his interest did not embrace art, literature, or music; to the harmonies of these spheres he was tone deaf. His brief and extemporary statement here is characteristic: art, letters, music are not valuable in themselves but take on meaning only when they become means to the end of social improvement.

. . . It is a somewhat general sociological principle that I am going to try to present to you in a word; and I might formulate it in these words: that in almost all the operations of mankind, the institutions of mankind and the activities of mankind, we find a law to exist, if we study and trace any of them back far enough—a law or principle which may be expressed in these words: that whereas most of these things began as ends there has been a universal tendency for them to be converted into means. A number of examples occur to me even now, without much reflection. If we take architecture, for I am going to pass over a great many others that might

Remarks on a paper by Mrs. J. Odenwald-Unger, "The Fine Arts as a Dynamic Factor in Society," *American Journal of Sociology*, XII (March 1907), 667–668; in *Glimpses of the Cosmos*, VI, 267–268.

be looked upon from the same point of view to illustrate the fact; but passing to architecture, it is obvious to anyone who has traveled at all about this world that architecture primarily was a fine art and it has become a useful art only by the proc- ess that I have been speaking about—the general tendency of that which started as an end to become a means. And if you travel in certain countries now: you need not go off of this continent on which you live—travel through the country of Mexico as I have myself, and you will see them prominently standing forth—the only great, beautiful architectural build- ings in any of the Mexican towns that I have ever visited are the churches, gilded and adorned and furnished with all the attributes of fine pieces of architecture. The human habitations are awful; and the contrast is striking to anyone from America —from the United States or from the North. But without elaborating that which all of you can see much more of than anything I have said, let us make a great leap and consider another art—the art of literature. In the eighteenth century, I might go back and repeat what is well known to all scholars, that poetry preceded prose and was accompanied with music and the dance—as Mr. Cooke has said, terpsichorean—but passing over even those earlier phases where even the laws were written not in rhyme but in poetry, we come down to modern literature. Take the literature of the eighteenth cen- tury. In the eighteenth century, especially in France, literature was a fine art—it was nothing else. It was an end. It was largely so in other countries; and as the center or the van of civilization advanced, the epoch in which literature was an end simply moved its position from one country to another. What is literature today? It is scarcely anything more than a means, and the only object in the world of fine writing is to express ideas. We admire the writings of a Huxley simply because they constitute a vehicle by means of which he was able to express the greatest thoughts of the age; and so with every other literary man today. He is of no particular impor-

tance from a literary point of view except as he is more capable
of expressing ideas and carrying thought from mind to mind
than other men are. Need I carry it any farther? Need I refer
to the other arts—for example, to painting? We speak of the
declining arts—especially of sculpture. Doubtless they are declining, and my implication is simply in so far as they fail to
become means and insist upon being ends in themselves there
is no demand for them. But there is demand for an artist like
Millet, who can paint an "Angelus" or a "Man with the Hoe,"
because those paintings carry ideas—not all intellectual ideas,
but mental ideas. And any great art today, whether it be painting, sculpture, or any other kind of art, that can carry emotions
or carry elevating influences through society will be in demand; and that kind of art will be capable of subsisting, of
surviving; all other kinds will fail under the law of the survival
of the fittest. I was trying to think if there was another; and
certainly there is, as Mrs. Unger has said. I cannot speak of
music. She can. But I can speak of the drama, because everybody knows what that is; and of fiction, because everybody
knows what the influence of that is. In speaking of fiction I am
almost going back to what I said about literature, but it is the
great modern renaissance as it is called—the great realistic
drama and realistic fiction; and the great works, if there are
any today; and the great works of nearly the last century—
certainly the last half-century—have all been great, or recognized as such, simply because they are what Mrs. Unger has
called dynamic. And what do we recognize as having value
in any great work of fiction or in any great drama unless it is
some social power to influence, and not only to influence but
to benefit mankind?

Viewed in this light then, which is certainly a true light, it
is obvious that the fine arts not only may become, but in a
great degree have already become, a dynamic factor in society.

29

WHAT BRINGS OUT

GENIUS

1907

Written for a popular audience, this was, as Ward tells us, "the most remunerative piece of work I ever did." It was also in all likelihood the most widely read, for it was published simultaneously in ten metropolitan newspapers. But though writing for a popular audience, Ward made no special concessions to that audience, unless the thesis itself may be regarded as a concession. The essay summarizes much that Ward had written in Chapters 9 and 10 of APPLIED SOCIOLOGY.

It goes without saying that civilization—whatever it is—has been made by men. But it wasn't always taken for granted. A great many people held the view for awhile that civilization was the work of certain blind, vague agencies of nature. They got into that way of thinking by opposing the view championed by the great historian Carlyle in his "Heroes and Hero Wor-

---

Sunday Magazine (December 22, 1907); in *Glimpses of the Cosmos*, VI 284–291.

ship." He maintained that demigods and heroes had made all our history. This seemed to many persons unscientific, and they took the other side.

Now the common sense view is coming back. As John Morley puts it, if men were all to fall into a Rip Van Winkle slumber for the space of a generation, they would awake surprised. They would find that the world had stood still during all that time, and would not resume its forward movement till they resumed their efforts. The same truth is proved by history, as when a nation—Spain, for example—sees fit to destroy or drive out its progressive spirits, its march is arrested and it falls into intellectual decay. And conversely, a country, such as Switzerland, which becomes an asylum for the victims of spiritual persecution, soon towers above all other lands in the display of genius. The conclusion is irresistible that the agents of civilization are men.

Not only is this true, but it is also clear that human progress is the work of genius; and therefore it is no wonder that great minds should regard as the problem of problems that of increasing the product of genius. But it is here that we arrive at the parting of the ways. One school contends that all the genius in the world is always in full action, and that the only way to increase its salutary effects is to increase its quantity in society. This is the doctrine of the irrepressibility of genius, and, as all now admit that genius is hereditary, it is seriously proposed to adopt a wholesale system of conscious and purposeful selection of superior progenitors of the race. But as breeders always breed for points; and as in man genius is regarded as the great "point"; furthermore, as genius is a function of the brain, and therefore brain increase is the great desideratum,—if this plan could be carried out we might have at length the race of men described by Mr. Wells: all head and no body. It therefore is probably fortunate that no such scheme can be forced upon a race of intelligent beings.

Rise of the Opponents

But this doctrine that genius is a fixed quantity, all of which constantly asserts itself, has now been successfully challenged, and an opposite school has arisen which declares that the greater part of all the genius of the race lies latent, and always has lain latent, and that all manifestations of genius are due to favorable circumstances of one kind or another that have made it possible for a relatively few of the indefinitely great number who actually possess genius to burst through the thick crust of conventional deposits that overlie the world. The statistical method, so freely employed by the hereditarian school, has been turned upon it in support of this later view, and with the most astonishing results. It is now proved that heredity is only one, though an essential one, of a great number of influences conducive to the manifestation of genius, and that without such other influences no degree of native genius can avail. These non-hereditary influences are of many kinds; but they may all be classed under one great group, and distinguished as environmental. In other words, the display of genius depends upon the two coöperating factors, heredity and environment, and a favorable environment is quite as essential to success as the native powers themselves.

A further analysis shows that the kind of environment which is effective either in the expression or the repression of genius is an artificial environment, that which society supplies and imposes, and not the natural environment under which the born genius lives. The physical conditions by which he is surrounded—climate, soil, mountains, lowlands, sea coasts, plains—count for little in determining his success. *Cælum non animum mutant qui trans mare currunt.* [They that roam change their skies above them, but not their hearts.] Even the race to which he belongs, the current belief to the contrary notwithstanding, has been found to be an almost negligible factor wherever a thorough test has been applied.

The All-Powerful Factors

The influences that count are always human or social influences, and these admit of a rough classification. Thus there are four kinds of artificial environment that affect directly the genius of man,—stifling it if unfavorable, stimulating it if favorable, and thus effectively determining its failure or its success. These are (1) the local environment, or the contact of men and things; (2) the economic environment, or the material means of subsistence; (3) the social environment, or the social class to which the possessor of native genius belongs; and (4) the educational environment, or the kind and amount of education that the born genius has received, especially in youth. These are the great, all-powerful factors in determining the expressions of latent genius, and unless one or more of them are favorable there is no possibility of such expression, however great that latent genius may be.

Statistical demonstration of this truth has been supplied for literary genius throughout modern times, especially for France, but also less fully for Italy, Spain, Germany, and England. A few of the general results are so striking that they cannot fail to command attention.

For the local environment, the great factor is found to be the cities as compared with the rural districts. Thus the number of eminent Frenchmen of letters born in cities was seventy-seven to the hundred thousand inhabitants, while those born in the country were only six to the hundred thousand, showing that the literary productivity of cities was nearly thirteen times that of the country. That of Paris was between eight and nine times that of the whole of France, and more than thirty-five times that of the rural districts. *Lex urbis lex orbis.* [The law of the city is the law of the world.] It is the material conditions which cities supply that stimulate and bring out the potential genius of mankind.

The influence of the economic environment is even more

powerful. It has been shown that only nine per cent. of the eminent literary men of France were of limited means, while ninety-one per cent. were rich or well to do. But as the poor formed ninety-seven per cent. of the population, it follows that three per cent. of the population furnished ninety-one per cent. of the talent. This means that the chances of success of a rich person are more than three hundred times as great as those of a poor person endowed with the same measure of native genius.

The social environment is closely connected with the economic, and the results are practically the same. In France during the modern period the upper classes—nobility, Government officials, liberal professions, bourgeoisie—furnished ninety and two-tenths per cent. of the eminent men of letters, while only nine and eight-tenths per cent. were low born. But these latter constituted at least eighty per cent. of the population. It follows that the chances of success of a person belonging to the upper classes are nearly thirty-seven times as great as those of one of the same native ability belonging to the lower. But the nobility alone, who constituted only about one per cent. of the population, furnished twenty-five and five-tenths per cent. of modern Frenchmen of letters. The chances therefore are nearly two hundred times as great for a person belonging to the nobility as for one belonging to the working class, all other things being equal.

Value of Education

Finally, as regards the educational environment, notwithstanding the claim openly made that for men of genius education is a negligible factor, it was found that out of eight hundred and twenty-seven Frenchmen of letters, the only ones whose early history in this respect could be ascertained, eight hundred and eleven received a thorough education in their youth, while only sixteen were self educated. It follows that for an educated man, other things equal, the chances of success are nearly fifty-two to one for a man who is compelled to educate himself.

Similar statistical tests have been made for the four other great literary countries of Europe, and the results do not vary essentially from those attained for France. The influence of great cities, of ample means, of high social position, and of early education is the same everywhere. But it can be readily seen that all these environments are educational. They are the means to education. It was found that the size of cities had less influence than other qualities, and that the most potent qualities were their educational facilities. It is true that Paris towers above all others; but aside from its population it is also the great seat of learning of Western Europe. Many large commercial cities, such as Havre, Toulon, Nantes, St. Étienne, Nice, rank very low in literary productivity, while other relatively small ones, especially the fifteen university cities of France, have been exceptionally fertile in literary talent. Of these, Dijon, Besançon, Grenoble and Aix are striking examples. All environments are favorable to the development of genius exactly in proportion as they are educational in the full sense of the word.

The thoughtful student of such facts as these cannot fail to perceive that genius is something that exists and only requires to be developed; that the amount of native talent in society is practically unlimited, and that its manifestation in the furtherance of civilization is mainly a question of opportunity. All that is needed to bring it forth in any required amount is that there be such a demand for it as shall really develop it. Not merely literary talent, but talent of every kind—artistic, scientific, practical,—lies latent in every land, waiting to be called forth.

Great astonishment has been expressed at the exuberant talent of the Greeks when that country was at the zenith of its history. The galaxy of historians (Herodotus, Thucydides,

Xenophon), statesmen (Lycurgus, Solon, Pericles, Cimon, Themistocles), orators (Demosthenes, Isocrates, Lysias), warriors (Miltiades, Nicias), sculptors (Phidias, Praxiteles, Scopas, Myron), painters (Zeuxis, Polygonotus), architects (Mnesicles, Ictinus, Callicrates), philosophers (Socrates, Plato, Aristotle), poets (Sophocles, Euripides, Aristophanes), and dramatists (Æschylus), that illumined the Grecian skies from the sixth to the fourth centuries before the Christian era has been the marvel of modern writers, and has led many to maintain that far more genius than existed than has ever existed since.

Must Be a Reward

But the true explanation is not difficult to find. It was simply due to the fact that Greece in that day, more than any other country at any later age, actually called out its talent and set it to work. Genius, like economic goods, is subject to the law of demand and supply. If it is demanded, it is forthcoming, and in any required amount. But the demand, as in political economy, must be a real, substantial demand, and not a mere velleity or a vain craving. No demand will be supplied unless it includes the wherewithal to labor and subsist. In the economic world the mere desire for or even the need of a commodity does not constitute a demand. An economic demand involves not only the wish for the thing demanded, but also the ability to obtain it in the market. And so a demand for the products of genius must be accompanied by the assurance that the man of genius shall be adequately remunerated for his services. He must be enabled to throw himself into his work without being haunted by the specter of want. It was this that Greece did, with the result that this substantial demand was abundantly supplied. Rome did something of the kind in the Augustan age. The Renaissance was largely a product of a serious demand on the part of both Church and State for great works of art. Even in medieval times and for several centuries later there was no lack of architectural talent to build the many great cathedrals and castles of Europe.

It is the same to-day. Every kind of genius for which there exists this real, living demand is even now at work. The supposed decline of literary and artistic genius is due entirely to the fact that those forms of genius are no longer demanded in this sense. But other forms of genius are in demand, and the demand is supplied. Genius is Protean in its nature. The inventiveness, which in the eighteenth century was expended upon fine figures of rhetoric, is to-day expended upon practical problems of life.

When the Department of Agriculture calls for experts in the prevention of the diseases of domestic animals and cultivated plants or in the discovery of improved fertilizers, they come forward in great numbers, and when set to work they display the highest genius, and soon devise means of saving the nation millions of dollars. They go beyond all that was expected of them, and invent processes for increasing wealth. In the study of soils they find ways, such as the introduction of nitrobacteria, of doubling or quadrupling the fertility of the land. Like results are obtained in other great practical undertakings: the development of mineral resources, the study of geological formations, the scientific mapping of the public domain, the great geodetic operations so useful to commerce and industry, the chemical investigation of the mineral, vegetable, and animal products, nutritive and medicinal, foreign and domestic. And along with this practical work the redundant genius of these trained experts always finds means of making strictly scientific discoveries and ingenious inventions never contemplated by the State, and thus of indefinitely expanding the domain of science, art, and industry.

Supply Would Follow Demand

Such are some of the ways in which the genius of to-day is displaying itself. These are the fields in which the demand exists, and it is always supplied. But I venture to say that if a demand of this substantial character existed for literary productions, for poetry and drama, for art in any form, sculpture, painting, ceramics, musical composition, it would be supplied in like manner, and would in every department prove to be a high order. The age of Pericles or Augustus could be reproduced, or perhaps surpassed, and almost immediately, by the simple process of calling out the latent genius of this or any other modern country in the same manner in which it was then called out. Genius is universal, all sided, unlimited; but the greater part of it is always latent for the reason that it is not demanded.

If the display of genius is to be increased, it must be done by creating a market for the products of genius. Intellectual production is subject to the same laws as economic production, and the spiritual resources of the world are as inexhaustible as are its material resources.

But the State should not be the only appraiser of genius. Society is its proper appraiser, and until society shall appreciate its geniuses and learn to reward them, few of them, relatively speaking, will ever come forward. The true market for achievement is the people, and when the people themselves shall demand it the supply will promptly meet the demand. The true way, then, to call out the dormant genius of mankind is to create this great popular demand, this world market, into which all the talent of the race will pour. How can this be accomplished? Only by the spread of ideas and ideals. There is no royal road to this goal, and the discussion of the ways and means transcends the limits of this article.

It has been maintained that a great difference exists in the respect between men of action and men of thought, between warriors and statesmen on the one hand and philosophers and scientists on the other. They tell us, and truly, that the Alexanders, Cæsars, Napoleons, Nelsons, Washingtons, and Grants, as well as the Solons, Catos, Richelieus, Gladstones, Websters, and Lincolns, have been simply the products of their respective times and countries, and would never have been heard from if they had lived under different political conditions. But we are assured that such men as Aristotle, Pliny, Galileo, Descartes, Leibnitz, Newton, Darwin, Franklin, Agassiz, and Marsh were the possessors of an intrinsic genius which is independent of circumstances. The same claim is made for literary and artistic geniuses as well as for renowned inventors.

This has been shown not to be the case. The law applies to all forms of genius. Most of those mentioned and scores of others have been investigated, and it has been found that without exception they have all owed their fame to the combination of genius and opportunity, that besides being native geniuses they have in a proper sense been called upon to display their talents in the direction in which they have displayed them.

American Geniuses the Same

When few systematic researches of this kind have been made for the leading American geniuses of any class, there is no reason to suppose that they are exceptions to this universal law, and upon those who maintain that they are such rests the burden of proof. That this law holds good for our generals and statesmen is too obvious to need stating. But for the Civil War, Grant, though he had a military training, would have remained an obscure tanner in Galena; Sherman, Sheridan, Custer, and the rest would have spent their lives at various outposts in the far West, known only to military circles. But for the great political questions that shook the country before that war, brought it on, and carried it through, as history records, even Abraham Lincoln would have never done more than grace the Springfield bar.

It would be easy, if space permitted, to take up other classes of eminent Americans and show how in one way or another the particular environment in each case was the decisive factor in their success. For example, Benjamin Franklin, though in somewhat straitened economic circumstances in his youth, was a printer by trade, and thus always able to earn a livelihood. But the printer's is one trade which has for its natural effect to bring its possessor into direct contact with the great men and great thoughts of the age. The average journeyman sets up the type from the copy before him without imbibing the thought that it expresses, but for a genius like Franklin every type touched with his finger is fraught with meaning, and a printing office is a university. If Benjamin Franklin had learned the shoemaker's instead of the printer's trade, he never would have captured the thunderbolt.

Anything connected with the press proves highly educative, even the selling of newspapers; and, as Elbert Hubbard has said, one never knows what future may lurk in a half-clad newsboy crying his wares. It is probable that the world is indebted to this "profession" for an Edison. But here, and not less in the case of Alexander Graham Bell, true genius found itself in the presence of a great public demand for its products, **and such a combination knows no failure.**

30

SOCIAL AND

BIOLOGICAL STRUGGLES

1906 1907

This essay was written originally in French for delivery to the Sixth Congress of the International Institute of Sociology, which met in London in July 1906. It is largely a defense of his position on "Social Darwinism," which he had formulated in Pure Sociology, *and which was under attack by the French sociologist, Jacques Novicow. The paper was first published in Volume XI of the* Annales de l'Institut International de Sociologie.

I

It has long been perceived that the "struggle for existence" is common to the human race and to the animal kingdom in general. Biologists are also aware that it extends to the vegetable kingdom and to all life. The sociologists, very few of whom are biologists in any proper sense, but most of whom have read the great leading works in biology, have themselves

---

"Social and Biological Struggles," *American Journal of Sociology*, XIII (November 1907), 289–299.

long been endeavoring to find the bond connecting the social with the biological struggle and the essential characters by which the two forms of struggle are distinguished. It is not too much to say, and is what might be expected, that the greater part of all that the sociologists say on the subject is wide of the mark, and exhibits an almost complete failure on their part to understand the true nature of the biological struggle.

The socialists, for the most part, regard the social struggle as a practical extension of the biological struggle into the human field, and the work of Karl Marx is frequently characterized as having the same relation to society that Darwin's work has to the organic world. For a long time the modern doctrines relating to life were regarded as highly favorable to socialism, and they are still so regarded by many. Nevertheless it is a fact that they are looked upon by most biologists who think at all on the subject, and by biological philosophers in general, as completely opposed to socialism, and as sustaining the old "let-alone" political economy.

The sociologists in the main deem it their duty to deny that there is any necessary connection between social and biological struggles. They are especially severe on all attempts to show that there is any redeeming virtue in social struggles, or that it is through them that social evolution has taken place, in any such sense as it is claimed that organic evolution takes place, viz., through the struggle for existence and the survival of the fittest. Considerable ingenuity has been shown in pointing out that the cases are not parallel, and that social struggles result in the survival of the unfit.

The sociologists generally confound the so-called "struggle for existence" with Darwinism, and very few of them have any adequate idea of what Darwin's phrase "natural selection" means. It is true that Darwin used both phrases, and also that he recognized the influence of direct effort, i. e., use and disuse, in modifying structures, although the discovery of that great law is more properly attributable to Lamarck, and constitutes the essence of Lamarckism as distinguished from Darwinism. But the sociologists are unable to see the distinction, and have only a confused idea of the whole process which they imagine to constitute Darwinism.

With this vague notion in their minds certain of them have invented the phrase "social Darwinism," and have set it up as a sort of "man of straw" in order to show their agility in knocking it down. There is of course much difference in the ability with which different authors have treated the subject, and a few have evinced some conception of the true merits of the question.

II

Darwinism has very generally been confounded with Malthusianism, and the fact that Darwin modestly admitted that he was led to the consideration of such subjects by reading Malthus on *The Principle of Population* has caused most of the sociological writers who graduated out of political economy into sociology, to identify the Malthusian law with Darwinism as a whole, and to imagine that when they have stated the former, which, as economists, they usually understand, they have stated Darwin's great biological principle, which they do not at all understand.

Darwin did not say nor mean to imply that the Malthusian principle embraced the whole of the biologic law. It is contained in the latter with certain qualifications, and naturally suggested the wider applications that Darwin made of it to the organic world; but it falls short of embodying even the principle of natural selection.

M. Achille Loria, in a very interesting chapter entitled "Social Darwinism,"[1] confines himself to a statement of the

---

[1] *Problèmes sociaux contemporains* (Paris, 1897), Sixième Leçon; *Le Darwinisme social*, pp. 113–35.

principle that "the quantity of subsistence existing on the earth is not sufficient for the nourishment of all organized beings, so that they are compelled to secure it at the price of an incessant struggle," and he bases his discussion entirely on that principle, saying:

It is natural that the weak should be defeated in this struggle, because, not being able to obtain any nourishment, or at least not a sufficient quantity, they perish, while the strong survive and triumph, so that the species possessing the "fittest" qualities improve little by little and rise to more perfect conditions of existence.

M. Loria then shows that certain sociologists apply this theory to social phenomena:

Men, too, they say, have carried on for centuries a terrible struggle for life, which, in our days, manifests itself in the unbridled competition of which we are witnesses; in this fierce struggle the victory is to the strong, and this constitutes the basis of evolution and progress. It is therefore wrong to deplore the bloody battles between men and the fierce competition which makes them trample upon one another in order to be first, since it is this competition which insures the triumph of the best, the most worthy; it is wrong to try to make laws to mitigate this struggle, since it is a valuable factor in progressive development. . . . Hence the most complete quietism, the happy calm of the philosopher and the *dolce far niente* of the legislator constitute the lesson taught by the Darwinian theory, according to these modern theorists.[2]

Such is the theory which, according to M. Loria, is called social Darwinism, but in his view these social applications of Darwinism are wholly false. He does not say who has defended this doctrine, but it cannot be denied that something near akin to it is held by many biologists who attempt to carry biological principles into human affairs, and that it is practically the attitude of most scientific men and evolutionists in so far as they

---

[2] *Ibid.*, pp. 117, 118.

have expressed themselves on the subject. It is the doctrine that I have characterized as the "gospel of inaction," and to the refutation of which I have devoted much effort.

M. Loria easily shows that there is no such parallel, and his comparison of the industrially successful class in society to parasites is ingenious and not wholly incorrect. He could have made his argument much stronger if he had recognized that all predatory animals are essentially parasites, since they live on the nourishment stored up by animals that take it from the vegetable kingdom, and do not differ in this essential respect from parasites that attach themselves to the bodies of other animals.

But the "struggle," if it can be so designated, between parasites and their hosts, including that between carnivorous and herbivorous animals, is only a very small part of Darwinism. In fact it may be said to form no part of it, since it was well understood long before Darwin was born. And yet, curiously enough, the so-called "social Darwinism" scarcely ever gets farther than this. I have never seen any distinctively Darwinian principle appealed to in the discussions of "social Darwinism." It is therefore wholly inappropriate to characterize as social Darwinism the *laissez-faire* doctrine of political economists, even when it is attempted to support that doctrine by appeals to the laws of organic development. That the *laissez-faire* doctrine is false and not sustained by biological principles I freely admit and have abundantly shown, but the fallacy is to be found in an entirely different department of scientific investigation.

III

There is another school of sociologists who, ignoring the economic struggle, confine themselves to the race struggle. These have still another form of supposed "social Darwinism" which they have conjured up in their own imagination, and against which they are battling as valiantly as Don Quixote battled with the windmills. With them social Darwinism is any attempt to maintain that human or social evolution has been influenced or furthered by the struggle of races, peoples, and nations. Their idea is that the only condition to progress is absolute peace, and that all disturbances of the peace of the world are retrogressive and even "pathological."

It is not my present intention to refute this doctrine. That has been done far more eloquently by history than it can ever be done by words, but I wish to protest in the strongest possible terms against the application of the term Darwinism to the race struggle. I know of no ethnologist, historian, or sociologist among those who see the real effect of the struggle of races, who has accepted this designation for that law. The general character of that struggle has always been known, and therefore it no more belongs to Darwin's teachings than does the law of parasitism. But the great discovery of precisely how the race struggle operates in the process of civilization, though clearly formulated by Gumplowicz in 1875 in a pamphlet[3] of whose existence Darwin could have known nothing, was not fully worked out until 1883,[4] one year after Darwin's death. That principle is to be ranked with the principle of natural selection, and may be appropriately called its sociological homologue, because, although an entirely different principle, it agrees with the latter in constituting a strictly scientific explanation of a great natural process, never before understood. I call it the principle of *social synergy*. It certainly is not social Darwinism nor Darwinism in any form. It would be difficult to find even an adumbration of it in any of Darwin's works, or, for that matter, in the works of any author prior to 1875 or

---

[3] Ludwig Gumplowicz, *Raçe und Staat. Eine Untersuchung über das Gesetz der Staatenbildung* (Vienna, 1875).

[4] Ludwig Gumplowicz, *Der Rassenkampf. Sociologische Untersuchungen* (Innsbruck, 1883).

even to 1883. But Ratzenhofer in 1893,[5] and especially in 1898,[6] took it up and greatly expanded it. But he acknowledges that it was Gumplowicz who succeeded in first establishing sociology as the science which forms the foundation of all political teachings.[7]

IV

One of the sociologists of the school now under consideration has recently made a general onslaught upon the new doctrine, but instead of going to original sources and analyzing the works which I have enumerated in which it was first promulgated and most elaborately expounded, he has seen fit to attack a work in which it is simply set forth by the author, though with all due credit to the discoverer and chief expounder, and without claiming any originality in the matter at all. He seems to be wholly ignorant of the works named and of their authors, except as he has met with them in the book which forms the object of his polemic. He does, indeed, mention Gumplowicz, and calls him a Pole, although he has been a professor in the University of Graz nearly all his life. He also mentions Ratzenhofer, whom he calls a German, apparently for no other reason than that his works have been mostly published in Leipzig. As a matter of fact this new and vital doctrine, like the new doctrine of value in economics, is essentially Austrian, and the discovery of both these principles is

---

[5] Gustav Ratzenhofer, *Wesen und Zweck der Politik als Theil der Sociologie und Grundlage der Staatswissenshaft,* 3 vols. (Leipzig, 1893).

[6] Gustav Ratzenhofer, *Die sociologische Erkenntnis: Positive Philosophie des socialen Lebens* (Leipzig, 1898).

[7] These are his own words, to which almost all his expounders neglect to call attention: "Nach vielen mehr oder weniger erfolgreichen Versuchen, das gesellschaftliche Leben wissenschaftlich zu erfassen, in welcher Hinsicht insbesondere Comte, Spencer, Tylor und Bastian bahnbrechend wirkten, scheint es Gumplowicz gelungen, die Sociologie als Wissenschaft festzustellen, welche die Grundlage der Lehre über die Politik bildet."—*Wesen und Zweck der Politik,* Vol. I, Preface, p. v.

probably due to the prolonged reflection of penetrating minds upon the series of social struggles which that land of many races has had to pass through.

But the author to whom I have referred has seen fit to direct his shafts at an American who is guilty only of having perceived that this principle lies at the foundation of sociology, as Ratzenhofer admits. This author characterizes the doctrine as social Darwinism, although none of the works treating it contain that or any similar expression. He is a peace reformer and any admission that there has ever been any social virtue in war is highly offensive to him.

We are interested now only in pointing out how completely this author misunderstands the teachings of Darwin whose name he so freely invokes. He sees in Darwinism nothing but war—*bellum omnium contra omnes*. Nevertheless, ten years earlier he had said:

Just as the perfect being wins in individual struggles, so the most perfect nation wins in international struggles. Darwin's law acts as inexorably in the case of collectivities as in that of individuals. The resultant of international struggles is also the triumph of the best.

But his mind seems to have undergone a great change since that date, and he now sees no good in social struggles, but only evil.

All his examples from biology refer to the relations subsisting between predatory animals and their prey, which he looks upon as a war of extermination; whereas, as Darwin clearly saw, a predatory animal cannot exterminate its prey without at the same time exterminating itself. In fact, between a predatory animal and its prey there is no struggle at all. A struggle implies some sort of reciprocity between the parties to it. But between a wolf and a sheep there is no mutuality. All the "struggling" the sheep can do is to escape from the jaws of the wolf. Even the most robust ram in such a case would have no instinct except that of flight.

This author makes the same mistake as Professor Loria in saying that the great difference between animal and human struggles is that the former are always between different species while the latter are between individuals of the same species. This is regarded as the final and conclusive argument. It simply shows how completely these authors fail to understand the most rudimentary principles of the biological struggle for existence. Darwin himself lays down the law that the struggle is always most intense between organisms that are most similar. The reason is obvious. It is essentially a struggle for subsistence. Any environment contains certain elements which a given organism can appropriate. Similar organisms appropriate similar elements. When too many organisms of the same general kind exist on a given area, all using the same forms of subsistence, it is evident that they will exhaust their resources, and there will be a struggle among them for the supply of their wants. This is a universal law in biology and applies to plants as well as to animals. To all outward appearances there is perfect peace. Any landscape in a state of nature presents an aspect of complete tranquillity, but the biologist knows that this is an illusion, and that there is going on an intense competition among all living things for the means of subsistence. If a given area is watched for a sufficient length of time changes will be perceived. Certain forms will be found to have gained the ascendant and advanced in number and vigor, while certain other forms have lost ground and begun to decline. The former will ultimately come to dominate the field, and the latter will disappear, having succumbed in the struggle for existence. The observing botanist will note the existence of varieties among plants. The leaves of some will be of a deeper or a paler hue, some will develop hairs, down, tomentum, bloom, etc. All these differences in outward appearance are due to corresponding differences in the minute structure and constitution of the plants, and these differences of structure in turn enable the plant to appropriate slightly different elements from the soil, air, sunlight, etc., and thus to escape in so far from the struggle for subsistence. It is thus that varieties arise. The differentiation at length becomes specific, and we have an explanation of the "origin of species." The great principle according to which all this goes on is natural selection, and it requires generations to effect the changes. Our anti-social Darwinists seem to have no conception of this law, and never get beyond the crude idea of bloody battles in which the weak are "devoured" by the strong.

It is true that closely allied species do compete with each other and one species often drives out another, but this is where both species require nearly the same food. Thus the brown rats in America have practically exterminated the black rats, which were formerly abundant. The latter seem to have been introduced earlier and flourished in our houses and barns until the brown or gray rats came. These required exactly the same kind of food, and being superior in certain qualities, they were able to multiply until they consumed all the food there was for rats, and the black rats, being unable to obtain any food, perished. The same occurs in a pure state of nature and on a large scale, but the great competition is always among individuals of the same species, resulting, as already described, in the gradual production of slightly different varieties and ultimately of distinct species, and thus causing all the variety and multiplicity that nature presents, and accounting for its power to appropriate all the elements of subsistence that the earth affords.

This competition is universal. It occurs among the most innocent and peaceful creatures, and even, as already remarked, among plants. But it also occurs among predatory animals, not as between them and their peaceful prey, but among themselves. If lions and tigers in the same area lived on precisely the same prey they would compete, and when the prey became scarce, the more successful of the two might exterminate the less successful. But it is probable that these animals in their native jungles live on quite different prey, and are thus both able to subsist together. Natural selection would bring about this result. The competition here is therefore the same as elsewhere, viz., between individuals of the same species. It may result in the production of varieties and new species, but its main effect is to keep down the number of individuals of each species, so that there can never exist more than a certain number of lions, tigers, leopards, etc., in a given region.

v

It is obvious how completely different this all is from the bloody picture drawn by the well-meaning persons whose biological vagaries we are considering. But their errors in biology are scarcely less gross than their errors in ethnology. I had not proposed to consider these here, but there is one that it may be well to point out as typical of them all. This is the much-discussed doctrine of "social pathology." This is one of the most specious and pernicious of all sociological fallacies. It consists in regarding all social phenomena that do not meet with the approval of these writers, as abnormal and as social diseases. The social phenomenon commonly called war is regarded as especially irregular and morbid, and comes in for the principal share of denunciation, which seems to be the form of medical treatment chiefly prescribed. But as the entire history of mankind has been characterized by incessant war, it follows that disease has been the prevailing condition and leading characteristic of human society. One might well wonder that mankind should have even survived, much more that the race should be able to present the robust appearance which it does present. If disease prevailed over health in any such degree among individuals surely we should have a moribund race of weaklings, even if they could exist at all.

It is therefore evident that the entire doctrine of social pathology must be fundamentally false, and that what is called war must be in a certain sense a normal condition. But a very little inspection shows that what is called war is simply the struggle of races for existence and for predominance, and is at least analogous to the biological struggle for existence, which no one would think of calling pathologic. Although, as I have shown, the principle involved in the race struggle is not the same as that involved in the organic struggle, still it has the same effect, and results in the survival of the fittest, which, as all know, are not always the ideally best. But in pure sociology we are not dealing with ideals any more than we are in biology. We are dealing with facts and searching for truth, and the fact is that the course of human development has been characterized and determined by the struggle of races, peoples, and nations, and whatever progress has been attained has grown out of this struggle, which is a perfectly normal and healthy condition, and, properly understood, does not possess the evil and immoral attributes that have been ascribed to it. It is ethically colorless, or, as they say, amoral or anethical, and is simply the consequence of a universal, even cosmical law of nature.

Nor has this historical study anything to do with the question of the abolition of war in the present advanced stage of civilization, unless, indeed, here as everywhere, an understanding of the past places us in a better condition for stating and solving that question. To accuse, as these writers do, the historical and scientific sociologists who have discovered and expounded the law and process of social development, of being for this reason apologists of war among modern nations, is a cheap rhetorical flourish, unworthy of anyone who aspires to be accounted a philosopher.

31

ARTIFICIAL AND

NATURAL INEQUALITIES

1908

In 1907 Ward was re-elected to the presidency of the American Sociological Society. These passages are from his second Presidential Address, delivered at the meeting of the society in Madison, Wisconsin. It must have been particularly gratifying to Ward that his distinguished disciple—and now his nephew-in-law—Professor E. A. Ross, of the University of Wisconsin, had just published his spectacular book, SIN AND SOCIETY, which was in a sense a variation on one of Ward's themes. It is not without interest, too, that Senator Vilas, who later endowed a group of chairs designed to encourage scholarly research at the University of Wisconsin, presided at this meeting.

. . . In simple assimilation the contending races are really equal, neither having as yet been conquered. The success of one in subjugating the other is in that case due to some special

---

"Social Classes in the Light of Modern Sociological Theory," *American Journal of Sociology,* XIII (March 1908), 623–627.

circumstance which chanced to give it the mastery. This may have nothing to do with any inherent superiority of the one over the other. In compound assimilation, which is the only form of which there are any historical examples, the superiority of the conquering race is usually due to its having undergone a larger number of assimilations than the conquered race, whereby it has acquired a higher social efficiency. This does not prove any inherent superiority, since the greater social efficiency is due to superior equipment. There are historical examples of the conquest and subjugation of superior races by inferior ones. When war became a business certain nations prepared themselves exclusively for war. They marshaled armies and invaded foreign countries where the arts of peace were being pursued, and easily conquered them. When in the year 1260 of our era Kublai Khan, trained in the art of war so successfully practiced by his grandfather Genghis Khan, marched his conquering legions into China, subdued it, and established the present Tartar Dynasty in the Celestial Empire, it was a case of a relatively low, semi-barbaric race conquering a far higher and more civilized race. Few Englishmen, I imagine, will admit that a Saxon is essentially inferior to a Norman Frenchman, yet the last great conquest of England was the Norman conquest.

A certain kind of inferiority of the lower classes to the upper is admitted. There is physical inferiority and there is inferiority in intelligence. This last is not the same as intellectual inferiority. Their physical inferiority is due entirely to the conditions of existence. As a subject race, as slaves, as overworked laborers or artisans, as an indigent and underfed class, their physical development has been arrested and their bodies stunted. These conditions long continued have told upon them through heredity and have brought about whatever physical inferiority they manifest. Their unequal intelligence has nothing to do with their capacity for intelligence. Intelligence consists in that capacity together with the supply of information for it to expend itself upon. We see therefore that both kinds of inferiority of the lower classes are extraneous and artificial, not inherent and natural.

I need not here go again over the ground already several times traveled, to show that, as a matter of fact, every time that the lower classes have been brought under conditions where they could manifest their natural and inherent equality with the upper classes they have done so in such a manner as to leave no doubt with regard to that equality. I shall therefore leave that aspect of the case and pass to the consideration of another quite different aspect upon which very little has ever been said.

I refer now to the admitted natural inequalities of men. This is observed on every hand by all, and so ingrained is the idea that the lower classes of society are such by reason of these natural inequalities that there has never been any attempt to analyze the subject with a view to ascertaining whether this is really true or not. Whenever the abolition of social classes is hinted at it is pronounced utopian, and the common and supposed final answer is that if we were to suppose them once really done away with, on account of the natural inequalities of men, they would almost immediately be restored, and every man would find his level. This usually closes the argument, and I have yet to see any attempt to answer it. And yet this is really such a superficial view that it falls to pieces upon the simplest inspection. It receives its death blow the moment we recognize the obvious fact that all these natural inequalities are to be found in all classes and within every class, and that no degree of intellectual deficiency is ever sufficient to cause its possessor to be removed to a lower social class. The weakest minds occur in the highest classes, and Lord Dundrearys are by no means rare. This does not make them any the less lords. We might well wish that social classes were based on some such rational grounds as this theory assumes. Unfortunately such is not the case, and not only are weak minds found in the higher classes, but, what is perhaps worse, strong minds are found in the lower, where they have no chance to work to any purpose. As Professor Huxley said of exceptional men, "no man can say where they will crop up; like their opposites, the fools and knaves, they appear sometimes in the palace and sometimes in the hovel."[1]

But this, while it completely overthrows the prevalent view that social classes are based on natural inequalities, is far from being the last word on that subject. We have seen that social classes are wholly due to artificial conditions, and that the inequalities which they manifest are all artificial inequalities. These have the effect to produce social cleavage or social stratification. They place one man over another regardless of his worth, and generate the whole series of inconsistencies and misfits with which society is afflicted.

Now natural inequalities also have a powerful effect on society. It is not the opposite of that produced by artificial inequalities. It is entirely different. As we have seen, they have no tendency to produce social classes, but they permeate every class alike. Moreover, their effect, instead of being injurious, is highly beneficial. Natural inequalities rarely tend to make one man superior or inferior to another. They simply make men different from one another. This is highly desirable. Of course there are brilliant minds and there are feeble minds. An excess of the latter quality relegates its victim to the class of social dependents. It becomes a pathological condition. Society cares for these wards, to whatever class they may belong. With them we have nothing to do. But the principal inequalities belong to normal minds. They simply represent mental differences. No two minds are exactly alike. Mind is capable of almost infinite variation. There may be a thousand varieties no one of which can be called inferior to another. Apparent inferiority is usually due to some peculiarity. Very few minds are perfectly bal-

---

[1] *Fortnightly Review* (January 1, 1878), p. 57.

anced. Some faculties are developed at the expense of others. No normal and sane mind can be deficient in all its faculties. The faculty called "common-sense," the one which makes its possessor appear normal and sane, may be poorly developed, while some other mental power may be greatly in excess. There is a kind of intellectual compensation by which all are equal but in very different ways. Many great geniuses, as all know, have been deficient in the commoner qualities. There is probably no one who does not have some strong side if it could be known. Many no doubt fail during their whole lives to find expression for the chief powers that they possess. If all could have adequate opportunities there would be no member of society incapable of performing some useful service.

Now it is these very inequalities, however extreme, that cause the efficiency of the human race. The actions of men are a reflex of their mental characteristics. Where these differ so widely the acts of their possessors will correspondingly differ. Instead of all doing the same thing they will do a thousand different things. The natural and necessary effect of this is to give breadth to human activity. Every subject will be looked at from all conceivable points of view, and no aspect will be overlooked or neglected. It is due to this multiplicity of viewpoints, growing out of natural inequalities in the minds of men, that civilization and culture have moved forward along so many lines and swept the whole field of possible achievement.

While therefore the effect of artificial inequalities may be said to be *vertical,* in producing social stratification and creating social classes with all their baleful consequences, that of natural inequalities may be called *horizontal,* spreading out in all directions and compassing the whole earth.

It follows that the great end of all social arrangements should be to discourage artificial inequalities and to encourage natural ones. It would be a great gain if the former could be abolished altogether, and could this be done, as we have seen, natural inequalities would have no tendency to re-establish them. We should have but one social class, or rather, we should have no social classes. All would stand on an equal footing and be enabled to put forth all their energies.

In the present state of society, even in the most advanced nations where the obliteration of class lines has already gone so far, about 80 per cent. of the population belong to what we still call the lower classes. These, although they possess natural inequalities as clearly marked as are those of the upper classes, are practically debarred from their exercise to any useful purpose. Statistical investigations, . . . prove that, notwithstanding their superior numbers, they furnish less than 10 per cent. of the agents of civilization, and that relatively to population they furnish less than 1 per cent. Their influence in the progress of the world is therefore practically nil, although their capacities are the same as those of the higher classes to whom, notwithstanding their small numbers, nearly all progress is due. This is entirely the result of the social stratification caused by artificial inequalities. The abolition of social classes, could it be accomplished, would therefore increase the efficiency of mankind at least one hundred fold.

It is no part of the purpose of this address to propose any method of social reform. Its aim is solely to put in a clear light the true nature of social classes, their historical and ethnic origin, and their wholly artificial character. It is hoped thereby to remove them from the list of superficial studies which start from no sound premises and lead to no safe conclusion, and to bring them fairly within the purview of scientific sociology.

32

EDUCATION

AND PROGRESS

1909

This was an extemporaneous address to the students of the newly organized Central Labor College at Oxford, an offshoot from Ruskin College. Not surprisingly, this address, which promised a bright future to the English working classes, was received with rapturous enthusiasm.

. . . The great demand of the world is knowledge. . . .

If I am right in that, then the great problem is to equalize intelligence; or, to simplify it still further, to put all knowledge in the possession of every human being. I call it the equalizing of intelligence because I maintain that the native capacity of mankind is equal in all classes of society. I have coined a new word in the English language, if I may be allowed to say so, and I have set it afloat and I hope it will be carried to the ends of the earth. I call this the principle of intellectual egalitarianism, the principle that—no matter what class of society you

The Plebs Magazine, I (November and December 1909), 218–221, 241–244; in *Glimpses of the Cosmos,* VI, 337–340.

may select from—taking a corresponding number from each—
the individuals from all classes of society will be equal in
their native capacity for knowledge; that those from any one
class will be equal in their capacity for knowledge to an equal
number from any other class of society.

It may be said that I have worked that out theoretically; it
is not entirely theoretical. I have observed as long as I have
lived; but I have never had brought before me any facts that
showed with such power and cogency the demonstration of
that principle as my experience of the last two days and these
last few moments before this audience.

Of course you cannot help seeing the bearing of all this upon
the problem of education, but you will all remember—those of
you who read my old *Dynamic Sociology* of 1883 know—what
I mean by education, because education is not the same thing
with me at all as it is with Oxford University. Education with
me is exactly that one thing, of imparting to the great mass of
mankind, all mankind, an equal amount of the essential knowledge that has been brought into the world.

When you all have that there will be no social classes. Social
classes are artificial; they are all made by man; they are all the
products of social organization and social phenomena. They
are all natural in one sense, in the sense that they have to be,
the same as everything else has to be; they have been produced, but they are not natural conditions. Social classes are
all artificial. I will go farther, and say that social classes are
based entirely—of course you will see the large ellipsis I have
to make here—upon inequalities in intelligence, and are the
effects of those artificial inequalities of intelligence on different
classes of mankind—on different men.

These inequalities tend, necessarily and essentially from
their very nature, to produce social stratification; in fact, artificial inequalities have what I call a vertical effect on the
stratification of society, raising one man above another in a
similar manner to the geological strata of the globe laid down

in the sedimentary rocks. That is what happens under existing social conditions and which constitutes the differences between the amount of intelligence possessed by different individuals.

I have said I have come to the conclusion that there is no difference in the native capacity of mankind so far as classes are concerned; that all mankind are equal; that the brain power of the world is the same at every level; even the lowest slaves and serfs that have ever existed on the globe have the same power for exercising their faculties, the same faculties as those who have had them under control, those who have owned them, those who have whipped and flogged them, those who have robbed them of their rights and liberty—there is no difference.

It is sometimes maintained; it has been a stock argument; that if we were to abolish the social classes, it would only be a question of time when the natural inequalities of mankind would bring about a stratification such as existed before. There is nothing more false in the whole domain of social sophism. One single fact will show it; you have here in England—and there have always been here and in all countries where they have had higher and lower classes of society—these inequalities, these natural inequalities, in the higher classes just as much as in the lower. You know perfectly well that a man being a lord of England does not ensure his being a philosopher; and I make bold to say that there is just as much difference in the higher classes, in your nobility, as there is in the lowest strata of your people, the common day labourer who has not so much as the skill of a trade—they all differ.

You ask me, do I deny natural inequalities? Not at all; I admit their influence much farther than those who maintain that they are the cause of social stratification. The great value of human life resides in the fact that the native capacities of mankind differ. And the simple answer is this: that the differences are qualitative and not quantitative. If every man had exactly the same kind of mind as every other man, the world would only have done one thing. But there are millions of men with different kinds of minds, and the consequence is that they have done millions of different things; and that is what I mean by asserting the intellectual equality of mankind, whilst maintaining the essential natural inequalities of mind. There are inequalities in the qualities of minds, and a great number of different kinds of minds; and if we were only supplied with data for exercising those minds we should have in them the bulwark of progress.

I use for the opposite of the natural inequalities the term horizontal, in distinction from the analogy of stratification, as, instead of producing a stratification, the tendency of the natural inequalities is to broaden out the functions and activities of mankind so that every object in the world will be looked into, everything in the world will be heard and seen and known; every thought of the world will be brought out, and the progress of the world will be a broad swath which sweeps over the whole of creation.

If I knew how many persons there were in this room I could tell how many different kinds of minds there were in this room; and, as all minds differ, every one will do something that no one else has done, and so broaden the course of human progress. That is what I mean by natural inequalities; and if there were no social inequalities there would be nothing to interfere with the full exercise of all those capacities of all mankind.

If we look at the question from this point of view, we can readily see what this great natural principle of inequality, or, as I call it, intellectual individuality, or individuality in achievement, is. Achievement has been the result of the immense individuality that has entered into it, due to the vast number and the great difference of human minds.

Now, the only thing that is needed is that all these minds shall be supplied with the means of their exercise. Human minds—admitting again for the sake of argument that these inequalities of the human mind exist—differ entirely in what they hold and not in what they are; and therefore, the great effort is to supply all minds with all knowledge. Of course you know that that is an ideal, but I adhere to that expression: that all mankind should possess all knowledge. I have not time here for the explanation of what I mean by universality, nor can I say now what I mean by universal education; but it is the same thing: a curriculum should actually embrace all the knowledge of the world.

I had intended to go into some other points, but the time is too short. One of these points refers to the position that all mankind are equally capable, no matter what position the social conditions may have placed the individual in. I will refer to two, and only two, further points. In the first place, the hereditarian philosophers; those who preach eugenics, and teach heredity, and insist upon an increase in the calibre of mankind: all admit that there have been self-made men all through history, and that there are hundreds of them at the present time. By self-made men they mean men who have risen from the lowest ranks of life to the very highest. What does that mean? It means that down in the very lowest ranks there are just as good brains as in the highest.

The second great proof, for any one who has studied the history of the world, is obtained from history itself. It is from the study of history that we have the knowledge that we now possess of these artificial social classes that have existed during human history. In Greece, at the time of its highest splendour, there were at least ten slaves to one freeman, probably more; in Rome it was about the same. What has become of those slaves? They are now in the other classes of society, they are completely mingled. What became of all the slaves of Europe when slavery and serfdom were abolished? They have all been mingled with the other classes of society. And have they not shown the same ability as their masters did before them? History shows nothing else more clearly than this: that class after class has been rising, one class after another; and the lower classes taking the powers of social organization under their control, taking the reins of human life in their hands, supplanting the other classes.

I trace it back to the system of caste in India, and I have shown that the classes of the eighteenth century were nothing but the holdovers of the old system of caste; that the lords spiritual and the lords temporal were nothing but the representatives of the Brahmins and the Kshatriyas, the spiritual caste and the warrior caste. Those classes have always existed; they existed down to the eighteenth century, and exist in some form to-day in some parts of Europe.

Then take the middle class: that class became, even in India, the business class of society; but in modern Europe that business class took the form of what are called in France the *bourgeoisie,* what you call in England the commons, and they gained the mastery. You know that the middle class, the third estate, came forward and assumed the power in society, and has held that power ever since. The third estate to-day contains and holds the brains of the world.

Many think the present social movement has to do with the French Revolution, that it is a verification of the old falsehood that history repeats itself. Nothing of the kind; the French Revolution had nothing to do with the fourth estate; it was carried on exclusively in the interests of the third estate. To quote Abbé Siéyès: "What is the third estate? Everything. What does it possess? Nothing. What does it desire? To become something." Before the French Revolution the third estate was nothing; it is everything to-day. The rise of the third estate was the French Revolution, and it was a grand work; and it showed that the third estate was capable of supplanting the first and second estates, and it has done so in France. What is the movement to-day? It is nothing but the same great movement. The first and second estates were supplanted by the third, and now the fourth estate is coming on and will ere long supplant the third estate. What do we hear all over the world? Nothing but the subterranean roar of that great mass of mankind, infinitely larger numerically than all the other classes put together; that class is rumbling and seething and working, and coming to consciousness; and when they do come to consciousness they will take the reins of power in their hands, and then will have been abolished the last of all the social classes.

33

SOCIOLOGY

AND THE STATE

1910

This is one of the last of Ward's essays, and one of the most polemical. In 1909, Professor Henry Jones Ford of Princeton had loosed a blast at all contemporary sociology and at Ward himself. Ford's essay was published in the AMERICAN JOURNAL OF SOCIOLOGY, *along with counter-blasts by Professors Small and Ellwood. Ford returned to the attack with a second article, "The Claims of Sociology Examined." It was at that point that Ward entered the lists with this essay on "Sociology and the State."*

I

Sociology must be something very bad because it is so much like vice. Most of those who hated it at first sight now embrace it and the rest are either in the enduring or the pitying stage.

As in the case of nearly all other sciences sociology was at first attacked and called a "pseudo-science." The sociologist is

---

"Sociology and the State," *American Journal of Sociology,* XV (March 1910), 672–680.

perfectly familiar with this, and it has ceased to trouble him. He has been hearing it from Lorenz Stein, Dilthey, Maurice Block, Bernheim, Lehmann, Treitschke, Martini, Van der Rest, and Leslie Stephen. They all say the same things, nothing more and nothing new. Some pains were taken at first to show that there were vast fields which no other science has ever touched or can touch without becoming sociology. But the need of sociology was so great and so keenly felt that there ceased to be any call to defend it. The people of all countries actually demanded the new science. None of the other sciences held out any hope of furnishing a theoretical and scientific basis for the study of the social problems of the day. Political economy had become a sort of quietism, and bade the people hush and cease to disturb the established order. But the people would not hush, and the unrest grew. Economics then vaulted over to the Austrian theory of value, which is a sociological principle, and then pretended that it had always been the "master science." Political science floundered about among a thousand fine-spun and wholly improbable theories of the state. It was both politically and socially hopeless.

When at last a science of both human origins and human welfare rose on the horizon it was immediately welcomed as that which had been so long looked for. Launched by Comte and fathered by John Stuart Mill, it moved, though at first slowly. Accepted by Herbert Spencer and recognized by several strong continental writers, it got on its feet during the last decade of the nineteenth century, and before the beginning of the twentieth century it had become the most popular of all the sciences. It began to be taught in one after another of the higher institutions of learning, and at the present time it seems there are about four hundred such in the United States alone in which sociology forms a part of the curriculum. Something analogous to this is true in other countries but I cannot quote any recent statistics.

Perhaps the surest index of the growth of sociology and of

the hold it has taken of all enlightened nations is the number of sociological societies that have sprung into existence during the period under consideration. Inaugurated by the formation of the International Institute of Sociology in 1893, followed by the Sociological Society of Paris in 1895, the movement spread to Brussels where the Belgian Sociological Society was founded in 1899, transformed into the Belgian Institute of Sociology in 1901, between which dates in 1900 there was founded at Budapest the Hungarian Society of Sociology. A Laboratory of Sociology was established in Palermo in 1901 and an Institute of Sociology at Madrid in the same year. In 1903 England fell into line and the Sociological Society of London was born. Our own American Sociological Society arose in 1905. Austria awoke in 1907 and produced the Soziologische Gesellschaft at Vienna, and on the occasion of the retirement of Professor Gumploicz from his chair in the University of Gratz in 1908 a sociological society was founded there in his honor. That same year saw the rise of two more sociological societies in Hungary, viz., at Nagyvarad and at Györ, and it was also in 1908 that the Institute of Sociology was founded at Catania. Finally, during the present year of 1909 the contagion reached Germany, and the Deutsche Gesellschaft für Soziologie was inaugurated at Berlin on January 3. It was also in January of this year that the Sociological Society of Birmingham was founded. Such is a bare enumeration, perhaps incomplete, of this movement for the scientific study of society.

The teaching of sociology in the great universities and its discussion before these learned bodies are paralleled by the activity of the press, both through the establishment of special organs devoted to it and through the writing of books on the subject by able authors in all countries. Any attempt to enumerate these would carry me far beyond the limits of this paper.

What are we to conclude from all this? Is the whole world, then, insane and chasing an *ignis fatuus*, a pseudo-science? I would be the last to fall back upon the old doctrines of *vox populi* and *quod ubique, quod ab omnibus,* as proofs of anything. Many grave errors have been long popular and well-nigh universal. But have any of the sciences had to be abandoned as false? Yes, they say, and point to alchemy. But alchemy was rather an art. There is a sort of social alchemy, and sociology is the social chemistry whose mission it is to supplant it. Society is a domain of natural phenomena, and there must be a science to deal with it. There was no such science till sociology came. It is not the same as the science of man (anthropology); it is not the same as the science of government and the state (political science). In a certain sense these all belong to sociology, or fall under it, as furnishing its data. They are special social sciences, and there are many more, but they do not, separately or together, constitute sociology. Sociology has been called the synthesis of all the special social sciences. It is that, but it is more. It gathers material from fields not included in any recognized science, but its great work is the co-ordination of all social facts, and the elaboration of a reasoned and systematized body of knowledge relating to social origins, social processes, social development, and social causation.

Notwithstanding the recruits that sociology is constantly receiving from all sides and the general silencing of adverse criticism by the logic of events, there ever and anon arises a new voice from some quarter reiterating the old cry that sociology is a pseudo-science. This, as we have seen, is of little consequence. Sociology has much more serious obstacles to overcome. It would be strange if among the hundreds of writers who have been attracted to this field there should not be some who would say foolish things. There is, for example, quite a large school of sociologists, who, though claiming to be such, are virtually denying that sociology is a science. Anyone who denies the existence of efficient causes in society does this. It does not mend matters to say that society is a domain of final causes. Final causes are nothing but the appropriation of efficient causes by intelligent beings. Of course sociology employs telic methods, and so does every other science. They are the only methods of which the intellect is capable. The higher mind works through final causes only. Telic is synonymous with intellectual. But in sociology as in all other true sciences, the mind deals with real things—the properties of matter and the forces of nature. Psychic forces are as real and natural as physical forces. In society psychic forces become social forces, and they are the true causes of all social phenomena. The virtual denial of this truth on the part of persons classed as sociologists, is doing sociology far more harm than all that the enemies of the science can do it. Several European sociologists must be so classed, as Ludwig Stein, Draghicesco, and Rivera. Nor are they wanting in America; at least passages may be cited to that effect, for example, by Dr. Small,[1] Professor Ellwood,[2] and Professor Hayes.[3] If the sociologists themselves admit that sociology is a pseudo-science how can we expect the enemies of sociology to see it in any better light?

I do not propose here to repeat any of my own proofs of the strictly scientific character of sociology when properly understood. My entire contribution to the subject consists essentially in heaping up these proofs. But I take pleasure in referring to Professor Giddings's papers on "Social Causation," as showing that not all Americans vacillate on this essential point. I may also be allowed to quote one Old World author, of whom fate has so recently and tragically robbed us, and this from the last book he ever wrote, the one he referred to as his *Schwanengesang*,[4] and which he probably never saw after it issued from the press. I refer to the posthumous little *Sozialphilosophie im*

---

[1] *Amer. Journ. Sociol.*, V, 811, 812.

[2] *Ibid.*, XIII, 341 ff.

[3] *Ibid.*, XI, 633; XII, 654, 834.

[4] *Ibid.*, XV (November, 1909), 412, 413.

Umriss of Ludwig Gumplowicz, a copy of which reached me on November 22 last through the kindness of his son, Dr. Wladyslaw Gumplowicz, of Vienna. On pp. 6–9 of this work he says:

We live in the state and in society; we belong to a social circle which jostles against its members and is jostled by them; we feel the social pressure from all sides and we react against it with all our might; we experience a restraint to our free activities and we struggle to remove it; we require the services of other men which we cannot do without; we pursue our own interests and struggle for the interests of other social groups, which are also our interests. In short, we move in a world which we do not control, but which controls us, which is not directed toward us and adapted to us, but toward which we must direct and adapt ourselves. . . .

Modern science knows the laws according to which the heavenly bodies move; it knows the laws of life of all organic beings; it knows the laws of the attraction, repulsion, and combination of atoms. What does it know of the social world? Nothing. In the world-conception of modern science this most distinctive human world is absent. There is no trace or intimation even of the laws of its movement in the prevailing philosophy of nature. This world does not exist for it. . . . That the will of man is controlled by his social environment, by the social group to which he belongs, in which he inheres and must inhere, that this influence is so exactly determined that we can calculate in advance the decisions of the wills of individuals from their social position and group attachments—of all this the modern philosopher of nature takes no notice; these factors which the phenomena of will call forth, do not exist for him. He knows only the organico-physical forces which set the human will in motion. The social environment of man with its impulses and suggestions, its coercion and compulsion, which determine the wills of individuals, these "forces" are as unknown to him as is the social world itself.

This final message of the author of the *Struggle of Races* fittingly supplements the splendid presentation by Dr. Ross of the great law of *Social Control,* and forces home to us anew the truth that sociology has to do with energy as certainly as astronomy, physics, chemistry, and biology. But this is only one side of the subject. It relates to the static aspect only. The dynamic aspect is even more striking and more important. To treat of that here would be but to repeat what I have been saying for thirty years.

II

On several occasions I have attempted to show that the tendency of sociology has been to seek to narrow it down to some one principle supposed to be adequate to embrace the whole field, and that there are many such principles, each of which is so regarded by some one writer or school of writers. When I made my principal contribution to this aspect of the subject in 1902, and discussed twelve such principles, all of which belong to sociology and constitute important factors in the completed science, no one had distinctly claimed that political science was the great comprehensive discipline, and that the whole field now usually embraced by the science of sociology falls under the single conception of the state. Such a claim has recently been made, and to it a moment's attention may now be given.

There is a doctrine usually ascribed to Comte and defended by a considerable number of sociologists, which has been sometimes called "objectification." Its chief form consists in declaring that society is the only reality, and that the individual is an abstraction. Comte is supposed to have said this but he only said that the man is an abstraction, and that there is nothing real but humanity.[5] The doctrine is metaphysical enough in any form, and it is such doctrines as this that have done most to discredit sociology in the eyes of scientific men. They judge all sociologists by the few who maintain such views, and the open enemies of the science have made the most of this.

---

[5] *Philosophie positive* (3rd edition, 1869), VI, 590.

We now have a new form of this doctrine of objectification, differing in nothing from the old forms, except that instead of humanity or society being called the only reality it is the state that is so regarded. The distinction between society and the state, however, is not clearly drawn, as may be seen from the following passage, which embodies the theory:

Instead of the genesis of society from individuals, what has taken place is the genesis of individuals from society; . . . . man did not make the state but the state made man . . . . it is an institution that existed before the human species was developed; . . . . the state includes society just as any entity includes all its parts.[6]

The author of this remarkable theory claims to be an orthodox Darwinian, and calls most sociologists anti-Darwinian, including those who are biological specialists and have sought to show the non-biological sociologists what Darwin really taught. It is a pity therefore that he could not have been contemporary with the great biologist in order to have told him how "species" were formed and developed, at least the "human species." That the "state" underlies the origin of species would certainly have been new to Darwin. That this "institution" is not confined to the "human species," but is of earlier animal origin, is, however, made clear in other passages, for example:

The state [which is here called a genus!], an integration that took place in the animal stock ancestral to the human species. All existing forms of the state have been evolved from primordial forms existing anterior to the formation of the human species. The state is the unit, of which all social structure and individual human existence are the differentiation. The state is a psychic unity and it is apprehensible only as it is objectified in institutions.[7]

Now certain sociologists have proposed some highly metaphysical and even absurd theories, and have "objectified" hu-

---

[6] *Amer. Journ. Sociol.*, XV (September 1909), 248.
[7] *Ibid.*, p. 255.

manity and society in ways that would have pleased a Scaliger, but none of them have ever approached this new doctrine as a specimen of mediaeval ontology. Yet its author is one of those who characterize sociology as a "pseudo-science" that has made a "false start." In his first attack upon it, published in a newspaper, and containing low appeals to popular prejudice, he simply repeated the old charges that have been so often made by the authors named at the beginning of this paper, and I was surprised that any answer was thought necessary. But the answer made him familiar with the face of the monster and lured him on to express his pity in a second attack, much subdued, in which at last he showed his colors, and advanced the astounding theory above stated. He has thus been good enough to tell the sociologists what they should have done and what a true "start" would have been. What might not sociology have been if it had only made this true start!

The comedy of all this lies in the fact that we now have a rational theory of the state. Morgan taught us in 1878 that political society supervened upon tribal society in Greece and Rome in the sixth century before Christ, and that it does not exist in most of the outlying races of men. Nothing that can be called a state exists in gentile society, and the state is a comparatively late factor in social evolution. Gumplowicz and Ratzenhofer have shown us just how the state arose as a consequence of race amalgamation. The ethnological and sociological proofs, although independently arrived at, harmonize completely and furnish us with the true natural history of the state. They teach us the origin in comparatively recent times of political society, states, and nations, as the result of prolonged struggles followed by periods of social and political equilibration and assimilation.

The state is the most important of all human institutions, and it is doubtless a recognition of this truth that has led to the innumerable attempts to explain its origin and nature. Some of the theories put forth may contain germs of truth, but the greater part of them are utterly worthless, as embodying no principle capable of explaining anything. Every writer imagined himself competent to formulate a theory of the state. I made bold to enter the lists in my initial work, which appeared in 1883. I was culpably ignorant of Morgan's great work published five years earlier, and Gumplowicz's *Rassenkampf* appeared the same year as my own book. Of course I knew nothing of his pamphlet, *Raçe und Staat*, 1875, which contains a clear statement of the principle. My guess was perhaps as good as the average, but was wide of the mark, and in the light of the great Austrian theory and of the ethnological proofs I do not hesitate to repudiate it and remand it to the same limbo as all the rest.

I would not have mentioned this had not this new interpreter of the state singled it out (instead of quoting *Pure Sociology*, chap. x, published twenty years later) and held it up as my theory of the state. This procedure may be compared with that of the Spanish court-martial in condemning Ferrer at fifty for what he said at twenty. It would of course be useless to argue with one who resorts to such methods, and I wished only to show that of all the worthless theories of the state that have been set afloat the theory proposed by him is the most absurd. To it Tully's famous saying perfectly applies: *Nescio quomodo, nihil tam absurde dici potest, quod non dicatur ab aliquo philosophorum.*

34

SOCIAL PROGRESS

1912

It is proper to conclude with this definition of social progress that Ward prepared for the Eighth Congress of the International Institute of Sociology, which was to have met at Rome in the fall of 1912. There is, to be sure, little here that Ward had not said at many times and in many places. But this restatement of the quintessence of his social philosophy, almost the last thing Ward wrote, dramatizes the consistency of that philosophy over a period of some thirty years.

There are two sorts of progress, structural progress and moral progress. Structural progress takes place not only in society, but also in plants and animals. One can even say that it takes place in the realm of the inorganic. Moral progress is limited to man, or, at least, to man and animals. By moral progress one does not mean to say progress in morality or ethics. The moral realm is the realm of sensation, and all that comprises sensation is moral. Moral progress comprises only that form of sensation that is called pleasure and pain. Everything that increases pleasure or diminishes pain is moral progress. It is therefore limited to the animal world. In this paper I

"Definition du Progress Social," *Annales de l'Institut International de Sociologie,* Vol. XIV (Paris, 1913), in *Glimpses of the Cosmos,* VI, 372–374.

am going to limit it to the human race. Since man always exists in society, all moral progress becomes social progress. The same is true for the structural progress of the human race. Consequently, social progress is of two sorts, structural and moral. The structural development within a society constitutes a culture. Therefore, one can characterize structural social progress as cultural progress, and the most elevated forms of culture have received the name of civilization.

Quite some while ago I defined civilization as "the utilization of the materials and the forces of nature," and I have repeated this definition several times. It can stand, then, as the definition of cultural social progress. It is "the human achievement," or "the conquest of nature."

But what, then, is moral social progress? Here are my first definitions, which, although slightly different in form, are substantially alike: "There is no real progress without a decrease in the totality of suffering, or an increase in the totality of enjoyment throughout society." "Everything which increases the sum total of human happiness." "Increase in human happiness." "Increase in human happiness, or negatively stated, decrease in human suffering."

The principal advancement that I have made beyond these definitions is to be found in a paper read in 1897 to the Third Congress of this Institute, entitled "The Regimen of Pain and the Regimen of Pleasure." In this paper I presented progress as consisting of an advancement from a regimen of pain towards a regimen of pleasure. Certainly, this same essential idea is to be found in the first definitions, but this latter one recognizes a true social movement in the indicated direction. There is no doubt about the reality of such a movement. By designating the pleasures with a *plus* and the pains with a *minus,* as I did in this paper, we can once more define social progress as *an increase in the algebraic sum of pleasure and pain.* It goes without saying that we are speaking here only of moral progress.

As I have already pointed out, the structural progress of society is quite simply the progress of civilization and I have always defined civilization as "the result of the utilization of the materials and the forces of nature." The tremendous degree to which the materials and forces of nature have been utilized cannot have failed to increase the pleasures and decrease the pains of existence. This result occurs fully for all those who are in a position to utilize effectively these materials and forces. The fact that civilization does not bring about moral progress is due exclusively to the circumstance that a large number of the members of society are excluded from the means to utilize the materials and forces of nature. It is the disorder of society which causes this situation. The utilization of the materials and forces of nature is the human achievement, but something that has yet to be accomplished is "the socialization of achievement." When all human achievement is socialized, in such a way that all members of society will share in its benefits, then civilization and progress will come to be the same, and all art will fulfill its usual function of increasing the algebraic sum of good and evil in the world. Sociology is the science which sets forth the principles and indicates the method for attaining this end.

INDEX